AN EDWARDIAN MIXED DOUBLES

An Edwardian Mixed Doubles

THE BOSANQUETS versus THE WEBBS

A Study in British Social Policy
1890–1929

A. M. McBRIAR

CLARENDON PRESS · OXFORD
1987

Oxford University Press, Walton Street, Oxford OX2 6DP
Oxford New York Toronto
Delhi Bombay Calcutta Madras Karachi
Petaling Jaya Singapore Hong Kong Tokyo
Nairobi Dar es Salaam Cape Town
Melbourne Auckland
and associated companies in
Beirut Berlin Ibadan Nicosia

Oxford is a trade mark of Oxford University Press

British Library Cataloguing in Publication Data
McBriar, A. M.
An Edwardian mixed doubles: the
Bosanquets versus the Webbs: a study in
British social policy 1890–1929.
1. Great Britain—Social policy
I. Title
361.6'1'0941   HN390
ISBN 0–19–820111–7

Library of Congress Cataloging in Publication Data
Data available

Set by Hope Services, Abingdon
Printed in Great Britain
at the University Printing House, Oxford
by David Stanford
Printer to the University

TO
MY MOTHER
ELIZABETH
WHO UNDERSTOOD

PREFACE

THE intention of this book is to provide an insight into the debate on social policy which began in late Victorian Britain and reached a climax in the Edwardian period. That debate is by no means a dead issue; it resonates into our own times, for it concerned the still unsolved problems of unemployment and poverty. The important role that the partnership of Sidney and Beatrice Webb played in the debate is fairly well known, although there remains much to be explored concerning the details of their contribution and their influence, which this study attempts to clarify. But the special part played by Bernard Bosanquet, the Idealist philosopher, and his wife, Helen (née Dendy), economist and social worker, has been overlooked by most historians, or submerged in general discussions of the Charity Organisation Society and of the Commissioners who formed the majority on the great Royal Commission of inquiry into the Poor Laws 1905–9. The significance of the contest between the Bosanquets and the Webbs did not, however, escape a shrewd contemporary, Lawrence Phillips, writing in the *Economic Review* of 1911: 'The economic "mixed doubles" between the Bosanquets and the Webbs is likely, unless a determined rally is made, to end in an easy victory for the latter.' (*Ec.R.* 21 (1911), 461.) His remark not only discerned the leading partners, but also compared their contest to the game, 'invented' (or at least codified) in the late nineteenth century, of lawn tennis. It has inspired our approach to their notable tournament, fierce indeed, but played more according to the 'rules of the game' than many similar encounters of our own times.

ACKNOWLEDGEMENTS

LIKE all historians, I am much indebted to the scholars who have preceded me in this field of study, and I have endeavoured to make acknowledgement to them and their work in the footnotes and bibliography of this book. I am also grateful to my colleagues and students in the History Department at Monash University for the inspiration I have gained from their discussion, fellowship and cordial goodwill. Special thanks are due to those who have made a direct contribution to the completion of the work. My wife, Marilyn, has had to put up with its slow development from inception to the last stages of proof-reading and index-making, and has offered perceptive criticism and great help at every stage. Alan F. Davies read through the whole typescript, and kindly tempered some incisive comment with general reassurance. So did Ian Britain, whose detailed comments in the margins not only curbed my tendency to use over-long sentences, but also gave me the benefit of his comprehensive knowledge, which must now make him the leading Australian scholar in the field of Edwardian British history. John D. Legge, Austin Gough and Jacqueline Templeton have looked over particular chapters, made helpful comments, and given encouragement. David Cuthbert assisted in a number of matters while on his own study leave in London. Norman MacKenzie has been very generous in allowing me to make use of the scholarly work which he and his wife have done on this period, and in helping me to negotiate certain difficulties of copyright. Deborah and William Kellaway made three study leaves in England delightful with their warm hospitality and experienced guidance.

I need to express my gratitude also to many owners of copyright who have given me access to sources or allowed me to quote from them: to the late Dr C. I. C. Bosanquet, who provided me generously with material, and to Mrs Barbara Bosanquet and Mr C. Jay Bosanquet, who have confirmed permission to make use of it; to the Director of the Family Welfare Association for permission to quote from C.O.S. publications; to the Librarian and Archivist of the British Library of Political Science, the Publications Officer of the London School of Economics, and Norman MacKenzie, and Virago Press for the use of Webb sources; to the Fabian Society; to the Society of Authors on behalf of the Bernard Shaw Estate; to the Right Honourable the Earl of Balfour for permission to publish extracts from letters of Lady Betty Balfour; to Mr R. W. Haldane for letters of Lord Haldane and Miss Elizabeth Haldane; to the Right Honourable Sir Zelman Cowen, Provost of Oriel College and Dr W. E. Parry, Vice-Provost and Librarian, for quotations from the Phelps papers; to the Director and the Palaeographer of the University of London Library, for use of the Charles Booth papers; to Constable and Co. for the quotation from George Lansbury's autobiography; and to the Government Printer for official material. I regret that I have not been able to trace the descendants of some other members of the Royal Commission on the Poor Laws of 1905–9, whose letters I have used from the Webb and Bosanquet sources, but I hope they will be magnanimous and forgive me in the cause of historical scholarship.

Secretaries of the Monash History Department, Audrey Allen, June Roder, Ray Goller and Val Edens, who typed early drafts of chapters of this book, and Bess Brudenell, who typed the final draft and did the photocopying, all have my sincerest thanks for their excellent work. Mr Ivon Asquith and his editorial team at Oxford University Press—Robert Faber, John Waś, Katy Whitmore and Dorothy McLean—have made the book's production a friendly and pleasant experience.

Alan M. McBriar

CONTENTS

ABBREVIATIONS

B.W.D.	Beatrice Webb, Diary
CCA	County Councils' Association
COR	*Charity Organisation Review*
COS	Charity Organisation Society
CUB	Central Unemployed Body
Ec.J.	*Economic Journal*
ILP	Independent Labour Party
IJE	*International Journal of Ethics*
LCC	London County Council
LGB	Local Government Board
LGR	*Local Government Review*
LSE	London School of Economics
MOH	Medical Officer of Health
NCPD	National Campaign for the Prevention of Destitution
NPLRA	National Poor Law Reform Association
QJE	*Quarterly Journal of Economics*
RC	Royal Commission
SDF	Social Democratic Federation
TUC	Trades Union Congress
WEWNC	War Emergency Workers' National Committee

I

The Players

OUR story begins, as all histories of the Edwardian period need to begin, in the last decade of Queen Victoria. At that time two matrimonial and intellectual partnerships were formed, which won a place for themselves amongst the most formidable players in the game of social theorizing in the years preceding the First World War. *Fabian News*, the internal information sheet of the Fabian Society, commented in its usual dry and matter-of-fact way in its issue chronicling events of July 1892 that 'Sidney Webb was married to Beatrice Potter on 23rd ult.'[1] The *Charity Organisation Review*, even more reticent about the private lives of its leading members, made no mention, three years later, of the marriage of Bernard Bosanquet and Helen Dendy. It took place on 13 December 1895 at the Unitarian chapel at Monton, near Manchester, which the bride's father had helped to establish, as secretary of its building committee, some twenty years before.[2] When these formidable partners joined, none of them was any longer young, and all of them had already achieved a measure of fame for their intellectual pursuits and social work. At the time of their marriages, Sidney Webb was aged thirty-three, Beatrice Potter thirty-four, Bernard Bosanquet was forty-seven, and Helen Dendy thirty-five.

Bernard Bosanquet

Bernard Bosanquet was the youngest of five sons of the Revd R. W. Bosanquet, of Rock Hall, Northumberland. The family, on the father's side, was descended from Huguenots, who had emigrated

---

[1] M. Cole, *Beatrice Webb* (London, 1945), p. 44. Half a century later, A. P. Herbert discovered the poetical possibilities of this kind of language: see his verse 'I heard the happy lark exult' in *What a Word!* (London 1935), p. 67.

[2] G. L. Lee, *The Story of the Bosanquets* (Canterbury, 1966), p. 85; H. McLachlan, *Records of a Family 1800–1933: Pioneers in Education, Social Service and Liberal Religion* (Manchester, 1935), pp. 128, 191.

to England at the time of the Revocation of the Edict of Nantes. Bernard's father had been Rector of Bolingbroke, Lincolnshire, until he inherited the family property of Rock Hall, where he retired. He was twice married, and had one son by his first wife and four by his second. Bernard Bosanquet's mother was Scottish, of the Macdowall family, Castle Semple, Renfrewshire. Four of the Bosanquet sons were to have distinguished careers. Charles, the eldest, became a barrister of Lincoln's Inn, and he played an active part in charitable work in London before he inherited the family estate: he was one of the founders of the Charity Organisation Society and its first secretary in the years 1870 to 1875. The second son, Robert Holford, was a man of diverse accomplishments: he was a mathematician and physicist, who became a Fellow of the Royal Society and of St John's College, Oxford; he was also a barrister of Lincoln's Inn, and furthermore, an accomplished musician and builder of organs; he held a Professorship at the Royal College of Music, and one of the organs he constructed is at Rock Church. The next brother joined the Navy and rose to become Admiral Sir Day Bosanquet and Governor of South Australia from February 1907 to March 1914. George, the fourth son, was a soldier in the 85th Regiment, who died young. Bernard, the philosopher, was to become the best known of them all.

Helen Bosanquet, in her memoirs of her husband,[3] records with affection the family unity and the patriarchal relations which the Bosanquets enjoyed with villagers and parishioners. Recollection of these relationships always remained important to Bernard Bosanquet, and many years later he was to write to his nephew: '. . . I can't help thinking sometimes how simple all social problems would be if the spirit that has ruled at Rock had ruled over the English town and country . . .'[4] Within the family, both mother and father provided an atmosphere promoting intellectual achievement, and the boys, not constantly distracted by the year-round boisterous outdoor life of those in sunnier climates, were encouraged to develop their own special intellectual talents. Their father's diary for 2 January 1867 noted, for example, 'Heavy snow all the forenoon; Holfy at his

---

[3] H. Bosanquet, *Bernard Bosanquet: A Short Account of his Life* (London, 1924).
[4] J. H. Muirhead (ed.), *Bernard Bosanquet and his Friends* (London, 1935), pp. 312–13. Cf. the autobiographical article by B. Bosanquet in J. H. Muirhead (ed.), *Contemporary British Philosophy: Personal Statements*, 1st series (London 1924), pp. 49–74.

shorthand and making his model organ; G. reading history and studying chess; B. reading all sorts of books.'[5] From his early years, Bernard began to develop his taste for literature encompassing the Classical languages and the main languages of Western Europe, which was to be reflected lavishly in his own writings. Homer, Dante, Shakespeare, and Goethe were his *lares et penates*, and his wide and discriminating knowledge of Romantic English poetry and of English and French Romantic and Realist novels seldom failed to illustrate and enrich even the more abstruse of his later philosophical disquisitions.

At the age of seven, Bernard was sent to boarding-schools: first to a preparatory school at Sherburn, then to Elstree, and finally to Harrow. At school he distinguished himself at study, but not at sport. In 1867 he won a scholarship to Balliol College, Oxford, and the four years he spent there as an undergraduate were most important formative years in his intellectual life. It was the time when Thomas Hill Green's influence was at its height, and when the personal conflict between Green and the great master of Balliol, Benjamin Jowett, added zest to the task of deciphering the 'fuliginous jargon' (as Jowett called it) in which Green was delivering the message of German philosophical Idealism to his students.

Bosanquet, like many others in those years, became a disciple of T. H. Green, though he was in later years to prove a critical one. He always acknowledged his debt to his tutor; and Green had an equally respectful opinion of his pupil's talents, describing him as 'the best equipped man of his generation'.[6] This was high praise, as his generation included men such as R. L. Nettleship and F. H. Bradley, who were to match, and in Bradley's case perhaps to excel, Bosanquet's own eminence in the philosophical field. But Green's estimation was borne out in his academic success. In 1870 Bosanquet took a first class in Greats, an achievement which had been denied both to Nettleship and Bradley;[7] and it resulted in his election as Fellow of University College, Oxford, ahead of Bradley, who also was an applicant for the post.

It was, in a way, a measure of Green's influence upon him that Bosanquet decided in the end not to become a clergyman, for he

⁵ H. Bosanquet, *Bernard Bosanquet*, p. 19.   ⁶ Ibid., p. 28.
⁷ M. Richter, *The Politics of Conscience: T. H. Green and his Age* (London, 1964), p. 14.

had clearly been the member of his family destined to find 'his station and its duties' in that sector of the Establishment. As a sign of the times it is interesting to note that Bosanquet and the three friends of his Harrow schooldays who went up to Balliol together,[8] all intended for a clerical career, decided, every one of them, not to enter the Church. The 'T. H. Green era'—the time from Green's arrival at Oxford as an undergraduate in 1855 to his death in 1882— comprehended the period from the opening of the University to students who were not professing Anglicans to its conversion from a largely clerical to an almost entirely secular institution. Until the reforms of 1871 the Fellows of Colleges were in Anglican orders, and celibate, and a high proportion of more senior students came from and was destined to return to the vicarages. Religious issues, or problems of faith and doubt, lay not far behind the major theoretical disputations of university life. In Jowett's and Green's Oxford, the adherents of liberal Christianity were engaged in a philosophical fight on two fronts: on the one side, against the religious dogmatism both of the Evangelicals and the High-Church Oxford Movement, and, on the other side, against the sceptical currents of thought linked with the progress of science— Utilitarianism, Comtist Positivism, Agnosticism, Materialism. It was the aim of men like Jowett and Green, in spite of the differences between them, to provide 'a quasi-metaphysical backbone which [liberal Christian] theology has always been in need of'.[9] They were in search of a philosophy which could reconcile the apparent conflict between science and religion—which would show this conflict to be mere appearance in the presence of the Reality revealed by philosophy. Jowett found what he needed in the philosophy of Plato and a modern rephrasing of some of the Church's intellectual formulae; but Green went further. Influenced by the German philosophers—Kant in particular, and to a lesser extent Hegel—he was prepared to make Idealist metaphysics a new universal theodicy, to abandon what was miraculous, dogmatic, and authoritarian in the Church's teaching and to identify Christian ethics with social humanitarian commitment. The popularity of

[8] They were R. G. Tatton, T. G. Rooper, and C. B. Heberden. H. Bosanquet, *Bernard Bosanquet*, pp. 20–1, 24.

[9] William James, quoted by J. Passmore, *A Hundred Years of Philosophy* (London, 1957), p. 49.

Mrs Humphrey Ward's novel *Robert Elsmere*,[10] in which T. H. Green was portrayed as Professor Grey, indicates that the fundamentals of Green's message had an attraction outside the ranks of the group of undergraduates at Balliol who were so fascinated by his teaching as to wrestle with the difficulties of his philosophical expositions.

While Jowett was concerned in launching his men into positions of power and influence, the effect of T. H. Green's teaching was to encourage them to devote themselves to self-sacrificing works of charity and social reform.[11] Bernard Bosanquet was a disciple of Green in this way too. He had left the Church, and did not return to it, although he always remained friendly to religion and later played an active part in the non-denominational London Ethical Society[12] and found much to attract him in Unitarian and Quaker groups. He was repelled by the dogmatic rejection of Churchmen of scientific biblical criticism,[13] yet he felt that Rationalism and a purely humanistic ethic was in danger of losing some of the metaphysical and moral truths which religion had won, however inadequately orthodox religion might have expressed them. Religious mysticism contained some genuine insights, and Bosanquet found it 'distressing' to find the religious and the non-religious each withdrawing to their entrenched encampments and abandoning the middle ground where their differences might be reconciled by a more comprehensive philosophy.[14]

Bosanquet's decision to abandon Oxford was partly the result of increasing dissatisfaction with the teaching and administration involved in the Fellowship at University College to which he had been appointed on graduation. Although he remained there for eleven years, he discovered too little of the enthusiasm amongst 'Univ.' undergraduates for the philosophical adventures which had inspired him and his contemporaries at Balliol. He was also anxious to write, and he found the task of teaching, which he fulfilled dutifully, prevented his getting ahead with original work. Later he

[10] See Richter, *The Politics of Conscience*, p 28, for Mrs Ward's statement of the sales of her book.

[11] C. D. Broad, in his *Five Types of Ethical Theory* (London, 1967), p. 144, took a sourer Cambridge view: he considered that 'T. H. Green . . . has probably made far more undergraduates into prigs than Sidgwick will ever make into philosophers'.

[12] It was founded in 1886. H. Bosanquet, *Bernard Bosanquet*, p. 44.

[13] Muirhead, *Contemporary British Philosophy*, pp. 53–4.

[14] Ibid., p. 59.

was to become a prolific author, but the only work he produced during his years as an Oxford Fellow was a translation of Schömann's *Constitutional History of Athens*. The teaching of Ancient Greek History absorbed a great deal of his time, and provided a stimulus to his permanent interest in the history and art of the Athenians. His artistic interests were also stimulated in a modern direction by his friendship with a colleague at Univ., the mathematician C. J. Faulkner, an associate of William Morris in socialist politics and a partner in his firm.

In 1881, Bosanquet decided to abandon his Fellowship and to follow the example of his half-brother Charles, by going to London to take up charitable and social work; he intended to devote his spare time to writing. A small independent income and the money he had saved while teaching at Oxford relieved him, at the age of thirty-three, of the need to earn his living. The inspiration to charitable work had been fostered by the teaching of T. H. Green, and he was also encouraged by another friend of his Balliol days, Charles Stewart Loch, who had succeeded Charles Bosanquet as Secretary of the Charity Organisation Society in 1875. Loch was to play a more active role in the COS than Bernard Bosanquet, but he never lost the respect of an Oxford Third for an Oxford First. At the time of Bosanquet's engagement Loch wrote to his fiancée:

It has made me think of the twenty-five years and thereabouts, when Bernard, as you will now call him, and I lodged on the same staircase in Balliol, I a mentally rebellious, uneducated and ignorant creature, and he well taught and trained, quick of memory, keen witted, scholarly. It was strange that we should foregather. In all things he was supreme and far above me—in possession of fields of knowledge that I could only mount my boundary wall to look over into. And so indeed it seems to me now, after all these years of the fight of charity organisation.[15]

Bosanquet, on coming to London, first lived in lodgings in Ebury Street. Some years later he took a terrace house at 7 Cheyne Gardens, Chelsea, which he furnished in the best taste of the time with Morris wallpapers and hangings, De Morgan tiles, parquet floors, and carefully chosen pictures. His role in the COS was mainly that of committee-man counsellor and theorist, rather than that of practical social worker. He found direct contact with the poor, when he attempted visiting, personally embarrassing and

---

[15] H. Bosanquet, *Bernard Bosanquet*, pp. 27–8.

uncongenial.[16] His committee work occupied about six to twelve hours every week, and his services as chairman were frequently in demand. He also took an active part in University Extension teaching, lecturing at Toynbee Hall and other university 'settlements', and finding the students at these classes much more receptive and appreciative than the ones he had taught at Oxford. They renewed his faith in teaching. But above all, Bosanquet now found plenty of time for his own study and writing. The books which were to make his reputation began to flow from his pen from the mid 1880s.

The diversity of his philosophical interests was impressive. He ranged through social and political philosophy, through logic and metaphysics, to aesthetics. He laid the foundations of his later writings by a series of translations from the German which he did himself or promoted: of R. H. Lotze's *Logic* and *Metaphysics* (1884), of the Introduction to Hegel's *Philosophy of Fine Art* (1886), and of A. E. F. Schäffle's *The Quintessence of Socialism* (1889) and *The Impossibility of Social Democracy* (1892). These were works that he felt English readers should know, although he was critical of some of the views of these German scholars. Bosanquet's interest in ethics and logic had been stimulated during his student days, and he had long been determined to write books on these subjects. But he was anticipated in both by F. H. Bradley, whose *Ethical Studies* appeared in 1876 and *Principles of Logic* in 1883. Of the first of these Bosanquet wrote: 'At first on reading Bradley's book I felt as if blown to the winds: I have been picking myself up since, but shall be much more cautious than I had meant to be in resolving to write.'[17] His response to the second of Bradley's books was mixed—he found much to agree with, and much to disturb him in Bradley's outlook—and he sat down at once to write a critical study, published in 1885 under the title *Knowledge and Reality*, which was the prelude to his full-scale work *Logic* that appeared three years later, in 1888.

At the same time, he was working at his studies of art and the philosophy of art. The rich resources of the British Museum and the National and Tate Galleries provided a superb training ground for his interest in ancient, Renaissance, and modern art, and the comments he made in his letters about the works of art he saw in

---

[16] Ibid., p. 54.
[17] B. Bosanquet to Peters 13 Aug. 1876, in Muirhead, *Bernard Bosanquet and his Friends*, p. 37.

his holidays in Germany, Italy, and Greece revealed a perceptive and cultivated taste. His liking for Ruskin's art criticism and the craftsmanship of William Morris, and his association with the Home Arts and Industries Association, founded in 1885 to encourage artistic handiwork in education, kept him in touch with some of the contemporary currents of opinion. Reactions to the first Post-Impressionist exhibition of 1910 provide a measure of contemporaries' views—'advanced' or 'reactionary'—concerning modern art, and a letter Bosanquet wrote to Professor Alexander on 7 December 1910 indicated that his opinions were decidedly 'advanced': 'We [*he and his wife*] were at the Post-Impressionists yesterday and we both rather like them. I thought the row in the papers indicated something good.'[18] Bosanquet's *History of Aesthetic*, published in 1892, has been regarded by some critics as his finest achievement as writer and philosopher.

The involvement with the Charity Organisation Society drew Bosanquet into the realms of social policy and social philosophy. In politics, he considered himself to belong in the Radical wing of the Liberal Party.[19] He occasionally took part in election campaigns on behalf of the Liberals, and by all the standard criteria his claim to be a radical Liberal seemed justified. He supported Irish Home Rule,[20] and although not a 'Little Englander' but a believer in the virtues of the British Empire,[21] he was a 'pro-Boer' at the time of the South African War;[22] he was a strong opponent of tariffs and an advocate of Cobdenite-Mazzinan notions of co-operative nationalism; he supported the Liberal Party's actions in its conflict with the House of Lords in 1910–11[23] and, during the First World War, while believing the Allied cause to be just, he deplored the war's necessity and the more heated forms of patriotism it aroused.

Bosanquet's social theory will occupy our discussion in later chapters. Here it is needful to say only that a good deal of it was produced in the way of incidental comment and lecturing arising

---

[18] Ibid., p. 134.

[19] Ibid., See also H. Bosanquet, *Bernard Bosanquet*, p. 97.

[20] Muirhead, *Bernard Bosanquet and his Friends*, pp. 309, 311; H. Bosanquet, *Bernard Bosanquet*, pp. 99–102.

[21] B. Bosanquet, *The Philosophical Theory of the State* (London, 4th edn. repr. 1925), p. lx.

[22] Muirhead, *Bernard Bosanquet and his Friends*, p. 95; H. Bosanquet, *Bernard Bosanquet*, p. 99. On this matter the Bosanquets disagreed with the Lochs.

[23] Muirhead, *Bernard Bosanquet and his Friends*, pp. 132, 134, 309.

directly out of his concern with COS activity. It took the form of articles, lectures later reprinted as articles, books of collected essays earlier written for journals, and chapters and prefaces to books by a variety of authors. In the late 1890s he recast some of his earlier essays and lectures to make his most important book on political philosophy, *The Philosophical Theory of the State* (1899). Except for two works on metaphysics which were given originally as Gifford Lectures at the University of Edinburgh in 1911 and 1912, *The Principle of Individuality and Value* (1912) and *The Value and Destiny of the Individual* (1913), the main lines of Bosanquet's philosophy in its various realms had been worked out by the end of the nineteenth century. Many of the writings of his later years were restatements of philosophical positions he had earlier adopted, and articles and pronouncements which had contributed to the lively philosophical debate characteristic of the first quarter of the new century. Bosanquet was always greatly involved in the professional debates of the philosophical confraternity. Indeed, he appeared on the scene as a philosopher just at the time when philosophers were ceasing to address the lay public in the main laymen's reviews. Whereas the generation of philosophers before his—that of J. S. Mill, Leslie Stephen, even Henry Sidgwick—had published their articles in the *Westminster*, the *Fortnightly*, or the *Contemporary Review*, the new generation published in the quarterly journal *Mind*, which was established in 1876, or in the *Proceedings* of the Aristotelian Society, an institution founded in 1880; these journals were addressed not to the public at large but to an audience of professional philosophers. Bosanquet was an active contributor to both: he joined the Aristotelian Society in 1886, became vice-president in 1888 and was its president from 1894 to 1898; and he was always an avid reader of and frequent publisher in *Mind*. There was loss as well as gain in the change: what was gained in rigour and professional expertise was counterbalanced by loss of much immediate intelligibility of philosophers' discourse to society at large, and even perhaps an increasing remoteness from other fields of scientific discussion.

After their marriage, the Bosanquets moved out of London into the country—'far enough out of London to be in the real country and out of reach of trivial engagements, while remaining near enough to carry on much of our work'.[24] They went first to

---

[24] H. Bosanquet, *Bernard Bosanquet*, p. 72.

Caterham, and then in 1899 they built a house at Oxshott in Surrey, next door to the house of their friends, the Lochs. There they lived until Bosanquet was invited to become Professor of Moral Philosophy at the University of St Andrews in 1903; but during this appointment, which Bosanquet held until 1907, they retained the Oxshott cottage, returning to it during the summer vacations.

Bosanquet found his teaching at St Andrews more stimulating than teaching in Oxford. He wrote in 1906 to his nephew:

These local universities . . . give one an insight into ordinary education and its demands which Oxford and Cambridge hardly do in the same way. Just because these latter educate the governing classes perhaps they do not in the long run educate the classes which govern? I like it; I am in this respect if no other like T. H. Green; I like these young fellows with their living to make . . . who, as a colleague said to me, 'do want to get something out of you'.[25]

But once again in the long run Bosanquet found that lecturing and teaching made it impossible for him to get on with his original writing, so he resigned at the end of the 1907 academic year and returned with relief to Oxshott and London. The only later academic post he held was that of Gifford Lecturer at Edinburgh in the winters of 1911 and 1912. Oxshott remained the Bosanquets' home until Bernard's health, which had been failing since 1915, made it necessary for them, in 1922, to move back permanently to London, to be near relatives in Golders Green. Bernard Bosanquet died on 8 February 1923.

Helen Bosanquet

Helen Dendy was the fifth of the nine children of John Dendy (1828–94) and Sarah Beard (1831–1922). Both of her parents came of old Nonconformist families. Her mother's father had been minister to a Unitarian congregation at Salford, on the west bank of the Irwell River from Manchester. Her father was of a General Baptist family that traced its ancestry to Edward Dendy, a Sergeant-at-Arms to Parliament in Cromwell's time, who had taken the warrant for his execution to King Charles I.[26] Trained for the General Baptist ministry at Manchester New College and Berlin

---

[25] Ibid., pp. 111–12.
[26] McLachlan, *Records of a Family 1800–1933*, pp. 121, 128.

University, John Dendy returned to hold several different appointments as Nonconformist minister in Cheltenham and Stourbridge between 1851 and 1858—appointments which suggest there was considerable interchange of ministerial services between Baptist, Presbyterian, and Unitarian churches in the English provinces. He resigned in 1859 and tried his hand at business in Manchester until 1883, in a concern which flourished for over twenty years but ended in disaster. He then returned to the Unitarian ministry to serve a congregation at Newport, Isle of Wight, for the last ten years of his life.

Sarah Dendy in her old age described her family as belonging to the 'aristocracy of talent'. So far at least as four of her children were concerned, she was justified in her opinion. John Dendy junior, the eldest son, became a successful lawyer, with a hobby of writing books of travel and lay sermons. Mary Dendy, the eldest daughter, after studying at Bedford College in London, became a teacher and later an eminent social worker concerned especially with the problems of defective children. Arthur, the second youngest son, achieved distinction as a biologist in two hemispheres—in Australia, New Zealand, and South Africa as well as at King's College, London. These three, together with Helen, were left in the family house at Manchester when their parents moved to the Isle of Wight, because John Dendy junior was in a legal partnership in the town, Arthur was studying science at Owens College, and Mary was teaching at the Manchester High School for Girls. In this intellectual environment Helen did most of the housekeeping. Up till then, her own education had come from her mother and from a German governess. As soon as her younger brother had graduated at the end of 1885 she decided her turn to acquire some higher education had come. She applied for entry to Newnham College, Cambridge, which had been established only in the previous decade with Anne Jemima Clough, the ardent campaigner for higher education for women and sister of Arthur Hugh Clough the poet, as its first principal. Although, at twenty-six, Helen Dendy was older than most of the first-year students, she was admitted, and she found those few extra years, her ability, and her experience of life gave her a special standing amongst her fellow students. She won their affection, and was known as 'Aunt Dendy' or 'T.R.' (signifying 'Tone-Raiser') by her class-mates.[27] She gained some

[27] Ibid., p. 186.

fame as a debater in the Liberal Party cause at Newnham, became a friend of Mrs Fawcett and an advocate of her brand of constitutional feminism, and she had outstanding academic success, specializing in Political Economy and graduating with a first class in the Moral Sciences Tripos in 1889. Despite these achievements, she did not discover at the Cambridge of her time the full acceptance that a woman of her ability might have been accorded in a later age. She does not appear to have found, amongst the famous dons of Cambridge in her generation—Sidgwick, Marshall, John Neville Keynes, Foxwell—the guru-figure that Bernard Bosanquet had found in T. H. Green at Oxford. In spite of the devotion of some of the Cambridge dons to the cause of higher education for women, and their willingness to teach women undergraduates, their attitude was still more than a little tinged with the patronizing belief in 'separate spheres': women were not admitted to the inner sanctum of Cambridge economists at that time and those of them who were qualified—such as Mrs Marshall and Mrs Fawcett, and Helen Dendy too—accepted that situation.[28] After a brief and unrewarding experience of part-time academic coaching at Oxford, Helen decided to follow her elder sister's example and go to London as a social worker.

In London she at once made contact with the Charity Organisation Society, became friendly with Charles Stewart Loch and his wife, and after only short experience in social work, was appointed, in October 1890, to the salaried post of District Secretary of the COS in Shoreditch.[29] She held this position until her marriage, living in rooms in Hoxton near her office. Her conscientiousness and efficiency as a social worker, as well as her intellectual grasp and ability to theorize her experience, soon brought her to the notice of other leading members of the COS. She also appeared to have drifted further away from orthodox religion at Cambridge, a tendency which was confirmed by experiences of squabbles amongst clergymen—the 'sky-pilots' as she called them[30]—in their charitable endeavours. This led her to take an active interest and share in the meetings and lectures of the London Ethical Society. In the course of these activities, she met Bernard Bosanquet in 1891. Not long after, he encouraged her to join him in becoming a

[28] J. M. Keynes, *Essays in Biography* (London, 1961), pp. 202, 205, 336–7.
[29] H. McLachlan, *The Records of a Family 1800–1933*, p. 186.
[30] Ibid., p. 190.

University Extension lecturer, and he took the trouble to give her advice about lecturing techniques.[31] He also secured for her an invitation to take on her first major scholarly assignment—the translation of Christoph von Sigwart's two-volume work *Logik*, especially important to English philosophers because of the close examination it made of the induction theories of Bacon, Hume, and J. S. Mill. Her translation was published in 1895, and in the same year she contributed seven of the eighteen essays in the important work of charitable and social theory, called *Aspects of the Social Problem*, which Bernard Bosanquet edited in 1895. Her articles ranged from studies of 'Children of Working London', 'The Position of Women in Industry', and 'Marriage in East London' and of 'Old Pensioners' and 'The Industrial Residuum' to explanations of the 'Origin and History of the English Poor Law' and 'The Meaning and Methods of True Charity'. Several of these articles had been published earlier in the 1890s in periodical journals, and brought together they demonstrated her dedication to literary enterprise in the intervals of busy charitable activity. The close association formed with Bernard Bosanquet at this time resulted in their engagement and marriage in 1895.

After marriage Helen Bosanquet continued her social work in an honorary capacity, writing occasional articles for the major reviews on social questions, and producing, every few years, a more substantial volume, which either drew together a collection of earlier published articles (*The Standard of Life and other Studies* (1898)) or essayed a lengthier exploration of a social problem: *Rich and Poor* (1896); *The Strength of the People: A Study in Social Economics* (1902); *The Family* (1906). She saw herself as an exponent of a down-to-earth form of applied social economics, and, together with her husband and C. S. Loch, she came to be recognized as a main formulator of 'orthodox' Charity Organisation Society ideology, in spite of persistent (not altogether ingenuous) claims that they were merely putting forward their own views and not wishing to commit the Society. Her eminence as social worker and social theorist was acknowledged in her appointment by the government as a Commissioner on the Royal Commission on the Poor Laws in November 1905. There she played a leading part, at the expense of her own health. At the end of the Commission's

[31] Ibid.

labours she resumed her full commitment to the COS, becoming editor of its journal, the *Charity Organisation Review*, in succession to C. S. Loch, a position which she held for the next twelve years. Apart from the COS activity she lived quietly in the home she and her husband had built, cultivating their fine rose garden and writing a history of the COS entitled *Social Work in London 1869–1912*, published in 1914. Although she was a strong supporter of women's suffrage, she disapproved of the militant activities of the Suffragettes, believing that the goal would be achieved inevitably by a change of opinion and by constitutional methods. Some of her other views also offended the more advanced feminists of her time: such as her rejection of anthropological theories of an original matriarchy,[32] her passionate defence of an ideal of a family that would combine equal partnership and a benevolent patriarchy (with the married mother's place in the home),[33] and her criticism of the recommendations of an extension of the grounds of divorce contained in the Majority Report on Divorce Laws of 1912.[34] She and her husband published in 1919 a slim volume of original verses and translations from the German called *Zoar* (a 'little one', from Genesis 19: 20–22), of unremarkable merit. But in 1921 her health as well as her husband's had declined, and the Bosanquets moved to Golders Green, to live near the family of her brother, Arthur. After Bernard Bosanquet's death, she wrote a brief memoir of his life and work in 1924, and her last essay 'Free Trade and Peace in the Nineteenth Century'—a defence of Liberal economic policies—was published by the Nobel Institute in the same year. Helen Bosanquet died on 7 April 1925.

Sidney Webb

Sidney Webb began his career without the family status or educational advantages of the Bosanquets and Dendys. His family was 'lower middle class' and cockney, living in the very centre of London, in Cranbourn Street running out from Leicester Square. In 1859, when Sidney was born, this district was on the commercial fringe of the working-class area stretching into Covent Garden. The

---

[32] H. Bosanquet, *The Family* (London, 1906), pp. 35 ff.

[33] Ibid., pp. 200, 335–6.

[34] H. Bosanquet, 'English Divorce Law and the Report of the Royal Commission', *IJE* 23 (1913), 443 ff., and see also a reply by E. S. P. Haynes and H. Bosanquet's rejoinder in *IJE* 24 (1914), 342 ff. and 451.

Webbs were fairly comfortably off for a family in their station of life, mainly because of the earnings of a successful hairdressing and millinery shop which Sidney's mother ran at 44 Cranbourn Street both before and after her marriage.[35] Sidney's father, Charles Webb, was the son of an innkeeper at Petham in Kent; he had acquired some training as an accountant or bookkeeper, but his economic role was supplementary: he helped in his wife's shop, kept its books, and acted also as bookkeeper and debt-collector for other shop-owners in the neighbourhood.[36] Much of Charles Webb's activity was devoted to Radical politics at the local level—he was said to have been a strong supporter of John Stuart Mill in the Westminster election of 1865, and to have served sometime as a vestryman, as a member of the local Board of Guardians, and in the rifle volunteer corps.[37] It was the mother, however, who appears to have been the dominant partner in the Webb household. Her parents had died when she was very young, and she had been brought up by one of her aunts, who belonged to a fairly prosperous family of Essex and Suffolk farmers and pilots of coastal ships. One of these relatives had advanced the initial capital for her independent and enterprising venture into business in London in 1848.[38] She was as good a housewife as she was efficient in her shopkeeping; and she was ambitious for the future career of her two male children, Sidney and his elder brother Charles—the younger sister, Ada, could not, at that time, expect equal opportunities. All the children received a primary education from a teacher with the remarkably Dickensian name of Mr Pincher, who ran a school for middle-class pupils in St Martin's Lane. But Mrs Webb then sent the two boys to Switzerland and Germany for their further education from 1872 to 1875—first to a school at Neuvéville near Neuchatel in Switzerland, to learn French, and then to a Lutheran pastor at Wismar, on the Baltic coast near Rostock, to learn German. Such a practice, as we have seen in the case of the Dendy family, was not uncommon with Nonconformists who had pastoral ambitions for their sons, but it was an unusually enterprising action for a London shopkeeper. Mrs

---

[35] B. Webb, *Our Partnership*, ed. B. Drake and M. Cole (London, 1948), p. 2.
[36] Ibid.
[37] M. A. Hamilton, *Sidney and Beatrice Webb: A Study in Contemporary Biography* (London, 1932), p. 17.
[38] B. Webb, *Our Partnership*, p. 2; N. MacKenzie (ed.), *The Letters of Sidney and Beatrice Webb*, vol. 1. *Apprenticeships 1873–1892* (Cambridge, 1978), p. 73.

Webb's aim was to provide her boys with a knowledge of languages which would establish them in good careers as correspondence clerks with substantial commercial firms, and, apparently, she took the advice of one of her customers about where to send them. Her elder son, Charles, did follow the path his mother had mapped out for him, and became in the end a successful City business man and, politically, a Conservative.[39]

Sidney, too, on his return from the Continent in 1875, worked for five years in the office of a City broker; but he found the situation uncongenial, and used his formidable talents as a student as a way of escape from it. He attended City of London College evening classes from 1876 to 1880, and won first class honours not only in French and German, in which he was fluent, but also in Bookkeeping and Arithmetic. Later, at the Birkbeck Institute, at which he studied in 1879 and 1880, he had excellent results in economics, history, and geology. In 1881 he sat for the Civil Service Open Examinations for the Lower Division, and won appointment as clerk in Inland Revenue. In the following year, he sat for the Upper Division Exam and gained entry to the Colonial Office at the same time as a graduate from Oxford, Sydney Olivier, who was to become one of his closest friends in his early manhood. In 1883 he won the Whewell Scholarship to Trinity College, Cambridge, but, as the Colonial Office would not give him leave to take it up, he felt he could not afford to risk resignation, and declined it (a cautious decision that he later regretted). Instead, he remained in the Colonial Office, and undertook a part-time law course at London University. Graduating very successfully in 1886, he was called to the Bar in Gray's Inn.[40]

The meagre information which survives of Sidney Webb's early life and student days does not suggest that he found a paragon in any of his teachers; but it does give the impression of widely eclectic study, with a utilitarian and scientific bias. He followed his father in being a Liberal-Radical in politics, and J. S. Mill's *Principles of Political Economy* and *A System of Logic* were amongst the university textbooks which he held in high esteem. But he also imbibed the criticisms which Mill's doctrines had been sustaining in the thirty years since the publication of these works in the 1840s.

[39] B. Webb, *Our Partnership*, pp. 3–4; Hamilton *Sidney and Beatrice Webb*, p. 18; MacKenzie, *Letters*, i. 73–4.
[40] Hamilton, *Sidney and Beatrice Webb*, pp. 19–21; MacKenzie, *Letters*, i. 74.

Webb did not ever break away from the Utilitarian line of thought; but he was strongly attracted by the evolutionary doctrines of the developing geological and biological sciences, especially in the application of their theories by analogical inference to the social sciences. Aspects of T. H. Huxley's and Herbert Spencer's thought particularly engaged him. He described Mill as the 'latest philosopher of the pre-scientific age', who had discerned the need for introducing a dynamic, evolutionary element into social theory, although remaining still too firmly anchored by the 'static' or 'abstract' approach of his Benthamite past. Sidney Webb appears to have got the elements of the concept of an evolutionary 'social organism' initially from Darwin, Spencer, and Huxley,[41] although he later realized that the organic analogy had a very much older history in social studies than it had in biology, and that it was merely reinforced by the doctrines of the new biology. His early writings show a considerable acquaintance with and use of the works of Spencer and Huxley. However, as Webb was coming to maturity as a social theorist at the time when those two old friends were beginning to diverge, even to fall out, in their social views, he was put on his critical guard, and one is inclined to believe that there was more of Huxley than of Spencer in his developing ideas. In the famous 'Historic' chapter in *Fabian Essays in Socialism*, where Webb made full obeisance to the concepts of 'evolution' and 'social organism', it was to Huxley's interpretation of 'evolution' in civilized society that he gave his allegiance,[42] while the section which he paraphrased from Spencer's *The Man versus the State*, listing in detail the recent developments in social control, was 'stood on its head' by his treating these developments as commendable rather than as something to be deplored.[43]

Webb's transition from Radicalism to Socialism was a fairly slow process. He was not favourably disposed to Marx's economics or to the politics of the Marxist Social Democratic Federation in the 1880s. He was not, at first, even a land nationalizer, as many of the extreme Radicals were; but he was prepared to give support to heavy land-taxes, though sceptical about the Land Reformers'

---

[41] L. Howard, 'The New Utilitarians? Studies in the Origins and Early Intellectual Associations of Fabianism', Ph.D. thesis (University of Warwick, 1976), pp. 4, 24–9, 35–41.
[42] G. B. Shaw (ed.), *Fabian Essays in Socialism* (London, 1889), p. 60.
[43] Ibid. pp. 46–53.

claims that they could abolish rent by this policy.[44] There is no convincing evidence that he came to Socialism through the loss of his religious beliefs, as some of his friends did: he seems to have lost any religious beliefs he may have had quite early, and he has left no record of mental anguish in the process of shedding them. Although his mother was an Evangelical Christian, 'who took the children to one church or chapel after another in search of an eloquent preacher free from sacerdotalism',[45] and although some of Sidney Webb's early speeches do show signs of typical Evangelical rhetoric, that may be evidence about the rhetoric of that period rather than of his residual commitment to a lost faith.[46] And we know nothing of Sidney's father's religious beliefs (if any), except, presumably, that he did not go church-visiting with the rest of the family on Sundays. London Radicals in general were not notable for their religious devotion. In 1885, Webb described himself as 'atheistic',[47] which meant that he had gone beyond Spencer's 'Unknowable' (one presumably had to know there was an 'Unknowable') and also Huxley's 'agnosticism' (where the evidence had to be at least debatable, if unconvincing). In later years, he would probably have agreed with a twentieth-century philosopher who, underestimating the loquacity of mankind, declared: 'Whereof one cannot speak, thereof one must be silent'[48]—for he withdrew, uninterested, from disputations of theological matters, even when his wife, to whom he was in other ways utterly devoted, discussed with friends the residual items of her religious belief.[49]

Sidney Webb's approach to Socialism came through a circle of friends he had built up in his days as a Colonial Office clerk. Sydney Olivier, his colleague in the Office, was the first of these friends, and he introduced Webb to his Oxford associate, Graham Wallas, who had become a schoolteacher in London. Both Olivier and Wallas were sons of the vicarage who had rejected a clerical career; both of them had become interested in the Positivist philosophy of Auguste

[44] MacKenzie, *Letters*, i. 79 (Webb to Shaw, 11 Aug. 1883).
[45] B. Webb, *Our Partnership*, p. 3.
[46] One remembers Bernard Shaw's story of the old lady, a very devout Methodist, who sat at the feet of Charles Bradlaugh for many years, entranced by his eloquence, without questioning his orthodoxy or moulting a feather of her faith (in Shaw's preface to *Man and Superman*).
[47] Webb to Wallas, 17 Aug. 1885, MacKenzie, *Letters*, i. 93.
[48] L. Wittgenstein, *Tractatus Logico-Philosophicus* (London, 1960), p. 189.
[49] B. Webb, *Our Partnership*, p. 292.

Comte at Oxford, and they introduced Webb, who had already made some contact with Comte's ideas through the writings of John Stuart Mill and of George Eliot, into deeper discussions of Positivist theory.[50] The three young men formed a close trio, dubbed the 'Three Musketeers' by Bernard Shaw, who no doubt saw his own role as that of D'Artagnan.[51] Webb became greatly interested in Positivism, in spite of the warnings and reservations which John Stuart Mill and Herbert Spencer had expressed about aspects of Comte's doctrines. Mill had incorporated a certain amount of Positivist philosophy, especially its doctrines concerning scientific and historical development, into his own system of logic,[52] but he rejected Comte's criticism of classical economics[53] and of 'subjective' psychology,[54] and he found Comte's proposals for a highly planned, collectivist society run by moralized capitalists and a priesthood of scientists utterly abhorrent. He described Comte's polity as 'the completest system of spiritual and temporal despotism which ever yet emanated from a human brain, unless possibly that of Ignatius Loyola'.[55] Herbert Spencer pointed out very adroitly that Comte's philosophy embodied many elements common to the English and French empiricist tradition, which made his doctrines appealing to a certain type of English intellectual, even if, like Spencer himself, they should reject everything that was special and original in Comte's own contribution.[56] Some of the English followers of Comte, such as Professor E. S. Beesley and Frederic Harrison, had given Comte's political and social aspirations a twist that appealed to young Radicals, by suggesting that one way to moralize capitalists was to have strong trade unions, and by interpreting Comte's 'priesthood of scientists' to mean highly trained administrators with careful 'scientific' knowledge of the facts, combined with an awareness of the forces of social

---

[50] M. Olivier (ed.) *Sydney Olivier: Letters and Selected Writings* (London, 1948), p. 60; M. J. Wiener, *Between Two Worlds: The Political Thought of Graham Wallas* (Oxford, 1971), pp. 16–17.

[51] Hamilton, *Sidney and Beatrice Webb*, pp. 14–15.

[52] J. S. Mill, *Auguste Comte and Positivism* (London, 1865), *passim*, and Bk. VI, ch. 10 of *A System of Logic* (London, 1879).

[53] J. S. Mill, *A System of Logic*, Bk. VI, ch. 9, pp. 481–5, and id. *Essays on some Unsettled Questions of Political Economy* (London, 1844), *passim*.

[54] Mill, *A System of Logic*, Bk. VI, ch. 4, pp. 422–32.

[55] J. S. Mill, *Autobiography*, (New York, 1944), p. 149.

[56] H. Spencer, *Reasons for Dissenting from the Philosophy of M. Comte* (London, 1884), *passim*.

evolution. Between 1883 and 1886 Webb's ideas were strongly influenced by Comtism and, even for some time after he joined the Fabian Society, he maintained that Comtism was a form of Socialism[57] (a view that Comte would probably not have shared) and that the moralization of capitalists might be a quicker way to Socialism than their expropriation. This last view was also influenced by the precepts of Thomas Carlyle (for Webb was an avid reader of Carlyle's writings too) that the greater capitalists should be persuaded to become socially responsible rulers, looking after the welfare of their workpeople and the community, rather than greedy and irresponsible competitive exploiters.[58]

Webb joined the recently founded Fabian Society on 1 May 1885, after earlier membership of several other small discussion groups in London. The Fabians had considered themselves to be 'Socialists' from the foundation of their society in January 1884, but neither the original members, nor Webb and his friends when they first joined, had worked out clearly what they meant by the term. The working out, which was to give definition to the meaning of Fabian Socialism, took place at a discussion circle of an inner group of Fabians, in which Webb, Olivier, Wallas, and Shaw played a leading part. Initially called the Karl Marx Club, and set up for the purpose of studying Marx's *Capital*, it had begun before Webb and his friends became Fabians and it was to be continued for several years as the Hampstead Historic Society. Although the formulation of Fabian doctrine was a collective achievement, Webb was emerging, by 1888, as the leading systematic expositor of its theoretical principles and practical applications.[59]

It has been well said that Webb 'became a Socialist when he became disillusioned with the idea of moralising capitalists'.[60] Webb from the first was hostile to Marx's economics, as expressed in *Capital*, and was a fierce critic of it at the Hampstead Historic meetings; but these discussions brought into vivid focus some central propositions of Socialism. He could not accept Marx's theory of 'surplus value' built as superstructure upon the classical

---

[57] S. Webb, 'The Economics of a Positivist Community', *Practical Socialist*, 1 (1886).

[58] T. Carlyle, 'Shooting Niagara: and After?', *Essays*, vol. i (London 1950), pp. 324 ff.

[59] A. M. McBriar, *Fabian Socialism and English Politics 1884–1918* (Cambridge, 1962), ch. 2.

[60] Howard, 'The New Utilitarians?', p. 65.

'labour theory of value', but he perceived the essential Socialist principle lurking behind what he considered to be Marx's antiquated and erroneous theorizing: the distinction between earned and unearned incomes—between those who contributed productively to society and the parasitic class of *rentiers*, who lived by owning rather than by working. The young Fabians, and Webb in particular, set themselves as their first Socialist task the replacement of Marx's surplus value theory with a 'Theory of Rent',[61] which would be compatible with the most up-to-date economic doctrines. Greater equality of incomes in society, promoted by government action, was a natural corollary of this theory: landlords and capitalists would be moralized not by ethical persuasion, but by social action. Webb continued to believe that moralization of the community so that it would accept Socialism, had to go along with legislation: it would be no use imposing changes by revolution or by mere force without community acceptance, and consequently the change to Socialism would need to be a very gradual and long-term process.[62] He also took the view that the extension of parliamentary franchise to the majority of the working class, which had occurred in 1884, and the further democratization of both central and local government which was expected to follow, would provide the basis of a change of opinion and the promotion of social legislation in a Socialist direction.

The immediate political task, as Webb saw it, was to 'permeate' the Radical wing of the Liberal Party, and encourage it to adopt a progressive social policy—both at the national and the local government level. The Fabian Society was to become a power-house of information and a directing centre of the campaign. Webb showed the way to his fellow Fabians with some of the Tracts and booklets produced in 1889–91: *Facts for Socialists*; *Facts for*

[61] McBriar, *Fabian Socialism and English Politics*, pp. 35–47; D. M. Ricci, 'Fabian Socialism: A Theory of Rent as Exploitation', *Journal of British Studies*, 9 (1969); W. Wolfe, *From Radicalism to Socialism: Men and Ideas in the Formation of Fabian Socialist Doctrines 1881–1889* (New Haven and London, 1975), pp. 202–14, 275–84. An essay worth adding to the primary sources cited in the above works, which reveals something of the inwardness of Webb's ideas concerning his 'Theory of Rent', is S. Webb, 'The Relation between Wages and the Remainder of the Economic Produce' (1889), reprinted in R. L. Smyth (ed.), *Essays in the Economics of Socialism and Capitalism: Selected Papers read to Section F of the British Association for the Advancement of Science 1886–1932* (London, 1964), pp. 65–73.
[62] S. Webb to Pease, 24 Oct. 1886, MacKenzie *Letters*, i. 101–2.

Londoners; *Figures for Londoners*; *Wanted a Programme: An Appeal to the Liberal Party*; *An Eight Hours Bill*; *Reform of the Poor Law*; *The London Programme* (for the newly formed London County Council). By the early 1890s, Webb, although still a civil servant, was emerging as a budding politician at the local level.

In January 1890 Sidney Webb first met Beatrice Potter, when she had been advised by a friend that he was the person to consult to gain certain information about the Labour movement that she needed for the book she was writing on Co-operatives. He soon fell head over heels in love with her, but not she with him. Barriers of class, family, an old love-wound, and her career stood between them, and it was only Sidney's undaunted devotion and persistence that finally overcame these. The marriage changed Sidney's life. Beatrice's private fortune enabled him to retire from the Civil Service and devote himself to their joint writings and to local politics. She had already contributed substantially towards his election expenses as candidate for Deptford in 1892 when he was elected to the London County Council.[63] As author of *The London Programme*, accepted as its manifesto by the Progressive Party (a Liberal–Labour combination) that had had a sweeping victory, he was destined for an important career in municipal politics for the next seventeen years, principally in the administration and reorganization of the whole educational system of the metropolis. He could hardly have extricated himself from his London commitments to enter national politics, as well as carried on with his and Beatrice's great works, before the 1905 general election, and Beatrice did not wish to see him do so; but he could, and perhaps should have made the attempt in 1905. In that period, however, the emergence of the Labour Party had made the political situation difficult for Webb. He had only in one moment of exasperation in 1893–4 given any real support to the formation of a separate working-class party,[64] and had fallen out with the Independent Labour Party over a number of political issues in the years at the turn of the century.[65] To have stood then for the first time as Liberal candidate might have estranged the Fabians from Labour. In addition, Beatrice

---

[63] N. and J. MacKenzie, *The First Fabians* (London, 1977), p. 157; S. Webb to B. Webb, 4 Jan. 1892, MacKenzie, *Letters*, i. 375.

[64] At the time of the 'To Your Tents, Oh Israel!' manifesto: McBriar, *Fabian Socialism and English Politics*, pp. 249–52.

[65] Ibid., pp. 305–6.

Webb was just beginning her own entry into the political arena, with membership of the Royal Commission on the Poor Laws, and Sidney was anxious to encourage and assist her in that enterprise. So he had to wait until he was entering old age (in 1924) before he began his career as a parliamentarian.

Sidney Webb turned out to be perfectly right, however, in his conviction that he and Beatrice would produce better scholarly work in partnership than as individuals. The first major project they tackled was one that she had already contemplated: a study of trade unionism, which she felt was the necessary sequel to her book on Co-operation. She dissuaded Sidney (probably wisely) from writing a new textbook on economics, which was his own plan for his first major work, for she knew it would have to compete with Alfred Marshall's recently published *Principles of Economics* and she feared that Webb did not have the experience to rival Marshall's '30 years of devotion to this subject'.[66] Beatrice also knew that she would not have much share in a 'partnership' in that sort of book. The result of the blending of their complementary talents was the production of two masterpieces, the *History of Trade Unionism* (1894) and *Industrial Democracy* (1897). The partnership then embarked on the great project, running in the end to ten volumes, *English Local Government from the Revolution to the Municipal Corporations Act*, which was to occupy them as their major studious task from 1898 to 1929, with the volumes coming out at regular intervals over that time: *The Parish and the County* (1906), *The Manor and the Borough* (2 vols., 1908), *English Poor Law Policy* (1910), *The Story of the King's Highway* (1913), *Statutory Authorities for Special Purposes* (1922), *English Prisons under Local Government* (1922), *English Poor Law History* (2 vols., 1929). The volume with the least inviting title, *Statutory Authorities for Special Purposes*, in the course of which they summed up their general conclusions about the evolution of local government in England, was probably the most brilliant of an admirable series.

After their marriage the Webbs lived first in a flat in South Hampstead, but Bernard Shaw suggested that 'a salon for the cultivation of the socialist party' was needed, and asked: 'Will Madame Potter-Webb take it on?'[67] So they moved to a terrace

[66] B. Webb to S. Webb, 23 Aug. [1890], MacKenzie *Letters*, i, 178.
[67] MacKenzie, *Letters*, vol. ii. *Partnership 1892–1912* (Cambridge, 1978), p. 2.

house at 41 Grosvenor Road, which they refurbished with William Morris wallpapers; it was on the Thames embankment close to the Houses of Parliament and the Tate Gallery. This house was to be their residence for the next thirty-five years, although they bought a country cottage, which they called 'Passfield Corner', at Liphook, Hampshire in 1923, for their prospective retirement. 41 Grosvenor Road was indeed to become a 'salon' (a rather severely intellectual and political one, for some of their guests' tastes) during all that time, and a centre for Fabian and high-level political 'permeation'.

The story of the Webbs' main activities in the Edwardian period, in the war years and up to 1929, will be told later in this book. Sidney Webb's involvement with the London County Council came to an end in 1910 when he did not stand for re-election. A great deal of the Webbs' occasional writing arose out of their involvement with the Poor Law Commission in the years before the War, and out of their wartime activities between 1914 and 1918. The First World War brought Sidney Webb for the first time directly into the ambit of the Labour Party, which resulted in his important contribution to the reorganization of the Labour Party in 1918, and the drafting of its first post-war programme.[68] He was appointed one of the mine-workers' representatives on the Sankey Commission of 1919 which investigated the future of the coal-mining industry, and, in 1920, he received nomination as Labour candidate for the mining electorate of Seaham Harbour in Durham, by which he was elected to Parliament in 1922. He was President of the Board of Trade in the first short-lived Labour Government of 1924; and in 1929 he was elevated to the House of Lords as Lord Passfield, and became Secretary of State for Dominion Affairs and Colonial Secretary in the second Labour Government of 1929–31. During that time, in addition to their production of the later volumes of their *History of Local Government*, the Webbs also published a study which analysed the functions of the Consumers' Co-operative Movement on the same lines as *Industrial Democracy* had done for the trade unions, and two Socialist manifestos, *A Constitution for the Socialist Commonwealth of Great Britain* (1920), and *The Decay of Capitalist Civilisation* (1923). Bitterly disappointed by the collapse of the Labour government in 1931, and disenchanted

---

[68] McBriar, *Fabian Socialism and English Politics*, pp. 341–5; S. Pierson, *British Socialists: The Journey from Fantasy to Politics* (Cambridge, Mass., 1979), pp. 340–2.

with the prospects of western Socialism during the Great Depression, the Webbs in their old age discovered merits in Marxism and the Soviet experiment, and made their 'pilgrimage' to Russia, resulting in *Soviet Communism: A New Civilisation?* in 1935. Sidney Webb suffered a stroke in 1938, which rendered him incapable of further work, and he remained an invalid for another nine years, dying at Passfield Corner on 13 October 1947.

Beatrice Webb

Beatrice Potter was born into 'the purple of commerce'. She was the eighth of the nine daughters of Richard Potter, chairman of the Great Western Railway, one of the 'railway kings' of the Victorian boom age. The fortune of the Potter family had been established by Richard Potter's father, through investment in Manchester cotton.[69] Richard Potter was educated at Clifton, and then, the family being Unitarian, he was sent for his tertiary education not to Oxford or Cambridge but to University College, London, where he studied law. His apparent destiny as a country gentleman with a career in politics was thwarted when the inheritance left by his father was almost swept away in the financial crisis of 1847–8.[70] Richard Potter had to turn to business enterprise himself to recoup his fortunes, and he proved to be even more successful than his father as an industrial entrepreneur on a large—eventually on an international—scale in many types of business, but especially timber and railways. As happened with many successful industrial capitalists, he shifted from the Nonconformity and Radical Liberalism of his youthful background to conformist Anglicanism and political Conservatism in his later years.[71] He was a genial man, with a wide, eclectic, detached interest in literature, fond of entertaining writers and intellectuals as well as his business associates in London during 'the season', or at his country houses—Standish House in the Cotswolds, Rusland Hall in Westmorland, or the Argoed in Monmouthshire.[72] Because of the Potter family's nomadic existence between its residences, Richard Potter's frequent business trips abroad, and his wife's preference for scholarly pursuits, the Potters did not establish roots in county society, and had to find their interests within the network of their

---

[69] B. Webb, *My Apprenticeship* (Harmondsworth, 1938), i. 18.
[70] Ibid., p. 19.   [71] MacKenzie, *Letters*, i. 1.
[72] B. Webb, *My Apprenticeship*, i. 27, 41.

own family and in the kaleidoscope of their father's associates and friends. Richard Potter was very fond of his daughters, and indulgent of them; he established a happy relationship early and, as they grew up, he took them in turn with him on his trips abroad. His expectations of them, however, were that they would marry successful men of the upper classes—expectations which all but the last two of them fulfilled.

Beatrice's mother, Lawrencina Heyworth, had come of the same social class as Richard Potter: her father had risen through his own efforts to become a rich Liverpool merchant. She was brought up pious and puritanical; she had been highly educated, and was a classical scholar and a brilliant linguist, who hoped to master twelve languages before she died. Her ambitions for a life of literary scholarly achievement with intellectual companionship from her husband had been shattered by the early slump in Richard Potter's fortune and the redirection of his activities, and by her lifetime of childbearing, even if the care and upbringing of the children was largely delegated to servants, nurses, governesses, and tutors. Beatrice remembered her mother as disillusioned and rather embittered, withdrawn and remote, ruling her domestic empire very efficiently from the fastness of her boudoir by orders transmitted through her personal maidservant.[73] Beatrice recorded that she really got to know her mother only in the last years of her life, when the elder daughters had married and Beatrice had taken over management of the household. She felt that she, even more than her sisters, had been separated from her mother because the only boy-child of the Potter family was born when she was four and died two years later: he had been 'the crowning joy and devastating sorrow of my mother's life'.[74]

One of Richard Potter's closest intellectual friends on the personal level was Herbert Spencer, although he remained detached and sceptical concerning Spencer's system and sociological ideas. Later on, Bernard Shaw was to say that Beatrice Webb's 'genial unmetaphysical father entertained [Herbert Spencer] much as he might have kept a pet elephant'.[75] Spencer had the role of tutor to the Potter daughters. There was no thought of sending any of them

---

[73] MacKenzie, *Letters*, i. 1; S. Letwin, *The Pursuit of Certainty* (Cambridge, 1965), p. 346.
[74] B. Webb, *My Apprenticeship*, i 28 ff.
[75] Ibid., G. B. Shaw's introduction, p. 12.

to a university; so the polymathic philosopher had a function in the household of this nineteenth-century plutocrat, of the kind that Adam Smith or Rousseau had once had in the establishments of eighteenth-century aristocrats. Beatrice was greatly indebted to Spencer, as she handsomely acknowledged, for information and inspiration, but she always retained something of her father's detached and ironic view of him, and evaded his attempts to make her a disciple or research assistant. In her diary,[76] at the time of his death in December 1903, she tried to sum up briefly what his teaching had meant to her; it included a scientific approach to social institutions, with special emphasis on the notion of functional adaptation, and an altruistic and disinterested search for truth with a belief that a scientific search for truth in social affairs was not in vain and could bring about consolation and reformation for mankind. By 1903 she had departed from Spencer's more specific ideas in economics, in politics, in sociological method, and in ultimate views about the nature of the universe, although earlier she had been influenced by them. Perhaps it was his religious views that had disturbed her from the beginning: she had felt, even as a girl, that his agnostic doctrine of an inscrutable Unknowable behind the phenomena of Nature did not satisfy the demands of her religious feelings, much as she tried to persuade herself that it left mystery in the universe in spite of the increasing discoveries of science. For many years, indeed up to middle life, she pursued her quest for a creed with a zeal worthy of her mother's piety. Intellectually, she sampled many forms of Christianity both Protestant and Catholic, as well as Hinduism, Buddhism, and the religion of Humanity of Auguste Comte. But, in the end, her critical faculty did not allow her commitment to any of the established creeds, nor did she think she had the capacity to construct a metaphysics of her own. It is revealing of her upbringing and education, indeed, that her search for a creed was conducted entirely in religious, scientific, and literary terms: at that time she was unacquainted with the works of contemporary metaphysicians. She emerged with a dualistic faith which involved sharp divisions between science and religion, reason and emotion, means and ends, a world which worked according to its own dynamics yet was subject to revelation from an impersonal 'Force working for good in the Universe' that could communicate with and aid individuals through the agency of prayer:

[76] B.W.D., 8 and 9 Dec. 1903, quoted in *My Apprenticeship*, i 56–7.

. . . it is by prayer, by communion with an all-pervading spiritual force, that the soul of man discovers the purpose or goal of human endeavour, as distinguished from the means or process by which human beings may attain their ends. For science is bankrupt in deciding the destiny of man; she lends herself indifferently to the destroyer and to the preserver of life, to the hater and to the lover of mankind. Yet any avoidance of the scientific method in disentangling 'the order of things', any reliance on magic or mystical intuitions in selecting the process by which to reach the chosen end, spells superstition and usually results in disaster.[77]

Beatrice Potter's impersonal Force remained largely undefined,but it was not as unknowable as Spencer's Unknowable.

At the same time as she was in search of a creed, Beatrice Potter was also seeking for some career which would engage her interest and her talents. Her experiments were enterprising, but she was ruthlessly self-critical. After her mother's death, she became a successful manager of her father's household, and hostess for his friends; but that did not satisfy her. She also acted as her father's private secretary and counsellor, and showed such shrewdness and judgement in business affairs that he suggested 'if she did not want to marry' she should become his associate and partner in his enterprises; but she had more intellectual ambitions. For a while she took seriously the idea of becoming a writer of novels, but finally decided that she had neither the special talents nor the urge to be a novelist; she also appears to have had puritanical doubts about the 'seriousness' of novel-writing. She dabbled in biology with encouragement from Herbert Spencer and her medical brother-in-law, William Harrison Cripps, and she studied mathematics under the tutoring of a local clergyman who was a Cambridge wrangler; but she felt that science was not her line of interest, in spite of her fascination with some great scientists to whom Herbert Spencer introduced her—Huxley and Tyndall, Hooker and Lubbock, but above all Francis Galton. Under the influence of her reading of John Stuart Mill's *System of Logic*, G. H. Lewes's *History of Philosophy*, and H. T. Buckle's *History of Civilisation*, and through the friendship of the Positivist philosopher Frederic Harrison and his wife, Beatrice made a study of the writings of Auguste Comte. Although she did not become an adherent of Comtism, she appears to have found some direction for her ambitions both from his 'sociology' and his collectivism. She

[77] Ibid., p. 127.

transcribed into her Diary the passage from Comte: 'Towards humanity, who is the only true great Being, we, the conscious elements of whom She is the compound, shall henceforth direct every aspect of our life, individual and collective'.[78]

Like many middle-class ladies of leisure, Beatrice Potter took up charitable work amongst the poor of London, in this following the example of her elder sister Kate. In 1883 she joined the Charity Organisation Society and became one of its 'visitors' in the slums of Soho, and later acted as a rent-collector on a housing estate run on lines prescribed by Octavia Hill in the East End of London. She remained in this activity until the end of 1885, when her father suffered a paralytic stroke and she was obliged to withdraw to attend to him and his business affairs. Later on, as Mrs Webb, she was to become a severe critic of the COS, but it appears from her Diary and letters that, in the period 1883–5, she was pretty firmly committed to the essential tenets of COS doctrine, although her personal association was mainly with Canon Barnett and his wife, and not with C. S. Loch, Bernard Bosanquet, or Octavia Hill. By the end of her stint she was finding the constant round of charity work futile and dispiriting: '. . . practical work does not satisfy me; it seems like walking on shifting sand, with the forlorn hope that the impress of one's steps will be lasting, and guide others across the desert'.[79]

During this time, in the years between 1883 and 1886, Beatrice had fallen passionately in love with Joseph Chamberlain, the Birmingham manufacturer who had risen to be leader of the Radical wing of the Liberal Party and who was thought to be (and saw himself as being) Mr Gladstone's successor as leader. She was miserably torn between her desire to become Chamberlain's third wife and her realization that marriage to such a man would mean the complete subordination of her interests to his. Finally she made him a frank declaration of love which he treated politely but coolly; she suffered a deep feeling of humiliation and a wound which left a scar long after they had gone their separate ways.[80] The only other thing which survived from their association was her sharpened

---

[78] Ibid., p. 173; N. and J. MacKenzie, *The Diary of Beatrice Webb* (London 1982–5), vol. i, p. 120.

[79] Ibid., *My Apprenticeship*, ii. 324; MacKenzie, *Diary*, i, 185.

[80] Cole (ed.), *Beatrice Webb's Diaries 1924–1932* (London, 1956), contains an appendix (pp. 311–16) on 'Beatrice Webb and Joseph Chamberlain'; see also MacKenzie *Letters*, i 15, 16, 23, 26, 36, 39, 44, 52, 58, 64, 66, 201–2, 231, 239.

awareness of politics, and an interest in his doctrine of 'ransom' which the rich owed to the poor.

She was rescued from depression and disillusionment by her cousin by marriage, Charles Booth, a retired Liverpool shipowner who had taken up social investigation in London. He invited her, in December 1886, to join his research team investigating the extent of poverty in London. As Beatrice remarked, Charles Booth 'delighted in upsetting generally accepted views, whether the free-trade orthodoxy of Manchester capitalism, at that time in the ascendant, or the cut and dried creed of the Marxian socialists'.[81] Influenced by Comtism, Booth was critical of orthodox economics, and he was keen to apply the new science of statistics to the measurement of London poverty. Beatrice sympathized warmly with his criticism of 'abstract economics', and attempted some critical articles of her own along those lines in papers[82] on 'The Rise and Growth of English Economics' and 'The Economic Theory of Karl Marx'. The first of these was important in developing her view that what was needed was a study of the history of social institutions as they actually exist, not in any assured perfection of development, but in all the changing phases of 'health or disease' that they have actually passed through. It was the first theoretical statement of the 'sociological history'—the study of the life-history of social institutions—which was to become the speciality of the Webb partnership later on. At the same time, she was serving her 'apprenticeship' as a social researcher with Booth, and though she praised his work, she also discovered that his way was not hers. She later came to criticize Booth for the 'static' nature of his investigation and his neglect of the 'historical method' of analysing the 'actual processes of birth, growth, decay and death of social institutions'.[83]

Her first book, which she began early in 1889, was to be a 'life-history' of the British Co-operative Movement. She was inspired in her attempt to study this subject by three influences: first, by a visit she had made in 1883, out of sociological curiosity, to a group of her maternal relatives in Bacup, who had remained in the working class and who were deeply concerned with local co-operative ventures; second, by the hopes of some progressive liberal economists that workers' co-operatives might be in some way a *via*

[81] B. Webb, *My Apprenticeship*, ii. 268.
[82] Ibid., ii. 338–42 and Appendix D, pp. 482–91.   [83] Ibid., ii. 292–4.

media between capitalism and socialism; third, by the attempts of Professor Alfred Marshall, whom she consulted about the topic, to dissuade her from attempting it, on the grounds that it was not a suitable subject for a woman to study, and to divert her on to the subject of women's labour. After her interview with Marshall, she noted in her Diary: '. . . with the disagreeable, masculine characteristic of persistence and well-defined purpose, I shall stick to my own way of climbing my own little tree. Female labour I may take up some day or other, but the Co-operative Movement comes first.'[84] It is worth noting, at this point, that Beatrice Potter was not a supporter of votes for women. In 1889 she had signed the women's petition, organized by Mrs Humphry Ward, against granting the suffrage to women. Subsequently, she came to regret this action, and twenty years later she publicly recanted. In trying retrospectively to explain why she had taken this 'false step', she gave several reasons: she was not herself interested in taking part in politics at that time; she had been put off by the fanaticism of some feminist agitators; she had not herself felt any frustration in being a woman, because of her father's treatment of his daughters; and she had discovered that there were advantages as a social researcher getting information in being female and outside politics.[85] She suspected that her anti-feminist views may have had something to do with Professor Marshall's wish to direct her investigations towards the question of women's labour; but it may have been only her sex.

Her little book, *The Co-operative Movement in Great Britain*, which appeared in 1891, won immediate recognition as an important study. The selection of the topic and the greater part of research was her own, but in the later stages, from January 1890 onwards, she received some help and much encouragement from Sidney Webb, to whom she had been recommended for advice. It marked the beginning of the Webb partnership, ardent from the first on his side, very reluctant at first on hers. He had much to gain from the union; she apparently had much to lose, especially the disapproval of her family and of most of the friends belonging to her social set, of such a match. She did not at first love him; and she made brutally clear that the terms were intellectual partnership, not conventional matrimony, giving him plenty of opportunity to

---

[84] Ibid., ii. 400.   [85] Ibid., ii. 400–2.

withdraw. Only a devotion as determined as his could have won through—and did, though on her terms. She did not, however, dare to marry him until her father had died. After their marriage, his relationship even with the more genial members of her immediate family did indeed prove to be somewhat difficult; but what hurt her more was that the Booths also took the view that Sidney Webb was a very unsuitable marriage partner for their socially eligible cousin.[86] Their personal aversion was strengthened by an ill-founded belief that it was Sidney's influence which had caused Beatrice to 'desert' Charles Booth as a helper in his great London survey.[87] The resulting estrangement lasted for almost a decade.

In spite of its somewhat inauspicious beginning, the Webb partnership flourished, developing from a 'working comradeship' into a deep and lasting personal attachment. They discovered reciprocal strengths which they would not have enjoyed as separate individuals. At first, their research interests followed the lines that Beatrice had planned—into a study of the history and functions of trade unions—but gradually she found herself drawn into the political activity of Fabian Socialism, and the Webbs' later extensive researches into the history of local government in England incorporated at least as much of Sidney's interests as hers. The money and the social *savoir-faire* which she brought to the partnership enabled Webb and his Fabian friends to permeate the political élite faster than that rising band of young intellectuals would have been able to do unaided, even though the still undeveloped bureaucracy of late Victorian and early Edwardian England provided a situation as favourable to outsider experts in social and political affairs as it had been to the Utilitarians in the early nineteenth century. Beatrice became the focus of the Fabian salon at 41 Grosvenor Road. Her main venture into politics in the years 1905–12 will be told later in this book. During the First World War Beatrice was drawn, along with Sidney, into active membership of the Labour Party. She played a supportive role to her husband in his parliamentary, ministerial, and constituency work, which interfered with her decision to retire and devote herself to writing her autobiography as well as sharing the writing of the other post-war works of the partnership. *My Apprenticeship* appeared in 1926, but she did not quite manage to complete for

[86] MacKenzie, *Letters*, i. 216, 274.
[87] Comments by C. Booth's son in Booth Papers.

publication the second volume, *Our Partnership*, which, edited by Barbara Drake and Margaret Cole, appeared posthumously in 1948. Beatrice was even more disillusioned than her husband by the Labour Party's collapse in the Great Depression; possibly it was she who took the lead in their 'pilgrimage' to Russia, and she lived long enough to be able to applaud the victory at Stalingrad that marked the turning-point in the fortunes of the Second World War. Active until almost the end, she died on 30 April 1943, before her invalid husband.

2

The Sports Arena

THE contest between our champions took place in the arena of
Poor Law policy and philanthropy. Although their interests ranged
well beyond that arena, their decisive encounter found its focus
there. In this chapter, we must try to explain why the Poor Law and
charity had such importance and attraction for their energies.

The English Poor Law had its beginnings in the Tudor period,
when the English monarchy, after the dissolution of the monasteries
and the subordination of the English church to the State, took over
with some reluctance the task of supervising and enforcing
provision for the help of the poor by setting up local bodies and
laying down general principles for its administration. The legislation
of the Tudor monarchs was consolidated in the famous statute
known as 43 Elizabeth, c.2, passed in 1601. With many amendments
through the centuries, the most notable of which was the Poor Law
Amendment Act of 1834, it remained the core of English legislation
concerning the relief of poverty until it was abolished by the
National Assistance Act of 1948. Following the precedent of the
Commissioners who framed the Poor Law Report of 1834, on
which the Poor Law Amendment Act of that same year was based,
we could flatly declare:

We do not think it necessary to prefix to the statement of the result of our
inquiries any account of the provisions of the 23 Elizabeth c.2, or of the
subsequent acts for the relief of the poor. Those acts are . . . to be found in
almost every treatise on the Poor Laws . . .[1]

Some salient points need to be emphasized, however, and the first
of these is the antiquity of the English Poor Law. It had deep roots
in the English legal tradition and social policy, differing markedly
from the situation in Scotland and Ireland, where the task of

---

[1] S. G. and E. O. A. Checkland (eds.), *The Poor Law Report of 1834*
(Harmondsworth, 1974), p. 72.

assisting the poor remained voluntary and largely the function of the local bodies under guidance from the Church until the nineteenth century, when a Poor Law on English lines was introduced into Ireland in 1838 and into Scotland in 1845.

The Tudor legislation made a division between the 'impotent' poor (the lame, blind, old, invalids, feeble-minded, and other persons not able to work) and those who were capable of working (later to be known as the 'able-bodied'). It provided for a compulsory rate to be levied on occupiers of land and houses, by Overseers of the Poor in each parish operating under the general jurisdiction of the Justices of the Peace—the Overseers being appointed yearly by the Justices from among the churchwardens and substantial householders. From this fund, which was intended to supplement donations from charity, the impotent poor of the parish were to be given 'necessary relief', and the able-bodied poor were to be 'set on work' on 'a convenient stock of flax, hemp, wool, thread, iron and other necessary ware and stuff'.[2] Able-bodied persons refusing to work, or wandering from their own parishes as 'sturdy beggars', were to be punished with Draconian severity. Provisions were also made to force parents, children, and even grandparents to support their poor relatives, and for the education and apprenticing of pauper children. The principles of the Tudor legislation appeared to have established certain legal—as distinct from moral—rights and obligations betwen the State and its poor citizens. But how far did these extend? What was meant by 'necessary relief' for the impotent? What was involved in being 'set on work'? The terms were so general, so much was left to the initiative of the fifteen and a half thousand parishes of England, and the principles proved so flexible of interpretation over the centuries that the actual practice of poor relief is still a vast field of exploration for local historians. It remained for the disciples of the classical political economists of the early nineteenth century to try to impose the centralization and uniformity upon the Poor Law which the earlier centuries had notably failed to achieve.

The motive of the Whig government, which appointed the Royal Commission on the Poor Law of 1832-4, was reform of the Poor Law rather than its replacement by a brand-new system. The Commission was instructed

[2] A. E. Bland, P. A. Brown, and R. H. Tawney (eds.), *English Economic History: Select Documents* (London, 1914), p. 380.

to make diligent and full inquiry into the practical operation of the laws for the relief of the poor in England and Wales . . . To report whether any, and what, alterations, amendments or improvements may be beneficially made in the said laws . . . and how the same may be best carried into effect.[3]

The recommendations of the Commissioners, however, were radical and sweeping, although they made obeisance to the Tudor legislation:

It is now our painful duty to report that in the greater part of the districts which we have been able to examine, the fund which the 43 Elizabeth directed to be employed in setting to work children and persons capable of labour but using no daily trade, and in the necessary relief of the impotent, is applied to purposes opposed to the letter, and still more to the spirit of that law, and destructive to the morals of the most numerous class, and to the welfare of all.[4]

Thus they were able to present their severe measures as a return to the true principles of Elizabethan Poor Law from the lax practices of intervening centuries. What they did in effect was to define in terms of their own day the operative phrases of the old statutes. The persons to be relieved were defined as those 'unable to labour, or unable to obtain, in return for [their] labour, the means of subsistence';[5] it was claimed that it had never been the intention of the Poor Law to relieve poverty which did not involve this extremity of indigence. The 'necessary relief' to be given to any pauper was defined as such amount as should not make his situation 'really or apparently so eligible as the situation of the independent labourer of the lowest class'.[6] Places where able-bodied 'may be set to work according to the spirit and intention of the 43 Elizabeth' were defined as 'well-regulated workhouses',[7] by which was clearly meant a place of strict discipline, hard labour, and adequate but minimum accommodation and provender. Able-bodied paupers were not to be given any aid, except for medical attendance and for apprenticeship of children, outside the workhouse. The workhouse conditions were to provide a test of the genuineness of the able-bodied pauper's destitution, and be sufficiently deterrent to persuade him to find whatever employment he could outside its walls in the open market. Needless to say, there was continuing

---

[3] S. G. and E. O. A. Checkland, *The Poor Law Report* p. 29.
[4] Ibid., p. 82.   [5] Ibid., p. 334.
[6] Ibid., p. 335.   [7] Ibid., p. 375.

debate, from the time of the publication of the Royal Commission's Report in 1834 to the twentieth century, about whether these definitions did in fact embody the 'spirit and intentions of the 43 Elizabeth'.[8]

The redefined principles were to be put into force by a new administrative system. At the local level, the fifteen and a half thousand parishes were to be united into Poor Law Unions large enough to provide a well-regulated workhouse for each Union. In every Union, there was to be a Board of Guardians elected by the ratepayers to administer the Poor Law, with its paid officials. A central Board of three Poor Law Commissioners, with Assistant-Commissioners to act as inspectors, was to exercise surveillance of the whole system, to issue general orders and regulations and policy directives to promote standard treatment and curb local deviations. The Poor Law Amendment Act of 1834 confined itself mainly to implementing these administrative changes, avoiding the more controversial policy recommendations of the Report, but leaving such matters to the discretion of the new Poor Law Commissioners, with an implication that the Royal Commission Report was to be their guide in policy. The Overseers of the Poor were not abolished: they continued to be appointed under the Act of Elizabeth, and the new Guardians could not interfere with their appointment, but as most of their duties were taken over by the Guardians, the Overseers' powers were restricted to the making and collecting of rates and payments. Justices of the Peace were provided with places on the new Boards of Guardians by allowing them to be Guardians ex officio, in addition to the elected members.

The central Poor Law Commission, set up by the 1834 Act, had a stormy career. The hopes of keeping it free of party conflict by making it independent and not subject to detailed parliamentary responsibility and control proved vain. Although the Commissioners had substantial initial success in introducing the New Poor Law into the agricultural south of England, at a time when the agricultural labourers' unrest of the early 1830s had been crushed, they encountered fierce opposition to their attempts to introduce

---

[8] There was a splendid tussle in cross-examination at the Royal Commission on the Poor Laws 1905–9 between the Fabian lawyer witness, John Theodore Dodd, and Helen Bosanquet, C. S. Loch, and Sir Samuel Provis concerning such matters, especially the validity of the term 'destitution': Cd. 4755, Min. of Ev., Appendix vol. iii, Qq. 25373 (sect. V, paras. 120–8), 25438–55, 25736–44, 25752–72, pp. 41, 48, 59–60.

'Poor Law Bastilles' into the north of England when they turned their attention there in the Chartist period of the later 1830s and the 1840s. The propaganda and novels of that time[9] helped to brand the New Poor Law with the mark of Cain. Above all, the strong tradition of local autonomy in social administration inspired a dogged resistance to the centralising efforts of the 'Three Bashaws of Somerset House'. In 1847 the unpopular Commissioners were replaced by a Poor Law Board, brought directly under parliamentary control by having a minister of the Crown as President. The Poor Law Board was superseded in its turn in 1871 by the ministry of the Local Government Board. In spite of the transformation from an autonomous Commission into a regular government Department, the general structure created by the Act of 1834 survived, with a central body, staffed by secretaries, legal advisers, and inspectors, supervising and issuing policy advice to the elected Guardians of the 646 Poor Law Unions, which were grouped into 14 Districts for inspectorial purposes.[10] Similar transformations occurred in Scotland and Ireland in 1894 and 1898.

The question whether, and to what extent, the government did or could or should achieve the objectives of the 1834 Poor Law Report provoked intense debate throughout the Victorian and Edwardian periods. In an age of 'small' budgets and earnest faith in retrenchment in government spending, the supporters and even some of the critics of the 1834 policies were prepared to believe that the new system saved England from bankruptcy and the people from the demoralization of increasing pauperism. Even Thomas

---

[9] Dickens attacked the workhouses in *Our Mutual Friend* and *Little Dorrit* as well as, most notably, in *Oliver Twist*; and Chartist propaganda was full of denunciations.

[10] The officials of the LGB, responsible for the administration of the Poor Law, were, at the end of 1908: J. Burns (President); C. F. G. Masterman (Parl. Sec.); Sir Samuel Provis (Permanent Sec.); A. D. Adrian (Legal Adviser); H. C. Monro, T. Pitts, J. Lithiby, N. T. Kershaw (Asst. Secs.); J. S. Davy (Chief General Inspector); W. T. Jerred (Private Sec. to President); H. J. Comyns (Asst. Private Sec.); A. V. Symonds, R. J. Simpson (Private Secs. to Parlty. Sec.); E. H. Rhodes (Private Sec. to Permanent Sec.); H. E. Boyce (Parl. Agent); J. W. Baines (Legal Asst.); A. H. Downes, J. S. Oxley, J. W. Thompson, N. Herbert, G. A. F. Hervey, B. Fleming, E. D. Court, E. B. Wethered, R. I. Dansey, The Hon. Gerald Walsh, A. B. Lowry, P. H. Bagenal, W. P. Elias, H. R. Williams (District General Inspectors); R. H. A. G. Duff, C. F. Boundell, Ina Stansfield, W. D. Bushell (Assistant Inspectors); A. H. Downes, A. Fuller (Medical Inspectors); E. P. Burd (Inspector of Audits); F. J. Willis (Inspector of Local Loans); Marianne H. Mason, Beatrix W. Evans, and M. O. Power (Inspectors of Boarded Out Children).

Carlyle, no friend of 'Benthamee' reformers or economic calculators, conceded that the

[Poor Law] Amendment Act, heretical and damnable as a whole truth, is orthodox and laudable as a *half*-truth; and was imperatively required to be put in practice . . . In fact, if we look at the old Poor-Law . . . we shall find it to have become insupportable, demanding, if England was not destined for speedy anarchy, to be done away with. Any law, however well meant as a law, which has become a bounty on unthrift, idleness, bastardy and beer-drinking, must be put an end to.[11]

Historians of our own times may cast an amused glance at the meagre saving made from so small an expenditure, and turn a sceptical eye upon the Commissioners' selection and handling of their evidence about the alleged corruptions of the old Poor Law; but one must take into account the prejudices of that age and the smallness of the national income, which enabled the 1834 Report to carry such conviction amongst the better-off classes.

The New Poor Law of 1834 was not successful in achieving fully any of its aims. Outdoor relief was never effectively replaced by the workhouse system for the able-bodied. Workhouses—particularly 'well-appointed Workhouses', which had separate accommodation for the different categories of paupers—were expensive to build and their complement of 'indoor' paupers more expensive to maintain than 'outdoor' paupers receiving small hand-outs of food and money.[12] Guardians were often notoriously parsimonious and unwilling to shoulder the extra expenditure to build new workhouses or to improve old ones, particularly when municipal funds were straitened and the government unable to provide financial help. The Guardians were also liable to be responsive to local opinion or subject to local pressures. In industrial towns they realized that outdoor relief could be a way of tiding workmen over temporary periods of unemployment, and they knew that it was virtually impossible to refuse outdoor relief in bad periods of trade depression. Even in rural areas it was said that farmer Guardians, although they were forbidden to give relief in supplement of low wages, gave outdoor relief to able-bodied men who were out of employment in slack seasons to maintain a reserve labour force.[13]

[11] T. Carlyle, 'Chartism' in *Essays*, vol. ii (London, 1950), pp. 176–7.
[12] D. Fraser (ed.) *The New Poor Law in the Nineteenth Century* (London, 1976), p. 132.
[13] Ibid., p. 157.

In certain Unions (those in Wales were the most notorious)[14] the popular sentiment in favour of giving outdoor relief was so strong that no alternative policy was practicable for the Guardians. The central Poor Law authority was never powerful enough to impose a uniform policy on the Guardians, and local variation remained the mark of Poor Law administration in practice.

Long before the difficulties of eliminating outdoor relief for the able-bodied had been fully appreciated, the central Poor Law Board had allowed an alternative under the Outdoor Labour Test Order of 1842. This provided for grants of outdoor relief on condition of work which would act as a test of the applicants' need and result in some financial return that would compensate for the relief expenditure. As it was hard to find some work for the paupers to do that was capable of being done by anybody, was more irksome than ordinary manual labour, and would not undermine by its competition the situation of independent unskilled labourers, this resulted in the setting up of labour-yards for stone-breaking in many Poor Law Unions—an occupation, as many of the men who were forced to it could have told their middle-class Guardians if they had deigned to listen to them, which required a good deal of skill that most unemployed did not possess. It demonstrated very well the difficulties inherent in the application of the 'less eligibility' principle: how could conditions in workhouses be made less agreeable than those of the least-favoured workman in independent employment without being made positively inhuman? Throughout the nineteenth and early twentieth centuries, there were too many unemployed or underemployed workmen battling for existence outside the bounds of the Poor Law system to allow any sharp demarcation, or the establishing of such a differential as was postulated by the New Poor Law. This situation also undermined another assumption of the Poor Law Commissioners of 1834: that there would always be work to be found in private employment if those out of a job were willing and eager to go and get it. Although

---

[14] See the evidence of F. H. Bircham to the RC on the Poor Laws 1905–9: 'There is great discredit in being an indoor pauper in Wales, but there is none in getting outdoor relief; so I do not think any circular or any change in treatment has had any effect in Wales of recent years. Wales has gone on in the tradition of past years, and that has been to give outdoor relief to poor people, rather than to build great palaces and barracks to stuff them in against their will. That they never will do.' Cd. 4625, Min. of Ev., Q. 5340, p. 273.

it is true that the 'less eligibility' principle can be, and has been, upheld on grounds other than this assumption, there is little doubt that the assumption did pervade the 1834 Commissioners' Report. They saw the workhouse as providing a suitable physical goad to moral rectitude in a social system that they believed would reward self-help.

The New Poor Law could hardly have been sufficient, or have survived social unrest, if it had not been supplemented on a lavish scale by private charity. In fact it implicitly relied on private charity to help the 'poor' as distinct from the 'destitute'. The range, variety, and multiplication of voluntary charitable institutions and of individual donations for worthy causes in Victorian England was a matter of comment by foreigners and of self-congratulation by the British. Public knowledge of the scope of philanthropic endeavour was increased by parliamentary commissions and inquiries from the early years of the nineteenth century. This eventually resulted in the passing of the Charitable Trusts Act of 1853, appointing Charity Commissioners with large powers of inquiry and registration, but only limited powers of supervision and interference to require the producing of accounts, to remove administrators, or to adapt old charities to new ones. The Commissioners prepared a Digest of endowed charities. By 1875 the income of charities in London, according to the 'least unsatisfactory' of estimates, was over £2 million, and that estimate included only 75 per cent of the 'approximately one thousand' charitable organizations in the metropolis, and it did not take into account personal and local church almsgiving.[15] This sum was about as much as the total expenditure by Poor Law authorities in London at that time. By 1908 a more reliable estimate suggested that the sum had risen to £8½ million, which far exceeded a metropolitan Poor Law expenditure calculated by Booth for 1904–5 at £4½ million.[16] The main trouble with this vast reservoir of philanthropic endeavour was, as its critics pointed out, its totally haphazard and uncoordinated organization and activity. Attempts at co-operation were often

---

[15] *Encyclopaedia Brittanica*, 11th edn. (Cambridge, 1910, vol. v, 'Charity and Charities', p. 883; D. Owen, *English Philanthropy 1660–1960* (Cambridge, Mass., 1965), p. 477; C. Booth, Memo A, Poor Law Unions: England and Wales: Abstract of Statistics, with Remarks, RC on the Poor Laws 1905–9, Cd. 4983, Min. of Ev., Appendix vol. xii, p.369.

[16] Owen, *English Philanthropy*, p. 478; Booth, Memo A, p. 369.

resented as an interference with the spontaneity of charitable giving or with the intentions of the benefactors, and the government was unwilling to become more than minimally involved in regulating this sensitive field of private enterprise. As a consequence, philanthropic patronage was very unevenly distributed, both geographically, and as between the many different types of good causes. While it must be acknowledged that voluntary philanthropy did a large amount of good work during the Victorian age in alleviating suffering and in pioneering advances in social welfare, there was plenty of scope for its critics to complain of its limitations. The main complaints concerned its patchwork coverage, its capricious functioning, its indiscriminate giving, and its failure to keep proper records and to exchange information. Such deficiencies resulted in much imposture and cheating and (so the extremer critics argued) in spreading the evil of pauperism it was intended to cure through undermining by gratuitous hand-outs the virtues of self-help and independence in the poor.

The simple picture of State assistance to the poor under the stringent conditions of a severe Poor Law was complicated further by the emergence of new social services provided by the central government or by municipalities from about the very time when the new Poor Law itself was established. The Municipal Corporations Act of 1835, by introducing elected councils, opened the way for an extension of municipal powers and municipal initiative through special Acts of Parliament. By the later nineteenth century, the provincial cities were well launched on a policy that became known in the last decades of the century as 'municipal socialism', although the actions they had taken were almost entirely pragmatic and innocent of any such ideology. London, which had been excluded from the Municipal Corporations Act on the grounds of its size and complexity, lagged behind the provincial cities in much local reform until it was made a County and the London County Council established by the Local Government (County Councils) Act of 1888. The central government itself, from the 1830s, had also invaded the social reform field, with Factory Acts to protect women and children, Education measures to supplement private or ecclesiastical enterprise in that field, Public Health Acts, Food and Drug Acts, Housing Acts, and the like. By 1884 Herbert Spencer in his *The Man versus the State* felt the need to make a last-ditch stand in defence of *laissez-faire* against 'the sins of legislators' and the wickedness of Socialists and 'those so-called Liberals who are diligently preparing the way for them'.[17]

The growing interest by the State in social welfare had its most direct impact on the Poor Law in the treatment of children and the sick. In the days before the passing of the Education Act of 1870, the proposal to provide education for pauper children in workhouses ran up against the 'less eligibility' principle. Should the children of paupers be given an education when the children of the 'lowest class of independent labourer' received little or none? Supporters of the idea of providing them with education (such as Dr James Kay, an Assistant-Commissioner of the Poor Law, public health reformer, and educationist, or Charles Dickens) argued that education would help the children to escape from pauperism. As smaller Poor Law Unions could not afford to provide a school in the workhouses, an Act of 1844 authorized Unions to combine to establish District Schools. Only a few of these were built, in the more populous areas, the larger of them getting a bad name as 'barrack schools', and a reputation amongst social workers as unsuccessful educational experiments.[18] Industrial schools for technical training, established by some of the larger Unions, were much more successful, and some workhouse schools in the larger Unions also appear to have been satisfactory. Children of parents on outdoor relief might have their educational fees paid by the Guardians under a permissive Act of 1855 if the Guardians chose to do so (and some did). But pauper children were mainly dependent on what the workhouse could or the Guardians would provide until the establishment of a national system of education by the Act of 1870. The resulting creation of Board Schools solved the Poor Law's problems, in that Guardians could send children to these schools, and an Act of 1873 required attendance at school as a condition of outdoor relief. From the 1870s several new methods in dealing with pauper children were attempted: boarding out children to foster parents or to institutions run by voluntary social workers; 'cottage homes', in which the children were divided into small groups in separate cottages, each supervised by a housekeeper, but with the cottages grouped together and the children all attending the same school; and 'scattered homes', with each unit in a different area, so the

[17] H. Spencer, *The Man versus the State* (Harmondsworth, 1969), pp. 110–2.
[18] The further extension of District Schools was stopped in 1896. M. Bruce, *The Coming of the Welfare State* (London, 1968), p. 117.

children could attend different schools and mix less conspicuously with the general community. The system adopted, however, depended on the local Guardians, and, as late as 1909, there were still as many as 3,000 children in workhouses in England and Wales and being educated at workhouse schools.[19]

The development of a more benevolent treatment in a patchwork way was also manifest in the treatment of sick paupers. Before the 1860s the sick were either granted outdoor relief or catered for in sick wards in the workhouses. The development of a Poor Law medical service was part of the general movement for improved public health. With small beginnings in the appointment by public tender of doctors to attend the sick in workhouses and district medical officers to care for the sick outdoor paupers, the service became salaried in 1842, and by the early twentieth century it was employing more than 3,000 district medical officers[20] and 6,000 nurses.[21] Though largely decentralized, it had acquired the appearance of organization under the general supervision of the Local Government Board, and the service had expanded to establish dispensaries, infirmaries, hospitals, and asylums throughout England. These were of greatly varying standards, but the best of them in London and the larger towns were as efficient as most voluntary hospitals. In the long run, such services could not be restricted only to paupers: they were extended to include persons whose form of pauperism was merely an inability to pay medical expenses, and in the 1870s and 1880s the principle of less eligibility for the sick receiving treatment by the Poor Law medical services was being abandoned. In 1885 the Medical Relief Disqualification Removal Act allowed that the receiving of medical relief alone should no longer involve the penalty of disfranchisement, which was one of the penalties of accepting poor relief.

Outside the Poor Law, another network of medical services was provided by the authorities established by the Public Health Acts

---

[19] This number did not include the 7,000 children in Poor Law sick wards and infirmaries; the number in Scottish poor-houses was 1,095 and there were over 5,000 in Irish workhouses: *Minority Report of the Poor Law Commission 1905–9*, ch. 4, sect. A, pp. 137–41 of the Kelley reprint of the 1909 Longmans edn.

[20] B. Webb, Memo B, The Medical Services of the Poor Law and the Public Health Departments of English Local Government, in their relation to each other, to the public, and to the prevention and cure of disease, RC on the Poor Laws 1905–9, Cd. 4983, Min. of Ev. Appendix vol. xii, p. 264.

[21] Bruce, *The Coming of the Welfare State*, p. 121.

from 1848 onwards. Very tentative for the first few decades—with merely permissive legislation and strong resistance by local authorities to centralized control—the 'sanitary idea' of Edwin Chadwick, John Simon, and their devoted assistants finally won public approval, with the aid of the cholera epidemics of 1854 and 1866. Public Health Acts of 1872 and 1875 consolidated earlier legislation and organized it into a modern system. The Local Government Board had been given the administration of Public Health as well as of the Poor Law in 1871, but these two divisions of its work were run as virtually separate branches, under the supervision of LGB medical inspectors. England was divided into Sanitary Authority areas, which sometimes coincided with Poor Law areas but more often did not, and in each of those Sanitary Authority areas the appointment of a Medical Officer of Health and sanitary inspectors was made compulsory—and here again, occasionally the same doctor was both MOH and Poor Law District Medical Officer, but usually these services were performed by different persons. Overlapping of functions inevitably took place; the main distinction was that the Health Service saw its function as preventive, searching out and remedying causes likely to be injurious to the health of the public in general, not merely of the poor, while the Poor Law Medical Service's function was curative, restoring to health the poor (not merely the paupers) who had become ill. Both services stepped outside the bounds of any narrow definition of the State's functions.

In the treatment of the aged paupers too, a more sympathetic attitude was taken of their plight in the last decades of the nineteenth century. Outdoor relief had traditionally been allowed to 'deserving' elderly persons, and the social investigator and statistician Charles Booth calculated that in 1903 nearly half of all those in receipt of outdoor relief were persons over the age of 60 (242,950 out of 487,038), and of those 64 per cent were over 70 years of age.[22] But 'the offer of the House' was often used by stricter Poor Law Guardians as a test of 'deservingness' and as a way of trying to force the families and friends of the elderly to help them, or to persuade them to seek help from charity. The 'undeserving' old people and those who were unable to look after

[22] C. Booth, Memo A, Poor Law Unions: England and Wales: Abstract of Statistics, with Remarks, RC on the Poor Laws 1905–9, Cd. 4983, Min. of Ev., Appendix vol. xii, pp. 355–6.

themselves, or find others to look after them, were taken into the workhouse. Those over 60 represented nearly 45 per cent of 'indoor' paupers in 1903.[23] Ultimate dependence on the Poor Law was a constant threat to working men and women as they advanced in years, and Charles Booth, in his studies of poverty in London in the 1880s and 1890, revealed that nearly a third of those who reached the age of 70 had become paupers.[24] From 1878, when Canon W. L. Blackley proposed a scheme for contributory old-age pensions, the problem of the elderly poor was brought to public attention, as the campaign for old-age pensions gained impetus because of the introduction of the scheme in Germany by Prince Bismarck in 1889, and the advocacy of the idea by Joseph Chamberlain and Charles Booth from the early 1890s. A later fillip was added by Old Age Pensions Acts in New Zealand (1898) and Victoria, Australia (1900). In the backwash of this campaign and the Royal Commission inquiries which it provoked, there came about a certain liberalizing of the treatment of old people by the Poor Law authorities. Elderly men in workhouses were provided with a ration of tobacco, elderly women with dry tea; outdoor relief was allowed more frequently to the aged, and money received from a Friendly Society up to five shillings a week was not to be taken into account in assessing need; and workhouse visiting societies were allowed more scope in giving old people excursions and treats. Conditions in workhouses of old people improved in the 1890s, but the view of some middle-class observers of the time that they were virtually being turned into 'sunset homes' needs to be treated with more than a grain of salt.[25]

The greatest breach with the principles and practices of the 1834 Poor Law was to arise, however, out of the problem of the unemployed. It is significant that the words 'unemployed' and 'unemployment' came into regular use in the 1880s as substantive nouns, for it meant that English society had become rich enough to afford an attack of conscience about 'poverty in the midst of plenty'. The Industrial Revolution's benefits in increasing the wealth of the nation had, by the 1870s, begun to filter down

[23] Ibid., p. 348.
[24] See table in C. Booth, *Old Age Pensions and the Aged Poor: A Proposal* (London, 1899), p. 14.
[25] See quotations in D. Fraser's chapter 'The English Poor Law and the origins of the British Welfare State' in W. J. Mommsen, *The Emergence of the Welfare State in Britain and Germany 1850–1950* (London, 1981), pp. 17–18.

noticeably to the working-classes, especially with the great fall in prices which began in 1873 and continued until almost the end of the century. The pessimism of the earlier classical economists about the chances of the working classes raising their levels of subsistence, except by the total wealth of society causing that standard of subsistence itself to rise, was beginning to be replaced by optimistic ideas of the possibility of the more respectable workers raising themselves to middle-class level, if not by sanguine visions of an egalitarian society.[26] The 'respectability' of the upper section of the working classes, which had persuaded Disraeli and Gladstone to give their blessing to an extension to them of the franchise in 1867 and 1884, and to allow larger scope to trade unions by legislation in 1871 and 1875, promoted a complete change of attitude. The problem for later Victorian social observers became one of distinguishing between the 'respectable' workers and the 'residuum'. For the political purposes of the franchise, the standard could be drawn cautiously high with a house occupiers' suffrage. A more generous rough distinction could draw the line between those who normally were in employment and those who were not. The problem became more difficult if the line of respectability or worthiness was to be extended into the ranks of the casually employed. Until the end of the 1880s there were no reliable statistical enquiries, so the size of the 'residuum' was entirely a matter of speculation.

The cyclical 'Great Depression of the 1880s', being to a large extent a depression in prices, benefited the workers in employment; but it had two other important effects. By reducing the incomes of the investing classes, it administered a mild shock to Victorian confidence in the stability of the capitalist system; and it created some areas of severe unemployment. In London, particularly, there was high unemployment in formerly skilled trades: shipbuilding, engineering, furniture-making, boot and shoe manufacture and leather goods generally, clothing, and furnishing industries. Falling prices and the adaptation to a mass-production consumer market played havoc with them. In the mid-1880s the fact had to be faced that the 'unemployed' were not simply the work-shy, but included a large component of 'respectable' workers who could not find jobs. Furthermore, there was by then a contingent of alienated middle-

[26] G. Stedman Jones, *Outcast London: A Study in the Relationship between Classes in Victorian Society* (Oxford, 1971), Introduction.

class Socialists prepared to expound to the politically conscious unemployed the Marxist doctrine of class conflict. The first English Marxist organization, the Social Democratic Federation, had emerged from an earlier Radical body in 1884. In the same year appeared the breakaway Marxist party led by William Morris, the Socialist League, and so also did the group of socialist intellectuals, influenced by but uncommitted to Marxism, the Fabian Society.

The large-scale riots by the unemployed in London in 1886 and 1887, which went beyond the ordinary protest demonstration, caused a temporary flurry of fear amongst the propertied classes that the 'respectable' unemployed might be joining forces with the 'residuum', under the leadership of Socialists, for some kind of Parisian *émeute*. The plight of the unemployed, normally a subject ignored by the well-to-do and the politicians, became an urgent matter. There was a shift in the interest of those concerned with the poor from the question of pauperism to the more general question of poverty. A need was felt to do something for those precipitated into unemployment through no fault of their own. Suddenly donations of charity shot up, and the Mansion House Relief Fund jumped, within the month of February 1886, from £3,300 to over £60,000.[27] Joseph Chamberlain, who in 1886 was President of the Local Government Board and had already embarked, as leader of the Radical wing of the Liberal Party, on a challenge for leadership in the Party, issued his famous LGB Circular on 15 March 1886, which suggested that as an emergency measure

What is required to relieve artisans and others who have hitherto avoided Poor Law assistance, and who are temporarily deprived of employment, is—(1) work which will not involve the stigma of pauperism; (2) work which all can perform, whatever may have been their previous avocations; (3) work which does not compete with that of other labourers at present in employment; and lastly, work which is not likely to interfere with the resumption of regular employment in their own trades by those who seek it.[28]

To achieve these aims, Poor Law Guardians were asked to confer with the local authorities in providing unskilled employment in local municipal works at wages lower than the wages ordinarily paid for such work. Believers in a firm Poor Law policy regarded

[27] Stedman Jones, *Outcast London*, p. 298.
[28] Circular reprinted in M. E. Rose, *The English Poor Law 1780–1930* (Newton Abbot, 1971), pp. 259–60.

this Circular as the *fons et origo* of a decline in the strict administration of the Poor Laws; Labour supporters regarded it as the first clear acknowledgement that the State recognized it had a duty to provide work outside the Poor Law for those whose unemployment was not their own fault.[29] And recognition of the need for public works for the unemployed was by no means confined to politicians of Radical persuasion; by the end of 1886 Lord Salisbury, the Conservative Party leader, had also—reluctantly— given his assent to the proposal.[30] Charles Booth in 1886 resigned from his managing directorship of an important shipping firm in Liverpool, and came to London to begin his first statistical inquiries into the extent and nature of London poverty—inquiries which were, as Beatrice Webb said, 'to stand out as a landmark alike in social politics and in economic science'[31] and begin to remove the problem of poverty from the realm of guesswork to the realm of scientific discussion.

Through the later 1880s, the 1890s and the early years of the twentieth century, the policy of the Chamberlain Circular remained the policy of both Liberal and Conservative governments concerning the unemployed. The special investigators for the Royal Commission on the Poor Laws of 1905–9 recorded that 'for the unemployed problem the history of the last twenty years is really the history of the effects of this circular'.[32] It led to a large number of diverse local and uncoordinated experiments to create work for the unemployed in the two decades between 1886 and 1905. None of these was designed to provide work permanently; they were seen as relief measures to tide over exceptional periods of distress. It must be remembered how very little was known about unemployment at this time. Apart from the statistics of the Poor Law section of the Local Government Board, which dealt with pauperism not unemployment, and Charles Booth's investigations into poverty in London, there were only the monthly reports of the Board of Trade from 1893 based mainly on returns from trade unions concerning

---

[29] G. Lansbury to B. Webb, 7 Feb. 1906. Webb Local Government Collection, vol. 286.

[30] Stedman Jones, *Outcast London*, p. 299.

[31] B. Webb, *My Apprenticeship* (Harmondsworth, 1938), ii. 263.

[32] RC on the Poor Laws 1905–9, Cd. 4795, Appendix vol. xix, C. Jackson and J. C. Pringle, Report on the Effects of Unemployment or Assistance given to the 'Unemployed' since 1886 as a means of Relieving Distress outside the Poor Law, p. 18.

unemployment of their members, a couple of investigations made by the Charity Organisation Society,[33] a few reports from the Mansion House Relief Fund,[34] the Report of a Liverpool Inquiry in 1894, and the Reports of a Select Committee of the House of Commons on Distress in 1896.[35] The resources for measuring the extent of unemployment were meagre indeed. But one thing these researches and experiments did uncover was the seriousness of the problem of casual labour. The relief works hardly catered at all for the section of the working class they were intended to help—the labourer normally in employment who was temporarily out of work—but they tapped a deep well in the casually employed. Lying between the 'residuum ' of paupers and the 'steady and respectable' upper crust of the unemployed that Chamberlain's Circular had been concerned with, there was a broad stratum of those casually employed—possibly representing as much as 10 per cent of the population of London.[36] It was the casual labourers who responded to the local authorities' attempts to offer temporary work to the unemployed in the form of manual jobs such as levelling, road-making, street sweeping, limewashing, and raised problems for which the municipal management was totally unprepared. The special investigators for the Royal Commission on the Poor Laws of 1905–9 summed up two decades of experience in these words:

The class who 'would endure any privation rather than ask the Guardians to relieve them out of the rates' were an object of supreme interest to politicians, local and imperial, in 1886, and have been ever since. They want 'work, not charity'. . . . They are temporarily out of work and will soon be in work again. It is stupid to leave them idle and distressed meanwhile.

This was the simple proposition, whose only error—apart from all questions of loafers and wastrels—was that it ignored the existence of casual and irregular work, the lot of millions, and all class distinction among the wage-earners. The best that relief works have accomplished has been to provide another—generally inconsiderable—odd job to honest men who have to live by odd jobs, because of the irregularity of so much of our industry. The man for whom they were designed is not known to have had work from them yet.[37]

[33] In Nov. 1886 and Nov. 1904.
[34] In Feb. 1886, Nov. 1887–July 1888, Dec. 1893, Nov. 1894.
[35] In July 1896.
[36] See G. Stedman Jones's calculations (*Outcast London*, p. 56) on the basis of Booth's figures, which are not easy to handle.
[37] Jackson and Pringle Report, Cd. 4795, p. 23.

A number of proposals, more enterprising than mere relief works, were put forward in the 1880s and 1890s for the setting up of 'labour colonies' for the unemployed, with either benevolent or disciplinary intentions (or both). They included ideas for 'farm colonies', which would train the urban unemployed as agricultural labourers. Two hopes lay behind such schemes: first that they would settle the unemployed on the land in England, thus solving the urban unemployment problem and the problem of drift of workers from the land to the cities in one blow; second, that the unemployed would receive a training preliminary to their emigration to the colonies, the assumption being that farm workers would be in great demand overseas. But there were also plans for industrial 'labour colonies' on the outskirts of cities that would (in the more optimistic schemes) use the unemployed workers' skills to create co-operative workshops, or (in the dourer versions) keep them employed at labour-intensive work for rehabilitation purposes or merely remove them from the city slums and prevent their competition from forcing down the standards of more respectable labourers. Only a few such schemes were given practical trial: the best known are those of the Salvation Army and of the Guardians of the East End London district of Poplar, under the inspiration of the Labour representatives on this Board of Guardians, George Lansbury and Will Crooks. Lansbury was a strenuous advocate of the policy of 'labour colonies', urging

That all able-bodied men applying for Poor Law relief should be sent to colonies or institutes in the country, where the entire work shall be reclamatory and in no way penal.

That it is cheaper to keep men under these conditions than in the workhouse.

That in this way the 'men and women may be scattered back again over the country' . . . [38]

Generous policies such as these were made possible in a few Poor Law Unions by the reform of Poor Law structure effected by the Local Government Act 1894. Under this legislation, ex officio and nominated Guardians were done away with, plural voting abolished, and the property qualification for Guardians replaced by a merely residential or rate-paying qualification—all of which enabled working-class men and more women to be elected. The 'progressive'

[38] Lansbury quoted by Jackson and Pringle, ibid., p. 22.

or 'Labour' policies adopted in Poplar were later to figure in the running fight the Poplar Guardians sustained with the Local Government Board, in the course of which such policies became known as 'Poplarism'.

Other tentative experiments made in the 1890s involved the establishment of labour exchanges or labour bureaux, designed to promote labour mobility by bringing those who were out of employment into contact with potential employers. There were, of course, private employment agencies in existence, but this was a demand for labour exchanges sponsored by the government. In 1892 the Trades Union Congress had passed a resolution suggesting 'that a Labour Exchange on the model of the Paris Bourse du Travail should be established and maintained by Public Funds in every industrial centre in the kingdom'.[39] Later, writers familiar with the Continental industrial scene, such as the Fabian Percy Alden,[40] were to point out that public labour exchanges were common in Germany, too. During the 1890s Labour Exchanges were established in some London vestries (and by their successors the borough councils) and in some provincial towns. The investigators for the Poor Law Commission 1905–9 found that some of them had 'done a humble but useful work',[41] but most of them were hampered by smallness of scope and lack of communication over a wider area. In 1905 a Central Employment Exchange was established in London under the general sponsorship of the body set up by the Unemployed Workers' Act of that year. It was intended to act as a clearing-house for local exchanges, and to remedy the fault of lack of communication. But the Poor Law Commission's special inquirers found that the identification of labour exchanges with relief of distress tended to kill the exchanges, by arousing the suspicions both of employers and of trade unionists.[42]

The Unemployed Workmen's Act of 1905 was an attempt to bring some system into the new practices, which seemed to be disrupting the uniformity of the Poor Law. The preliminary work for this measure had been done by the Conservative President of the Local Government Board in 1904–5, Walter Long, a Tory squire of warm social sympathies and paternalistic leanings. At the end of the

[39] Quoted ibid., p. 95.
[40] P. Alden, *The Unemployed: A National Question* (London, 1905), pp. 49–52. The biographer of William Beveridge points out that he gained a number of his ideas from Alden: J. Harris, *William Beveridge: A Biography* (Oxford, 1977), p. 116.
[41] Jackson and Pringle Report, Cd. 4795, p. 97.   [42] Ibid.

Boer War Long found himself faced with a recurrence of severe unemployment, with demonstrations and 'hunger marches', backed by the Labour movement.[43] Long's first expedient was to reconstruct an organization in London similar to the earlier Mansion House Committee, but on a larger scale, making an attempt to co-ordinate the efforts of voluntary and public enterprise dealing with unemployment. He called for the setting up in each London borough of a 'distress committee'. These were to include representatives from borough councils, Poor Law Guardians, and voluntary charitable groups. The 'distress committees' were to elect representatives to a Central Unemployed Body for the whole of London, which was also to contain members co-opted by the CUB itself or nominated by the Local Government Board. The main task of the local committees was to determine which of the unemployed should be dealt with by the Poor Law and which should be helped outside it. The Central Body's function was one of co-ordination and superintendence, and the running of services such as a central labour exchange, labour colonies,[44] or other special projects. Funds were to be raised mainly by public subscription (Queen Alexandra's Appeal in November 1905 raised over £150,000). Local authorities could make grants if they chose to do so, but only for administrative purposes. A similar structure was made compulsory in all municipal boroughs and urban districts of 50,000 inhabitants or more in England by the Unemployed Workmen Act of 1905. This was introduced by Gerald Balfour, who succeeded Walter Long as President of the Local Government Board in 1905.

The Unemployed Workmen Act of 1905 was a compromise, and an unstable one. It did not reconcile the warring ideologists. Its machinery was ramshackle and not very effective. It pioneered no new policy and merely continued with the eclectic mixture that had emerged in the 1890s. Its method' of funding could not be permanent. This was the situation that engaged the energies of our protagonists and was to be the scene of their great encounter.

---

[43] K. D. Brown, *Labour and Unemployment 1900–1914* (Newton Abbot, 1971), pp. 37–49.
[44] The CUB established the labour colony of Hollesley Bay on the site of a former Colonial Agricultural College with the assistance of the American philanthropist Joseph Fels (concerning whom, see p. 104 below). The question of its success or failure became a matter of hot dispute between its Labour Party supporters and John Burns and his LGB officials.

3

Practice Matches With One's Own Side: The Bosanquets

THE CHARITY ORGANISATION SOCIETY AND ITS NON-SOCIALIST CRITICS

DURING the 1870s and 1880s the Charity Organisation Society had established itself as the leading authority on matters concerning the Poor Law and charity. The Society had been founded in April 1869 as the Society for Organising Charitable Relief and Repressing Mendicity, but soon took its better-known title. Bernard Bosanquet's half-brother, Charles, had been its earliest secretary, and he was succeeded in 1875 by the formidable Charles Stewart Loch, who had been Bernard Bosanquet's closest friend at Balliol. The COS attracted into its ranks a number of vigorous and able social workers and theorists, including Octavia Hill, Sir William Chance, Sir Arthur Clay, Thomas Mackay, William A. Bailward, and the Revd. Samuel (later Canon) Barnett. Its primary objective had been to bring some order and system into the chaotic profusion of London charities,[1] an objective which might be regarded as part of the tidying-up process that was going forward so vigorously in many fields of administration in Victorian England. The COS fell very far short of accomplishing its primary aim: like many other administrative institutions, private or governmental, local charitable societies put up a resolute resistance to the efforts of reformers to tidy them up and organize them. But the COS compensated for its lack of success in that direction by achievements in other ways. It became a pioneer in England of systematic social casework,[2] an

---

[1] C. L. Mowat, *The Charity Organisation Society: Its Ideas and Work* (London, 1961), p. 21; B. Bosanquet, 'The Principles and Chief Dangers of the Administration of Charity', *IJE*, 3 (1893), 323 ff. gives an admirable picture of the aims, methods, and organisation of the COS in London.

[2] Mowat, *The Charity Organisation Society*, pp. 38–9; K. Woodroofe, 'The Charity Organisation Society and the Origins of Social Casework', *Historical Studies, Australia and New Zealand*, 9 (1959), 19–29.

exponent of Octavia Hill's method of improving housing and living conditions for the poor, a deviser of new methods for charitable care and treatment of the incapacitated, the feeble-minded, and of neglected children: in short, the COS was responsible for introducing an element of trained professionalism and scientific investigation, previously little known or appreciated, into the field of charity and social work. As a result, it commanded the allegiance of many of the more intelligent members of the upper and middle classes of later Victorian England who felt a desire to do something to help the poor.

In 1881 Bernard Bosanquet resigned his Oxford Fellowship and joined his friend Loch in charitable and social work in London, and during the 1880s and early 1890s Loch and Bosanquet between them worked out a systematic philosophy (any less grandiose term would hardly do justice to its scope) concerning the role of charity in the universal scheme of things. Bosanquet, with a certain flexibility and modesty, claimed that this philosophy was the view of its authors alone, and not of the COS as a whole, and that it represented 'an early attempt to apply the philosophy of T. H. Green to current problems';[3] but it is doubtful if C. S. Loch, a man of firmer and more dogmatic temperament, had such reservations. In matters of charity work proper, Loch felt he knew what was what, however much he deferred to his friend as a philosopher. Helen Dendy joined them in 1890. She brought to the theorizing her knowledge of political economy, in which she had specialized at Cambridge, and after a few years' experience, her claims to an intimate acquaintance with social work in its detailed application, which could flesh out and verify the theory.

At its elementary level, COS doctrine depended upon the Victorian belief in self-help. This was the central concept of C. S. Loch's ideas of charity, and of those of most of the older members of the Society. The aim of all charitable work and action, they believed, must be the strengthening, or at least not the weakening, of the individual's will to help himself. The individual should be persuaded, but if necessary goaded, into achievement through his own efforts. Charity, whether from private sources or from public funds, should never be handed out indiscriminately, for the money at best would be wasted or, worse still, it would serve to increase

---

[3] B. and H. Bosanquet, 'Charity Organisation: A Reply', *Contemporary Review*, 71 (1897), 112.

'pauperization'—that is to say, it would encourage the poor to join the class of those whose initiative to work had been weakened by reliance on a bounty levied on the more industrious members of society. Down that Gadarene slope had rushed the proletarians of the Roman Empire (so Loch and the Bosanquets believed), dragging their civilization to destruction with them.[4] A puritan sense of the attractiveness of evil and of the strenuous effort needed to sustain good conduct was a marked feature of the doctrine; it took the form of a fear that men would prove shamelessly eager to quarter themselves idly on the labour of their fellow-citizens if they were given a chance to do so. What is more (and at this point the theories of Malthus entered the picture) these shameless ones would breed fecklessly and reproduce their pauper kind. It was at the price of eternal vigilance that the forces of light were winning the battle against pauperism during the nineteenth century.

In the eyes of all COS theorists, the Poor Law Amendment Act of 1834, and the Royal Commission of 1832–4 which gave rise to it, represented mighty engines for promoting good and healthy social relations. None of the COS theorists and historians had any doubts that the stern measures introduced by the 1834 Act had rescued England from the demoralizing effects of the humanitarian but disastrously mistaken policies of the older Poor Law. Mrs Bosanquet was particularly given to fervent disquisitions on this theme:

It may be doubted whether it has ever before happened that a nation so far on the way to decay has checked its downward course and recovered itself so completely.[5]

1834 may be called the Renaissance of the working class.[6]

The great lesson, then, of the nineteenth century is this, that the English people is strong, but only when it is not tempted into weakness; that it easily succumbs to the suggestion of dependence, but that it responds nobly when called upon to assert its manhood.[7]

The pre-1834 Poor Law policy of giving outdoor relief had resulted (so the COS theorists believed) in demoralization of the working

---

[4] C. S. Loch, *Charity and Social Life: A Short Study of Religious and Social Thought in Relation to Charitable Methods and Institutions* (London, 1910), pp. 433–4.
[5] H. Bosanquet, *The Strength of the People: A Study in Social Economics* (London, 1902), p. 155.
[6] Ibid., p. 168.   [7] Ibid., pp. 170–1.

classes, increasing pauperism, and the prospect of financial bankruptcy for the State. The New Poor Law of 1834—severe, unpopular, but salutary—had administered shock treatment to restore the social organism to health. Its principles, the COS leaders asserted, were sound. A person receiving poor relief should remain in a condition 'less eligible' than the worker in independent employment, to discourage people from asking for assistance from the poor-rates except in extreme need. Outdoor relief should be reduced as much as possible; and able-bodied adult paupers 'offered the workhouse'. There was, however, as we shall see, considerable division of opinion amongst COS members about the applicability of the 1834 principles to modern circumstances.

A more immediate and vital question to the thinking of COS spokesmen concerned the relation between charity and the Poor Law. They held that the destitute could be separated out into two categories, which they at first labelled the 'deserving' and the 'undeserving' poor. Later, with more sophistication, they changed these labels to the 'helpable' and the 'unhelpable',[8] because they felt that the terms 'deserving' and 'undeserving' appeared to place too much emphasis on the moral faults which had brought the pauper to his sorry condition, whereas they really wished to place the emphasis on the question whether or not he possessed the moral qualities to rescue himself from his plight. The 'helpable' were those whose character or will to struggle for self-maintenance had not been destroyed. They were fit objects of such discriminating voluntary charity as would remove the obstacles to their development and set them once again on their feet. And in order to be discriminating, voluntary charity needed method, system, a scientific approach to social problems, and theory to guide its work: all these the COS set out to provide by case-studies, by research into social conditions, and by theorizing. As for the 'unhelpable' poor, they would profit not at all by charitable assistance; they needed a deterrent Poor Law to goad their weak wills into habits that would strengthen them. The Poor Law should confine its activities to the 'unhelpables', but as the 'helpables' were acknowledged, on the

---

[8] Sometimes, but more rarely, the terms 'likely to benefit' and 'not likely to benefit' (from charitable assistance) were used. It is possible that the new terminology was introduced by the Bosanquets; if not, they were active in advocating it. See B. Bosanquet (ed.), *Aspects of the Social Problem* (London, 1895), pp. 171–2.

basis of COS experience, to be only a minority of the destitute, this left ample scope for Poor Law administration. Co-operation between the two fields of activity was desirable. It was necessary to sort out the 'helpable' cases from the mass of applicants for Poor Law relief and hand them over to organized voluntary charity for proper attention. This could best be achieved by Poor Law Boards of Guardians keeping in close touch with the local COS, and by the COS encouraging its members to seek election to the Boards. But the dispensing of charity and the administration of the Poor Law should be regarded as separate, though complementary, functions. The Guardians and administrators of the Poor Law should keep out of the delicate field of charitable endeavour and never regard themselves as dispensers of charitable help.[9] All attempts by Poor Law administrators to soften the stern principles of the Poor Law should be opposed.

Like Thomas Malthus before them, one or two COS theorists[10] may have nurtured idealistic visions of abolishing the Poor Law altogether. They looked back in admiration to Dr Thomas Chalmers, who in the early nineteenth century had fostered a 'natural' charitable system amongst his parishioners of St John's, Glasgow, most of whom were very poor. He believed (according to COS historians) that there was a great chain of sympathy and support in the social organism; the poor helped the poor and knew best how to do it. Chalmers maintained that intrusions of official helpers or outside philanthropists who did not understand the working of the interrelationships could be harmful, because they might check the flow of this vast invisible fund of charity, and encourage false expectations, waste of effort, lying and cheating. The role of the true helper (like that of a modern anthropologist studying a primitive community) was to understand the working of the system, and to refrain from interference that might upset it. Nevertheless, despite the doffing of their hats to Dr Chalmers, most

---

[9] Ibid., ch. 14 (by C. S. Loch); L. R. Phelps, *Poor Law and Charity* (Oxford, n.d. [?1887]), p. 5; id., 'Poor Law and Charity', *Proceedings of Poor Law Conferences 1901–2*, pp. 51–5; H. Bosanquet *The Administration of Charitable Relief* (The National Union of Women Workers of Great Britain and Ireland, Tract 6; London, 1898), pp. 4–5.

[10] H. Bosanquet, in a review of the COS historian Thomas Mackay's *Public Relief of the Poor*, in *IJE*, 12 (1902), 529: 'We surmise that an England without a Poor Law would have been more satisfactory in the author's opinion . . . '.

COS theorists, including the Bosanquets,[11] recognized that it was in practice impossible to restore a self-operating charitable system once a national Poor Law had come into existence. The only progress towards a euthanasia of the Poor Law, if progress there was to be, was that charted by the Royal Commission of 1832—through the restriction of outdoor relief to a minimum.

Divisions appeared in the COS ranks when its members faced the problem of the application of the 1834 principles in the social and intellectual environment of the 1890s. What did modern conditions call for in the case of the unemployed and the non-able-bodied poor—widows and deserted wives, the elderly, the children, the sick? The COS members fell into two broad categories in face of these practical issues—the 'strict' and the 'less strict'. Most of its 'old guard' theorists fell into the 'strict' category[12] (though there were some minor differences between them, depending on the degree of their strictness). The Bosanquets must be regarded as coming into that category, although they were not by any means extremists. This can be demonstrated by their performance in several encounters with non-socialist opponents in and outside the COS.

Bernard Bosanquet versus William Booth

Many clergymen and adherents of Christian churches were, from the outset, not happy with the COS's attempt to make charity 'scientific'. Neither the extent of this opposition, nor its unity, must be exaggerated. Indeed, it is surprising how much support COS principles and practice found in Christian ranks, even amongst Roman Catholics. And probably more opposition came from clergymen defending a traditional occupational field against the intrusion of self-styled 'experts', than from those who had serious objections to COS ideas. But it is possible to detect a certain disquiet amongst some Christians at what was felt to be an element of unfeelingness, hardness, and constriction of true Christian

---

[11] B. Bosanquet expressed this opinion of Chalmers in his article 'The Meaning of Social Work', *IJE*, 11 (1901), 300: 'Only a democratic church, perhaps, could use Chalmers' method with the fullest effect; but the essence of his principle is a permanent gain to the economics of social work; the only serious advance, it might almost be said, since Aristotle.'

[12] Including Octavia Hill, Sir William Chance, Sir Arthur Clay, Thomas Mackay, W. A. Bailward, and C. S. Loch.

sentiment towards the poor in the teaching of the COS.[13] The strongest Christian reaction against the COS teaching came from the Salvation Army. In the East End of London and the slums of other great cities the Salvation Army scorned the arguments of these Pharisees, and established its 'shelters' and soup-kitchens and distributed charity indiscriminately in the name of the Lord. Opponents of the COS had the temerity to argue that the effects of its strict policies were wholly offset by the Army's generosity.

In 1890 General William Booth published *In Darkest England, and the Way Out*.[14] In this book he publicized and attempted to justify the Army's methods of helping without asking questions, and he set out a grand scheme for a labour colony which would train the poor and unemployed for reabsorption in agriculture or industry at home or for emigration abroad. Immediately Bernard Bosanquet entered the lists with a pamphlet *'In Darkest England' on the Wrong Track*.[15] He claimed that General Booth's case was based on two false assumptions: first, that the extent of poverty in Britain was enormous; second, that it was a stagnant pool, not constantly being renewed, which could be drained. In fact, Bosanquet argued, pauperism had decreased both in actual numbers and even more as a proportion of the rising population over the three decades from 1857 to 1887, and this decrease had been brought about by 'stricter' methods. In the second place, because pauperism was something that was constantly being renewed, it could not be 'drained like sludge' as General Booth had expressed it in one of his metaphors; his operation of removal would produce more than it took away. Booth's indiscriminate charity would encourage the poor not to provide for themselves. Bosanquet could turn a fine metaphor himself: 'Your Lifeboat Brigade are really wreckers in disguise, who decoy ships on to the rocks by false lights!'[16] General Booth's colony scheme would do nothing to touch the real problem; Bosanquet was willing to allow that a *'very carefully discriminatory small* [*his italics*] scheme'[17] of a farm colony might serve as a 'healthy open air workhouse' for the few cases who slipped through the COS's fingers and who might be

---

[13] The attempt of the COS to keep itself free from denominational entanglements, which was on the whole a source of strength, raised some unjustifiable suspicions that it was a wholly secular body, not interested in traditional Christianity.

[14] W. Booth, *In Darkest England, and the Way Out* (London, 1890).

[15] B. Bosanquet, *'In Darkest England' on the Wrong Track* (London, 1891).

[16] Ibid., p. 33.   [17] Ibid., p. 34.

restored to industry, but he was sure that a big scheme would prove disastrously unsuccessful. He concluded loftily that the Salvation Army's claim to have proper experience in treating the poor was not true, and advised its members to get some real social work training. In the pamphlet, Bosanquet invoked no high-level theory, but conducted the argument at the level of assertions of fact and of established COS working doctrine: he preferred to take the line that the Salvationists were mistaken or misguided in their social policy. But clearly, the whole issue involved an interpretation of what Christian charity really meant, and Bosanquet raised that problem in a theoretical work he published later.[18] From an evangelical point of view, his interpretation must have seemed distinctly heterodox. He argued that scriptural passages which appeared to be recommending unqualified alms-giving were 'ideas gathered from other soils and climates, and rightly applicable only in the spirit, but not in the letter'.[19] Ideas for dealing with the poor applicable in a small community, as were the Jews, could not be transferred directly to 'a vast community whose industrial organisation rests on the individual will'. In the former case, alms could be distributed to individuals to promote industry; in the latter, indiscriminate alms-giving to an anonymous class of poor would merely perpetuate the existence of that class. Modern society and modern religion could no longer recognize poverty as a permanent class-function: 'Self-sacrifice for the poor should not mean a tribute to the maintenance of a vicious status, but an abiding and pervading sense of the claims which the weaker humanity has to be made strong.'[20]

C. S. Loch and the Bosanquets versus Samuel and Henrietta Barnett

The second important Christian revolt against COS doctrine came from within the ranks of the COS itself. It was led by Samuel and Henrietta Barnett. The Revd. Samuel Barnett began his career as Vicar and Poor Law Guardian in Whitechapel as a firm adherent of 'strict' COS principles. But from the middle 1880s he began to move beyond the limits of COS orthodoxy. His wife's warmly

---

[18] *The Philosophical Theory of the State* (originally published in London, 1899); pp. 294–8 of the 1925 edn.
[19] Ibid., p. 295.
[20] Ibid., pp. 297–8.

humanitarian sympathies[21] helped to change his opinions, and the liveliness of discussion at the university settlement of Toynbee Hall, of which he became the centre, helped in the shaping of them. In 1886 Barnett was associated with the Mansion House Fund, established in the aftermath of the unemployed riots of that year in London in order to do something to assist the workless. He regarded that enterprise as a failure, and not only wrote an interesting account of its failure but also put forward some tentative suggestions for a better policy. These were not as yet very radical proposals, and revealed how gradually Barnett broke away from his former associates. He still held to the principle that outdoor relief to the able-bodied should be reduced to a minimum; but he now put forward the view that the work in workhouses should take the form of educational retraining, supplemented by street-cleaning work (of which there was great need in the East End) provided by the local authorities. The willingness to undertake these would be sufficient 'test' of the unemployed person's genuine desire for work. Barnett also suggested that the qualification for Poor Law Guardians should be abolished, and the elections democratized, in order to allow the election of working men to the Boards and their involvement in the responsible work of helping their fellows. He already recognized casual labour as a major problem in unemployment, and suggested that promotion of the organization of unskilled labour was a major task, but he did not say how this could be done. There would still be ample opportunity for organized charity in providing tools, loans of money, and fares for emigration to the 'helpable'. While Barnett still felt the need for more efficient organization of voluntary charity, he expressed some doubt about its full realization:

The ideal [organization of the helpers of the poor] is in its fullness impossible until there be a really national Church, in which the denominations will preach their truth, and in which 'the entire religious life of the nation will be expressed'.[22]

Two years later Canon Barnett had elaborated his notion of retraining for the unemployed into a plan for a training farm which would fit the unemployed men for agricultural work and emigration

---

[21] H. Barnett, 'Passionless Reformers', *Fortnightly Review*, N.S. 32 (1882).
[22] S. Barnett, 'Distress in East London', *Nineteenth Century*, 20 (1886), 678 ff.; quotation from p. 691.

to the colonies. It was a time when such 'back to the land' schemes were in the air,[23] and Barnett had obviously also been influenced by his reading of Thomas Carlyle's *Chartism*, which he quoted. He was much exercised by the question whether control of the training farms should be in hands of the Boards of Guardians or a voluntary agency, but he finally decided in favour of the Guardians, as providing greater stability. These farms were not to be confounded with 'such pernicious establishments as the national workshops of political [Socialist] dreamers': the State's object should be not to give work but to give training.[24] A further evolution of Barnett's opinions took place in the early 1890s, when he came into closer association with the sociologist Charles Booth, with Fabians such as Sidney and Beatrice Webb and W. C. Steadman, with such progressive politicians as John Williams Benn and Sydney Buxton, and with fellow clergymen of radical sympathies such as Scott-Holland and Price Hughes. These men furnished ideas for a study group on the Poor Law and unemployment at Toynbee Hall,[25] and Barnett used its conclusions in a wide-ranging restatement of his views. He still clung to his former opinion that indoor relief should be the aim for the able-bodied poor, but it should be indoor relief which brought hope, not despair. The workhouse should be replaced by institutions that would provide farm or industrial retraining. His emphasis now was on industrial retraining, because he had become persuaded that farm colonies were an anachronism so far as England was concerned, although they might provide suitable training for emigrants. This training, together with street-cleaning, would be a sufficient test to separate the unfortunate from the idle. Houses of correction with severe discipline would be necessary only for those who were recalcitrant. As far as the non-able-bodied poor were concerned, the tendency had been towards more generous treatment, and it was merely a matter of seeing that what was attempted was done well and that free space was left for the activities of voluntary charity. However, Barnett was indeed recommending an extension of welfare services: though he believed the general tendency in the education of Poor Law children was in

[23] Revd H. V. Mills (*Poverty and the State: or Work for All* (London, 1886)) and the Social Democratic Federation were its chief advocates.

[24] S. Barnett, 'A Scheme for the Unemployed', *Nineteenth Century*, 24 (1888) 753 ff.; quotation from p. 761.

[25] E. K. Abel, 'Canon Barnett and the First Thirty Years of Toynbee Hall', Ph.D. thesis (University of London, 1969), pp. 41–2

the right direction, he hoped it would become even better as public opinion became more intelligent; for the sick, he went far in the direction of recommending that everyone should have as much right to help from the parish doctor as from the parish priest; and for the aged, he wholly embraced Charles Booth's scheme for universal, non-contributory old-age pensions at 65. While he was anxious to distinguish these recommendations from socialism (stressing that they were 'scientific palliatives', not fundamental remedies for poverty or proposals for reconstruction of the social system), he realized that they would be anathema to the 'strict school' of COS theorists, and he did not hesitate to throw down the gage. He now said bluntly that the COS had proved a failure in its attempts to organize voluntary charity; and that the doctrine of its 'strict' theorists that 'discipline, and discipline only, is necessary to deal with the unemployed' was not only false but also dangerous, because it fostered class antagonism:

They forget that the unemployed represent human beings not one of whom is incapable of rising to better things, and that society owes to each one the gift of hope. Such stern treatment justifies antagonism and often brings the help of the generous to the side of the unworthy. The strength of the idlers is the injustice meted to the honest . . . [26]

These strong words ended in a bitter personal confrontation between Barnett and C. S. Loch at a COS meeting in July 1895.[27] The argument passed beyond the particular matters of the desirability or otherwise of old-age pensions, free medicine, and special treatment of the unemployed into general accusations that the COS had become idolators of out-of-date ideas and ripostes by Loch that Barnett's views changed with every wind of current philanthropic opinion.[28] The Bosanquets sided with their friend Loch; and Loch's views remaining ascendant, the Barnetts withdrew from the central organization of the COS, though they kept their membership of its Whitechapel committee. Barnett's Parthian shot was wounding:

A mind must be thin and narrow, timid and hard, which lives under the law

[26] S. Barnett, 'Poor Law Reform', *Contemporary Review*, 63 (1893), 322 ff.; id., 'The Unemployed', *Fortnightly Review*, N.S. 54 (1893), 741 ff.; the quotation is from p. 744 of the latter article.
[27] *Charity Organisation Review* (Aug. 1895).
[28] H. Barnett, *Canon Barnett: His Life, Work and Friends* (London, 1921), ii. 267.

and not under the spirit. The mind of the Council [of the COS], constantly concerned for its dogmas and its forms, tends thus to become thin, i.e. unable to hold the enthusiasm of the day, narrow, i.e. unwilling to leave the ruts it has made ... It has a sort of panic at the suggestion of socialism, and in fear of its presence ruthlessly destroys some of its own good work ... [29]

Thereafter the Barnetts favoured the establishment of Councils of Public Welfare, organizations which would be less exclusive than the COS and would try to achieve the co-operation of a wide variety of philanthropic organizations and workers and social investigators. Canon Barnett became the Chairman of the Stepney Council of Social Welfare when it was eventually established in 1903, and Toynbee Hall was the meeting point for its activities. The young followers of the Barnetts,[30] when they remained members of the COS, formed something of a critical non-official opposition to its 'Old Guard'.

C. S. Loch and the Bosanquets versus Charles Booth and Alfred Marshall

The Bosanquets chose to remain faithful members of the 'Old Guard', but they left the personal dispute with Barnett to their friend Loch. They realized that the theoretical forces behind Barnett were the arguments of Charles Booth and the arguments of Socialists, and they decided to direct their fire against these supporters. Indeed Charles Booth was treated by the Bosanquets, mistakenly, as a 'Socialist' on the strength of his advocacy of universal, non-contributory old-age pensions (a cause which was warmly taken up by Socialists), and of some remarks in volume i of his *Life and Labour*, where he declared that he wished to enlarge the area of 'Socialism' in social provision for the poor.[31] However, the arguments need to be considered separately, because Booth was not in fact a socialist, and the arguments against him are more particular and less wide-ranging than those attacking the Socialists. The two items in dispute with Booth were the methods and conclusions of his poverty survey, and the pensions remedy which he proposed for poverty arising from old age.

[29] Ibid., p. 268.
[30] Three of them were to be appointed Commissioners on the RC on the Poor Laws 1905–9: Thory Gage Gardiner, Hancock Nunn, and Lancelot Phelps.
[31] C. Booth, *Labour and Life of the People* (London, 1891), i. 167. And see p. 188 below.

At first, Bernard Bosanquet was not at all hostile to Charles Booth's survey. In his pamphlet directed against General Booth of the Salvation Army, Bosanquet drew a great deal of ammunition from the work of the other and very different Booth. He claimed that the facts and figures of Charles Booth's great poverty survey provided an 'annihilating . . . criticism' of William Booth's projects[32] and he used them to some effect.[33] And elsewhere Bosanquet quoted Charles Booth with approval.[34] There was a decade of disputing with Booth about old-age pensions and of 'misuse' (as the Bosanquets thought) of his survey statistics by Socialists and extreme Radical Liberals before they decided to launch a full-scale attack on the methods and conclusions of his *Life and Labour*.

The dispute about old-age pensions had begun in the early 1890s, when C. S. Loch had tackled both of the main proponents of different schemes of pensions, Joseph Chamberlain and Charles Booth. His debate with Joseph Chamberlain had been featured in *The Times* of 28 January 1892 and his criticism of Booth in the *Charity Organisation Review* of September 1892. Two years later, in an article in the *Economic Journal*,[35] he contested the whole argument of Charles Booth's book *The Aged Poor in England and Wales*,[36] challenging the evidence on which Booth's statistical conclusions were based, the methods by which his calculations were made, and the conclusions that were drawn. Loch did not mince his words:

Those who wish to justify a happy-go-lucky administration can find no better friend than Mr Booth.[37]

It is a matter for sincere regret that . . . statistical tables so elaborate and yet so incorrect in their conclusions, and so insufficient, should have been published under Mr Booth's name and auspices.[38]

In 1895 Bernard Bosanquet edited a book, which consisted of a selection of essays on charity and social work, entitled *Aspects of the Social Problem*, and the essay on 'Pauperism and Old Age

---

[32] B. Bosanquet, *'In Darkest England' on the Wrong Track*, pp. v–vi.
[33] Ibid., pp. 38–9, 45, 47.
[34] B. Bosanquet, 'The Principles and Chief Dangers of the Administration of Charity', *IJE* 3 (1893).
[35] 'Mr Charles Booth on the Aged Poor', *Ec.J.* 4 (1894).
[36] (London, 1894).
[37] 'Mr Charles Booth on the Aged Poor', p. 481.   [38] Ibid., p. 487.

Pensions' in this work was written by Loch. In it, Loch rehearsed the central points of his arguments against Chamberlain's[39] and Booth's[40] proposals. Chamberlain's voluntary and contributory scheme for providing old-age pensions at the age of 70 was dismissed on the grounds of its inadequacy. Persons who were able to insure themselves voluntarily seldom became paupers, fewer than one in three lived to be 70, and there were already in existence provident fund schemes that were cheaper than the public one Chamberlain was intending to create. It was better to leave well alone. The argument of inadequacy could not be urged with such force against Booth's scheme for a pension, paid for out of general taxation, to everyone at 65 except those convicted of crime or in receipt of Poor Law relief in the ten years before they became 65; but Loch noted shrewdly that 'probably about 46%' of paupers over 65 became paupers before they were 65, and this might lead to a demand for dropping the age limit, which would nearly double the cost of the scheme. As it was, the cost 'would represent a transfer of £12 million from the richer to the poor classes'—an imposition which only Socialists could approve! Worse still, Loch claimed, the prospect of old-age pensions would weaken the independence of the workers by sapping their will to save for their old age; it would weaken ties of family affection, because children would no longer feel an obligation to provide for their elderly parents; and generally it would undermine the sense that dependence on State funds was degrading. The battle was joined when Booth rebutted this argument by claiming that saving by the working man was the consequence of a vision of hope, not fear of destitution— that saving was not in fact done by those living in fear of destitution. Booth believed that the prospect of a small pension would stimulate saving, rather than check it. Saving for insurance and other purposes would still be needed, and he did not believe that the pension would put a stop to the amount of help old people might expect from their children.

Somewhat to the dismay of the COS spokesmen, Professor Alfred Marshall, the formidable Cambridge economist, had intervened in the debate at its earlier stage with a compromise solution.[41] He thought it would be unwise for the Government to commit itself to

---

[39] Op. cit., pp. 163–6.   [40] Ibid., pp. 155–63.
[41] A. Marshall, 'The Poor Law in Relation to State-aided Pensions', *Ec.J.* 2 (1892), 186 ff.

old-age pensions without a full-scale inquiry into the whole problem: to introduce pensions, but leave the Poor Law standing unchanged would, he considered, result in 'a most expensive garment made up of patches'.[42] On the other hand, he deprecated the notion of the 'stern school of Poor Law reformers' that assistance from the Poor Law should always involve disgrace. Britain's National Income had increased so much (fourfold) since 1834 that it was financially possible to treat the poor with greater generosity. Professor Marshall threw in his lot with those who believed that outdoor relief, though apt to be abused, could be capable of being put to good use. Any poor person who could demonstrate that he had made a reasonable attempt to save during his working life (such as by subscribing to a Friendly Society a sum standing in some reasonable relation to his wages) could be allowed outdoor relief without any mark of public disgrace. This would encourage saving—and Professor Marshall also raised the question whether 'severe' Poor Law methods did not in fact *discourage* saving. To help his proposed concession work, a close association between Poor Law Guardians and the Charity Organisation Society would be required, and it would be advantageous to involve working-class representatives in the active administration of the Poor Law. Marshall proposed that the COS bodies be given 'semi-official status' in their advisory role with Guardians, and that working-class representatives be strongly enlisted in responsible Poor Law administration, even perhaps to the extent that this administration be done by the working classes and not for them.

Bernard Bosanquet acted as the COS champion in replying to Professor Marshall.[43] He undertook to correct 'a misapprehension' by the Professor of the practical situation. The division of labour in administering relief by which the Poor Law dealt with 'hopeless' cases while private charity or Guardians' Relief Committees took on the helpable was not caused by 'strict' Poor Law notions—or for that matter anyone's notions. It was 'the necessary result of the working of a machinery' which could not do more than it was functionally capable of doing. Poor Law Guardians *as Guardians* had to act according to general rules and with a care for public funds. In so far as Guardians' Relief Committees concerned themselves with questions of character or capacity or restoration of

---

[42] Id., 'Poor Law Reform' [a reply to Bosanquet], ibid., p. 371.
[43] B. Bosanquet, 'The Limitations of the Poor Law', ibid., 369 ff.

families to self-support they were '*acting as volunteers and in their private capacity*' [*his italics*] and taking on the work which properly belonged to private charitable agencies. In their official capacity there was for the Guardians 'an essential sameness of the conditions under which Poor Law relief is still carried on, and so far as we can judge always must be carried on, with those pointed out by the authors of the Report of 1834'. If many respectable people were induced by lavish hand-outs to resort to the Poor Law, its 'inherent limitations' would not be removed. The London COS opposed outdoor relief—first on the ground of its likely effects on recipients and the community, secondly with a view of promoting thrift, and thirdly because of its tendency to lower wages.

Professor Marshall was distinctly unamused by Bosanquet's insinuation that he was unaware of the practical situation.[44] He retorted sharply that he had spent more than thirteen years studying the Poor Law, and was acquainted with COS work too, through his wife's experience as an active member of the Oxford and Cambridge Charity Organisation Societies. The conditions of administering the Poor Law were *not* the same, as Bosanquet had alleged, as those of 1834. The National Income was so much larger, more and better educated officials could be employed, the causes governing wages were better known, and the co-operation of working-class leaders and Charity Organisation Societies could now be enlisted. These factors made a change of policy possible. Marshall said he opposed the policy of the 'extreme lenient' school as much as Bosanquet did. Perhaps lavish out-relief might lower wages, but his cautious scheme would not do so; it would promote, not discourage, thrift. The 'best leaders of the working class'[45] now understood the danger of a reckless Poor Law policy, but they needed to be convinced that the existing system was not 'needlessly harsh, offensive and patronising'. They had contended that a man who had not grossly misconducted himself, and who had saved, had an equitable claim to receive back in the case of need part at least of what he had contributed to the poor-rates; and this contention had not been proved wrong. There was no chance that

[44] Marshall, 'Poor Law Reform', ibid., p. 371 (reply by Marshall).

[45] By the 'best leaders of the working class' Marshall did not mean those who were then pressing for the formation of the ILP; Marshall to T. Mackay 25 Aug. 1892: 'I think that after the old Poor Law the Independent Labour Party is the greatest danger of the present century: both being powerful engines for preventing people from making the best of their abilities' (COS records).

outdoor relief would be abolished: the real choice lay between his policy and the COS's restrictive one.

There the argument between Booth, Marshall, and the COS rested, without being resolved, right through the Aberdare Royal Commission on the Aged Poor of 1893–5, on which Booth and Loch served as Commissioners and to which Professor Marshall gave evidence. The Bosanquets were not swayed by their opponents' views, and up to 1907 (that is, the year when the Liberal government was actually beginning to draft legislation on old-age pensions) they were still denouncing both extended outdoor relief and old-age pensions as likely to be socially disastrous. As they went on, their arguments became broader and more colourful. In her book *Rich and Poor* (1896) Mrs Bosanquet warned that the expectations that were being raised about the introduction of old-age pensions would cause the workers to cease providing for their old age;[46] and in her *Strength of the People* (1902) she claimed that the rise in the statistics of old people applying to the Poor Law between 1892 and 1900 showed that it had had this effect.[47] She maintained that Bismarck's (1890) contributory pensions plan in Germany had led to social friction between masters and men and it had not been a stimulus to thrift;[48] that the Danish (1891) non-contributory scheme had caused a check to independent provision for old age by the working class;[49] and that New Zealand's 'experimental' legislation (1898) would merely demonstrate that it was not possible to withdraw from such an experiment once it was undertaken.[50] The agitation for old-age pensions was, she declared, 'entirely a middle-class movement in its origin, and in no sense emanate[d] from the working class themselves', but, once launched, the workers were bound to take it up, because 'it is not in average human nature to persist for ever in refusing to take 5/– a week'.[51] In her *Strength of the People* and *The Family* (1906), the argument was elaborated that old-age pensions would undermine the cohesiveness of the family which was 'the strength of the nation and the salt of the earth'.[52] In spite of her rather sentimental approach and armchair anthropologizing about the benevolent patriarchal nuclear family of which she so strenuously approved, Mrs Bosanquet was undoubtedly right in saying that, in the absence of

[46] Op. cit., p. 190.
[47] Op. cit., pp. 243–5.
[48] Ibid., pp. 251–2.
[49] Ibid., pp. 252–3.
[50] Ibid., pp. 253–4.
[51] Ibid., p. 247.
[52] *The Family*, p. 337.

public provision, the family usually was the support of the old. Whether this made family ties more harmonious was something that she asserted rather than investigated. As for more generous outdoor relief,

it is the most remarkable, but best ascertained phenomena of Poor Law administration that where out-door relief is restricted, the numbers of those who go into the workhouse are diminished; that where out relief increases in lavishness, the numbers of those who go into the workhouse increase,

because 'out relief is a preparatory school for total dependence'.[53]

In the meantime, Bernard Bosanquet was elaborating a complete social philosophy (to be discussed more fully in Chapter 6 below), which in its particular reference to more generous outdoor relief and old-age pensions stressed the 'communal mind' and 'general will' of social groups, whether small ones like the family or large ones like the State:

A community of people is a living mind. It has its affections, its duties, its obligations, its foresight, its pride and its delicacy . . . it has its own innate strength, its own variety, its own recuperative power. If you wish to help it make the most of itself, you must understand it, sympathize with it, and meet it on the right path.[54]

Social workers would need to create their own theory—their own sociology. Economic science as it stood was useless or misleading, for it had very little to say about the social and psychological forces central to social work. The idea of society as embodied in will, mind, and character was avoided by economics. The new theory would need to grow out of practice, when a generation of competent exponents of the new theory would appear.[55]

This growing hostility to Cambridge neo-classical economics as expounded by Professor Marshall and his followers was accompanied by similar increasing hostility to the social investigations of Charles Booth and Seebohm Rowntree. Those investigations appeared to be providing too much ammunition for reformers of a socialistic bent, especially when, during the Boer War, the rejection of many recruits as physically unfit caused a stir in military official circles and the press concerning the health and nourishment of the people.

---

[53] *The Strength of the People*, p. 175.
[54] B. Bosanquet, 'The Meaning of Social Work', *IJE* 11 (1901), 299–300.
[55] Ibid.

Helen Bosanquet took up the challenge in her book *The Strength of the People: A Study in Social Economics* (1902), and later expanded the criticism of Booth which she made there into an Occasional Paper for the COS[56] and an article for the *Contemporary Review*, 'Physical Degeneration and the Poverty Line'.[57] In its expanded version, she set out to refute sensational claims, allegedly based on Booth's and Rowntree's statistics, that one-third of the population of the United Kingdom was incapable of maintaining itself in physical efficiency. Her arguments were sharp. First, she pointed out that these were surveys based on London and York, and that it was a 'gigantic step' to generalize from them to the United Kingdom as a whole, without establishing that those places were really representative. She thought it to be likely, on the contrary, that both London and York were special cases. Next, she pointed out the discrepancies between the 'poverty line' of Booth and Rowntree, in spite of superficial resemblances. Booth's poverty line was based on 'opinion only'—the opinion of School Board Visitors of what it would cost to maintain a man, wife, and three children in minimum comfort, which was estimated by them at 21–2 shillings a week. Rowntree, who arrived at a similar minimum (21s. 8d. for a man, wife, and three children), claimed to base this on his knowledge of what one large firm and certain other employers paid for unskilled labour, plus the application of a standard derived from dietetic experts. Neither of these could be regarded as hard evidence, especially as the alleged dietetic experts' opinion was 'contradictory of every housekeeper's experience'.[58] In any case, Booth did not say that the 30 per cent of the population rated below his poverty line were on the verge of starvation or ill nourished or badly clad, and Rowntree rated only 9.91 per cent of his people as in 'primary poverty' (meaning that they had incomes below what was necessary for physical efficiency) and arrived at the 27.84 per cent below his poverty line by adding to them the 17.93 per cent in 'secondary poverty' (which was comprised of those who had incomes above starvation level if they had not misspent it). Therefore it followed either that there was no real similarity between Booth's and Rowntree's figures and the poverty in York was only one-third of that in London, or that Booth's figures below

---

[56] COS Occasional Paper No. 11, 3rd series, n.d.

[57] *Contemporary Review*, 85 (1904), 65 ff.

[58] Ibid., p. 72; H. Bosanquet, *The Strength of the People*, pp. 101 ff.

the poverty line also contained a large majority whose incomes were also sufficient if they had not been misspent. Mrs Bosanquet was inclined to think that the second alternative was the true one, and that in fact Booth's survey shuld have revealed that one-tenth rather than one-third were really in dire straits in London too.

Mrs Bosanquet went further: she was not convinced that even this apparent one-tenth of real poverty did not make the problem seem more serious than it really was. She raised doubts about whether the methods of enquiry of either Booth or Rowntree were satisfactory to establish firm conclusions about *any* proportion of absolute poverty. She criticized Booth's reliance on the evidence of School Board Visitors, and the validity of the statistical methods he used to generalize them over London as a whole, and she pointed out that he had no *direct* evidence concerning the incomes of heads of households, let alone of families as a whole. She found the specimen pages of Rowntree's investigators' notebooks defective in the same way concerning the constitution of each family and its occupations. Her general conclusion was that the main problem lay with what Rowntree called 'secondary poverty'—the misspending of family earnings rather than the absolute want of enough money to spend. It was a problem that needed to be attacked by charitable workers through families—persuading men to take home their earnings, wives to spend it sensibly and feed and clothe their children well. It was only through families that poverty could be remedied, even the poverty of the lowest tenth—if tenth it were.

The Bosanquets versus J. A. Hobson and L. T. Hobhouse

The Bosanquets had also to contend with a younger, more radical group of Liberals who were to become known as the 'New Liberals'. These young men sought to retain the internationalist and libertarian values of the liberalism of Cobden, Gladstone, and J. S. Mill, but to abandon the old Liberal attachment to *laissez-faire* and come to terms with the demands of labour and moderate socialism. The Bosanquets encountered in particular the two leading theorists of this group, who were more inclined to the left in their views than most of their immediate associates: Leonard Trelawney Hobhouse and John Atkinson Hobson. Both of these men had careers as distinguished journalists; Hobhouse was later to become the first Professor of Sociology at the University of London, but equivalent recognition was denied to Hobson because he was regarded as an 'economic heretic'.[59] Hobson was, indeed, the boldest and most original economic thinker of his group. Amongst his many economic 'heresies', the one which was central to his approach to problems of poverty and unemployment was his firm conviction that poverty was produced by social causes, due fundamentally to economic imbalance and distortion resulting from the inequitable distribution of incomes. But he did not agree with the Socialists that these faults were incapable of remedy within the capitalist framework: he believed that given suitable radical reforms, a 'socialized' liberal capitalism could provide the means to a good and happy life for all citizens, though he did not draw a hard and sharp line between Socialism and his brand of Liberalism when he added guardedly that there might be no 'economic or moral finality' in the social order he was advocating.[60]

Hobson's book *The Problem of the Unemployed: An Enquiry and An Economic Policy* (1896) accepted that Charles Booth had exposed the 'disgraceful fact that a third of the working class in the richest country ever known in the history of the world was living in the state of physical and moral degradation'.[61] He claimed that that situation could be remedied without much difficulty. As 'palliative' measures he supported all the remedies that the COS had opposed or questioned: old-age pensions, generous treatment of Poor Law children, experiments of various kinds for providing work and training for the unemployed. But he insisted that these were no more than 'palliatives';[62] the real solution of unemployment and poverty was not to be sought in these, any more than the deepest causes of unemployment were to be found in separate and exceptional factors, such as ignorance of the market, want of business confidence, speculation, changes in taste or fashion, strikes, or the impact of new machinery.[63] The 'root-cause' of unemployment lay in cyclical trade depressions produced by 'under-consumption'—the failure of consumption to keep pace with productive power.

---

[59] J. A. Hobson adopted this description of himself in his autobiography, *Confessions of an Economic Heretic* (London, 1938).

[60] J. A. Hobson, 'Poverty: Its Causes and Cures', reprinted in his *The Crisis of Liberalism: New Issues of Democracy* (London, 1909), p. 173.

[61] Ibid., p. 161.

[62] J. A. Hobson, *The Problem of the Unemployed: An Enquiry and an Economic Policy* (London, 1896), ch. 8.

[63] Ibid., chs. 3–5.

It was Hobson's next theoretical move which brought down on his head the anger or contempt of orthodox economists. He claimed there could be too much 'saving'.[64] This appeared to be questioning the virtue of thrift—the most sacred of economic dogmas associated with both economic· growth and individual economic prudence. 'Over-saving' (and consequent over-investment in capital goods, whose productivity could not be matched by increasing consumption) was caused, Hobson believed, by the maldistribution of incomes in favour of the richer classes. The remedy lay in State action to redistribute incomes in favour of the poorer citizens, who spent more of their incomes on articles of consumption. This was the point at which orthodox professional economists would not—or, perhaps, to do them justice, could not—see that Hobson had demonstrated the economic mechanism by which unemployment would be diminished by a diminution of saving, even if more equal distribution resulted (as it probably would) in less saving.[65] The established orthodox doctrine of the time was that investment created its own purchasing power (except, perhaps, occasionally when there might be 'miscalculation' in particular industries or 'over-saving' in periods of 'disturbed confidence'). This ruled out *general* 'under-consumption' or 'over-saving' and unemployment as caused by it. Hobson's fundamental argument was therefore regarded as cranky, not only by the orthodox neo-classical economists of the Cambridge school,[66] but also by the less orthodox academic establishment of the London School of Economics;[67] to the COS it was anathema as an apparent invitation to improvidence.

---

[64] This 'heresy' was first formulated by Hobson in conjunction with A. F. Mummery in their joint publication, *The Physiology of Industry* (London, 1889). The book by their disciple J. M. Robertson, *The Fallacy of Saving* (London, 1892), may have attracted, by its challenging title, more attention than the original statement. As J. M. Keynes later pointed out in his *The General Theory of Employment, Interest and Money* (London, 1936), pp. 364–71, the weakness of Hobson's 'heresy' consisted in his 'orthodoxy' in identifying saving and investment. For an excellent analysis of the difference between Keynes's and Hobson's views see P. Clarke, *Liberals and Social Democrats* (Cambridge, 1978), pp. 227–34.

[65] See, e.g., Edwin Cannan's review of Hobson in *Ec.J.*, 7 (1897), 87–9.

[66] A. Marshall, *Principles of Economics* (London, 8th edn., 1925), pp. 711–12.

[67] For Fabian views, see remarks about Hobson in *Fabian News* (May 1895 and May 1910). Relations between the Webbs and Hobson were somewhat distant, a coolness which probably dated to the early 1890s when Hobson published his article on the 'Law of the Three Rents', giving a Radical-Liberal version of the Theory of

Hobson inflamed the Bosanquets' hostility by launching a fierce attack on COS doctrines entitled 'The Social Philosophy of Charity Organisation', a review article of the Bosanquets' *Aspects of the Social Problem* in the *Contemporary Review*, November 1896. He damned the COS with faint praise for having set itself up as a company of 'expert middlemen' to police and organize charity in a situation where the act of giving had lost its traditional neighbourly and personal virtue and had become a 'sort of conscience money' by which a segregated moneyed class sought to 'reconcile the sentiment of pity for vaguely known distress with a sensitive shrinking from closer personal contact with concrete cases of suffering'. Hobson allowed that the COS in its work had established some general rules which had won wide recognition ('even the clergy hear and tremble'), but *Aspects of the Social Problem* had the more ambitious aim of interpreting these empirical rules in the light of 'superimposed and externally derived principles' and aspired to be an 'authoritative revelation of the Charity Organisation philosophy'. It amounted to an attempt to bolster the opposition of the propertied classes to the claims of the poorer classes for more social support in gaining decent material conditions of life—through such reforms as old-age pensions, free meals for schoolchildren, and work for the unemployed. The older COS arguments that these concessions would sap responsibility and initiative, weaken incentive, and destroy the unity of the family, all of which had come under attack on empirical grounds, were being reinforced by philosophical arguments about human nature and social causation and a new justification of property. Doles degraded, the Bosanquets claimed, because such windfalls upset the workman's rational planning of his life and detached enjoyment from effort. But, Hobson asked, what about gifts and bequests to the well-to-do and the unearned incomes of the rich? Bernard Bosanquet's answer to this question was, Hobson declared, a piece of 'effrontery'. It amounted to saying that Poor Law relief was a gift to a person who was already a social failure, it provided no remedy, it was not within the pauper's control and management, it was in

Rent, without an acknowledgement or even a reference to Webb, in the very journal in which Webb had published his own article on the Theory of Rent four years earlier: S. Webb, *QJE*, 2 (1888), 188 ff.; J. A. Hobson, *QJE*, 5 (1891), 263 ff. As late as 1929 Webb was still referring to Hobson's 'crankiness': S. Webb to Robson 27 Feb. 1929 in N. MacKenzie (ed.), *The Letters of Sidney and Beatrice Webb*, vol iii. *Pilgrimage 1912–1947* (Cambridge, 1978), p. 310.

fact a 'payment for idleness'; whereas a large pension or gift of property to a man not demoralized was quite different: it enabled him to choose his work, which was a great indulgence, but justified if the recipient considered the gift as a 'trust' to be put to good use.

Hobson contested that argument at every level. He denied that poor relief was any more temptation to idleness than an unearned income; he was sure that Bosanquet would not welcome the suggestion of raising out-relief to 20 shillings a week (the wage above Booth's 'poverty line') to ensure its adequacy; he knew that the COS opposed Booth's pension scheme which would in fact put the pension-money within the recipients' control. Concerning Bosanquet's argument about the difference between doles and gifts to the rich, Hobson was forthright:

Speaking candidly this talk about a . . . 'trust' is a wanton abuse of language, applied as it is to describe elements of income which pass to the owners from exercise of sheer economic might . . .

The ground-landlord who 'realises himself' in the rents he draws from his slum property is preventing the docker and the seamstress from realising themselves, and is destroying for them the possibility of rationally organising life.

Hobson went on to challenge the COS claim that individual families were all able to achieve material comfort if they exerted their will. Poor Law statistics were useless as a proof of poverty; and the claims of COS investigators that poverty was nearly always associated with personal defects were no proof that moral factors were more important than social forces as causes. The fact that some persons could rise from poverty by their own efforts was no guarantee that social forces did not set a limit to such successes, by making it impossible for sufficient moral energy to be generated in an environment of poverty. The Bosanquets' philosophy that 'character was the condition of conditions' was therefore a 'mischievous half-truth'—the other half of which was espoused by cruder forms of Socialism. Though it might be true that moral reform was prior 'in the nature of things', and that social reforms could only be effectual if they acted as a means of elevating character, nevertheless social reform was 'prior in time'. COS methods were 'sterile', because

the poor feel and know that they are not fairly matched with their 'friendly visitors'; that in fact 'it is all very well' for these well-dressed, nice-spoken ladies and gentlemen to come down and teach them how to be sober, thrifty and industrious; they may not feel resentment, but they discount the advice and they discount the moral superiority. In a blind, instinctive way they recognise the superiority is based on better opportunity—in other words, on economic monopoly.

Helen and Bernard Bosanquet retorted with a brief dismissive reply to Hobson in a later issue (January 1897) of the *Contemporary Review*. They denied that *Aspects of the Social Problem* purported to be an authoritative statement of the views of the COS: it represented the views of the individual authors alone. They wondered what Hobson could have meant in talking about the opposition of the propertied classes to such reforms as old-age pensions, feeding of schoolchildren, and public work for the unemployed, considering that every one of these demands emanated from the propertied classes, not from the workers. Their objections to these proposals were simply that they were ill-adapted to meet social needs. They were not rejecting practical reforms as such, or defending vested interests or ground-rents. But 'no kind of economist could seriously attribute the poverty of the seamstress to the ground landlord', and the practical social results of out-relief and property windfalls to the well-to-do were sufficient to differentiate between them. Out-relief *was* a 'payment for idleness' because 'as the law stands, out-relief must be withdrawn in proportion as the recipient earns'. They could not see why Hobson should object to the suggestion that private property was a 'trust'. While they were quite aware that a diminution in the statistics of pauperism did not necessarily mean a diminution of poverty, they claimed to know from practical experience and careful investigation of districts where pauperism was reduced that poverty also was reduced. Their belief in the superiority of moral to environmental factors was supported by the observation that the 'industrial residuum' lived in the same environment as those who did 'hard, solid and effective work'. This did not mean a neglect of economic forces; but '. . . what we do say is that though at any moment misfortune may make circumstances seem insuperable, yet, given time, character—if not thwarted—will reassert itself, and mould circumstances to its own support'. The COS aimed to help sufferers from economic as from other causes to tide over difficult times and increase the will-power they possessed. The real difference between themselves and Hobson, the Bosanquets asserted, was that Hobson was one-eyed—he wanted to derive poverty from a single cause: the occasional disorganization of industry by economic crises. They maintained on the contrary that poverty had many causes, including many economic causes, some of which were periodical and abnormal, others regular and normal, and of these they considered the regular and normal ones to be more important. Concerning Hobson's derision of COS workers,the Bosanquets declared that to say 'there can be no true sympathy between members of different classes is to sin against human nature'. They concluded by accusing Hobson of knowing nothing about the social visiting he condemned, and with a plea to all readers who were interested to come and see the COS at work.

L. T. Hobhouse did not make J. A. Hobson's personal acquaintance (which was soon to ripen into close friendship) until 1899,[68] but he was already familiar with his writings, and took a favourable view of them. He did not go the whole way with Hobson's under-consumptionist theorizing, but he was willing to agree, on ethical grounds and in terms of their common belief in a 'Theory of Rent', with Hobson's condemnation of the evils of gross economic inequality and maldistribution,[69] and to accept all the 'palliative' measures to raise the status of the underprivileged which Hobson supported. Hobhouse and Hobson had both been students at Oxford—Hobson in the later 1870s, Hobhouse in the early 1880s—and both of them (Hobson at Lincoln, Hobhouse at Corpus Christi) had been relatively insulated from the influence of T. H. Green and his disciples. They had been educated firmly in the English empiricist tradition as transmitted by John Stuart Mill, and modified by scientific-evolutionary doctrines of Darwin, Huxley, and Spencer. Later on, Hobhouse discovered a respect for T. H. Green, finding him to be in spirit a 'true successor' of Mill, although obscure;[70] but he never lost his aversion to the more full-blooded Hegelianism of Green's immediate followers.

In a sour few months, in December 1901 to February 1902, towards the end of the Boer War, and after the 'Khaki election' of

---

[68] Clarke, *Liberals and Social Democrats*, p. 90.

[69] Ibid., p. 126; S. Collini, *Liberalism and Sociology: L. T. Hobhouse and Political Argument in England 1880–1914* (Cambridge, 1979), pp. 63–4.

[70] L. T. Hobhouse, *Democracy and Reaction* (Harvester Press repr., ed. P Clarke; Brighton, 1972), p. 224. But cf. M. Freeden, *The New Liberalism: An Ideology of Social Reform* (Oxford, 1978), pp. 16–19, 55–60, on the influence of T. H. Green and Idealism.

1900 had reaffirmed the Conservatives in power, Hobhouse contributed a series of articles to the Liberal journal, the *Speaker*, which later formed the basis of his book *Democracy and Reaction*, published in 1904.[71] The articles and the book were intended to examine and arraign those elements which, in his view, had engendered a mood of public opinion that justified the Boer War and Conservative reaction against the principles of Liberal internationalism and humanitarianism. Amongst the intellectual elements responsible, the influence of German Hegelian philosophy was given an important role in 'swell[ing] the current of retrogression'.[72] In words which were to be reasserted by Hobhouse himself during the First World War[73] and by others during the Second World War,[74] Hegelian Idealism was identified with Prussian conservatism,[75] and claimed

to sap intellectual and moral sincerity, to excuse men in their consciences for professing beliefs which in the meaning ordinarily attached to them they do not hold, to soften the edges of all hard contrasts between right and wrong, truth and falsity, to throw a gloss over stupidity, and prejudice, and caste, and tradition, to weaken the bases of reason, and disincline men to searching analysis of their habitual ways of thinking . . . [Men] can, therefore with lightened intellectual conscience revert to the easy rule of authority and faith, a rule particularly attractive to a society which has been afraid of further progress and is lusting after the delights of barbarism.[76]

This fierce tirade revealed Hobhouse's long-standing smouldering distrust of German Idealism; any immediate cause of the explosion has not so far come to light. Presumably he was speaking of what he felt to be the tendencies of Hegelianism in general; he was certainly not particularizing the views and teachings of the tiny band of British philosophers whom one might describe roughly as Hegelians (Bosanquet,Bradley, the Cairds, Haldane, McTaggart, Ritchie, Stirling, and Wallace). Most of them, with the exception of

[71] Hobhouse, *Democracy and Reaction*, P. Clarke's introduction, p. xv.
[72] Ibid., p. 78.
[73] L. T. Hobhouse, *The Metaphysical Theory of the State: A Criticism* (London, 1951 repr.; first published in 1918), pp. 5–6, 23–5, 134–7.
[74] e.g. K. Popper, *The Open Society and its Enemies* (London, 1945), vol. ii, ch. 12.
[75] Hobhouse attributed the establishing of this link to the former Fabian, William Clarke.
[76] Hobhouse, *Democracy and Reaction*, pp. 78–80.

Bradley and Stirling, were Liberals, and some of them, particularly Haldane and Ritchie, might have had a better claim than Bosanquet to describe themselves, at least on matters of social policy, as 'advanced Liberals'.[77] It is true that Liberalism at the time was still torn with bitter factional division, and Hobhouse thought, rightly or wrongly, that some Liberal Hegelians were flirting too intimately with Imperialism and its concomitant evils, or with ideas of 'National Efficiency' current at that time.[78] But all of the small band mentioned (or at least the six of them still surviving) could reasonably have objected to Hobhouse's sweeping condemnation. If it came to their attention, however, they chose to ignore it publicly. But one critic favourable to Hegelian views, Henry Jones, Professor of Moral Philosophy at Glasgow University, did remonstrate with Hobhouse for overgeneralization and misinterpretation,[79] and Hobhouse in his second edition of *Democracy and Reaction* in 1909 conceded that he had 'modified some sentences which appear to do less than justice to the elements of positive value contributed by Idealism to social ethics';[80] but he stoutly maintained that Hegelianism's view that the world order is rational led to a conservative acceptance of things as they were: 'If all that is real is rational, it is difficult to resist the view that what wins is right'.[81] Hobhouse's assault misfired at the time, but it opened a style of attack which was to become more familiar later on.

In the early years of the twentieth century, Hobhouse's views (and his friend Hobson's) represented the most advanced point reached by New Liberal thinkers. On practical matters of social policy there was little to distinguish them from Fabian Socialists. Hobhouse held very favourable opinions of trade unionism and the Co-operative movement.[82] He considered the problem of better distribution of wealth to be more important to society than

---

[77] For Helen Bosanquet's description of her husband as 'always an advanced Liberal' see her memoir *Bernard Bosanquet* (London, 1924), p. 97.

[78] See G. R. Searle, *The Quest for National Efficiency* (Oxford, 1971) for a full account, especially of Haldane's involvement.

[79] Prof. Henry Jones's reply to Hobhouse was published in the *Contemporary Review* (1907) and later incorporated in his volume *The Working Faith of the Social Reformer and Other Essays* (London, 1910), chs. 7 and 8 ('Idealism and Politics: The Accusation and the Defence').

[80] Hobhouse, *Democracy and Reaction*, pp. 276–7.   [81] Ibid., p. 274.

[82] L. T. Hobhouse, *The Labour Movement* (originally published London, 1893; reprinted from the 3rd edn. (1912) by the Harvester Press, Brighton, 1974), chs. 1 and 2.

increased production,[83] and favoured progressive, redistributive taxation, falling heavily on 'unearned incomes'.[84] He carried this principle far, envisaging.

... great national works giving the nation control over the vital industries; ... a still greater development of municipal works; and ... supplementing these, voluntarily formed Co-operative Associations on the existing model, united by the Federal principle, and ultimately, co-extensive with the community ... many branches of industry would, as to their immediate direction, remain in private hands. But over all the State would exercise a supreme control, regulating and correlating economic forces which are now left to adjust themselves as they may.[85]

It is hardly surprising that, of the many relatives of Beatrice Webb, Leonard Hobhouse was one of the few whose social views met with the thorough approval of Sidney Webb,[86] although Hobhouse shied at the label 'Socialist', and clung firmly to his attachment to the Liberal Party, and took exception to the Webbs' occasional flirtations with the Tories. Hobhouse wanted a social order which rested neither on untrammelled individual ownership nor on full state ownership:

As in feudal days men held the land, not in absolute ownership but as tenants of the king, and conditionally on the discharge of certain duties, so in the State system which is gradually emerging out of individualism the owner holds of the community and subject to the duties which the community requires. It is not the business of the State, as some of the narrower forms of Socialism seem to suggest, to get all property into its own hands and to serve out to individuals such necessaries and comforts as seem good to a committee of officials. It is its business rather to impose such a use of property and such arrangements of industry as secure to all who live honestly the means of directing their own lives on the lines which they find most suitable to themselves, and this it does, not by abolishing private property, but rather by extending to all its citizens a certain lien upon the common stock. .... Its true function is not to supersede but to supervise, to guide, to harmonise. The State is too big a body and its methods are too mechanical to admit of its dealing directly with the endlessly varying needs of the individual.[87]

On the specific Poor Law questions, however, Hobhouse and the

---

[83] Ibid., p. 14.   [84] Ibid., ch. 3.   [85] Ibid., p. 127.
[86] S. Webb to B. Webb 21 May 1892: '... Leonard Hobhouse ... , for whom I have an overwhelming admiration'. MacKenzie, *Letters*, i. 413.
[87] Hobhouse, *The Labour Movement*, pp. 90–2.

Fabians were very close. Hobhouse favoured the imposition by the State of 'national minimum' standards, in wages, health, industrial conditions, and hours of work;[88] he was an enthusiastic supporter of old-age pensions financed out of taxation;[89] he believed that unemployment was due to social causes, and was a social responsibility[90] and he considered that the demand for the 'Right to Work' was legitimate if it was interpreted, as it could be, as a demand conducing to the good of society;[91] he supported the movement for establishing Trade Boards in 'sweated' industries;[92] and he mocked the 'refined anxiety' of well-to-do persons who tormented themselves 'lest men should be "spoon-fed" with too much of the goods of this world if the aid of the State be invoked to secure . . . a minimum wage, regular employment, and five shillings a week at seventy'.[93] Hobhouse and Hobson must not be regarded as typical, even of the New Liberals in general. They stood noticeably to the left even of their immediate colleagues. But their stance does reveal the wide spectrum of Liberal Party views on social policy in the Edwardian age.

The Bosanquets were far to the right of these young Radicals. In the early years of the twentieth century they still maintained their faith in the policy which had been succinctly formulated in a COS statement:

The working man does not require to be told that temporary sickness is likely now and then to visit his household; that times of slackness will occasionally come; that if he marries early and has a large family, his resources will be taxed to the uttermost; that if he lives long enough, old age will render him more or less incapable of toil—all these are the ordinary contingencies of a labourer's life, and if he is taught that as they arise they will be met by State relief or private charity, he will assuredly make no effort to meet them himself. A spirit of dependence, fatal to all progress, will be engendered in him, he will not concern himself with the causes of his distress, or consider at all how the condition of his class may be improved; the road to idleness and drunkenness will be made easy to him, and it involves no prophesying to say that the last state of a population influenced after such a fashion will certainly be worse than the first.[94]

---

[88] Ibid., p. 38.
[89] Ibid., p. 134.
[90] Ibid., p. 107.
[91] Ibid., p. 149.
[92] Collini, *Liberalism and Sociology* pp. 112–13.
[93] Hobhouse, *The Labour Movement*, p. 15.
[94] Quoted by Mowat, *The Charity Organisation Society*, pp. 42–3.

On 15 November 1907, in an address to the Edinburgh COS,[95] Bernard Bosanquet defended the 'old guard' COS position as the true *via media* between the dangers of the do-nothing policy of *laissez-faire* Individualists and the 'rough and mechanical' reforming methods of Socialists. The Individualists were right in seeing that social change should come through individual character and intitiative, but wrong in thinking the community could do nothing to help. The Socialists were right in wanting to help their fellow-man, but wrong in trying to provide for people 'as a crowd . . . whose lives are to be broken up into a series of wants, each to be satisfied as it arises, like the needs of a child or a dog'.

It is a method which in every case involves the destruction of some shape of mind or purpose—the Family, the Friendly Society, the Provident Medical Institution—which men have with pains and labour and with lofty faith created to realise, through their joint foresight and energy, their common good.

Bosanquet took several examples of misguided socialist proposals: the state feeding of schoolchildren; free medical provision for the working class; universal State old-age pensions; and he also indicated (without elaborating) that his remarks could also apply to proposals for the 'right to work' and for the 'endowment of motherhood'.[96]

He rejected out of hand, in the case of underfed schoolchildren, any proposal that the State should attempt complete provision of school meals, on the grounds that it would undermine family responsibility. He also objected, though less severely, to the notion that the State might provide meals at school and try to collect the cost from the parents. The idea he favoured was the appointment of Relief Committees—of 'trained ladies', with the help of health inspectors—attached to each school. The Committee would make investigation of the need of the children, and consult and encourage the family. They would have power to arrange whatever help was necessary, 'preferably out of voluntary funds'. No feeding should be done at the school. If the family was really incapable of looking after the children, then a more drastic remedy was required—'the

---

[95] B. Bosanquet, *The Social Criterion: or How to Judge of Proposed Social Reforms* (Edinburgh, 1907).

[96] 'Endowment of motherhood' was a Fabian-sponsored proposal for State child-endowments to widows and deserted wives who were not engaged in industrial work. Fabian Tract 149.

Poor Law, with excellent maintenance and education for the children'.[97] The ideal situation in the case of medical attention for members of the working class, in Bosanquet's view, was attendance of the chosen family doctor (arranged through subscription to provident societies); but when special attention was needed this could come from a hospital or infirmary, with after-care once again from the family doctor. 'Rough and mechanical' State intervention, however, had brought about a system where hospitals, Poor Law dispensaries, free charitable dispensaries, and 'cheap doctors' shops' competed with each other to provide routine medical treatment for the working class; and now there was a demand for free medical treatment by state salaried doctors as a remedy for the confusion. This, Bosanquet averred, would ruin medical clubs and provident dispensaries and take away from patients their choice of doctor.

Old-age pensions provided from State funds would have a similar deleterious effect, Bosanquet claimed again. They would discourage people from making their own provision against old age; they would diminish the wage of the wage-earning class; and they would cause charitable endeavour to fall away. The Bosanquets clearly went into the contest arising in the Poor Law Commission of 1905–9 with their style of play well prepared for the great game.

[97] Elsewhere the Bosanquets agreed that children should be well treated. They should be 'entirely separated from workhouse surroundings' but 'they could not be taken out of the control of the Poor Law—because of the effects of such action on poor families which were just managing by themselves, and because of the bad consequences which would flow from the management of the children by one authority and their parents by another'. H. Bosanquet, *Rich and Poor* (London, 1896), pp. 170, 187–8.

4

Practice Matches With One's Own Side: The Webbs

THE FABIAN SOCIETY AND ITS SOCIALIST CRITICS

By the mid 1890s there were three main teams representing Socialism in Britain: the Social Democratic Federation, the Fabian Society, and the Independent Labour Party.[1] The SDF was the earliest of the Socialist groups which had emerged in the 1880s to put forward a clear and distinctive doctrine concerning poverty and the Poor Law, based on what its theorists believed to be a 'correct' interpretation of the ideas of Karl Marx. But the main styles of our three teams' play in this field were developed at much the same time—in the late 1880s and the early 1890s. There were many things in common between them; but in others they differed noticeably. Their differences concerning the Poor Law—as well as their considerable agreements—may be brought out by way of a discussion of the views of some leaders of these groups.

The Webbs versus Hyndman

Before they had met, Sidney Webb and Beatrice Potter had each made acquaintance with some of the major writings of Karl Marx in the middle 1880s—Sidney at the Fabian Society's Hampstead Historic group in 1885–6, and Beatrice in the course of her private studies in 1886. Although the Social Democratic Federation (*ci-devant* Democratic Federation) had been preaching a form of Marx's doctrine at least since 1883,[2] Marx's writings were not extensively known in England, and the Webbs' acquaintance with them appears to have been confined at that time to the *Communist Manifesto*, *Capital*, a few pamphlets of Engels, and interpretations offered by such SDF disciples as Henry Mayers Hyndman, Ernest

---

[1] The Socialist League had disintegrated in the early 1890s.
[2] The Democratic Federation could be regarded as a Radical Group until 1883, when it adopted a 'Marxist' programme.

Belfort Bax, Edward Aveling, and William Morris. Although Sidney and Beatrice were interested in some aspects of Marx's thought—and particularly in his views of historical development— neither of them was greatly impressed by Marx's economic theorizing in detail, nor by that of its SDF interpreters, although Sidney had been attracted (more than has often been appreciated) by the speeches and writings of William Morris during Morris's SDF days and later.[3] The general atmosphere of the SDF (and that of the short-lived Socialist League of William Morris) was too doctrinaire, too Bohemian, and too revolutionary for their tastes. What was worse, the political tactics of the SDF and its leader Hyndman appeared to Sidney Webb to be disastrously foolish and incompetent in alienating the Liberal-Radicals. Nevertheless Hyndman and the Webbs shared certain convictions relating to questions of poverty and the Poor Law. Above all, they were in agreement that, although the wealth of the community was increasing rapidly, the existence of poverty could not be solved while the capitalist system endured. The only remedy in the last resort which would abolish poverty was the total supersession of the capitalist system. Hyndman's pronouncements on this matter were notorious; but here is Sidney Webb's expression of what amounts to the same view in terms of his 'Theory of Rent' in an early Fabian Tract which he had a main share in drafting: 'the need for Poor Relief would cease if the owners of land and capital were compelled to restore to the workers collectively the tribute of rent and interest which is now exacted from them individually.'[4] It is true that, during the 1890s, the Webbs became more impatient of the latent 'Utopianism' which they felt characterized Hyndman's utterances about the coming of socialism. They took the view that much thought and effort needed to go into the devising of administrative machinery to cope with social problems, that this machinery could precede the advent of Socialism, making the transition easier and more gradual, and possibly even surviving to make a positive contribution in the new order. To Hyndman, who had been schooled in Marx's notions (drawn from the experiences of the great French Revolution and the Paris Commune of 1871) about the need for the Revolution to dismantle the old State and spontaneously create its own new institutions, the Webbs' views were nothing but bureaucratic

[3] R. H. Tawney, 'In Memory of Sidney Webb', *Economica*, 14 (1947), 245–53.
[4] Fabian Tract 17, *Reform of the Poor Law* (London, 1891), p. 4.

heresy.[5] This represented a fundamental difference between Fabianism and Marxism, but perhaps it was a difference of means and methods rather than of principle? At least Hyndman and the Webbs agreed that, until the advent of Socialism, some public organization for the relief of poverty would be needed, even if Hyndman persisted in saying this was merely a matter of 'palliatives'.

Karl Marx had left to his later socialist followers two separate, though complementary, explanations of the causes of poverty. One was his analysis which attempted to show that the condition of the working class must inevitably get worse with the progress of capitalism—his so-called 'theory of increasing misery'; the other was his demonstration that economic crises were a recurring and irremediable feature of the capitalist economy. The SDF theorists held firmly to both doctrines, without adding much of interest to Marx's arguments, and often tending to vulgarize his analysis. But Hyndman was an effective popularizer, who could write lucidly and well. One of his best works was a little book entitled *Commercial Crises of the Nineteenth Century* (1892), which J. A. Hobson praised as a pioneering achievement in descriptive economic history, although he criticized it for its explanatory deficiencies.[6] The Webbs, of course, were not committed to the defence of either of these doctrines of Marx, as they did not base their expectations of the advent of Socialism on 'increasing misery' or industrial crises. Webb was perhaps willing to allow that 'increasing misery' would probably be the result of a completely *laissez-faire* system, but he was quick to point out that capitalism had long since moved away from *laissez-faire*, and had been modified for the better by government intervention, stimulated by the progress of democracy and the government's response to the demands and needs of the working class.[7] He could quite happily admit that the general condition of the British workers had been improving, not worsening, in the late nineteenth and early twentieth centuries. As for the theory of industrial crises, the Webbs accepted cyclical crises as descriptively true of the working of the capitalist system; but they did not display much interest in the causal analysis of them, or

---

[5] H. M. Hyndman, *The Record of an Adventurous Life* (London, 1911), p. 310.
[6] Hobson's preface to the 2nd edn. of *Commercial Crises of the Nineteenth Century* (London, 1932).
[7] See, e.g., S. Webb's 'Historic' essay in G. B. Shaw (ed.), *Fabian Essays in Socialism* (London, 1889), *passim*.

make a significant contribution to the discussion of counter-cycle measures before 1905. A fashionable theory of the time, that crises would become less and less severe as the industrial system grew older and better established, held some attractions for them,[8] because this stabilization could be attributed in part at least to the specific stabilizing effect of government intervention and municipal expenditure, which they were advocating.

All socialists shared a fundamental belief that the major causes of poverty were social, not individual moral causes; and in committing themselves to Socialism, Sidney and Beatrice Webb came to share that belief. If the major causes of poverty could be demonstrated to be social, it could be argued that it was the duty of society to provide the remedies. Little was known scientifically about the dimensions or the particular causes of unemployment or poverty before the end of the 1880s; but the early Socialists did make some attempt at investigation. Hyndman said that the SDF conducted a systematic and careful inquiry into a sample of working class streets and buildings in different quarters of London and arrived at the conclusion (to which it gave extensive publicity) that 25 per cent of workers were living on an income which was insufficient to save them and their families from physical deterioration. He claimed that Charles Booth, then about to begin his own great investigation, came to see him to protest that this percentage was an exaggeration.[9] In 1886, at the depth of the 'Depression of the 1880s', Sidney Webb also was investigating London poverty as a member of a Fabian Society committee considering unemployment. The report of that committee, which was not issued publicly as an official Fabian Society document because of disagreements, and which bears the signs of divergent opinions on the committee, is interesting as showing the state of thinking of young Socialists at that time.[10] It divided the unemployed into three categories: those out of work through 'temporary interruption' caused by the trade cycle; those unemployed because they worked in seasonal trades dependent on the weather or fashion; and the permanently unemployed or only casually employed—the 'Residuum'. The causes of unemployment which it canvassed were a somewhat 'mixed bag': indiscriminate

[8] *Fabian News* (May 1901) (review of Edwin Jones's *Economic Crises*).
[9] Hyndman, *The Record of an Adventurous Life*, pp. 330–1.
[10] *The Government Organisation of Unemployed Labour* (printed for the information of members (London, 1886)).

almsgiving by private charities; casual labour; declining trades; seasonal and cyclical fluctuation of trade; migration of rural workers to the cities; the employment of boys and girls too early in dead-end jobs with lack of training and technical education; foreign immigration; and absence of labour mobility. The Report reveals that the young Fabians were alert to a number of particular social causes, though they lacked statistical and other evidence to assess their relative importance. The same was true of the SDF at that time.

As a result, the Socialists were dependent on the work of social investigators—of Charles Booth above all. Booth's conclusions about the causes of poverty were taken by Socialists to mean that scientific investigation had tipped the balance decisively in favour of social causes of poverty being more important than individual failings. The later survey of Seebohm Rowntree in York in 1901 was taken to confirm Booth's conclusions.[11] In addition, the attention which social investigators of the 1880s and 1890s following Booth paid to the problem of casual labour helped to make this aspect of poverty and unemployment a chief concern of Socialists and social reformers. So much was common ground.

There was a large measure of agreement also between the Webbs and Hyndman concerning remedies, particularly so far as the non-able-bodied poor were concerned. They agreed that the 'Socialist and Labour' aim was to advance as near as possible to a society where no man or woman would be out of work who was willing to work and no poor person be in need because of sickness and misfortune. Children should be properly fed, clothed, housed, and trained. Improvements in the treatment of pauper children should be continued and extended, particularly in the direction of providing well-appointed schools where, after their elementary school course, they could receive technical education which would fit them for better employment than their usual prospect of domestic service for girls and low-grade jobs or emigration for boys. The medical service already available to the sick poor should be extended to provide curative treatment in their own homes and in well-equipped infirmaries and hospitals. The elderly poor should receive an 'honourable pension' sufficient to live upon and, until that was introduced, adequate outdoor relief: and if they were

---

[11] Hyndman, *The Record of an Adventurous Life*, pp. 332–3.

unable or unwilling to live in their own homes or with relatives they should be provided with almshouses or old people's homes.

Such disagreements as arose between the Webbs and Hyndman about policy towards the non-able-bodied concerned matters of detail. While they both backed Charles Booth's scheme for universal and non-contributory old-age pensions, and opposed Canon Blackley's and Joseph Chamberlain's proposals for a contributory scheme, the Webbs were willing to go all the way with Booth in recommending pensions at 65 with perhaps 'at first' the pensions granted only to those who could show they had made some attempt at saving for old age, although the 'thrift condition' should be made easy enough to be satisfied by the poorest class of persons of 'average foresight and strength of character'.[12] Hyndman demanded pensions at 50 with no qualifications.[13] Sidney Webb's phrase 'at first' indicated that his suggestions were 'Fabian' tactics to win the support of the hesitant. The other point of detail which involved some disagreement concerned the provision of meals in schools for needy schoolchildren. The SDF was strongly in favour of this policy and had included it in its programme since 1893;[14] the Fabians became divided and doubtful about it. At first they had been favourable to the idea, and Graham Wallas had taken the initiative in setting up the London School Dinners Association in 1889 to co-ordinate the activities of London charitable organizations in this enterprise.[15] By the mid-1890s, however, Wallas had become rather disillusioned with the results of the Association's activities and was impressed by a COS survey which claimed to demonstrate that in only 20 per cent of the cases studied was school feeding the appropriate remedy to help the undernourished children.[16] Consequently he turned in an unfavourable report to the Fabian Society which influenced the views of the Webbs.[17] Fabian opinion was divided on the issue and the Society did not agree on publishing Wallas's report; but the Webbs became distinctly cool about this item of social reform until it was revived in the early years of the

[12] S. Webb, 'The Reform of the Poor Law', *Contemporary Review*, 58 (1890), 105.
[13] M. Beer, *A History of British Socialism*, vol. ii (London, 1953 edn.), p. 268.
[14] Ibid., p. 267; C. Tsuzuki, *H. M. Hyndman and British Socialism* (Oxford, 1961), pp. 50, 148.
[15] J. Harris, *William Beveridge: A Biography* (Oxford, 1977), p. 53.
[16] H. Bosanquet, *The Administration of Charitable Relief* (London, 1898), p. 25.
[17] *Fabian News* (Feb. 1896).

twentieth century by Margaret McMillan and other educational reformers.[18]

Remedies and treatment for the able-bodied poor occasioned more dispute. Most Socialists of that period were prepared to admit that some distinction would need to be made between those who were willing to work but could not get work and the 'loafers'. The early Socialists, like their COS opponents, subscribed to the Victorian 'gospel of work', considering deliberate idleness to be wicked and an imposition on more industrious fellow-citizens. Of course, they applied this moral judgement to both ends of the social scale. (It was not till 1918, that an aristocratic Socialist dared to make the shocking suggestion that the National Income was sufficiently large to provide everyone, idle or not, with a minimum subsistence, and allow the industrious ones to get more.[19]) There were substantial differences of opinion about the seriousness of the 'loafing' problem, ranging from John Burns's view, expressed after his career as a SDF agitator had ended, but quite early in his career as an independent Labour MP, that the loafer, the lazy, and the undeserving represented a substantial element amongst applicants for poor relief and charity and needed stern treatment,[20] to the view of the kind-hearted George Lansbury that 'it is really astonishing how few men there are who are born tired' and ' . . . I for one never see a man or woman right down in the gutter, without remembering what was said years ago by a wiser man than me—"There, but for the grace of God, go I." '[21] As a rule, Socialists were concerned to emphasize the magnitude of involuntary unemployment, and to minimize the amount of deliberate idleness. But they were usually under some pressure from their non-Socialist opponents not to appear to be sentimental dupes. Their varying degrees of toughness in deciding what to do with the 'loafers' had an individual

[18] S. Ball in his article in *IJE* 7 (1897), 85, said that the Fabian Society was proposing to publish G. Wallas's paper as a Tract; but it did not appear. See A. M. McBriar, *Fabian Socialism and English Politics 1884–1918* (Cambridge, 1962), pp. 218, 335, and B. B. Gilbert, *The Evolution of National Insurance in Great Britain* (London, 1966), ch. 3, on the subject generally.

[19] B. Russell, *Roads to Freedom: Socialism, Anarchism and Syndicalism* (London, 1954; first published in 1918), pp. 118–20.

[20] J. Burns, 'The Unemployed', *Nineteenth Century*, 32 (1892), 855. His opinions seem to have hardened between the publication of this article and his Fabian Tract 47, based on it, although Burns was not a member of the Society.

[21] G. Lansbury, 'The Position of the Poor Law in the Problem of Poverty', *Proceedings of Poor Law Conferences 1904–5*, pp. 631, 635.

psychological, as well, perhaps, as a class dimension. Those Socialists who were more directly in touch with the working classes, and with the unemployed in particular, tended to be softer in their pronouncements on this subject than those who were not. The Webbs were tougher in their remarks than Hyndman; but Sidney Webb did temper his proposals for disciplinary treatment of obdurate cases with the proviso that the discipline should be of a curative nature, calculated to 'raise and stimulate, never to depress'.[22]

All Socialists believed that the State should do something to provide work for those who were involuntarily unemployed; and in principle there seemed to be no reason why they should have had any doubts about recommending extension of the State's powers of intervention, ownership, or management to achieve it. Nevertheless, even if they were prepared to discount the general prejudices of 'capitalist economists' to extensions of State activity, Socialists had to confront specific theoretical objections to the provision of employment by the government. Such provision would be necessary, as a rule, in a time of economic depression, and the fear was raised that if the government tried to provide employment it would divert resources of land, capital, and technical skill from private investment at a time when it was necessary to encourage such investment. If the government raised capital on the money market it would raise the interest rate and thus reduce loans to private employers. If the government competed in the industrial field it might destroy some private enterprise through its competition and create more unemployment. In any case, increased government expenditure would increase taxation at a time when it was desirable not to do so. There seems no doubt that these arguments appeared to be compelling to Sidney Webb in the earliest days of his contact with the problem.[23] Other Socialists, including some Fabians, wished to argue, on the contrary, that 'in times of depression . . . the appearance upon the market of the Government as a large borrower of capital, and as a large employer of labour [would have] a salutary effect'.[24] But the upholders of this economic 'heresy' were not able to present their argument in a theoretical form which seemed convincing to those

---

[22] RC on the Poor Laws 1905–9, Cd. 5068, Min. of Ev., Appendix vol. ix, pp. 186–90.
[23] *The Government Organisation of Unemployed Labour*, pp. 11–13.
[24] Ibid., p. 15.

who, like Sidney Webb, had been trained in orthodox economic thinking.

This fundamental difference of opinion was not resolved at the time. It was got round by suggesting fields for government activity which would not interfere much with private investment or divert workers from private employment. As these activities were the only ones the government was likely to be persuaded to engage in, no doubt it seemed an unprofitable exercise in dialectics to the Webbs to bother with the large-scale argument. By the time of the Royal Commission on the Poor Laws even the SDF was concentrating on suggesting areas of activity for the government which did not attract much private capital.[25] The activities recommended by both Hyndman and the Webbs fell, for the most part, well within the confines of 'permissible' government activity as defined by John Stuart Mill and even by earlier political economists: the making and repair of roads, reclamation of foreshores, afforestation, the provision of new water-supplies, the construction of arterial drainage or of defensive fortifications, reconstruction work on canals and (perhaps) railways, labouring work in public gardens, and street sweeping.

The disagreements arose concerning slightly more daring suggestions than these. Amongst English urban workers the mystique of 'Merrie England' lingered far into the late nineteenth and early twentieth centuries, in spite of the plight of British agriculture after the middle 1870s. The notion of returning unemployed urban workers to the land persisted, and the SDF sponsored the notion of State action to establish farming labour colonies, based on intensive cultivation and intended to be self-supporting. In conjunction with these rural ventures, it put forward proposals for experiments with State-established co-operative workshops, using the skills of urban unemployed craftsmen, and exchanging their industrial products for the products of the rural colonies so that the products of neither would come on to the ordinary competitive market.[26]

These ideas awake echoes in the mind of anyone familiar with the history of socialism of the early 'Utopian' socialists, Robert Owen, Louis Blanc, and Pierre-Joseph Proudhon. Some members of the Fabian Society, too, in its early days, had entertained beliefs in these

[25] RC on the Poor Laws, Cd. 4755, Min. of Ev., Appendix vol. iii, p. 62.

[26] Ibid.; and see G. Lansbury's draft of an article 'The Unemployed and the Land', written for *Landward Ho!* (n.d.), Lansbury Papers, vol. 29a.

projects.[27] But from the early 1890s Sidney Webb set his face against such ideas. He denounced them in Fabian Tract 51, *Socialism, True and False* (1894) in the course of a general repudiation of 'Utopianism'. He declared firmly that it was unimaginable that 'a Parliament of landlords and capitalists' would vote the necessary capital to found them; but, even if it did, there was no hope that they would be successful. Above all, the notion that the gathering of 'a mixed crowd of unemployed' into a co-operative enterprise, whether a farm or a workshop, could offer any 'hopeful way of ushering in a Socialist State' argued 'a complete misconception of the actual facts of industrial and social life'. These were corollaries of views Webb had already put forward in the report to the Fabian Society, *The Government Organisation of Unemployed Labour* in 1886. He thought it was simply foolish to believe that work created specially for the unemployed could be linked in any way with larger schemes of social regeneration. Unemployed relief works had to remain relief work; and relief work had to conform to certain criteria. It had to cater mainly for unskilled workmen; it had to be employment which could be suddenly begun or ended as general economic conditions get worse or better; it had to be the kind of employment that would not be interrupted in winter when it would be most needed; it should not compete with private employment in a way to displace other men from their jobs; and it ought to be work of distinct though not necessarily of immediate utility, in order to retain the self-respect of the workmen and to recoup some of its cost. These ideas, already implicit in the Fabian Society's first attempt at considering unemployment, were reiterated but also extended in two Tracts published just at the time the Royal Commission on the Poor Laws began its inquiries in 1906.[28] The second of these Tracts announced that there should be no 'making work' of an artificial or useless kind for the unemployed, nor any 'recalling to earth [the] ghosts of national workshops'; there was plenty of work which society needed:

There are slums to clear, houses to build, land to redeem, and waste places to afforest. To get this work done there is need of armies of workers,

---

[27] A. Besant's contribution 'Industry under Socialism' to Shaw, *Fabian Essays in Socialism*, pp. 153 ff.

[28] Tract 126, *The Abolition of Poor Law Guardians*, and Tract 127, *Socialism and Labour Policy*, both of 1906; the quotations are from Tract 127.

engaged not temporarily to tide over a depression, but permanently to complete an undertaking, the amount undertaken swelling or diminishing each year according to the state of trade.

Employment of that sort provided by municipalities could act as a *preventive* measure against unemployment.

Hyndman and the SDF, from the 1880s onward, played an actively militant role in unemployed demonstrations of all kinds, including mass rallies, marches and processions, street-corner oratory, parades to churches, deputations to Boards of Guardians, local councils, officials, and politicians, and strikes and protests in labour yards or on relief works. The aim of this agitation was to apply pressure on the authorities to give more generous relief or provide more work for the unemployed, or to stir up public sympathy; but its success was conjectural.[29] After the 1880s the Fabians distanced themselves from that kind of activity—or at least were selective in their support of it. The Webbs were very concerned to maintain that, while they were sympathetic to the cause of the unemployed, they did not favour a chief objective of the agitation—the gaining of a 'lax' administration of the Poor Law.

What they meant by this came out clearly in their views of the Poor Law Amendment Act of 1834 in contrast with SDF views of the same legislation. Harry Quelch, Hyndman's disciple and close colleague, acting as SDF spokesman on the subject, maintained that the 1834 Act was a totally repressive measure, treating the workers harshly in the interests of nascent capitalism. Its aim, in accordance with the then prevailing philosophy of *laissez-faire*, had been to set the narrowest limits upon assistance from the state in order to drive the workers helpless into the capitalist labour market.[30] The British workers had neither forgotten nor forgiven its iniquity; and he contrasted the New Poor Law of 1834 unfavourably with the relative benevolence of the Old Poor Law which it replaced.[31] While the Webbs agreed with certain points of this indictment—that the Act of 1834 was severe, that it did reflect 'Individualism triumphant', and that it had 'never received the support, or even the assent, of

---

[29] M. Dober, 'The Unemployed in England 1880–1914', MA thesis (University of Melbourne, 1981), chs. 4–6.

[30] RC on the Poor Laws 1905–9, Cd. 4755, Min. of Ev., Appendix vol. iii, Qq. 25800, 25811.

[31] Ibid., Q. 25819.

the great mass of the wage-earning class',[32] they were nevertheless inclined to follow Thomas Carlyle's view of the New Poor Law. It was a harsh measure but necessary to reform a system which had become corrupt through indiscriminate distribution of outdoor relief. Like Carlyle, they thought the New Poor Law was a 'half-truth'—sound in its principle that able-bodied persons should work, but deficient in that that principle needed to be extended to the whole community, not merely to the working class. In its time, however, it had 'reformed great evils and arrested a disease [of sloth and dependence] which might have proved fatal to the moral health of the community'.[33] The New Poor Law had work to do; but this work had been done. 'The main evils against which it was directed have now virtually disappeared. The chief objects of the Commissioners have been attained.'[34] There were dangers in two false paths: first, in continuing with harsh measures after they were no longer required, and, second, in a return to the laxity of the system which made the Act of 1834 necessary. A continuation in the first path might indeed lead to a stampede to the second through 'some wave of popular feeling [which] should sweep away . . . many of the provisions of the existing system which experience has shown to be valuable'.[35] What was needed was a well-chosen middle line, which would retain what was best while accepting modern advances, not retrogressing to earlier practices.

The Webbs and the SDF, in early years of the twentieth century, diverged substantially in their opinions about reforms to Poor Law administrative machinery. Earlier both of them were chiefly concerned to 'democratize' the existing 647 Poor Law Unions and Boards of Guardians. This move, which was an item in the Liberal programme, was achieved by the Local Government Act of 1894, when the special property qualification for Guardians (other than that of being a ratepayer) was abolished, nominee members of the Boards were removed, and married women allowed to be elected. Up to that time, even the Fabians had asked for few changes beyond that. A main exception was their demand for the establishment of a central 'Poor Law Council'—similar to the London County Council or the London School Board—to co-ordinate the work of

---

[32] S. Webb, 'The Reform of the Poor Law', p. 95.
[33] Ibid., p. 97, and Fabian Tract 126 (1906); the quotation is from the latter, p. 8.
[34] S. Webb, 'The Reform of the Poor Law', p. 97.
[35] S. Webb, 'An English Poor Law Reform Association', *QJE* 5 (1891), 371.

the 30 Boards of Guardians of London. The proposal was for it to be elected at the same time as the local Boards of Guardians, with the persons getting the highest votes composing the Council as well as sitting on their local Boards. This central Poor Law Council would take over the 'equalization' of rates between richer and poorer districts performed by the existing Common Poor Fund for London; it would take over the Metropolitan Asylums Board, and the general administration of all workhouses, casual wards, and Poor Law schools; and it would have discretionary authority over the local Boards of Guardians.[36] In the 1890s they made no demand that county councils should take over Poor Law administration, or that Poor Law union areas should be assimilated with other areas of local government, and outside London they thought it unnecessary to make any alteration at all. 'No one would propose to transfer [the Poor Law] to the county councils, which are quite unfitted for the detailed examination of individual cases which should form the leading feature in Poor Law administration', wrote Sidney Webb.[37] Furthermore, he considered that local rating should remain the method of raising Poor Law finance; it was a guard against extravagance and so it should not be made a national charge.[38]

Hyndman and the SDF did not favour even a centralized 'Poor Law Council' for London. They set little value on purely bureaucratic alteration. The only change they thought necessary after the 1894 reform was that the Poor Law should be financed from the national exchequer, not from local rates (though a small proportion of the financial burden might be borne by the locality, to make it aware of its responsibilities). The centralization of funds was needed to ensure adequate help and an equal burden of sacrifice throughout the country. Otherwise, the popularly elected Boards of Guardians should be allowed full powers, free from the control, prohibition, and restrictions imposed upon them, in the name of out-of-date ideas, by the bureaucrats of the Local Government Board. The SDF was always scornful and suspicious of mere changes in administrative machinery, and believed firmly in the virtues of participatory democracy. The main concern of the SDF was in using the new democratic machinery of the Poor Law to gain improved conditions for the poor and to remove the stigma of

---

[36] Fabian Tract 17 (1891), p. 18.
[37] Ibid.   [38] Ibid.

pauperism from help allowed by the State. The Social Democrats did not believe that the abolition of the Poor Law was essential to the gaining of these better conditions or the removal of the stigma.[39]

Before 1905, the organizational implications of 'humanizing' the Poor Law remained fragmentary and not consistently worked out, even by the Webbs and the Fabians. Sidney Webb had at one stage suggested a Hospitals Board for London that would take over Poor Law dispensaries and supervise voluntary hospitals as a step in the direction of separating medical and hospital relief from the Poor Law system;[40] but on the whole he was more concerned with his proposal for some general Poor Law Council for London. By the end of the 1890s he had become interested in the method of administering old-age pensions through the Post Office, as introduced in New Zealand in 1898.[41] Much earlier, he had suggested the possibility that government labour bureaux, when they were introduced, might also be operated through the Post Office.[42] And ever since the Order issued by Joseph Chamberlain when he was President of the Local Government Board in 1886 there had been much interest in the possibility of dissociating work provided for the 'real' unemployed from the Poor Law by having it administered by the ordinary municipal authorities, not by the Guardians. There was no clear idea of any 'break up of the Poor Law' until the early years of the twentieth century.

The first plan for bolder administrative change came from the Fabian Society about the time of the setting up of the Royal Commission. In 1903 H. G. Wells had electrified the Fabians with his lecture on 'The Question of Scientific Administrative Areas in relation to Municipal Undertakings', publicized in the following years as an appendix to his book *Anticipations*. In both the lecture and the book he developed the theme that the Fabians' thinking about 'municipal socialism' was as obsolete as Dogberry and Shallow in view of modern scientific advances in electricity, transport, and communications. Under Wells's impact, the Fabian Society set up committees to think about a number of administrative

---

[39] See statement and evidence to the RC on the Poor Laws 1905–9, presented by Harry Quelch on behalf of the SDF, Cd. 4755, Min. of Ev., Appendix vol. iii, pp. 61 ff.

[40] S. Webb, 'The Reform of the Poor Law', p. 111.

[41] Fabian Tract 89 (1899) gave publicity to the New Zealand scheme.

[42] *The Government Organisation of Unemployed Labour*, p. 11.

regional problems and to publish their findings in a series of 'New Heptarchy'[43] Tracts. The report of the Committee dealing with the reform of the Poor Law was presented to the Society on 8 December 1905, and was published in February 1906 as a 'New Heptarchy' Tract under the title *The Abolition of the Poor Law Guardians*.[44] The new policy was announced with a trumpet-blast of principle: 'It may be laid down as a general rule that there is a presumption against the efficiency and modernity of any piece of government machinery which has run without complete overhauling for more than a generation.'

The Guardians had been established in the early nineteenth century for the specific purpose of giving effect to a Poor Law reform which was now out of date, and later they had other duties loaded on to them. Their areas were *ad hoc*, and bore no relation to other areas of local government, which was confusing to the 'busy citizen'. The elections were often a 'farce', ignored by the majority of qualified voters or fought on party or personal issues irrelevant to the administration of the Poor Law. The working classes were demanding that new social services such as old-age pensions, meals for needy schoolchildren, and provision of work for the unemployed should be administered, when they were enacted, by machinery 'wholly dissociated from the obnoxious Poor Law'. *Ad hoc* bodies were now 'generally admitted' to be clumsy and inefficient. All Boards of Guardians, and the Metropolitan Asylums Board of London should be swept away; the counties and county boroughs should become the authorities for dealing with indoor poor relief and have charge of workhouses, almshouses, cottage-homes, hospitals, labour colonies, and asylums. Medical relief, outdoor relief, and special provision of work for the unemployed should become the responsibility of the local sanitary authorities, that is, of urban and rural district councils and borough and metropolitan borough councils. The funds were to be raised mainly through county and county borough rates, though a small part might be raised by the local sanitary authorities to keep them in touch with expenditure. So the Fabians in 1905 had quite abandoned their

---

[43] The reference to the Heptarchy of the Anglo-Saxon kingdoms was intended to indicate that the Fabians were thinking of local government in terms of a new regionalism. The idea was not followed up as much as it should have been after Wells left the Society in 1908.

[44] Fabian Tract 126 (1906).

former objections to transferring Poor Law services to the ordinary local authorities. They were inspired to this change of mind by their belief in the success of the Education Acts of 1902–3, which had swept away the *ad hoc* School Boards and absorbed their duties into the ordinary machinery of local government by handing them over to Education Committees of the county and county borough councils. However, perhaps with some memory of their former objection that county councils were unfitted to examine individual cases, they proposed that the new authorities should draw up an elaborate scheme of Poor Law classification and decide on suitable relief for each class, leaving it to a 'well-paid superintendent relieving officer' accompanied by a member of the council ('as a stipendiary is assisted by the local justice of the peace') to decide into which class a particular case should fall; alternatively, the council could adopt the German Elberfeld system where 'volunteer committees are systematically enlisted to examine and report on applicants for relief'. So Beatrice Webb had more than one stroke prepared for her racquet at the time when the Royal Commission was just beginning. The SDF, however, refused to play this game and was later to denounce the Webbs' proposals to abolish the Guardians as an attempt to withdraw the whole Poor Law from the view and control of democracy.[45]

The Webbs versus George Lansbury

George Lansbury, a partner in a small veneer-cutting business in the East End of London, became a member of the SDF in 1892, and retained his membership until the early years of the twentieth century, when he transferred his allegiance to the ILP and Labour Party. His attachment to the SDF (of which he became the leading member in Bow, Bromley, and Poplar) rather than to the ILP in the 1890s must be explained in terms of the strength of the SDF and the relative weakness of the ILP in the East End of London at that time.[46] Lansbury seems to have been by nature an ILP rather than SDF type of person: his devotion to Christianity was only

---

[45] H. Quelch, 'The Prevention of Destitution', *Social-Democrat*, 14 (1910), 340–3.
[46] See P. Thompson, *Socialists, Liberals and Labour: The Struggle for London 1885–1914* (London, 1967), chs. 1–7, on the political situation in London.

temporarily submerged by his SDF commitment in the 1890s;[47] Marxism did little to systematize his warm-hearted enthusiasms; and his theorizing was unrepentantly eclectic. He took a leading role in experiments in farming labour colonies, in which he received backing both from the SDF and the ILP. He argued[48] that an important cause of unemployment was migration to the cities (and in particular to London) from rural areas. Men were lured to the cities in the hope of bettering their condition; but experience had shown that industry, even if it was expanding, could never provide full employment. The State was unwilling to be generous, for maintaining the unemployed in idleness involved wringing increased 'taxation from an already overtaxed people'. (The modern mind boggles at what men brought up in the principles of Gladstonian finance thought was overtaxation, but they clearly *did* think it!) An increased use of land was therefore the 'one possible direction to look for an adequate remedy'. The state should use its influence to check the drift from the land by promoting intensive cultivation, fostering the development of new or insufficiently exploited crops (sugar-beet, flax, and timber were given as examples), and making village life more attractive. The main difficulties in the way were lack of capital and technical knowledge and the conservatism of landowners and farmers. A beginning should therefore be made with the setting up of 'example farms' to point the way and encourage the others. Trade unions, co-operative societies, capitalists, wealthy benefactors, and the state could all lend a hand; and finance might be raised by the creation of 'people's banks' or the advancing of loans by the municipalities. That, however, was a long-range project; something had to be done for the unemployed at once. The most immediate action might need to be public works such as road repair, etc. But farming labour colonies, based on intensive cultivation and intended to be self-supporting, to avoid heavy burdens on the rates and any taint of pauperism, were the real road to longer-range agricultural renewal, Lansbury believed, although he was not unaware of the dangers, difficulties, and tentative nature of his proposed experiments.

[47] G. Lansbury, 'Why I Returned to Christianity', in G. Haw (ed.) *The Religious Doubts of Democracy* (London, 1904). For further description of Lansbury, see p. 191 below.

[48] The following arguments, which Lansbury put forward at different times and places, are consolidated in the proofs of an article he wrote for *Landward Ho!*, Lansbury Papers vol. 29a.

When lansbury was elected to the Poplar Board of Guardians
in 1893, he was determined to reform Poor Law conditions after his
first visit to a workhouse, of which he gave a moving recollection in
his memoirs:

My first visit to a workhouse was a memorable one. Going down a narrow
lane, ringing the bell, waiting while an official with a not too pleasant face
looked through a grating to see who was there, and hearing his unpleasant
voice—of course, he did not know me—made it easy for me to understand
why the poor dreaded and hated these places, and made me in a flash
realise how all these prison or bastille sort of surroundings were organised
for the purpose of making self-respecting, decent people endure any
suffering rather than enter. It was not necessary to write up the words
'Abandon hope all ye who enter here'. Officials, receiving-ward, hard
forms, whitewashed walls, keys dangling at the waist of those who spoke
to you, huge books for name, history, etc., searching, and then being
stripped and bathed in a communal tub, and the final crowning indignity of
being dressed in clothes which had been worn by lots of other people,
hideous to look at, ill-fitting and coarse—everything possible was done to
inflict mental and moral degradation.[49]

In his task of 'humanizing' the Poor Law and making Poplar the
model of a 'Labour' Board of Guardians, Lansbury was strongly
supported by Will Crooks of the Coopers' Union (G. K. Chesterton's
choice as the ideal British working man), Harry Kay of the Dockers'
Union, and other socialists and radical clergymen.[50] Workhouse
conditions were changed by changing the attitude of officials
(sometimes by replacing the officials), by providing a new dietary,
better clothing, and more generous terms of leave for the inmates.
The barrack-like school for pauper children at Forest Gate,
Stratford, was converted into the Poplar Training School and
ultimately, in 1907, moved to Shenfield in Essex. It was claimed
(though this claim was contested) that the Poplar Guardians gave
outdoor relief pretty freely.

Even more controversial was the experiment of establishing a
farm colony near Laindon in Essex to provide work and training
for selected able-bodied unemployed men outside the workhouse.[51]

[49] G. Lansbury, *My Life* (London, 1928), pp. 135–6.
[50] R. Postgate, *The Life of George Lansbury* (London, 1951), p. 62; Thompson,
Socialists, Liberals and Labour, pp. 22, 129; G. K. Chesterton's opinion is given in
his introduction to G. Haw, *From Workhouse to Westminster: The Life Story of
Will Crooks, M.P.* (London, 1907), pp. xiii, xvi–xx.
[51] RC on the Poor Laws 1905–9, Cd. 5077, Min. of Ev., Appendix vol. xxv,

The Laindon colony was only one of a number of such colonies established in the 1890s and 1900s in England. It was set up in 1904, and was made possible by a donation by a philanthropic American capitalist, Joseph Fels, a disciple of Henry George and founder of the Vacant Land Cultivation Society. Fels bought the farm, which had almost fallen into disuse, and leased it to the Poplar Guardians for a peppercorn rent for three years with option of purchase by the Guardians at the end of that time, and the Guardians employed some two hundred out-of-work men to redevelop it as small farm and market garden. The Guardians supplied clothes and maintained the families of the men working there; but, as they were not empowered to pay them any wages or allowance, Fels provided each man with sixpence a week as pocket-money. The value of Laindon as an experiment was to become a matter of hot dispute between the Poplar Board of Guardians and the officials of the Local Government Board. John Burns, when he became President of the Local Government Board in the new Liberal Ministry of 1905, viewed this and other experiments in labour colonies with unvarying hostility.[52] The Webbs, also, were sceptical, for the reasons set forth in the last section. They were totally distrustful of labour colonies, of whatever type, as experiments in economically productive enterprises, or useful for any purpose other than as training (or retraining) establishments to fit carefully selected applicants for future employment. Furthermore, the Webbs regarded Lansbury as a 'thorough-going sentimentalist',[53] and were prepared to believe reports that the Poplar Board of Guardians had been lax, reckless, and extravagant in its use of public funds.[54] Lansbury, for his part, did not begin with any great affection for the Webbs, as he connected them with Canon Barnett and the Toynbee Hall 'experts', for whom he had an inveterate hatred.[55] But the tenuous approval that the Webbs gave to labour colonies as training establishments helped to avoid outright hostility.

Statistical Memoranda, Part xiv, The Work and Cost of Labour Colonies, pp. 788–95; Postgate, *The Life of George Lansbury*, pp. 67–71.

[52] See e.g. J. Burns's Diaries, 5 June 1906, 4 Apr. 1907, 13 Apr. 1907, 28 Aug. 1908, 16 Jan. 1909, 2 Mar. 1910, 19 Oct. 1910, 15 Dec. 1910. Burns Papers.

[53] B. Webb, *Our Partnership*, ed. B. Drake and M. Cole (London, 1948), p. 337.

[54] Ibid.

[55] Lansbury, *My Life*, pp. 130–1.

The Webbs versus Keir Hardie

Keir Hardie was a member of the Fabian Society from 1890 onwards; but he was not one of the Labour leaders close to the Webbs. They took an unfavourable view of him in his roles as Member of Parliament from 1892 to 1895, as one of the founders of the Independent Labour Party, and as its first Chairman. The rhetorical 'demonstration method' which Hardie employed in Parliament to draw attention to the grievances of the unemployed was considered by the Webbs to be unfitting 'posturing'[56] and useless; they considered the founding of the ILP in 1893 to be inopportune; and Hardie's tactics (in the 1890s) of hostility to the Liberals ran counter to the Webbs' tactics of 'permeation'. At the personal level, the Webbs regarded Hardie as muddle-headed and incapable of 'constructive thought'[57] about social problems. Indeed, the blend of socialism which Hardie concocted from the writings of Ruskin, Carlyle, Morris, Kropotkin, the Christian Fathers, old Radical myths, and the romantic history of Alice Stopford Green, with an admixture of Marxism and Fabianism,[58] was not likely to appeal to well-trained theoretical minds. But the Webbs underrated the emotional force of what they would have called 'sentimental socialism' as propaganda, and they underrated Hardie as a shrewd politician. Ethical fervour combined with shrewd politics was precisely the Gladstonian style with which the Radical working man of England had been long familiar, and Hardie knew instinctively how to play that kind of game. There was an especially passionate quality in Hardie's propaganda about the Poor Law—a passion that derived in part from the moral exhortations of Nonconformist religion with which Hardie and so many other ILP leaders had been imbued, and in another part from the direct and immediate experience of poverty and its consequences which had caused many of the ILP rank and file to rally to the Socialist cause.

There was, of course, much agreement between Hardie's ILP, the Fabians, and the SDF concerning the Poor Law. This ranged from the general assertion that poverty and unemployment was inherent in the capitalist system and could only finally be abolished with capitalism's replacement by Socialism down to the detailed plans by

---

[56] B. Webb, *Our Partnership*, p. 127.   [57] Ibid., p. 122.
[58] See e.g. J. K. Hardie, *From Serfdom to Socialism* (London, 1907) for a good example of Hardie's eclectic propaganda mixture.

which it was sought to 'democratize' and 'humanize' the existing system. On certain important disputed items, Hardie and his followers tended to side with the SDF rather than with the Fabians. The ILP favoured non-contributory old-age pensions at 50, without qualifications.[59] It did not share the Fabians' doubts about the advantages of providing meals at school for needy schoolchildren, and in fact was instrumental in carrying forward this campaign when the Fabians' interest showed signs of flagging. And like the SDF, the ILP believed in a generous use of outdoor relief and of assistance for the involuntarily unemployed as part of a 'labour' policy for Guardians. But Hardie's paper, the *Labour Leader*, made an original contribution to unemployed agitation by resurrecting and popularizing the slogan of the 'right to work'. It was a cry which went back to the earlier socialists of the 1830s and 1840s, but in the 1890s the ILP made it a central feature of its propaganda. It was a rousing slogan for the workers; but it was repugnant to Utilitarians and historians like the Webbs, for it recalled social demands based on abstract natural rights and historical memories of the chaos of the French 'National Workshops' of 1848.[60] As the ILP propagandists did not bother with fine theoretical distinctions, it is difficult to say how far their slogan really was based on a resurrection of a 'natural rights' style of thinking. There is some evidence that it was,[61] but it was also associated with historical-legal claims that the Elizabethan Poor Law had promised to 'set the poor on work', or with Marxist claims that the worker had such a right because 'it is the labour by hand and brain of the worker that produces all wealth'. The SDF when making use of the slogan preferred a Marxist gloss for it. Fabians who became associated with the Right to Work movement somewhat uneasily explained that it meant that certain legal rights ought to be written into the statute book in the interests of general welfare.[62] The slogan, however, was popular and persistent: when the Labour Party brought forward a bill in Parliament in 1907 dealing with unemployment it was immediately nicknamed the 'Right to Work' Bill.

[59] ILP programme adopted at the Annual Conference, Apr. 1895; P. Poirier, *The Advent of the Labour Party* (London, 1958), p. 53.

[60] Fabian Tract 127 (1906).

[61] K. D. Brown, *Labour and Unemployment 1900–1914* (Newton Abbot, 1971), p. 18.

[62] Fabian Tract 127, p. 7.

In December 1902, at the end of the Boer War, the ILP took the initiative in establishing a National Unemployed Committee under the secretaryship of Percy Alden, who had been Warden of Mansfield House University Settlement, and who was to become a Fabian-Liberal MP in 1906. The objectives of this organization, endorsed by a conference at the Guildhall in February 1903, included agitation and propaganda for the provision of work for the unemployed by local government authorities; but Alden's longer-range objective was to be the establishment of a government department headed by a Minister of Cabinet rank to deal exclusively with labour and unemployment, and be responsible for disseminating information about labour conditions and organizing unemployed labour on roads, in forest work, and in farm colonies.[63] This long-range administrative proposal was, however, not on the immediate agenda, and rested in the ILP armoury for several years. The so-called 'Right to Work' Bill of 1907 showed that the ILP was still mainly concerned with the provision of work by local authorities. This Bill, as first drafted, cast upon the ordinary local government authorities the duty of setting up unemployed committees and appointing local commissioners to register the unemployed persons of their areas and either provide them with work or maintain them and their families. The Bill also contained compulsive powers to penalize those who refused to work. The Local Government Board was left as the central authority, with the duty of appointing inspectors; during normal periods the LGB was to have power to decide whether local or national funds should be used to finance unemployment schemes, but in times of exceptional distress the central exchequer was to pay. There was provision also for the King by Order-in-Council to establish a central unemployment committee to act as advisory body to the LGB in co-ordinating local schemes of work, and the LGB was to be obligated to put into operation a central scheme of national employment, paid for out of national funds, in periods of exceptional distress.[64] The emphasis in this Bill was still on the municipalities; its proposals for central control and national action remained secondary.

Six months later the ILP had moved forward to their more

---

[63] Brown, *Labour and Unemployment*, p. 22.
[64] 7 Edw. VII, c. 3: A Bill to promote work through public authorities for unemployed persons.

5

Practice Shots Between the Webbs and the Bosanquets

HOW THEY BECAME RIVAL SOCIAL THEORISTS

WHEN Beatrice Potter was in London for the 'season' of 1883, she became a member of the COS and worked for it intermittently during the next three years, at first as a visitor in the slums of Soho and later as a rent-collector in one of Octavia Hill's housing projects in the East End. She did not seek to become one of the inner, committee group of the COS because her duties in looking after her father occupied most of her time; but as a rank-and-file charitable worker, she was able to become acquainted with a fair range of the Society's methods of work. In later years she became very critical of the COS's pretensions to 'scientific' diagnosis and treatment of poverty; but at the time of her active membership she does not appear to have strayed far from the kind of views which were being moulded into formal doctrine by C. S. Loch and Bernard Bosanquet. Beatrice's first article, entitled 'A Lady's View of the Unemployed in the East End', which was published in the *Pall Mall Gazette* of 25 February 1886, expressed impeccably orthodox COS opinions, and she clearly implied, in a letter to Joseph Chamberlain[1] when he was President of the Local Government Board, that she sided with C. S. Loch rather than with him in their dispute concerning stern or less stern treatment for the poor. Her abandonment of the COS came when she was encouraged by Charles Booth to devote her limited time to his Survey rather than to charitable activities. No doubt in this change of direction she was persuaded by Charles Booth that the COS did not know as much about the extent and causes of distress as it pretended, and that only his full-scale sociological inquiry could discover these things;

---

[1] B. Potter to Chamberlain n.d. [early Mar. 1886], N. MacKenzie (ed.), *The Letters of Sidney and Beatrice Webb*, vol. i. *Apprenticeships 1873–1892* (Cambridge, 1978), pp. 53–4.

but there was no sudden or dramatic breach with her former associates. Bernard Bosanquet spoke favourably of the work which 'Miss Potter' published under her own name in connection with Booth's survey and in her study of the Co-operative movement.[2] The game became less friendly when Beatrice became associated with the Fabian Socialists, for by 1890 signs of conflict between the COS and the Fabians were already appearing. Sidney Webb's first reference to Bosanquet had been cordial: in his essay 'Socialism in England' (1889),[3] he had listed Bosanquet's translation of the Austrian-German economist Dr Albert Shäffle's *Quintessence of Socialism* as one of the Socialist books published by British academics; a reference which Bosanquet was presently to make clear involved a misunderstanding of Schäffle's position (and his own). So far as Schäffle was concerned, this was evident when a work of his which had appeared in German first in 1885 was translated in 1892 by A. C. Morant into English, with a preface by Bernard Bosanquet, under the title *The Impossibility of Social Democracy*. There Schäffle made it plain that he was a Christian conservative and monarchist of social-reforming sympathies, an opponent alike of German Social Democracy and of the authoritarian features of Bismarck's policy. Socialism in both its Marxist and Lassallean forms he criticized and rejected both in theory and practice (although he had a kindly word for Rodbertus), but he felt that Bismarck's Anti-Socialist Laws were oppressive and unnecessary. The dangers of Socialism and Democracy could be met in two ways: first by a departure from *laissez-faire* Liberalism in the direction of a 'positive' social policy (or 'Social Positivism', as he called it, adding however that this was not 'Positivism' in Auguste Comte's sense);[4] and second, by 'supplementing' manhood suffrage by adding to the existing Reichstag representatives of municipal bodies, public and private corporations, professional associations of many kinds, the Church, and universities 'either as a separate Chamber, or as a portion of both chambers'.[5] These measures were designed to substitute an 'organic' State for the

---

[2] Ibid., p. 323; B. Bosanquet's preface to A. Schäffle, *The Impossibility of Social Democracy* (London, 1892), p. v.

[3] S. Webb, 'Socialism in England', *Publications of the American Economic Association*, 4 (1889), 41.

[4] Schäffle, *The Impossibility of Social Democracy*, p. 42.

[5] Ibid., pp. 388–9.

'spirit of Individualism', of which both Liberalism and Socialism were the offspring 'like a pair of Siamese twins'.[6] Schäffle's 'positive social policy' amounted to an approval of public and private corporative bodies in industry, independent except for State supervision, and the 'harmonious working' of corporative and private systems of management, of co-operative and endowed societies. He thought that private capital was more fit to manage most businesses, and he foresaw the need to nationalize only railways, banks, electricity, heating and lighting, coal mines, water-supply, and power, and the tobacco industry. 'Further than this', he wrote, 'I do not anticipate the advance of public and associated industrial management.'[7] The main control by the State in the future would come through its 'constant furthering, protecting, and regulating power of the will and force of the whole community over the play of private, associated, and corporative action and inter-action'.[8] Schäffle approved of strong trade unions and collective bargaining, industrial arbitration, labour bureaux, universal contributory insurance, progressive taxation—and peasant proprietorship. He accused the Socialists of being materialists, atheists, and republican revolutionaries, and of wishing to weaken the family and the stability of the marriage bond, of basing their philosophy on the 'subjective speculations of Hegel', and of aiming at the unattainable and socially disruptive ideal of equality. Unless Socialism could purge itself of these dangerous ideas, it had to be regarded as a malign force, to be combated in the only way it could be effectively checked—by the introduction of his positive social reforms.

Bernard Bosanquet took the opportunity of making explicit his views concerning Schäffle in the preface he wrote to *The Impossibility of Social Democracy*. He considered that some of Schäffle's ideas were of permanent value, but others were so much related to peculiarities of German politics and economic organization which were 'so far inferior to [those] of England'[9] as to make them irrelevant. On the latter ground he was prepared to set aside attacks on Socialism in terms of its alleged materialism, atheism, or disloyalty to monarchist principles, to ignore Schäffle's proposals for 'superseding' democratic voting, and to regard some of Schäffle's more particular proposals for strengthening economic

[6] Ibid., p. 18.   [7] Ibid., p. 45.
[8] Ibid., p. 39.   [9] Ibid., p. v.

organization as having been already solved by English developments in trade union, co-operative, and trade management organization. Furthermore Bosanquet considered that the idea that Socialism was really based on Hegel's philosophy to be a 'ridiculous fallacy'—a 'confusion between distinct tendencies which bear a certain external resemblance'.[10] On the other hand, Bosanquet believed that the main form of Schäffle's 'Social Positivism or Social Policy', which he said—going even further than Schäffle himself—had 'no reference whatever to Comtism',[11] was commendable; he 'thoroughly assent[ed] to the author's conviction that the basis of Socialism is as yet individualistic';[12] and he approved his warnings of the 'serious risks' involved in 'any fundamental aggression on family unity and parental responsibility'.[13]

This was not, however, Bosanquet's first exegesis of Schäffle's ideas: he had read his books much earlier in German, and his first variation on Schäffle's theme had been presented as a paper to the Fabian Society, as an invited outside speaker, on 21 February 1890. The title he chose for that paper was 'The Antithesis between Individualism and Socialism Philosophically Considered';[14] but, instead of presenting the Fabians with a clear-cut antithesis familiar in popular controversy, he invited them to consider that Economic Socialism, which he defined as a collective and publicly directed organization of property, did not automatically involve Moral Socialism, which he took to be an organic society where the good of the social whole was seen to be identified with the moral essence of the individual. In fact, Economic Socialism was likely to appear when egoism (Moral Individualism) was rampant, and to appear as an attempt to use public force to coerce egoistic individuals for the good of the whole, when it could not, apparently, be attained by the moral power of the social purpose. In those circumstances, Economic Socialism substituted public compulsion, sanctions, and machinery for morality, continuing to rely on Moral Individualism. That was far removed from the ideal state of affairs, and the ideal society, which could only be achieved if Economic Socialism could be combined with Moral Socialism. Then the economic regulations of society would reflect the real character and moral will of the community, and would assist morality, not substitute the machinery

---

[10] Ibid., p. vii.   [11] Ibid.   [12] Ibid., p. vi.   [13] Ibid.
[14] Printed in *COR* 69 (1890) and in B. Bosanquet, *The Civilization of Christendom and Other Studies* (London, 1893), ch. 10.

of coercion for moral choice. Economic Socialism based on Moral Socialism would be 'heaven', whereas Economic Socialism based on Moral Individualism would be 'hell'—far worse than the existing system. Unfortunately there were many indications that Economic Socialists were taking the wrong track, away from Moral Socialism.

Bosanquet gave four examples in support of this contention. The polemics of Economic Socialists against the principle of private property cut them off at once from the 'two greatest expounders' of the organic view of society—Aristotle and Hegel: he recommended Socialists to study the 'deep and complex' teaching of Hegel's *Philosophy of Right* on the subject. However much the forms of property might have changed since Aristotle's, or even Hegel's time, the correct view for Moral Socialists must be that private property should be maintained but modified. Total hostility or disrespect for private property implied 'an entire blindness to the essential elements of the social organism'.[15] Second, Bosanquet claimed that Economic Socialists tended to disparage thrift and saving; but thrift and saving were signs of 'that foresight and self-control which is, and always must be, the ground and medium of all Moral Socialism'.[16] Third, Economic Socialists were inclined to attack the strict administration of the Poor Law. Bosanquet here restated the Charity Organisation Society's principles wth belligerent emphasis:

I want all ordinary cases of destitution to be treated in the workhouse, with gentleness and human care, but under strict regulation and not on a high scale of comfort. I want all cases of exceptional misfortune, which has finally frustrated foresight and persistent effort, to be treated by private skill and judgment, apart from the Poor Law, through the dutiful care of relatives or neighbours. I want the State supplementation of the resources of those who are poor but not destitute, known as out-relief, to cease altogether. . . . And with out-relief I class all inadequate treatment of the symptom of the social evil which is known as poverty. I mention especially large-scale organisations for free dinners at popular schools, and large-scale arrangements for giving employment to the casual unemployed.[17]

His fourth and final argument against the Economic Socialists criticized them for pursuing the aim of complete equality and the abolition of classes. The organic society of Moral Socialism implied structural positions and organic functions of different kinds and levels. There should not be *castes* of workers, but *classes* must

---

[15] B. Bosanquet, *The Civilization of Christendom*, p. 329.
[16] Ibid., p. 336.   [17] Ibid., pp. 342, 346.

endure 'because the increasing material of human knowledge and endeavour will more and more consume the entire lives and thoughts of those upon whom its burden falls'.[18] In the end, the impression was left that Bosanquet thought the Economic Socialists had gone a long way down the wrong track; and in conclusion he flung out the challenge that Moral Socialism was 'the only thing for which any healthy human being, at the bottom of his heart, cares a single straw'.[19]

As might be expected, Bosanquet's address was not greeted with universal approval by the Fabians. The Society had only recently emerged from a period of earnest internal debate about the merits of Moral as opposed to Economic Socialism[20] and it had finally settled for the Economic. Sidney Webb, who had played a very active part in those debates, was understandably impatient of this attempt to revive the issue in a new form. The acridity of the later exchanges between him and Bosanquet seems to need to be explained on some such ground, for there seems little reason why a large measure of what both Schäffle and Bosanquet were saying should not have been accepted by such extremely moderate Socialists as most of the Fabians were. The main fire of Schäffle and Bosanquet was directed, not at the Fabians, but at the Marxists, Anarchists, and extremer Socialists. Schäffle was professedly anti-Socialist, but there was a lot that was 'socialistic' in his economics, and there seems little doubt that his works attracted the attention of the Fabians.[21] Bosanquet appeared to be more 'progressive' than Schäffle, for he was claiming at this time to be a 'Moral Socialist' at least, and he was described by an anonymous writer in the *Charity Organisation Review* of June 1890 (almost certainly his friend. C. S. Loch) as 'a sympathetic critic of the Fabians'.[22] But his sympathies, such as they were, did not long survive the acrimonious exchanges of the next few years, inflamed by the very unsympathetic

[18] Ibid., p. 355.
[19] Ibid., p. 351.
[20] W. Wolfe, *From Radicalism to Socialism: Men and Ideas in the Formation of Fabian Socialist Doctrines 1881–1889* (New Haven, 1975), chs. 7 and 8 and Conclusion; S. Pierson, *British Socialists: The Journey from Fantasy to Politics* (Cambridge, Mass., 1979), pp. 30–4.
[21] Sidney Webb's reference to Schäffle in his 'Socialism in England' essay has already been mentioned; and Bernard Shaw appears to have made some mocking reference to his best-known works in the titles of his *The Quintessence of Ibsenism* (1891) and *The Impossibilities of Anarchism* (1893).
[22] In an article discussing *Fabian Essays*, p. 259.

attitude to Socialists, including the Fabians, adopted from the outset of her literary career by his future wife, Helen Dendy.

Shortly after Bosanquet's address was presented to the Fabians, Sidney Webb decided to launch the Society into a campaign for the reform of the Poor Law. His first article on the subject appeared in the *Contemporary Review* for July 1890, and it was reprinted as Fabian Tract No. 17 at the beginning of the following year. There was a good deal in these publications that was calculated to be irritating to the spokesman of the COS. In advocating universal non-contributory old-age pensions, the complete separation of medical and hospital relief from the Poor Law system, and the establishment of a central Poor Law Council for London, Webb made a direct challenge to the ideas of Bosanquet and Loch. But he also accompanied these proposals with arguments that adroitly tried to stand familiar COS arguments on their heads. He contended that harsh Poor Law policies discouraged thrift and savings: a man needed £150 of savings to provide for himself and his wife in old age as well as the Poor Law provided; anything short of that minimum was not worth saving, because the Poor Law was restricted to the destitute. The COS claimed that old-age pensions would discourage attempts at saving; but Webb retorted that if pensions were made independent of small savings, it would be worth while to make them. At present many grown-up children would not help their aged parents because their contribution merely saved the rates; if small gifts were permitted, filial feelings might be awakened and personal character elevated. And Webb made other indirect jibes at the ignorant adherence of certain Poor Law 'experts' to the doctrines of 'an obsolete political economy', and at the hopes of 'a certain school of Poor Law reformers' to 'return to the medieval millenium in which all almsgiving was left to voluntary goodwill'. The Fabian proposals were presented as a safe middle way between the dangers of a too strict system on one side and too lax a one on the other. The arguments were supported by statistics, which had already been printed in the earlier Fabian Tract No. 8, *Facts for Londoners*, claiming that one person in five in London would die in a workhouse, Poor Law hospital, or insane asylum, that one in eleven of the whole metropolitan population would be driven to accept Poor Law relief in any one year, and that in 1888 there were twenty-nine deaths in London from starvation. On the basis of this propaganda and programme, Webb encouraged the formation of a Poor Law Reform Association with a broad, non-political membership in 1891.[23]

The COS took up the challenge, and launched a counter-attack. The first blow was delivered by C. S. Loch in a paper entitled 'Returns as an Instrument in Social Science' read to the Economic Section of the British Association at its meeting in Edinburgh in 1892. In this paper he illustrated the dangers of a careless or unscrupulous use of statistics, using as his example the Poor Law statistics from the Fabians' *Facts for Londoners*. While he did not dispute that the figures correctly reproduced those from the Registrar-General's Reports, he claimed that in the raw and unanalysed way in which they were presented in the Fabian pamphlet they were being used merely as an instrument for Socialist propaganda. He gave reasons why, in estimating deaths in public institutions, it was important not to lump together workhouses with Poor Law hospitals, infirmaries, and asylums. The latter institutions housed a large number, perhaps a majority of patients who might never have gone to a workhouse; many people preferred to go to these hospitals and infirmaries in spite of the legal stigma of pauper status it involved, because the treatment in many of them was as good as that in voluntary hospitals; they took accident cases and admitted many workpeople who normally earned good wages but who had to be treated for a long and difficult illness. The more people who resorted to them, the greater the number of deaths; but the Fabian Tract implied that the more people treated, the worse the condition of the poor. Loch also argued that, in handling returns of deaths by starvation, it was important to make reference to the series of returns of which the particular figure was part. The returns of a whole decade showed a marked decrease in the number of cases. In any event, there were remarkable fluctuations in the figures which often reflected the policy of the coroner in recording a verdict, when the coroner's jury attributed death to more than one cause. And, finally, Loch disputed the validity of the multiplier used in arriving at the figure of one in eleven of the metropolitan population being driven to accept Poor Law relief during the year. This paper of Loch's was published in the *Charity Organisation Review* of September 1892, and reprinted again in the book of essays *Aspects of the Social Problem* (London, 1895) edited by

[23] S. Webb, 'An English Poor Law Reform Association', *QJE* 5 (1891), 370 ff.

Bernard Bosanquet. The Webbs simply ignored it, and reprinted their figures again in subsequent editions of the Fabian Tract and in their book *Problems of Modern Industry* (London, 1898). This stung Mrs Bosanquet to fury. She wrote of these later Tracts that she regarded 'the particular methods of handling facts and figures, adopted by the Socialist Propagandists' as 'superficial and immoral'[24] and, reviewing *Problems of Modern Industry*, she declared:

... the most serious blot upon the book, and one which is likely to discredit it with all fair-minded students, is the deliberate reproduction, in the essay entitled 'The Reform of the Poor Law', of figures and misinterpretations of figures which have already been subjected to a searching and annihilating criticism. Many of the so-called facts quoted in that essay originally appeared in a Fabian tract, and were exposed in a paper read before the British Association in 1892; and to offer them again in support of seriously suggested reforms without a word of explanation or justification is, to say the least of it, a grave oversight.[25]

Between 1889—the year in which both *Fabian Essays* and Bernard Bosanquet's *Essays and Addresses* were published—and 1895, both the Webbs and the Bosanquets were working out the implications of their social philosophies. The main problem for the Webbs was to define their Socialism in relation to the somewhat ambiguous position they occupied between 'Progressive' Liberal-Radicalism and the emerging Independent Labour movement. The Bosanquets had already taken their stance firmly with the COS, and with the Liberal Party's Radical wing—though somewhat to the right of its extremist section. Their problem, as they saw it, was to present an up-to-date version of T. H. Green's social philosophy which would define the practical and theoretical criteria of desirable Liberal social reform. The Bosanquets inevitably viewed the Webbs' 'permeative' tactics between Liberals and Labour as dodgy, disingenuous, and potentially dangerous. Helen, reporting for the *Charity Organisation Review* in June 1894 a meeting of the London Reform Union (an organization supporting the Liberal-Labour Progressive Party on the London County Council), was shocked and indignant at the tactics of the Fabians in trying to force 'Socialist' resolutions concerning the reform of the Poor Law upon

[24] H. Bosanquet in an additional note to B. Bosanquet's reply to S. Ball's article of 'The Moral Aspects of Socialism' in *IJE* 6 (1896).
[25] H. Bosanquet, 'Review of the Webbs' *Problems of Modern Industry*', *IJE* 9 (1899), 251.

this meeting. She felt that a proper hearing had been denied to some COS stalwarts by the disruptive behaviour of the younger Fabians; and her indignation was tempered only by her feeling that the meeting had ended in farcical confusion. She decided to give a satirical account of the proceedings; but her account was too angry for effective satire, and too satirical for the serious moral reprobation which was needed if her anger was justified. Some of her remarks were bound to give offence: not only those about 'picturesque young Fabians, with flowing locks and motley garb', but also her references to Bernard Shaw as 'the facile Fabian' and to the earnest Graham Wallas as 'protesting with manly energy against the barbarity of feeding schoolchildren on rice pudding'. Even the solemn Oxford lawyer, Theodore Dodd, was mocked as being 'very much to the fore with Bluebooks and Acts of Parliament'.[26]

Some months later, early in 1895, Helen Dendy developed her dislike into a full-scale, direct assault on Socialism. Addressing the Council of the COS on 8 April 1895,[27] she raised the question whether there was necessarily any antagonism between Socialism and the COS, and answered with an emphatic yes. Even those Socialists who might have sound ideas on the evils of indiscriminate charity had aims and tendencies that were directly antagonistic to the COS's fundamental principles. The COS believed that economic independence for all was desirable, and that this could be achieved by a 'wise administration' of charity and the Poor Law; Socialists, on the contrary, aimed at an economic dependence on the State which would be degrading to the working class and to the whole community. So much was evident, even though Socialist ideals were vague and remote, amounting to little more than the demand that capital and land should be nationalized, without adequate explanation of the way industry would actually be carried on under those conditions. All Socialists maintained that a comfortable living was to be secured to everyone, irrespective of skill and energy, so long as they did not actually refuse to work. This policy, so Helen Dendy claimed, had been tried in England at the beginning of the nineteenth century, under the Old Poor Law, with the result (as Malthus discerned) that there was a rapid increase in population accompanied by a degradation of the conditions of the working

[26] H. Dendy [Bosanquet], 'The Farce of the Fabians', *COR* 10 (1894), 268–9.
[27] *COR* 124 (1895), 211–12.

class. Propaganda in favour of such irresponsible notions was doing great harm to the uneducated; it was undermining their character and determination to be self-helping, as also were Socialists' sneers at thrift, temperance, and industry, and their attempts to 'break down family life', by throwing all responsibility for the welfare of children on the State and by their direct criticisms of the institution of marriage. She went on also to attempt to demolish some other ideas, less central to her argument, which she claimed to be advocated by Socialists, such as the fixing of minimum wages and maximum prices, the belief that Britain could subsist on its own food supplies, and the notion that the economic waste and friction which existed under capitalism could be eliminated under Socialism.

Her arguments were given a more elaborate and detailed statement soon afterwards, this time in the form of an outright challenge to the Fabians, in an article on 'Socialist Propaganda' in the *National Review*.[28] Making particular reference to *Fabian Essays* and the Fabian Tracts, she claimed that little was being offered by the Fabians but 'brilliant caricatures of society under the so-called capitalist system' and imaginary sketches of the past. *Fabian Essays* placed its hopes in examining the forces which were supposed to be leading to Socialism, but in Sidney Webb's essay all that in fact was presented was a long list of what were supposed to be socialistic measures achieved so far. Taken altogether, these measures covered only an insignificant part of the whole industrial world. Such straws might show the way the historical current was flowing, but could tell little about where the river would lead. The possibility of its leading to a system which could preserve the vigour and freedom of private enterprise within a large scheme of State control and regulation had been ignored. Socialists should leave off abusing the present order and offer some solid proof of their claim that industry run by the State and its salaried officials would be the best one.

Helen Dendy ventured to give the Fabians some advice about the problems they should be considering. Would the new system work at least as well as the one it proposed to supersede? Would a Socialist system lead to such a slackening of incentives that it would seriously diminish the national income? Would State-controlled industry mean more routine and less freedom for the craftsman?

[28] *National Review*, 26 (1895–6), 108 ff.

What methods could be used to equalize different kinds of work under Socialism? Would the increase in population which would be produced by guaranteeing comfort to all (Helen Dendy still took the Malthusian argument for granted) result in an increasing proportion of inefficient to efficient workers? How could Socialism get along without the entrepreneur (she refused to accept the Fabians' contention that entrepreneurial functions could be performed by salaried managers)? Would the evils of monopoly be meaningless under Socialism? What would be the position of trade unions under Socialism: would the State be obliged to assert its full authority over them or would the trade unions (or a section of them) capture the State? Even where the Socialists appeared to be giving answers to some important questions, they spoke with a double tongue, she declared. For example, *Fabian Essays* and Fabian Tract 15 gave different answers to whether there would arise a 'new spirit' to replace existing incentives, under Socialism. Some Fabian Tracts (17 and 47) took a stern line with 'loafers', but the Fabians had supported a motion at a London Reform Union meeting claiming that these people were 'victims of the present system'. *Fabian Essays* proposed a scheme of labour colonies for dealing with the unemployed but Tract 47 rejected labour colonies. These vaguenesses were 'doubtful in wisdom and honesty': they pandered to the vague desires of the masses. The joint *Manifesto of English Socialists* (1893), subscribed to by the Fabians, called for 'free maintenance of all necessitous children'. That amounted to an insidious attack on the family and parental responsibility, and ignored the well-known fact that the defects of 'institution children' were an ever-recurrent problem. A worse example was the disparagement of thrift, temperance, and industry by Robert Blatchford in his *Merrie England*. The Fabians were countenancing, even though they were not indulging in, grosser forms of Socialist preaching amongst the masses, based on envy, cupidity, and class hatred. Webb and his friends needed to do some hard thinking before they went further with their propaganda for Socialism.

Not content with attacking the Webbs in their capacity as preachers of Socialist doctrine, Helen Dendy also sponsored an indirect criticism of them as historical writers. In 1894 the Webbs' *History of Trade Unionism* appeared, and in the following year Helen Dendy published in the *Economic Journal*[29] a summary of

[29] *Ec. J.* 5 (1895), 488 ff.

the criticism that the German historian Dr Brentano had made of it in *Archiv für Soziale Gesetzgebung und Statistik*. Although she noted that Brentano 'in the main recognise[d] the great value of the work', she underlined his criticism of the 'party standpoint' of the book, which led to 'misrepresentations of facts when they may conduce to further certain principles which the authors have at heart'. She also spoke of the 'difficulties of style' and contrasted the 'larger and more comprehensive views' of Dr Brentano on the subject with the 'narrow' views of the Webbs.[30]

A more general definition of the Bosanquets' outlook was given to the world in 1895 with the publication of a volume of eighteen essays, collected and edited by Bernard Bosanquet. Nine of the essays had been published before, and nine were written specially for the volume, which appeared under the title of *Aspects of the Social Problem*. Although he was careful to say that the book was not an official statement of the opinion of the COS as a whole—he perhaps needed to do so, as six of the essays were written by himself and seven by his future wife—the work soon became a focus of attention both of COS adherents and of its opponents. Its special standing was, indeed, asserted in Bosanquet's claim in the preface that all the studies in the volume had 'a single principle at their root'.[31] This claim seems, at least at first sight, surprising, considering that the articles in the volume ranged from descriptions of 'Marriage in East London' to theoretical dissertations on 'Socialism and Natural Selection'. But the single principle was said to be the view 'that the individual member of society is above all a character and a will, and that society as a whole is a structure in which will and character are "blocks with which we build" '.[32] It may be as well to begin by trying to explore the ramifications of this belief in the ideology with which Bosanquet was trying to fascinate the COS and confute its supposed opponents.

The antithesis of the view that character (or will) determines social structure is, presumably, the view that social structure

---

[30] She did not specify what she meant by 'difficulties of style'. In fact, *The History of Trade Unionism* is written in the best British mandarin historical style, and it had the benefit of revision by Bernard Shaw and Graham Wallas. The 'more comprehensive views' of Dr Brentano included his belief in the connection of modern trade unions with medieval guilds, which the Webbs considered to confuse descent and connection with similarity.

[31] B. Bosanquet (ed.), *Aspects of the Social Problem* (London, 1895), p. v.

[32] Ibid.

determines character. As Bosanquet was well aware, the latter view had been put very strongly by Robert Owen, often considered the earliest of British Socialists.[33] J. S. Mill, in his *System of Logic*,[34] had tried to escape from the rigid social determinism of Owen's view by suggesting that the individual himself had a significant part in shaping his own character. The individual's character, or permanent disposition of behaviour, he thought, was partly determined by his environment, especially by the educational influences which bore upon him, but partly also by the choices it was possible for him to make amongst alternative influences that were being offered. The choices, hardening into habit, formed his 'character', and from that his behaviour pattern could be predicted in future circumstances. And Mill believed that a 'character' of this kind could be discovered in social groups as well as in individuals: for example, social classes would acquire class characteristics, and States might be said, when certain forms of behaviour had become institutionalized or traditional, to have a 'national character'. While Mill's view did something to justify the 'common-sense' opinion that the individual (or group) could properly be praised or blamed for its character or characteristic actions, because he or she or it had some 'free-will' in shaping them, it did not solve the question of *how far* character was shaped by circumstances or by choice. This was a problem which was left by Mill to be solved by a new science of 'ethology'—the science of character-formation, which he proposed.

It may be doubted whether Bosanquet ever really got beyond this point, in spite of his application of Hegelian philosophy and, later, the psychology of William James and James Ward. Nevertheless, he was prepared to make large speculative claims for the capacity of the individual will to shape character, and of character to readjust social conditions, going well beyond Mill's cautious suggestions, and even, perhaps, beyond his master Hegel's socio-metaphysical determinism. In the Preface to *Aspects of the Social Problem* the importance of character was announced in great trumpet-blasts:

. . . circumstance is modifiable by character, and so far as circumstance is a name for human action, by character alone [p. vi]. . . . Only give scope to character and it will unfailingly pull us through [p. vii] . . . the disposition of the mind as a whole [i.e. character] is the determining condition of all

[33] R. Owen, *A New View of Society* (Harmondsworth, 1970 edn.), pp. 129, 140, 150.
[34] J. S. Mill, *A System of Logic* (London, 1879), vol. ii, bk. VI, chs. 2, 5.

conditions [p. vii]. . . . In social reform, then, character is the condition of conditions . . . [p. viii].

These formulae were elaborated and illustrated in a later chapter, entitled 'Character in its bearing on Social Causation', where the moral or ethical or idealist viewpoint (all three terms were used interchangeably at different times) was contrasted with the economic viewpoint. The moral view was said to be 'concrete', in that it dealt with man in his essential completeness as an active being; while the economic view was 'abstract', as dealing only with a small portion of the influences acting upon him. Economic science abstracted or isolated a few definite and simple influences for study: its methods, depending on such narrow theorizing, on crude empirical observation, and on the purely literary or arithmetical researches of the bookman and statistician, put severe limitations on the range of its causal analysis. The moral view did not discard the findings of economics, but it criticized and adjusted them in the light of a fuller and deeper knowledge and experience of man's nature. This fuller knowledge presumably was to be derived from a study of what the great philosophers had written concerning human nature and from the experimental knowledge of it gained by the personal contacts of trained charity workers. That knowledge was not displayed by most modern economists and reforming publicists.[35] The moral view treated men not as economic abstractions, but as living beings with a history and ideas and a character of their own. It stood to the economic view not as an opposite but as an inclusion, not as less but as more. It should not be confused (as its opponents tried to confuse it) with a view which held that social problems could be solved by apportioning blame to the unfortunate. Neither did it wish to belittle the force of material conditions nor deny that external misfortune might sometimes drag a man down. But it did assert that in most cases material conditions were not an insuperable obstacle in the way of achieving a good life. Ideas and character were all important; if the will was there, economic and material disabilities could normally be overcome.

These principles were given precise application by Helen Dendy in her chapter on 'The Meaning and Methods of True Charity'. She argued that the terms 'deserving' and 'undeserving' poor, earlier used by charity workers, needed to be abandoned, because they

---

[35] B. Bosanquet, *Aspects of the Social Problem*, p. 106.

appeared to concentrate attention on the question whether the condition of the poor was or was not their own fault. The real concern should be with consequences: did the poor man possess the character to rescue himself from his plight, and what kind of assistance was necessary to enable him to do this? There was need to substitute another term for 'deserving' to convey this idea, and all she could suggest was 'the barbarism "helpable" '. The 'case' to be helped needed to be studied in terms not only of his circumstances and of his social relationships (as a member of a family, church, trade, etc.), but also in terms of his character. And the stress she laid on character emerged when she expressed her lack of sympathy for the plea that a man was 'out of work through no fault of his own'. *'There is always some reason'* [*her italics*], she said, 'why the man who knows his trade cannot get employment';[36] and the clear implication was that the reason lay in him.

She carried this argument further in her chapter on 'The Industrial Residuum'.[37] This purported to be a descriptive analysis of the character of the 'unhelpable' poor of London, as she had observed them. It was an impressionistic essay, uncluttered by statistics or 'hard' evidence; and she did not set out the methods or criteria she used to arrive at her bold generalizations concerning the character of these classes. The reader consequently is left puzzled to decide how much was based on the shrewd observation of an active social worker, and how much simply on her *a priori* theorizing. However, he is left in no doubt about Helen Dendy's opinions. The Residuum, she asserted, displayed all the defects of character which rendered it industrially incompetent: absence of foresight and self-control; recklessness; aimless drifting; self-indulgence; an insuperable aversion to steady work; low intellect; degradation of the natural affections to animal instincts; looseness of family ties and feelings of family responsibility; a disposition unfavourable to the acquisition of skills; and many other vices of similar kind. Members of the class could be divided into two groups: first, those who followed factitious employments that were no real use to the community; and second, those who had casual or irregular employment. What could be done for them? Helen Dendy's answer, in effect, was: nothing—at least for the men—beyond what the Poor Law provided. (As a feminist, she felt that many women workers who

---

[36] Ibid., p. 179.
[37] This had been published earlier in *Ec. J.* 3 (1893), 600 ff.

fell into the class of casual labourers represented a 'genuine economic problem'). Attempts to enforce minimum wages would simply deprive members of this class of such employment as they had. Organization of labour, if it were possible, would have the same effect. Labour bureaux would encourage casual employment. All that could be hoped was that, with industrial progress, the Residuum would gradually disappear. But this tendency 'would be delayed by any scheme, however well devised, which seeks to deal with it in the mass and as a permanent institution, or in any way fosters its reluctance to yield to the pressure of circumstances'.[38]

Bernard Bosanquet, taking up Helen Dendy's conclusions, argued explicitly elsewhere[39] that the history of attempts to assist the unemployed revealed that no scheme or agency for this purpose had been successful which did not exclude the Residuum from its help; that meant 'that no general agency for helping the unemployed is successful except in so far as it excludes those whose supposed needs have called it into existence'.[40] What was more, 'the mere spreading of the idea that something must be done [for the unemployed] . . . is in and by itself a potent factor in the creation of the miserable class whose existence we deplore',[41] because it encouraged its gambling expectations. It had the same effect as indiscriminate charity and a recklessly lax Poor Law. He claimed that local governments and 'even the Labour party' were coming to see that no good could be done in helping the 'genuine' unemployed unless they began with 'immense exclusions'. But, winding up the discussion on a 'hands-off' note even as far as the 'genuine' unemployed were concerned, he remarked:

I add, however, that it would seem disastrous to adopt any policy which should discourage the Trade Societies from giving out-of-work benefit, or should recognise that a man whose annual income is sufficient, though his trade is seasonal, is to be maintained in winter at the expense of ratepayers poorer than himself.[42]

He approved the discouragement, so far as possible, of intermittent employment, despite its harsh results for the Residuum. But the only other positive recommendation that he and Helen Dendy had to offer was that something might be done by Education authorities

---

[38] Ibid., p. 616.
[39] B. Bosanquet, *Aspects of the Social Problem*, pp. 109 ff.
[40] Ibid., p. 109.   [41] Ibid., pp. 113–14.   [42] Ibid., pp. 115–16.

to help place children in work on leaving school and to provide higher education after Board School, to prevent children entering dead-end jobs.[43]

Bernard Bosanquet was quite aware that negative aspects of their teaching would invite accusations from their opponents that they were, deep down, advocates of a *laissez-faire* policy. This would have been reinforced by the chapter republishing C. S. Loch's criticisms of Chamberlain's and Booth's schemes for old-age pensions, and his attack on the idea of State pensions altogether. Helen Dendy's chapter on 'The Origin and History of the English Poor Law' would have had the same effect, for she praised the Poor Law policy in those phases where it turned a stern face to 'an outcast class for whom there is no function in the industrial organism', and condemned it when its softness enabled that class to 'perpetuate itself as a parasite upon the community'.[44] In order to redress the balance, Bernard Bosanquet tried to make clear where the contributors stood, reiterating some points that he had made in his earlier writings. He not only dissociated himself entirely from the *laissez-faire* views of Herbert Spencer but also he delivered a forthright attack on Herbert Spencer's use of 'Natural Selection' to defend *laissez-faire*.[45] Spencer exemplified 'the necessity which modern culture appears to be under of attempting to designate well-recognised phenomena of civilized society by names drawn from the evolution of the plant and the lower animal world'. It caused 'plain and well-known facts to be disputed by new-fangled analogies'.

For this evil we have largely to thank Mr Herbert Spencer, and in spite of his great abilities and untiring industry, or rather because of them and their abuse, I think that a Dante of philosophers ought to grant him the distinction of the lowest circle in the inferno.[46]

Bosanquet argued that 'natural selection and struggle for existence' did not adequately describe human adaptation, for humans and human societies did not aim at mere survival but at a certain kind of survival. It was wrong to identify these concepts with economic competition without qualification, or to treat the 'survival of the fittest' as a mere tautology, or (as T. H. Huxley did in *Evolution and Ethics*) to claim that in human society the struggle was for enjoyment. In human society the struggle was for a certain standard of life, determined by the moral ideas accepted by the community. What the standard was conceived to be varied in the course of human evolution, but the ideas that had successively imposed themselves as moral on the human race were marked by organic quality and development. Those, like Bosanquet himself, who believed that the development of human reason was the ultimate power immanent in the evolutionary process, must believe that the 'survival of the fittest' in human terms was the survival of the most reasonable. But the retrogression of any particular society was possible if it allowed the standard of life it represented and was upholding to deteriorate. Bosanquet made a brief statement of his credo in the following terms:

I believe in the reality of the general will, and in the consequent right and duty of civilised society to exercise initiative through the State with a view to the fittest development of the life of its members. But I am also absolutely convinced that the application of this initiative to guarantee *without protest* the existence of all individuals brought into being, instead of leaving the responsibility to the uttermost possible extent on the parents and the individuals themselves, is an abuse fatal to character and ultimately destructive of social life. The abolition of the struggle for existence, in the sense in which alone that term applies to human societies, means, so far as I can see, the divorce of existence from human qualities; and to favour the existence of human beings without human qualities is the ultimate inferno to which any society can descend.[47]

He explained what he meant by the words 'without protest' by saying that in civilized human society it was impossible forcibly to prevent the birth of individuals lacking co-operative qualities, or to starve them when they were born; but society could 'express protest' by want of encouragement or by some penalty.

The role of the family was the subject of lengthy discourse both in this chapter and in another chapter on 'The Duties of Citizenship'. Both its importance and its social fragility were stressed. The modern monogamic family was the creation of Roman law as modified by later civilizations, and it could be destroyed by hostile state action. The co-operative individual could only be created in the family. Law and public opinion should hold the 'author of a family' responsible for providing for its material

[47] Ibid., pp. 290–1 (my italics. A. McB.).

and moral needs. In order to produce energetic and productive individuals it was better that even family existence should not be absolutely secure: 'I desiderate for every one, for their own sake, some possibility of falling into distress by lack of wisdom and exertion.'[48] This should not extend to terror of starvation (an 'animal motive'), but 'We are all of us poor creatures; and the most high-minded is none the worse for being kept up to his work'.[49] Too great an absorption in one's family could be undesirable, as cutting a person off from the larger community; but normally the family acted as a 'half-way house' to wider interests. Free schools, co-operative dwellings, factories, libraries, clubs, organizations of labour could all be agencies for enriching family life; but they could also be agencies for destroying it. Misguided interference by philanthropy, the Poor Law, and the State constituted the greatest dangers. A list of instances of the advocacy of dangerous proposals was given from Socialist literature concerning the 'free maintenance of schoolchildren'—from *Fabian Essays, Merrie England,* the *Manifesto of English Socialists,* and from Morris and Bax's *Socialism: Its Growth and Outcome.* Bosanquet took a further step away from Socialism by repudiating this 'true Socialism' which aimed at arresting competition and guaranteeing existence without protest to all individuals; he still declared himself willing to accept a kind of 'Socialism' which would regulate the competitive struggle while enhancing the efficiency of competition—but to accept that kind alone.[50]

The 'Reality of General Will' demanded a separate chapter. It was a reprint of an article, published in the previous year,[51] in which Bosanquet had given his first definition of a concept that was later to prove central to his chief work in political philosophy, his *Philosophical Theory of the State* (1899). Its interest in the present context lies in demonstrating the reality of his philosophical or moral 'collectivism', in spite of his repudiation of Socialism *nudis verbis*. The conception of a 'general will' was implicit in the teaching of Bosanquet's mentor, T. H. Green, that 'will not force' was the basis of the State, or as J.-J. Rousseau had put it a hundred years earlier in his *Social Contract*, ultimately it was the will of the people which justified or made legitimate the 'social chains' which the State enforced. Hegel had taken up Rousseau's idea and given it a

---

[48] Ibid., p. 300.   [49] Ibid., p. 301.   [50] Ibid., p. 291.
[51] B. Bosanquet, 'The Reality of the General Will', *IJE* 4 (1894), 308 ff.

wider significance, arguing that the institutions of society and the State itself—the political and social organization, law, morals, culture, and the whole civilization of a society—were the outward embodiment of the sentiments, valuations, and habits (the 'general will' or *Volksgeist*) of its citizens. It was this Rousseau-Hegel doctrine which Bosanquet espoused. As he put it: 'man's social life in a functioning community is his will seen from outside'; the 'external life' of action 'reflected' the 'inner life' of the citizen's thoughts and will or the ideas held in common by the citizens of that society. So far as the State's legislation and activity gave expression to this 'general will' it was justified. The implication was (and Bosanquet had stated it plainly elsewhere)[52] that there was no necessary antithesis between liberty and legislation, as earlier Liberals had supposed there was: legislation, social restrictions, and compulsion could increase freedom providing they were in accord with the general will and adapted to producing a rational and civilized life. Later on, Bosanquet was to develop his argument concerning the general will with great complexity; but in this first essay he was mainly trying to face the difficulties which Rousseau also had had to face in specifying ways of discovering it. Like Rousseau, he found himself mainly specifying ways in which it could *not* be discovered. It could not be discovered by voting results on particular issues, because the general will was not static but changing and developing; it was not to be identified with 'public opinion', because that merely expressed reflections on the course of events, not the ideas producing that course; it was not just another term for the *de facto* tendency of the actions of the community, but the ideas behind that tendency. Bosanquet's conclusion appeared to be (like Hegel's) that, despite the general will's potent force in shaping the present, it could only be discerned and described in retrospect, by a philosophical history concerned to discover the 'inside' of historical happenings.

The limits of the 'moral collectivism' expressed in this chapter on the general will were made clear once again in another chapter, in which Bosanquet gave a fuller and more elaborate exposition than ever before of 'The Principle of Private Property'. Dismissing earlier and rival theories of the justification of private property as inadequate, he claimed that the true explanation lay in the

---

[52] B. Bosanquet, *The Civilization of Christendom*, ch. 11 ('Liberty and Legislation').

recognition by society that rights of property ownership would best develop citizens as moral and rational beings and thus promote the common good. Private property gave the adult citizen the means of organizing his own life and welfare, and his intelligent self-assertion and grasp of reasonable possibilities depended on such a relation with the material world. Bosanquet contrasted this adult and responsible attitude to life with that of a child or an animal. For animals and young children life was from hand to mouth; it had no future, no past: they lived in the present, and what they had and did in no way expressed their own previous actions, choices, or character. The adult person had learnt to measure his resources, to predict, to assess his own competence and character. Any rejection of the principle of private property in favour of the communal for all needs and wants amounted to the preferring of the ideal of the child to the ideal of the reasonable and responsible adult. Those who did so forgot that the reason why the workhouse was a miserable place for a grown man or woman was that 'the forward look to the unity of life is abandoned, and an adult has accepted the status of a child'.[53]

Bosanquet went on to argue that the recognition of the principle of private property did not involve either the acceptance of the unlimited acquisition of wealth, or the acceptance of existing economic arrangements. Indeed, in any actual social system its 'spiritual expression' would be to some extent distorted or obstructed. The means for its realization had to be treated as a practical problem, and could vary in accordance with the nature of the particular society. In present-day society the property of the majority of the people consisted in salaries and wages. These, to fulfil the requirements of the principle of private property, needed to be permanent and calculable—capable of being foreseen and of being invested—in order to allow the making of plans for the future. The problem of apportioning property to capacity and to services rendered to the community was desirable, but could run into practical difficulties. Unearned incomes were not necessarily and in all cases to be condemned. Corporate private property was obviously different from individual property, and raised new problems of control; but any destruction of small industries managed by individuals would certainly be a bad thing. Above all,

---

[53] B. Bosanquet (ed.), *Aspects of the Social Problem*, p. 314.

instances of the misuse of property, demonstrated or probable, were not in themselves an adequate complaint against the institution of private property, though they might be a reason for demanding restrictive legislation. At the end of the chapter Bosanquet had left no doubt that his bias was in favour of a capitalist order, though a lot of doubt remained about just how far he was prepared to go in putting it under social regulation.

Aspects of the Social Problem excited a good deal of comment, and it was not long before it provoked a reply from the Fabians. The Webbs did not need to take the lead in this, because Sidney Ball, the doyen of Oxford University Fabians, volunteered to leap into the fray. Ball, a former Oriel student who became a Fellow of St John's College, seemed eminently qualified for the task, for he, like Bosanquet, was a disciple of T. H. Green and a Hegelian, although his main interests lay in politics and ethics, not in metaphysics. His essay 'The Moral Aspects of Socialism', published first in 1896 as an article[54] and subsequently (in revised form) as a Fabian Tract,[55] was a sustained critique of *Aspects of the Social Problem*, and the Webbs thought highly of it. Sidney Webb still described it, twenty-five years later in an obituary article on Ball, as 'the best exposition of the relation of Socialism to Ethics and Philosophy'.[56]

Although the tone of Ball's essay was vigorously controversial, he acknowledged that it was easy for outsiders to misread the nature of modern Socialism, for, he said, modern or 'scientific' Socialism was only just emerging or evolving from earlier forms of Socialism which had spoken with many different voices, some of which were still vociferous in the street. The new Socialism of middle-class intellectual theorists was separating itself from the Socialism of the street so noticeably that, he remarked ironically, it might soon come to enjoy an unpopularity equal to that of the Charity Organisation Society. This modern Socialism claimed to be 'scientific' in the sense that it was in tune with the modern scientific spirit and conception of life in its approach to social problems. Fabianism, now that it had for the most part sown its wild oats, was the most thoughtful expression of it. The retrogressive rather than progressive ideas of the older Socialism were being abandoned

---

[54] In *IJE* 6 (1896), 290 ff.   [55] Fabian Tract 72 (1896).
[56] O. H. Ball (ed.), *Sidney Ball: Memories and Impressions of 'an Ideal Don'* (Oxford, 1923), p. 233.

or repudiated—such ideas as the 'right to work', payment according to needs, denial of 'rent of ability', expropriation without compensation, minimizing of wants, catastrophic 'impossibilism' and revolution, the elimination of all competition, complete equality, and the manufacture of mechanical Utopias. He gave this definition of scientific Socialism:

Modern Socialism recognises the laws of social growth and development . . . ; it recognises the moral continuity of society in its consideration for 'vested interests'; it does not base industrial organisation on 'the right to work' so much as on the right of the worker, not on 'payment according to needs' so much as 'payment according to services'; it recognises the remuneration of ability, provided that the ability does not merely represent a monopoly of privileged and non-competitive advantage; it is aware of the utility of capital, without making the individualist's confusion between the employment of capital and the ownership of it, between productive and proprietary classes; it is not concerned about inequality of property, except so far as it conflicts with 'equality of opportunity' or 'equality of consideration' for all workers; it does not so much seek to minimise as to rationalise wants, and attaches the utmost importance to the qualitative development of consumption . . .[57]

Ball claimed that Bernard Bosanquet and Helen Dendy, in the 'underground polemic' against Socialism which ran through their writings, constantly misrepresented modern scientific Socialism by attributing to it ideas generalized from earlier Socialism. Above all, this was the case with their central accusation that Socialism denied or neglected the importance of character. Even if it could be established that Socialists spent more time talking about the 'machinery' of reform and did not put character into the foreground of their discussion, it had to be remembered that machinery was only a means to an end, for Socialists as for everybody else. The end, or objective at which Socialists aimed, was the development of human nature in scope and powers of life and enjoyment. This implied the development of character, and the acceptance of a higher standard of life than the existing system could provide. This higher standard involved shorter working hours, dignity and continuity of status, participation in responsibility, and the creation of working conditions which would encourage the worker to find satisfaction in his work and give of his best.

[57] S. Ball, 'The Moral Aspects of Socialism', p. 294.

Modern Socialism was not merely concerned with the worker alone: it was equally concerned with the consumer, with promoting superior standards of consumption, not merely quantitatively but also qualitatively. Ruskin, so Sidney Ball affirmed, had shown that such higher standards of consumption were not incompatible with better conditions of work for workers. These ethical ideals, which he summed up as the increase of human power over circumstances, increase of humanizing wants, and increase of powers of social enjoyment, were essential indeed to Socialism. Without them, the machinery of Socialism would be an empty shell:

Mere 'nationalization', or mere 'municipalization', of any industry is not Socialism or Collectivism; it may be only the substitution of corporate for private administration; the social idea and purpose with which Collectivism is concerned may be completely absent.[58]

This implied an effort of will and character on the part of citizens and the action of a 'general will (which is, of course, also the will and purpose of individuals)'.[59] If public industry did not maintain the ideal, or if an employee through want of will and character failed to enter into the social purpose, there would be just as much a mechanical and material relation to the work as was now to be found in private employment. Those who took a low and cynical view of human nature, and treated present conditions as 'normal', might accuse Socialists of being too idealistic. But Socialists claimed that present 'machinery' and present conditions based on a 'plutocratic ideal' were positively degrading. Bosanquet wanted to attain 'Socialist' ethical ideals, while maintaining present economic and social arrangements. That was impossible. It was mere 'abstract' moral idealism and transcendentalism'.[60] What was there in modern society to suggest to a capitalist that he should fulfil a duty to society rather than make his fortune? How could a man on ten shillings a week or depending on casual employment regard property as 'the unity of his material life'? How could that condition be realized under a system of violent contrasts between careless ease and careworn want, a system which apparently made it the interest of the employer that the employed should not have property? Socialists were obliged to insist on the two-way link between social conditions and institutions on the one side and character (and ideals arising from it) on the other, against

[58] Ibid., p. 300. [59] Ibid., pp. 300–1. [60] Ibid., p. 308.

Bosanquet's attempt to make it a one-way process, with ideas and character having a 'spontaneous generation' and 'indefinite possibilities'. The Socialist view was: 'If institutions depend on character, character depends on institutions'.[61] Neither could work without the other. Sidney Ball was careful to avoid committing himself to the view which was the opposite of Bosanquet's—the view that institutions and circumstances produced a particular character or set of aspirations; he was content to argue their mutual dependence, and the ineffectiveness of the one without the other. He claimed this was demonstrated by the weakness of merely empirical social reform which tried to remedy 'social evils' without consciousness of the workings of the system and of the full range of 'machinery' changes needed to achieve a better world:

As a rule, [merely empirical social reform] means the modification of the system by an idea which does not belong to it, with the result that it is either ineffective or that it hampers the working of the system itself.[62]

By contrast, he claimed, modern Socialists had both a higher ideal, and a comprehension of the institutional changes necessary to achieve it.

Descending from this high level to more particular matters, Sidney Ball engaged the Bosanquets on their charges against the Socialists concerning lax Poor Law methods, relief works for the unemployed, old-age pensions, free meals for schoolchildren and breaking up the family, and abolition of private property. On some of these matters, he went further than perhaps some of his Fabian colleagues, including the Webbs, were prepared to go, in arguing that none of these things were logical deductions from Socialist or Collectivist principles.[63] The Poor Law itself was in no sense a Collectivist institution (as the COS considered it to be); it was the 'waste-receiver of private enterprise':[64] 'The Poor Law system, so far from being a concession to Socialism, is a device of Individualism, which, indeed, could not 'work' unless its logical consequences were intercepted by the work-house and the infirmary.'[65] Neither lax administration of the Poor Law, nor outdoor relief itself, nor organization of charity had anything necessarily to do with Socialism. It was not the Socialists (but, he implied, men such as Joseph Chamberlain) who were taking the lead in the campaign to

[61] Ibid.   [62] Ibid., p. 299.
[63] Ibid.   [64] Ibid., p. 296.   [65] Ibid.

'ransom' the capitalist system by old-age pensions and relief works for the unemployed.[66] 'Socialism means the organisation not of charity, nor of relief, but of industry, and in such a way that the problem of finding work which is not apparently wanted, and of devising pensions for no apparent service, would not be "normal".[67]

If Bosanquet was prepared to allow that salaries—on which present society was largely, and Socialist society would be wholly based—fulfilled the conditions of private property, then Socialism was not averse to private property. Socialism should not be confounded with Communism. The apportioning of salaries to capacity and value of services rendered, and their permanence and calculability, were quite acceptable to Socialists, who would mainly require the universalization of these principles, at present unattainable. Hand-to-mouth existence, the ideal of the slave or the child, was really encouraged by fluctuation and lack of organization of capitalist industry. In so far as an 'economy of high wages', and permanent salaries, had become a feature of capitalism, it was a result of the development of industrial organization—of trusts, combines, and syndicates—and the elimination of wasteful rivalry between competing firms. This development, which was 'a normal development of modern business', represented a 'higher type of industrial organisation':

It has become, in fact, no longer a question between 'competition' and Collectivism, but between public and private monopoly, between monopolies controlled by private capitalists and monopolies controlled by the community.[68]

In a sense, this 'higher organisation' represented a step towards Collectivism. Socialism would 'give to the possession of property character and propriety',[69] and the collective provision of such institutions as art galleries, libraries, and parks would all add to the possessions of citizens.

Ball went on to argue that Socialism did not logically involve any necessary conflict with the 'idea of the family'. But here he struck a more uncertain note. He admitted that Socialists had criticized the existing family, and that such criticism had sometimes gone beyond justifiable criticism of abuses. He considered that modern Socialists should recognize that the family had deep roots in human

[66] Ibid., p. 313.
[67] Ibid.
[68] Ibid., p. 297.
[69] Ibid., p. 315.

nature. It was because of this that both the selfishness and the unselfishness of human nature could express themselves so intensely in it. Care was needed in social interference to remedy abuses but respect the institution. He agreed there was a danger that Socialists might trust too much to State regulation and override individual responsibility; and he admitted Bosanquet and Dendy were right in thinking that 'free maintenance of all necessitous schoolchildren' by the State would 'destroy the moral idea of the family'.[70] However, if the State made it compulsory for parents to provide a certain standard of maintenance for their children, that would 'fall within the lines of "scientific" Socialism'.[71]

Sidney Ball's essay was not published anonymously, as were Fabian Tracts which had the general agreement of members of the Society: it was published as a signed Tract, which meant that the author was individually responsible for the opinions it expressed. However much Sidney Webb admired its more general argument, it is difficult to imagine that he would have been quite so dismissive of old-age pensions, at least, as a mere palliative.[72] But Webb did not enter the argument until it reached its second stage. This it did with considerable speed, after a sharp reply from Bernard Bosanquet and Helen Dendy (now Mrs Bosanquet) to Ball's criticisms.[73]

On the central question of the primary importance of character the Bosanquets were unmoving; they reasserted their proposition, and Bernard Bosanquet reaffirmed his belief that this did not involve the underrating of material conditions. But the reply was mainly taken up with answering the charge that they had failed to discriminate between a 'higher' and a 'lower' Socialism. Bosanquet reminded Ball that he had given a lecture to the Fabian Society[74] in which he had tried to do that very thing. In a scarcely veiled reference to a recent Fabian Tract by Sidney Webb called *Socialism: True and False*, he said it would have been possible for him to have represented his own views, including the recognition of the family and private property, as 'the only true Socialism' and to have stigmatized the lower form 'as a barbarous Individualism, which

---

[70] Ibid., p. 319.   [71] Ibid.

[72] In fact, the changes in the Fabian Tract version are interesting (notably the more guarded remarks about old-age pensions, and the omission of discussion of school feeding and the family).

[73] *IJE* 5 (1896), 503 ff.

[74] 'The Antithesis between Individualism and Socialism Philosophically Considered' (1890).

we fully believe it to be'. But he had put aside that temptation, as infringing 'the copyright of names', and as likely to cause himself to be credited with views he did not hold. Consequently, he took Socialism and Collectivism to mean 'the views of recognised Socialist bodies in England, as expressed in their authorized publications and manifestoes'.[75] On that criterion, Ball's ideas, though interesting and often commendable, were not those of the main Socialist groups, including the Fabian Society. The 'Joint Socialist Manifesto' which had been 'signed in the most formal manner' by Sidney Webb, Bernard Shaw, William Morris, and the secretaries of the Social Democratic Federation, Socialist League, and the Fabian Society, had called for 'the free maintenance of necessitous children', and had also declared: 'Thus we look to put an end forever to the wage-system, to sweep away all distinctions of class, and eventually to establish national and international communism on a sound basis.'[76] Why then did Mr Ball claim airily that Fabians attached no importance to the first demand, and that they were content to base their Collectivism wholly on the wage-system? Why did he suggest the Bosanquets confounded Socialism with Communism?

Bosanquet said he was aware that Sidney Webb had given a new interpretation to the 'abolition of the wage-system' in his Fabian Tract No. 51, *Socialism: True and False*, but in signing the Joint Socialist Manifesto he spoke with a divided voice, and other Socialists, including Mrs Webb in her *Co-operative Movement*, did not appear to agree with his later view. Old-age pensions were strongly advocated by Webb in his Fabian Tract No. 17, *The Reform of the Poor Law*, and his diatribes in that pamphlet and elsewhere against the 'harshness' of the Poor Law did not suggest a resolute stand against softer policies. The Independent Labour Party, which proclaimed itself a Socialist organization, openly advocated 'relief works'. The principles concerning wages policy and the responsibility of the head of the family for his family's maintenance, which were upheld by Mr Ball 'with praiseworthy audacity', were not mentioned at all, or were treated with 'extreme timidity' by other Socialist writers. Even the illustrations on the cover of the most important Fabian book illustrated their duplicity regarding 'higher' and 'lower' forms of Socialism:

[75] *IJE* 6 (1896), 503.   [76] Ibid., p. 505.

The difference between the higher views of Socialists and their working Socialism might be illustrated by the difference between the higher and lower priced edition of the Fabian Essays. The former presents on the cover an allegorical design, which may be taken to mean the contrast of Greed and Humanity. But the latter has a plainer device,—a gentleman in top-boots and old-fashioned hat, with 'privilege' inscribed on his ample waistband, stands upon a ladder marked 'Capital' that leads to fruit-bearing trees, aiming, with a revolver in either hand, at a pair of working-men who are approaching to dislodge him. This disgusting presentation of class-hatred has gone out by the thousand among workingmen.[77]

The distinctness of Socialism's 'lower' side contrasted with the vagueness and superficiality of its 'higher' side. Its leaders and spokesmen had not acquired any real vision of social welfare and did not appear to care whether the masses were elevated or brutalized by its impact. If Ball thought the people would pay more attention to his 'academic suggestions of the chair' than to 'lower' forms of Socialism, he revealed his lack of experience of the urban working population. Helen Bosanquet added a brief note, drawing attention to what she had already said in her earlier article of 'Socialist Propaganda'.[78]

Sidney Webb intervened in the exchange at this point. With more anger than accuracy, he declared: 'Mr Bosanquet and I suffer from an apparently incurable incapacity to agree on any one point, and I hope he will forgive me if I leave his personal references undebated'.[79] Bosanquet had implied that Ball's views were out of accord with those of the Fabian Tracts. This was not so:

. . . it so happens that immediately on the appearance of Mr Ball's article, the executive committee of the Fabian Society asked Mr Ball to allow it to be issued as one of the Society's series, and this proposal was unanimously endorsed at the next members' meeting of a Society.[80]

The Bosanquets' attacks on the accuracy of Fabian Tracts were unjustified. Exceptional pains were taken to make them as correct and educational as possible, whatever might be said of other Socialist propaganda. There were many different versions of Socialism current, and had Bosanquet chosen he could have 'refuted' every point in Ball's paper by quoting a contrary statement from some Socialist or other. But

this is exactly what, on Mr Ball's hypothesis of an evolution in Socialist

[77] Ibid., p. 507.   [78] Ibid.   [79] *IJE* 7 (1897), 80.   [80] Ibid.

doctrine, we should expect to find. In the biological world the contemporary existence of an infinite variety of types is one of the strongest proofs of the development theory.[81]

Therefore the important thing for the philosopher to discover was not what the movement had been, but what it was becoming. Webb's contention about the diversity of views amongst Socialists were borne out by two further Fabian contributions. Sidney Ball, returning to the fray,[82] reasserted his argument that the Bosanquets' version of Socialism, while true enough of popular Socialism, was no longer true of 'educated Socialism'. He quoted the opinions of the French writer Paul de Rousiers, and cited instances of Webb's disagreements with local and continental Social Democrats, in support of his contention that Webb's Socialism was different. He justified the Fabians' signing of the Joint Socialist Manifesto by the need to compromise to avoid breaking altogether with popular Socialism. The Fabian Tract advocating free meals for schoolchildren was 'obsolete' and he claimed that the Fabian Society was considering issuing a new tract by Graham Wallas opposing this policy. Ball resented the suggestion that his argument was purely academic: he pointed out that he had experience in the COS in London and on the Board of Guardians at Oxford to match that of his opponents. The other newcomer to the debate, Fred Brocklehurst[83] a member of the Independent Labour Party and also a Fabian, argued that there was really no difference between the principles expounded by popular Socialists and by 'Socialists of the Chair'. Neither considered school meals, old-age pensions, and relief works to be Socialism: they were 'palliatives' required by the evils of the existing economic system, an 'expression of the spirit of opportunism in its best sense in social politics'.[84] Socialists—and others—needed to be cautious in making pronouncements about the family. It had changed much over time and showed a great variety of forms in present society. There was no reason to assume the permanence of the male-dominated family and it was hard to know how the family would develop in the future. Brocklehurst was also inclined to dismiss the controversy between 'materialists' and 'moralists' as resulting from an insistence on half-truths on both sides.

Bernard Bosanquet concluded the bout by reaffirming his own position:[85]

[81] Ibid., p. 81. [82] Ibid., pp. 85 ff. [83] Ibid., pp. 91 ff.
[84] Ibid., p. 94. [85] Ibid., pp. 226 ff.

My own position is not one which any careful thinker could call Individualist. The opposition to the ideas of Herbert Spencer, and of Mill in some of his moods, which I share with the Socialists, has therefore imposed on me the task of discrimination between Socialism and the main stream of social theory due to the great thinkers of the world . . . Socialism has a core of ideas in common with the great political and social philosophy of the world, and adds to these a number of misapprehensions and extravagances which are all its own.[86]

He would not accept, as a 'rule of the game', that one must be either a Socialist or an Individualist. He would continue to deplore the particular views of some Socialists, but even more the general policy of 'intellectual drifting' which seemed to be characteristic of the Fabians. It might be the case that the tendency of evolution would be to purge away the extravagances, but would the result be Socialism? It was too soon to judge of the Fabian Society's new policy, if it had one. If it really produced a literature 'worthy of our century and our ethical standpoint',[87] he would hail it; but it certainly had not produced any so far.

[86] Ibid., p. 227.   [87] Ibid., p. 228.

6

Developing the Styles

IN the next ten years both the Webbs and the Bosanquets were
indeed to produce books worthy of their century and their ethical
standpoint. Both managed to refine and elaborate their styles in
social and political theory. Although their main preoccupations
were very different—Bernard Bosanquet's being philosophical,
Helen Bosanquet's centred in social work, and the Webbs' in
politics and administration—they nevertheless had two special
theoretical interests in common. They wanted to break away from
'abstract' economics (as represented by the neo-classical Cambridge
school led by Professor Alfred Marshall) and attempt to forge a
new style of 'social' economics or sociology; and they were
concerned to define their attitudes to democracy. The outstanding
works that arose from these quests were the Webbs' *Industrial
Democracy* (1897), Bernard Bosanquet's *The Philosophical Theory
of the State* (1899), and Helen Bosanquet's *The Strength of the
People: A Study in Social Economics* (1902).

Sociology and Social Economics

Beatrice Webb had been, for a long while, a critic of 'abstract'
economics: her criticism had begun in discussions she had had with
Herbert Spencer about the scope and nature of English economics
several years before she had met any of the young Fabian theorists.
In papers which she had written and sent to Herbert Spencer in
1886–7, she had argued that both Ricardian and Marxist
economics were based on abstract, deductive assumptions (or, as
we should say today 'models') of human behaviour and the way
society worked that were, to say the least of it, imperfectly based on
actual observation. She argued (in the style of Comtean Positivist
critics of classical economics) that what was needed was a
'sociological' or 'historical' approach to economic problems, not

based on 'abstract' or 'ideal' assumptions about human nature or the nature of capitalist society, but studying the working of social institutions as they actually existed—studying the actual 'life-histories' of these institutions:

Whether competitive profit-making or capitalism promotes greed and oppression, and depresses public spirit—like the analogous accusations that State employment favours slackness and lessens initiative, and that vocational organisation furthers exclusiveness and stale technique—*are all alike questions to be investigated* . . . I believe we have here a most fruitful field for enquiry. We might discover that each type of organisation (or absence of organisation), each social institution, has its own peculiar 'social diseases', which will lead to senility or death unless arrested—arrested, possibly, by the presence or the development of another and complementary social institution.[1]

In the long debate that was to rage between exponents of 'deductive' and 'historical' economics, Beatrice had early chosen her side. When Herbert Spencer tried to argue in defence of 'model-building' that it was necessary to have some assumptions about the 'normal' working of the economic system before one could know what 'pathological' conditions would be like and prescribe a 'course of treatment', Beatrice (who considered her approach to be that of an unbiased social scientist) reacted angrily, perhaps missing Spencer's more serious argument:

I have no intention of presenting a course of treatment, and his reference to it proves that his observation and reasoning on social subjects are subordinate to a *parti pris* on the art of government. . . . The first step is surely to find out what are these ['normal'] relations. . . . But, as I understand Ricardo's economics, he does not attempt to discover, he merely assumes. It is possible that his assumptions may turn out to be an account of normal action, but he does not prove that his assumptions represent fact. But then he does not seem to think that proof is necessary . . . The object of science is to discover what is; not to tell us according to some social ideal what ought to be.[2]

In her first book on the Co-operative movement, Beatrice Webb demonstrated what she meant by her new approach to the study of

---

[1] B. Webb, *Our Apprenticeship* (Harmondsworth, 1938), ii., 484.
[2] Ibid., pp. 340–2. It was a pity that Spencer had not used some apparently 'neutral' science like ballistics in arguing his case for the importance of 'perfect models' and calculating deviations from them; but no doubt that was too much to expect in an age obsessed with biology.

economic institutions. This little work, *The Co-operative Movement in Great Britain* (1891) was a pioneering analysis of both types of co-operation—producers' (or as she called it then 'individualist') co-operation and consumers' (or as she called it then 'democratic') co-operation, demonstrating the failure of the former and the success of the latter. It destroyed many myths dear to the hearts and hopes of certain middle-class reformers. Although she was sympathetic to the Owenite ideals of the co-operators, she pointed out ruthlessly the practical limitations of the Co-operative movement: the smallness of its scope, and the social, economic, and administrative barriers to its expansion, and the need (if it were to become a major reforming force in Society) for its efforts to be integrated with those of the trade union and the Socialist movements.

The Co-operative Movement in Great Britain set the style for the Webbs' later studies. As we have seen earlier, Beatrice dissuaded Sidney from pursuing work in abstract economics which he had begun in the company of his young Fabian associates. Although he always remained proud of his contributions to the 'Law of Rent', and brought these into their later joint writings, Sidney perhaps did not require a great deal of persuasion to refrain from going on in that field. It seems unlikely that he could have done more with his first theoretical insights than J. A. Hobson was able to do; and the bent of his own encyclopaedic and fact-oriented mind found attraction in a down-to-earth approach that promised to undermine and topple the cloud-castles of speculative thinkers. Becoming Beatrice's helper and intellectual partner in her enterprise was a condition of their marriage, and both love and political ambition argued in its favour. In addition, the popular interest in the upsurge of New Trade Unionism in the late 1880s and early 1890s made the study of trade unionism, which was her chosen next subject of study, an exciting and topical one.

Their combined talents made their *History of Trade Unionism*, published in 1894, a masterpiece which still stands as the authority in spite of almost a century of criticism. It was not a history of individual trade unions, but an evolutionary account of trade unionism—the story of the development of more complex and sophisticated forms of trade union organization during the nineteenth century. The fruit of immense research and systematic organization, it not only brought the importance of trade unions into full focus, but also demonstrated precisely the method of writing the life history of institutions that was to become the Webb speciality in their later studies of English local government. Was this a contribution to a new 'sociology'? The Webbs were aware that some of their critics did not think so, and that those critics were inclined to relegate the *History of Trade Unionism* (and their later works of that kind on local government) to the category of history—a novel and useful institutional history, perhaps, but still history. So they decided to write the supplementary volumes of *Industrial Democracy* to reveal the fuller sociological implications of their approach, which was to be built up on the foundations of their life history of institutions. In the *History of Trade Unionism*, they conceded, the

student has . . . before him a picture of those external characteristics of Trade Unionism, past and present, which—borrowing a term from a study of animal life—we may call its natural history. These external characteristics— the outward form and habit of the creature—are obviously insufficient for any scientific generalisation as to its purpose and its effects.[3]

But they went on to argue that 'Sociology, like all other sciences, can advance only upon the precise observation of facts', and that it was necessary to dismiss as useless 'conclusions, theoretical or practical, . . . arrived at by arguing from "common notions" of Trade Unionism [or] by refining these into a definition of some imaginary form of combination in the abstract'.[4]

Industrial Democracy (1897) was to be the Webbs' most ambitious attempt to 'rewrite economics' or to show the way to a new sociological approach. Combining historical, analytical, and theoretical methods, it contained a thorough description and criticism of trade union structure and functions in their varying forms, and concluded, in the third part, with a severe evaluation of economists' opinions, a theoretical interpretation of their own, and some predictions and judgements about the future of the trade union movement. The preface to the work gave an outline of the research methods they had adopted in gathering and handling their material. The Webbs were particularly fascinated by the way the evolution of trade unions had matched the evolution of the modern state. 'Functional differentiation' was demonstrated in the larger and more important unions, with the emergence of national organization, centralized funds, representative institutions, and a

[3] S. and B. Webb, *Industrial Democracy* (London, 1913 repr.), p.v.
[4] Ibid.

salaried staff chosen for their special capacity. This had arisen directly out of the needs of the greater unions, in the same way that analogous development had arisen out of the need for specialization of function in the modern mass state:

> . . . Trade Union experience points clearly to an ever-increasing differentiation between the functions of three indispensable classes of Citizen-Electors, chosen Representatives and expert Civil Servants.[5]

Trade unionism had also adapted itself to 'functional differentiation' in the economic sense in a way that made the 'old-fashioned' classical economists' simple categorical distinction between labourers and capitalists 'seem almost ludicrous'. Instead:

> we see Trade Unionism adopting and strengthening the almost infinite grading of the industrial world into separate classes, each with its own corporate tradition and Standard of Life, its own special faculty and distinctive needs . . .[6]

and furthermore trade unionism was extending itself amongst the brain-working directors of industry:

> In place of the single figure of the 'capitalist entrepreneur' we watch emerging in each trade a whole hierarchy of specialised professionals—inventors, designers, chemists, engineers, buyers, managers, foremen, and what not—organised in their own professional organisations, and standing midway between the shareholder, taxpayer or consumer, whom they serve, and the graded army of manual workers whom they direct.[7]

Trade unionism was helping to integrate the workers into the new democratic society; but it was also changing that society. Here the Webbs coined the slogan of the 'National Minimum',[8] which was to acquire an important role both in Fabian Socialist and in New Liberal thought. In the course of defending trade union practices against their opponents, they argued that the enforcement by trade unions of minimum standards within their industries was positively beneficial to industrial efficiency: it encouraged the employment of the best workmen and the introduction of better machinery and organization; and, when it put an end to 'parasitic' trades, which kept workpeople in employment at standards incompatible with health and vigour, that was a good thing too.

---

[5] Ibid., p. 844.   [6] Ibid., p. 843.   [7] Ibid.
[8] Possibly earlier usage of term may be discovered, but the Webbs made it their special slogan, popularized it, and introduced it in political and intellectual circles.

They pressed forward with this notion to argue that National Minimum standards, enforced by the State (as exemplified by Factory Acts and Public Health Acts), had a similar beneficial effect. It would come gradually to be recognized, they claimed, that the State had a duty to preserve certain standards below which no citizen should be allowed to fall. And henceforward, a great deal of Fabian Society propaganda was to be presented in terms of winning a National Minimum standard. The Fabian Society's advocacy of extensions of the factory acts, its campaign against 'sweating', its demands for arbitration, the eight-hour day, and the extension of workers' compensation, its support for old-age pensions, improved housing conditions, extension of educational facilities, and reform of the Poor Laws were all justified by the 'National Minimum' slogan, advocating the raising of the status of the underprivileged. Although the Webbs regarded these demands as Socialist in tendency, they recognized that the National Minimum was designed only to 'secure the base of the pyramid';[9] they appealed to sympathetic non-Socialists for support in the reforms they promoted under that slogan, and they did not realize until much later that they were presenting a useful name for a halting-place to New Liberals who were willing to go so far but no further.

The establishment of the London School of Economics in 1895 with money left to the Fabian Society by one of its members symbolized the Webbs' high hopes of their new approach to social science. The model for the new foundation was the École Libre des Sciences Politiques in Paris, and its purpose was to teach not specifically 'Socialist economics' but to foster the practical 'socio-logical' economics that the Webbs were advocating. The School's first director was W. A. S. Hewins, a young economic historian from Pembroke College, Oxford, of Conservative inclinations politically, but who had impressed the Webbs by his talents and his criticism of Oxbridge economics. The Webbs put much effort into selecting a distinguished band of lecturers. From very small beginnings and with much soliciting of donations, they gradually built up the School, finally securing its fortunes by incorporating it into the reorganized University of London in 1900. The Webbs did not in fact prescribe any 'line' of teaching at the LSE, but their influence in early selections of staff and their own personal

---

[9] *Industrial Democracy*, p. 839.

enthusiasm and interest in its early affairs gave it a distinctive flavour, recognizably different from older university institutions. Later, as the Webbs' critics in the Fabian Society had predicted, it grew away from them, particularly in the teaching of economics and sociology.

The Bosanquets did not regard the Webbs' 'life-history of institutions' (even when extended into structural and functional analysis) as sociology at all. Bernard Bosanquet wrote dismissively:

Any independent researches, such as Mr and Mrs Webb's *Industrial Democracy*, may of course be ranked under the heading 'Sociology'. But works of this kind do not, as a rule, attach themselves to the peculiar method and language of sociological writers.[10]

The severity of the remark was softened, however, by his later observation that

no such serious successes have as yet been won in the name and by the special methods of sociology as have been achieved by many investigators approaching their problems directly and with an immediate interest; whether in the sphere of political economy proper, or in dealing with various questions of social and ethical importance, such as pauperism, charity, sanitation, education, the condition of the people, the comparative study of politics, or the analysis of material and geographical conditions in their reaction upon social and artistic development.[11]

All the same, he made it clear that these empirical successes were mere chips and fragments compared with the ambitious aspirations of the sociologists to become the Newtons of social science. He admired the aspiration, which he saw as foreshadowed in aspects of the work of Plato and Aristotle in the ancient world but as having its true modern beginnings with Vico and Montesquieu, then transmitted by Comte, Marx, and Spencer (in various limited naturalistic forms) to their abler successors of the French sociological school: Le Bon, Durkheim, and Tardé.[12] Bosanquet did not criticize sociology for its attempt to formulate its conclusions in terms of general theory, but for its positivistic approach and what he considered to be its attempt to explain social life in terms which reduced explanations of mental activity to the level of explanation in physical science (Comte), biology (Spencer), or economics

---

[10] B. Bosanquet, *The Philosophical Theory of the State* (London, 1925 edn.), p. 20 n.

[11] Ibid., p. 21.   [12] Ibid., ch. 2 *passim*.

(Marx). In the latter case, he allowed that 'political economy' had been 'indisputably successful as a science of explanation'[13] within the narrow scope of its own definitions, and the influence of economic conditions on social behaviour was undeniable, but it would not do to formulate a sociology in which 'economic conditions were a sort of iron girders put up to begin with and civilisation was the embellishment of them. It is the old story of forgetting that the skeleton is later than the body, and is deposited and moulded by it.'[14] Economic structure was an aspect of the structure of the human mind, and the relation between ideas and economic facts would need to be entirely restated.

Bosanquet found it refreshing that the French sociologists of his own day were turning to psychology for their explanation of social behaviour, as revealed by their use of such terms as the 'mind of the crowd', 'social consciousness', *logique sociale*. They were on the right track, for, he averred: 'Explanation aims at referring things to a whole; and there is no true whole but mind'.[15] But, although this was the right track, the psychology they espoused would not take them all the way, because contemporary psychology was also positivistic and reductionist. Only when psychology found itself impelled, by its own development, to recognize the insights of (Hegelian) Philosophy about human nature and human society would it reach its true destination. Bernard Bosanquet did no more than sketch lightly, in the penultimate chapter of *The Philosophical Theory of the State*, expounding Hegel, and in his concluding chapter, some leading ideas of his approach to a new sociology or social economics. The elaboration of these ideas was left to his wife.

During the 1890s, Helen Bosanquet had been a prolific writer of articles on problems of social work, social conditions, and economics in a number of journals, notably the *Economic Journal*, *Charity Organisation Review*, *International Journal of Ethics*, and *Contemporary Review*. She had gathered the best of these writings into two volumes of essays, *Rich and Poor* (1896) and *The Standard of Life and Other Studies* (1898). They had included descriptions of life in the East End of London, dealing with the workings of local government, the conditions of women and children and their education and industrial training, and the financial plight of poor families; they dispensed general advice to

---

[13] Ibid., p. 26.   [14] Ibid., p. 28 n.   [15] Ibid., p. 40.

charitable workers, and advice to working-class families about how to manage on their meagre incomes; and they ventured into more controversial fields of social theory in esays criticizing the Marxist theory of class struggle, defining the terms of industrial conflict, and specifying the elements of a psychology of social progress. Encouraged by the success of these volumes, Helen Bosanquet in the first years of the twentieth century embarked on her first full-length book of social theory, which appeared in 1902 as *The Strength of the People: A Study in Social Economics.*

She claimed that the new Social Economics would coincide with earlier Political Economy in some respects; but it would differ from it in being an applied science, useful to practical administrators.[16] The main differences seem to consist in its Idealist insistence that the mind makes the man—and moulds his circumstances; and in the explicitness of its other moral judgements throughout. One of the book's reviewers remarked sharply, but not altogether unjustly, that it 'unfortunately has a slightly patronising tone as of (say) a Bishop's wife lecturing to Curates'.[17] All the same, the economic argument began in an orthodox enough way, stating the aim as being the development of resources so as to yield maximum wealth, and the distribution of the wealth so as to render the produce as useful to society as possible. Helen Bosanquet took the view that the problem of distribution was the more important one in her time, although she argued that it was necessary to remember that distribution was essentially bound up with production. The three major questions concerning distribution were: (1) what distribution encouraged maximum production (she called this the 'business-man's question')? (2) what distribution was most useful to all members of the community ('the philanthropists' question')? and (3) what was the best method of distribution ('the statesman's question')?[18]

She recognized there was a *prima-facie* case that extremes of poverty and wealth of the kind that would potentially discourage maximum production did exist, and that a more equal distribution might set it right. But great difficulties arose when one tried to estimate its extent or to remedy it. Poverty was often too quickly

[16] H. Bosanquet, *The Strength of the People: A Study in Social Economics* (London, 1902), p. vi.
[17] C. P. Sanger, *IJE* 13 (1903), 388.
[18] H. Bosanquet, *The Strength of the People*, pp. 60–3.

assumed to be the cause of the inefficiency of the poor and wealth the inefficiency of the rich, when other causes, more deeply rooted in mental habits and attitudes, might be more potent. The undernourishment of schoolchildren might be the result of the ignorance of parents rather than of their poverty. The 'most impressive waste', that of failure to employ satisfactorily 'the woman-power of the community',[19] was probably due more to prejudice than to families being able to afford industrial training only for boys. She admitted that a more equal distribution would cause a substantial improvement in the lot of the unskilled labourer, but thought it would probably not effect much improvement for the skilled worker. It was difficult to say what result this would have in terms of greater efficiency over all. Diversity of quality was essential even to the maintenance of quantity; and diversity of quality required inequality of distribution:

The man who is training to be a doctor must pass through a longer unproductive period than the man who is to be an artisan; the artisan again than the unskilled labourer. The scholar must have more teachers and books; the man of science more expensive apparatus. The artist and the poet need leisure and freedom from anxiety; the statesman immunity from the pressure of his own personal wants.[20]

She criticized Professor Marshall for demanding to know why numbers of people should be doomed by hard work to provide the requisites of a refined and cultured life for others and not share it themselves. She claimed that the lower-paid workers were not producing the 'requisites of a refined and cultured life'; they were occupied always in producing things for consumption by their own class: 'Badly paid tailors are making cheap clothing that no rich man would look at; badly paid servants are rendering services [to their own class or the class just above them]'.[21] The requisites of refinement were produced by professional people and skilled artisans, who were not exploited by the rich.[22]

The tasks of the philanthropist and the statesman were to ensure that goods went to those who needed them most, and to devise the best means of doing so. This differed from the task of the business man who merely had to distribute them to persons who would pay for them. In this connection, Helen Bosanquet considered Jeremy

[19] Ibid., p. 67. [20] Ibid., p. 69.
[21] Ibid., p. 71. [22] Ibid., p. 72.

Bentham's argument (as reformulated by Professor Sidgwick) that a more equal distribution would be beneficial on the ground that an increase in a person's wealth would produce an increase in his happiness but in a decreasing ratio the more he had of it.[23] She was sceptical of the possibility of calculating in this way different persons' needs or happiness, except in a community 'practically homogeneous in its wants and interests and power of handling wealth'.[24] There were too many assumptions about 'other things being equal' in economists' arguments. In the real world, other things were not equal, yet decisions still had to be made. She cited a number of instances where increase of wealth had not brought happiness but had resulted in the degradation, moral and economic, of many people—where the extra wealth had been dissipated in fecklessness, drink, and debauchery. She claimed, in particular, that an increase of wealth not achieved by one's own exertions but coming from outside sources almost invariably produced a diminution of the individual's own efforts. This was so, because in modern civilized communities it was not the spur of hunger or the fear of starvation which provided the incentive to effort: in modern times the alternatives were independence and dependence, and the incentive consisted in the *will* of the individual to preserve his independence. Anything that undermined that will to independence, even if it were the provision of old-age pensions that relieved workmen from having to think of providing for their future or the provision of school meals which removed from parents the responsibility of providing for their offspring, would have fatal social consequences. In italics Mrs Bosanquet emphasized that an increase in wealth alone could not bring benefit or happiness, it could do so *only when the power to use it wisely is present*.[25] The main task for the philanthropist, and the main method to be promoted by the statesman, was to encourage such inner virtues, whether directly, through schools and the teaching of household management to mothers or, more importantly, indirectly, through influences actually involved in persons' lives such as their families and those they emulated, and through claims that the community actually made on them. She declared that she had no objection to a more equal distribution 'than we have at present'[26] but reasserted

---

[23] Ibid., p. 74.
[25] Ibid., p. 82.
[24] Ibid., p. 83.
[26] Ibid., p. 100.

that it would be effective only under the conditions she had specified.

Surely there never was a time when society believed so entirely in the power of money to effect all its good works for it. The strong can help the weak, there is no doubt about that; they may even help the poor to be less poor; but money will play a very subordinate part in their work.[27]

Her view was directly opposed to that of the Fabians, or even to that of Conservatives like Charles Booth or of Liberals like Seebohm Rowntree, when she went on to claim that 'poverty lines' meant very little when the same income could mean neatness and comfort in one home and squalor in another. She asserted boldly:

I speak confidently, and with full knowledge of all the difficulties of a small income, when I say that there are comparatively few families in London [*there was a footnote here excepting families dependent solely on women's earnings*] through whose hands there had not passed in the course of a year sufficient money and money's worth to have made a life free at any rate from hunger and cold, and with much of it good.[28]

The Webbs never commented directly on Mrs Bosanquet's version of social economics; but the Fabian opposition to this kind of view was expressed with unqualified violence by Bernard Shaw in his preface to *Major Barbara* a few years later:

. . . to deplore [the desire of the poor for more money] . . . is to strain towards the extreme limit of impudence in lying and corruption in hypocrisy. The universal regard for money is the one hopeful fact in our civilization, the one sound spot in our social conscience. Money is the most important thing in the world. It represents health, strength, honor, generosity and beauty as conspicuously and undeniably as the want of it represents illness, weakness, disgrace, meanness and ugliness. Not the least of its virtues is that it destroys base people as certainly as it fortifies and dignifies noble people . . . : money is the counter that enables life to be distributed socially: it *is* life as truly as gold coins and bank notes are money . . . The crying need of the nation is not for better morals, cheaper bread, temperance, liberty, culture, redemption of fallen sisters and erring brothers, nor the grace, love and fellowship of the Trinity, but simply for enough money.[29]

He was willing to allow that, as things were, the working classes might use extra money unwisely, but he considered that to be a self-

[27] Ibid., pp. 108–9.   [28] Ibid., p. 101.
[29] B. Shaw, *Major Barbara* (Harmondsworth, 1945), p. xii.

remedying problem: '[the poor] want very much to wallow in all the costly vulgarities from which the elect souls among the rich turn away with loathing. It is by surfeit and not by abstinence that they will be cured of their hankering after unwholesome sweets.'[30] If the Webbs ignored Helen Bosanquet, she did not quite ignore them. The last part of her book was devoted to a criticism of their argument for Wages Boards and Minimum Wages.[31] She accepted that the experiments of Wages Boards in Victoria, Australia, had raised wages (slightly) in sweated trades, and that restrictions of women's hours of work had not lowered wages, but she argued that any attempt to introduce a universal Minimum Wage by legislation would result in employers reducing their wages bill either by replacing workmen by machinery (and thus causing unemployment) or by raising the price of their commodity. While advocates of the scheme, such as the Webbs, might regard the second alternative with equanimity, on the assumption that the working classes, although 80 per cent of the population, consumed only one-third of the annual aggregate of products and services, she pointed out that the production of the sweated trades was almost wholly consumed by the wage-earners, and therefore the increased cost would be borne by the workers. She took the view that it was necessary to relinquish all ideas of raising wages by Act of Parliament, and to abandon any notion of substituting a new system for the existing one. Her conclusion was that 'no new method is necessary, but only a better working of the old'.[32]

The Bosanquets' enthusiasm for 'social economics' resulted in the Charity Organisation Society's training school for social workers, which had been established in 1896, assuming the grander title of School of Sociology and Social Economics in 1903. This new enterprise began on a small scale, with one man, E. J. Urwick, an Oxford graduate, former sub-Warden of Toynbee Hall, as part-time lecturer and tutor to the sixteen students (he was also President of the Morley College for Working Men and Women). A good deal of the lecturing, then and later, was helped out by visiting speakers, the Bosanquets and other leaders of the COS taking a large share in it. Later Dr James Bonar, economist and historian of

---

[30] Ibid., p. xi.
[31] H. Bosanquet, *The Strength of the People*, pp. 287–95. *Industrial Democracy* was referred to at p. 292.
[32] Ibid., p. 295.

economic ideas, became President of the School. The original plan was to have four disciplines of 'new knowledge' taught: social history, social economics, social philosophy, and psychology. But in fact the work of the school became divided into three departments: sociology, social theory, and practical instruction in charitable and poor law administration.[33] No doubt the venture had been inspired by the success of the LSE; but, unlike the LSE, it did not thrive. Its founders lacked the Webbs' ability at administrative organization and the promotion which would attract financial support. Besides, the COS had left its run too late: the LSE's fortunes were made by gaining a foothold in the reorganized University of London; so, to the chagrin of its founders, the School of Sociology and Social Economics had to solve its financial difficulties by being absorbed into the LSE in 1912.

Democracy

When the Webbs were writing their *Industrial Democracy*, they found that it was necessary to provide some clarification and definition of what they understood by 'democracy'. Characteristically, they avoided approaching this task by way of the style of theorizing of political philosophy. Their approach was institutional and matter-of-fact—political science, as they saw it, rather than political philosophy. Yet, of course, they did have a theory, and recognized they had one, for Sidney Webb was not content to let it rest implicit in their discussion of trade union functions: he extrapolated it into the form of six lectures on 'The Machinery of Democracy', which he delivered to the Fabian Society at fortnightly intervals from 2 October to 11 December 1896,[34] just before *Industrial Democracy* was published. Basically, the Webbs' idea of democracy was the Representative Democracy of John Stuart Mill, but the Mill of *Representative Government* rather than the Mill of *On Liberty*. Sidney Webb, in the mid 1890s, was becoming more impatient of metaphysical and theoretical speculation about politics, partly because he had made up his mind about certain fundamental problems, partly because he was becoming completely absorbed in down-to-earth details of administration and politics, and partly because he was anxious to avoid potentially divisive conflicts

---

[33] K. Woodroofe, *From Charity to Social Work in England and the United States* (London, 1962), p. 137.

[34] These were reported in *Fabian News* (Nov. and Dec. 1896 and Jan. 1897).

within the Fabian Society by limiting the issues on which it claimed to speak with a collective voice. As a result, the more speculative problems were deliberately shunned by Webb himself and by the Society when it was speaking in its collective capacity. Bernard Shaw and the Secretary of the Fabian Society, Edward Pease, voluntarily went along with Webb in this policy. Shaw revelled in his divided roles as responsible Fabian spokesman and irresponsible individual artist;[35] Pease repressed his former extra-mural enthusiasms.[36] Beatrice Webb occasionally—in private—found some of the restraints irksome, but reflected that abstinence was a condition of accomplishing the main tasks that she and Sidney had set themselves.[37]

Sidney Webb's religious and philosophical scepticism, and the limits imposed on Fabian doctrine, excluded from effective theoretical influence the few eminent philosophers whom the Fabian Society numbered in its entourage in the mid 1890s. The fact that these philosophers—Professor D. G. Ritchie, a modified Hegelian, Henry Sturt, a Personal Idealist, and Bertrand Russell, a Cambridge Realist—were sharply divided in their metaphysical views also probably helped to neutralize such theoretical influence as they might have had. When he gave his address on democracy to the Fabian Society, Webb was able to dismiss blandly the lecture on Natural Rights which Professor Ritchie had given to it earlier (and which formed the basis of Ritchie's notable book on the subject[38]) by remarking that, whatever the validity of Natural Rights doctrine, it was no help in deciding whether particular individuals should or should not have a vote for a rural district council![39]

Neither of the Webbs attempted to work out a coherent system of political philosophy. Only in their economic Theory of Rent did Sidney Webb (in association with his Fabian friends) ever try to scale theoretical heights. Otherwise their approach to abstract theory was eclectic—borrowing from others such items of theory as

[35] M. Meisel, 'Shaw and Revolution: The Politics of the Plays', in N. Rosenblood (ed.), *Shaw: Seven Critical Essays* (Toronto, 1971).
[36] I. Britain, *Fabianism and Culture: A Study in British Socialism and the Arts 1884–1918* (Cambridge, 1982), pp. 46, 166.
[37] B. Potter to S. Webb [n.d. ?24 Oct. 1890], N. MacKenzie (ed.), *The Letters of Sidney and Beatrice Webb*, vol. i. *Apprenticeships 1873–1892* (Cambridge, 1978), pp. 225–6; B. Webb, *Our Partnership*, (London, 1948), p. 292.
[38] D. G. Ritchie, *Natural Rights: A Criticism of some Political and Ethical Conceptions* (London, 1895).
[39] *Fabian News* (Nov. 1896).

served their turn in argument and occasionally giving them a characteristically individual twist. But this approach was not purely opportunistic: they were selective in their choice, and their ideas had a firm underpinning of beliefs which they had arrived at through much thought and study by the early 1890s. So far as their views on democracy were concerned, they were conscious of their Utilitarian heritage; Beatrice wrote: '. . . Bentham was certainly Sidney's intellectual godfather; and though I have never read a word of him, his teaching was transmitted through Herbert Spencer's very utilitarian system of ethics . . . '[40] Lest this conjuncture between Bentham and Spencer might seem a little ill placed, Beatrice went on to make clear that what she meant by 'utilitarian' here was the very general concept that 'human action must be judged by its results in bringing about certain defined ends'.[41] But she and Sidney found it difficult to accept the Benthamite formula which defined the 'end' as 'the greatest happiness of the greatest number', because of the vagueness and possible ambiguity of the term 'happiness'. They preferred a definition not in terms of a single end, but in terms of ends: the promotion in the community of noble characters, intellectual achievement, love, truth, beauty, and humour:

. . . we differ from the Benthamites in thinking that it is necessary that we should all agree as to ends, or that these can be determined by any science. We believe that ends, ideals, are all what may be called in a larger way 'questions of taste' and we like a society in which there is a considerable variety in these tastes.[42]

This amounted to pursuing further the line of thought begun by John Stuart Mill, when he had introduced the notion of different 'qualities' in types of happiness, but promoting Mill's 'qualities' to the status of ends. The Webbs do not seem to have considered the difficulties arising out of the obvious generality and incompleteness of their list of ends, and out of their introduction of the notion of 'questions of taste' if these arguments were pressed. One notes with surprise, for instance, that the list above (taken from a passage in Beatrice Webb's Diary) does not include equality (in some form or

[40] B. Webb, *Our Partnership*, p. 210. Spencer in his *Principles of Ethics* had been concerned to reconcile Utilitarianism and Evolutionism; late in his life he was inclined in his *The Man versus the State* to abandon Utilitarianism in the political sphere for a return to Natural Rights.

[41] B. Webb, *Our Partnership*, p. 210.

[42] Ibid., pp. 210–11. MacKenzie, *Diary*, ii, 200.

other), which one would have thought to be fairly central to the ethical demands of Socialism (and which elsewhere they stressed). Would a complete list require at least an outline sketch of an ideal society? The idea that ethical judgements be treated as matters of personal taste suggests an agreeable tolerance, but obviously could not (as the words 'a considerable variety' imply) go the whole way for such puritanical citizens as the Webbs without some limits and standards. Perhaps they believed the democratic process would bring about the necessary agreement?

While the Webbs remained Utilitarians of some sort, there is indication that (if they are to be considered Hedonists of any kind) they went beyond the Universal Hedonism of Bentham and Mill, in which the criterion was the promotion of the general happiness in society including one's own, towards Altruistic Hedonism, where the criterion was the promotion of social happiness at the expense of one's own.[43] The austere regimen they imposed on themselves in their devotion to public service and social investigation and research, with their renunciation of many pleasures they might have enjoyed, inspired respect or lent itself to malicious caricature. But they were not puritan fanatics: they recognized that they had deliberately chosen this way for themselves and, despite Beatrice's occasional tut-tuttings about her friends' indulgences in her private diary, they were reasonably tolerant of others taking an easier path.[44] The Webbs' personal austerity was connected with a feeling of guilt that they were living on an unearned income from rent and interest: they felt that, so long as the social system which permitted and legally endorsed this situation existed, and was incapable of being altered by individual action, that they had to regard themselves as 'stewards for the community' of this wealth, not entitling them to special privileges, except that of choosing what work they would do for the community (amounting to not less than a solid eight hours a day) and for social change to a juster social order.[45]

Their commitment to the community and its welfare entitled them truly to call themselves 'Collectivists'. Later generations,

[43] See C. D. Broad, *Five Types of Ethical Theory* (London, 1967), pp. 240–1 for a discussion of the differences.
[44] The whole matter has been discussed with admirable balance and discretion by I. Britain, *Fabianism and Culture*, pp. 113–42.
[45] S. Webb to J. Burdon-Sanderson, 25 Nov. 1887. MacKenzie, *Letters*, i. 109–12.

which have seen such enormous increases in State power and 'collectivism' of the totalitarian sort, may flinch for some of the less-qualified utterances of these late Victorian and Edwardian Collectivists, as for instance Sidney Webb's remark that '. . . the perfect and fitting development of each individual is not necessarily the utmost and highest cultivation of his own personality, but the filling, in the best possible way, of his humble function in the great social machine'.[46] At other times (or, in the case of his famous 'Historic' chapter in *Fabian Essays in Socialism*, at the same time) Webb, with a blithe disregard of consistency in metaphor, used the concept of 'social organism' rather than 'social machine' to express his collectivist views: '. . . we must take even more care to improve the social organism of which we form part than to perfect our own individual developments.'[47] But the historical context must be kept in mind: the Webbs were making use of the organic concept, and stressing the importance of the community because *laissez-faire* Liberalism had stressed the importance of the individual at the expense of the community. The Webbs were denying that the social good automatically followed from individuals striving after their own welfare, and they were demanding that the State should pay direct attention to the social good. The Welfare State in England was only in its beginning, and for most of their lives, the Webbs were engaged in promoting hardly more than State provision of a National Minimum. So it is perhaps understandable that they were impatient of 'Gladstonian Liberalism', which thought of freedom in a negative way as the individual's freedom from State control, and opposed the positive freedom which State intervention could offer. Sidney Webb had, quite early in his career, criticized and rejected John Stuart Mill's attempt in *On Liberty* to distinguish between 'self-regarding' actions of the individual, with which the State should never interfere, and 'other-regarding' actions, where State interference was justified if harm was done.[48] Webb considered that all actions affected other people. He did not appreciate, any more than Mill did, that the criterion of 'doing

---

[46] G. B. Shaw (ed.), *Fabian Essays in Socialism* (London, 1889), p. 58.

[47] Ibid.; this quotation directly precedes the one above.

[48] S. Webb, 'Anarchism', Passfield Papers, VI. 18, quoted in W. Wolfe, *From Radicalism to Socialism: Men and Ideas in the Formation of Fabian Socialist Doctrines 1881–1889* (New Haven, 1975), p. 278; and S. L. Howard, 'The New Utilitarians? Studies in the Origins and Early Intellectual Associations of Fabianism', Ph.D. thesis (University of Warwick, 1976), pp. 187–8.

harm to others' could stand independently of the attempted distinction between 'self-regarding' and 'other-regarding' actions. But, in any case, he was not anxious to restrict the possibility of State interference to promote actively the good of its citizens.

Webb's notion of the citizen's duty as 'the filling, in the best possible way, of his humble function in the great social machine' also sounds too much like the Conservative F. H. Bradley's notion of 'My Station and its Duties'.[49] But here again it is necessary to notice the qualifications which Webb placed upon this concept, as revealed in his work in promoting education in London. He believed that this was not being achieved in existing conditions, and that it would not be achieved until everyone was, as far as possible, 'placed' according to each individual's ability (and not according to birth or wealth):

. . . the really democratic purpose of public education was not to dole out elementary education to all and sundry, nor yet to develop a race of scholarship winners, but to train up the most efficient and most civilized body of citizens, making the most of the brains of all, and, in the interests of the community as a whole, developing each to the 'margin of cultivation'. . . . What Collectivists demand is the equipment of the whole body of citizens, each in accordance with his particular aptitudes and capacities, for the service of the community, as far and as freely in each case as the interests of the community require.[50]

There seems little doubt that the Webbs, in the 1890s, were thinking of society as evolving a new class structure. In their *Industrial Democracy* they claimed to discern, 'instead of the classic economist's categories of "the capitalist" and "the labourer" ', the development of 'an almost infinite grading of the Industrial world into separate classes, each with its own corporate traditions and Standard of Life, its own specialised faculty and distinctive needs'.[51] Both the bourgeoisie and the proletariat were becoming split and diversified into hierarchies of specialized functional groups, organized into their own trade or professional associations. This provoked discussion within the Fabian Society about whether the Socialist society of the future would be a 'classless society' or a society in which classes would be based on status and function

[49] F. H. Bradley, *Ethical Studies* (London, 1927; first published in 1876), pp. 173–4.
[50] *Fabian News* (Jan. 1903).
[51] S. and B. Webb, *Industrial Democracy*, pp. 842–3.

instead of ownership of land or capital.[52] Later on, H. G. Wells was to make much play with the latter alternative; while Bernard Shaw strongly repudiated it.[53] The Webbs made no pronouncement, so their position remains arguable; but their views in *Industrial Democracy* aroused some suspicion that they favoured a hierarchically disposed order topped by managing 'experts'. This may have been unfair, because, in *Industrial Democracy* the Webbs went on to point out the 'paradox of democracy': that each citizen was both master and servant. He was servant of the community in the work he did for his subsistence (that is, in the work where he was most expert, namely, the craft to which he devoted himself); he was master in having a voice in matters in which he was no more expert than anyone else, namely, the general interests of the community as a whole.

In this paradox, we suggest, lies at once the justification and the strength of democracy. It is not, as is commonly asserted by the superficial, that Ignorance rules over Knowledge, and Mediocrity over Capacity. . . . It is only by carrying along with him the 'average sensual man', that even the wisest and most philanthropic reformer can genuinely change the face of things. Moreover, not even the wisest of men can be trusted with that supreme authority which comes from the union of knowledge, capacity and opportunity with the power of untrammelled and ultimate decision. Democracy is an expedient—perhaps the only practicable expedient—for preventing the concentration in any single individual or any single class of what inevitably becomes, when so concentrated, a terrible engine of oppression.[54]

This makes fairly explicit that the Webbs saw their 'experts' as operating within a framework of democracy. The people were to be '. . . served by an elite of unassuming experts, who would appear to be no different in status from the common man'.[55]

Their fully explicit discussion of democracy, however, was confined to 'The Machinery of Democracy'—the title of the series of lectures which Sidney Webb delivered to the Fabian Society from October to December 1896.[56] These followed the lines of the later

[52] See, e.g., the report of a lecture by Halliday Sparling in *Fabian News* (Mar. 1894).
[53] A. M. McBriar, *Fabian Socialism and English Politics 1884–1918* (Cambridge, 1962), p. 156.
[54] S. and B. Webb, *Industrial Democracy*, pp. 844–5.
[55] B.W.D., 21 Aug. 1928; I. Britain, *Fabianism and Culture*, p. 264 (I am indebted to Dr Britain for this reference).   [56] See footnote 34 to this chapter.

chapters (from Chapter 5 onwards) of J. S. Mill's *Representative Democracy* but were lavishly illustrated with conclusions drawn from the Webbs' own study of trade unionism. They amounted in general to a stalwart defence of representative democracy against 'direct democracy', the origins of which are nowadays traced back to Rousseau[57] (though Sidney Webb attributed them to the later followers of Saint-Simon) and which was sponsored by the Social Democratic Federation and extremer Radicals. Webb sternly rejected democracy of the mass meeting, such devices as the Referendum and Initiative, election of administrative officials, rotation of office, and the derogation of the representative to a mere delegate. The government of a large-scale democratic society demanded division of labour, he argued. The electorate—the collective, popular will—was capable of expressing only broad general principles in non-technical language on matters affecting the whole nation; but most modern legislation was technical, detailed, and often dealing with matters affecting only a section of the nation. The mass of electors could judge such laws only by results, not in anticipation. The central requisite was to secure legislators and administrators who would devote their time to the specialized task of legislating and administrating. This was achieved by a representative system giving the electorate a choice of potential legislators, and by open examination and selection committees picking the civil servants.[58] In short, Webb gave his approval of the existing—or rather, emerging—system of democratic government in England: the Fabian Society as a whole agreed, expressing it succinctly in Tract 70 of 1897:

When the House of Commons is freed from the veto of the House of Lords and thrown open to candidates from all classes by an effective system of Payment of Representatives and a more rational method of election, the British Parliamentary system will be, in the opinion of the Fabian Society, a first-rate practical instrument of democratic government.

By the middle 1890s, the Webbs were disillusioned with the

---

[57] 'Direct democracy' is nowadays usually referred to as 'participatory democracy' (a less satisfactory denomination). For a recent discussion attributing its origin to Rousseau see C. Pateman, *Participation and Democratic Theory* (Cambridge, 1970), Ch. 2.

[58] J. A. Schumpeter expressed a view similar to Webb's in a more controversial manner (which consequently has attracted more attention) in ch. 22 of his *Capitalism, Socialism and Democracy* (London, 1966; first published 1943).

political party scene. Their attempts to persuade the Liberal Party to adopt an advanced social policy, and to make political concessions to the trade unionists, had been a failure; and Sidney Webb's momentary spasm of anger, which led him to publish a factious article 'To Your Tents, Oh Israel!',[59] had deeply offended the Liberal leaders and occasioned the resignation of some devoted Liberal Party supporters from the Fabian Society. The Webbs could not conceal their opinion that the Liberal Party's disastrous rout at the 1895 general election was its own fault. But the even more overwhelming defeat of the Independent Labour Party at the same election convinced them that attempts to establish a third party in England were at least premature and in all probability quite hopeless. They reassured themselves with the belief that the historical 'stream of tendency' in public administration was inevitably in the direction of Socialism, whatever party might be in power. So the Webbs gave their undivided attention to the study and practice of public administration and social policy, sure that whatever promoted rationality, efficiency, scientific investigation, and expertness in this field would help along the cause of Socialism. They were ready to make available their vast store of knowledge and advice to anyone who would pay attention, and in the later 1890s and early years of the twentieth century they believed that they had found more willing listeners in the 'Imperialist' faction of the Liberal Party and in some leading Conservatives (including Arthur Balfour) who were concerned with the quest for 'National Efficiency', than among the more Radical wing of the Liberals. This association caused further defections from the Fabian Society at the turn of the century and alienated the Webbs from the Radicals, who accused them of having a 'narrow', 'mechanistic', 'bureaucratic' outlook, and, even less fairly, of lacking a 'moral' or truly democratic approach to Socialism.[60] These labels stuck, and have remained current to this day.[61]

[59] The reasons for the publication of this article are discussed in A. M. McBriar, *Fabian Socialism and English Politics*, pp. 249–52.

[60] '. . . Mr Webb and his friends do not really believe in "the will of the people" as the true source of governmental power: if it is for them a force at all, it is only as so much fuel to be utilised by the superior wills of a virtually self-appointed aristocracy of talent.' Thus L. T. Hobhouse in the *Nation* (13 June 1908), quoted by P. Clarke, *Liberals and Social Democrats* (Cambridge, 1978), p. 262. If the word 'élitist' had been in currency then, no doubt it would have been used too.

[61] P. Clarke on the Webbs as 'mechanical reformists', ibid., pp. 86, 88–9, 119–20.

Unlike Sidney Webb, Bernard Bosanquet revelled in the higher realms of philosophy, and the book which enshrined his views on democracy was appropriately entitled *The Philosophical Theory of the State*. It presented a coherent system of political philosophy, not confined to the special problem of democracy, but embracing the whole theory of political obligation, from the city-state of ancient Greece to the nation-state of the modern world. Our interest here is limited to his views of the modern democratic state.

Bosanquet did not, like his Balliol contemporary F. H. Bradley, look upon the teaching of Jeremy Bentham and John Stuart Mill with total hostility and contempt;[62] his criticism was more measured. Bentham he allowed to deserve the title of a 'philanthropic reformer', whose 'rule of thumb' concerning 'the greatest happiness of the greatest number' was attended with 'magnificent success . . . in the practical work of reform'.[63] Mill's *On Liberty* was treated as well intentioned but confused. Bosanquet could not accept that either of them had furnished a principle to solve the problem of liberty and authority in the modern state, or, as he called it, 'the paradox of self-government'. He concluded:

For Bentham all solid right is actually in the State, though conceived by himself as a means to individual ends; for Mill it is divided between the State and the individual, by a boundary which cannot be traced and therefore cannot be respected . . .[64]

Herbert Spencer, who in his late work *The Man versus the State* had abandoned the Utilitarian criterion for a return to Natural Right, got much shorter shrift:

Herbert Spencer . . . has recourse to one of those hypotheses of tacit consent which would reduce a community to the level of a joint-stock company *minus* a written instrument of association . . . ; for Herbert Spencer all right is in the individual, and the State has become little more than a record office of his contracts and consents.[65]

The views of all three theorists were relegated by Bosanquet to a category he called 'theories of the first look', and he summoned his readers to turn with him to the underrated genius Jean-Jacques Rousseau for a profounder treatment of the 'paradox of self

---

[62] R. Wollheim, *F. H. Bradley* (Harmondsworth, 1959), pp. 14, 19.
[63] B. Bosanquet, *The Philosophical Theory of the State* (London, 1925 edn.), pp. 53, 56.
[64] Ibid., p. 75.　　　　　[65] Ibid., pp. 71–2, 75–6.

government'. There followed one of the acutest and most insightful expositions and criticisms of Rousseau's political theory ever written. Bosanquet's choice of Rousseau as his ritual ancestor was a startling one, for Rousseau's doctrines (whatever Rousseau's real intentions) had come to be considered, through historical and theoretical association, to belong to the ultra-Radical left of politics.

Bosanquet's interest in Rousseau centred upon Rousseau's doctrine of the General Will, which Bosanquet recognized to be the foundation of Hegel's concept of the *Volksgeist*.[66] In the light of the writings of later thinkers, such as T. H. Green and Hegel, he attempted to give a consistent development to an idea not fully worked out by Rousseau. In the mind of each individual (though with varying degrees of consciousness of it) there was what he called a 'real will' as well as an 'actual will'.[67] The 'actual will' sought satisfaction of the individual's immediate desires, including ill-considered, momentary, and transient impulses; the 'real will' exercised the more critical function of thinking beyond immediate particular ends and means, to more permanent and moral satisfactions, including the harmonizing of the individual's wants with those of others. The real will thus became identified with a social way of living: with the 'general will' of the community. It did so, because the customs, laws, and institutions of society were the embodiment of the 'general will' of past and present citizens of the community; the individual had been socialized within their framework, and their rules provided an easier (if imperfect) guide for the individual to moral conduct than would the exercise of the individual's real will on each separate occasion.[68]

This emphasis on the importance of the social whole indicated that Bosanquet, too, was a 'Collectivist'. He took over Bradley's notion of 'My Station and its Duties', stressing the place of the individual as a function in the social organism, a 'heart beat in its system',[69] his very mind and being as a production of the communities—the family, the neighbourhood, the profession and class, the social groups, the State—to which he belonged. Ultimately, the basis of the individual's political obligation of loyalty to his community and State was that its 'collectivism' provided him with protection and opportunity for developing his talents, not only for

---

[66] Ibid., pp. 221–3.   [67] Ibid., p. 110.   [68] Ibid., p. 115.
[69] The phrase was Bradley's: *Ethical Studies*, p. 163.

the purpose of fulfilling his role in his social station, but also, in the case of gifted individuals, for achieving a perfection, in advance of where society at any moment stood,[70] in the arts and sciences, as well as in social virtues and personal cultivation. This striving towards perfection was an essential aspiration of the general will. The individual was raised to higher levels of morality by the standards set by the groups to which he belonged, and the larger the community the wider the moral union achieved. So far as historical progress has gone, the nation-state is the largest community created by mankind to have attained the comprehensiveness and cohesion necessary to establish itself as a universal, concrete reality. The claims of other communities to higher unity than the nation-state, such as the Church, humanity in general, and international organizations, have to be dismissed, as things really stand. The community of the universal Church has been eroded by religious division and the growth of unbelief: its claims to universality now rest on dogmatic authority or sectarian fanaticism.[71] 'Humanity in general' and such international organizations as exist remain wishful ideals as communities rather than real facts, and sensibility to their claims is not common amongst mankind at present.[72] Beyond the nation-state there is only the greatest of all universals, the Absolute, the ultimate reality and all-inclusive unity of the universe-as-a-whole, in which all contradictions are explained and transcended, but which we can only partially (although perhaps increasingly) come to know.

Bosanquet was persuaded that logic and the unity of thought implied the existence of the Absolute, not as transcendental but as immanent in the universe as the values and the covert but real meaning of the appearances of our phenomenal world.[73] Its quality as the perfection and goal of natural harmony and human aspiration was capable of being glimpsed in the highest achievements of the

[70] B. Bosanquet, *The Philosophical Theory of the State*, p. 310. Bradley also held this view: see Essay VI in *Ethical Studies*. The point is important, because Bosanquet—and more often Bradley—have been accused by critics of placing too much emphasis on the part conformity plays in morality: see G. H. Sabine, 'Bosanquet's Theory of the Real Will', *Philosophical Review*, 32 (1923), 633 ff.

[71] B. Bosanquet, *The Philosophical Theory of the State* (1925 edn.), p. 265.

[72] Ibid., pp. 306–9; B. Bosanquet, 'Philosophical Importance of a True Theory of Identity', *Mind*, 13 (1888), 365.

[73] B. Bosanquet, 'On the True Conception of Another World', ch. 19 of *Science and Philosophy and Other Essays* (London, 1927); first published in 1886 as an introduction to a translation from Hegel's *Aesthetic*), p. 325.

human mind and spirit—in art, science, philosophy, religion, citizenship, and even in more mundane accomplishments:

The highest praise, perhaps, is felt to be conveyed by [the popular mind] in any and every topic of experience, when it judges of anything it cares for— a game, a speech, a policy, a play or a fight, a poem or a piece of music, a great religion or a great character—that in it you have 'the real thing'.[74]

Bosanquet's attempt, in his ethical theory, to satisfy a common human craving to be reassured about the harmony, order, and justice of the universe, a need also catered for by religion, did not satisfy orthodox Christian theologians, who accused him of Pantheism (an accusation which Bosanquet denied).[75] But he also encountered criticism at more down-to-earth level from Cambridge philosophers, who regarded the Oxford Idealists' ethical criterion as belonging to a type of theory refuted by David Hume and inferior to the Utilitarianism developed by Henry Sidgwick[76] or (later) to the non-naturalistic Utilitarianism of G. E. Moore. The unkindest stroke of all came from the Cambridge Idealist, J. M. E. McTaggart, from whom Bosanquet might have expected some support. McTaggart declared that metaphysical ideas or philosophy as such were too abstract to give constructive guidance in social reform or political actions; and therefore some kind of hedonistic Utilitarian formula was as far as one could go in the way of a general ethical criterion for practical, empirical affairs.[77] Bosanquet defended himself strenuously against McTaggart's subtle and wicked attack. But in the course of his defence he made the rather damaging admission:

I agree that philosophy by itself can say nothing decisive as to what is best to be done about property and the family. But if, for example, from bad philosophy, or a mental twist equivalent to bad philosophy, measures are proposed on the ground that certain conditions are incompatible, which we know to be in a general way inseparable and reciprocally intensifying,

---

[74] B. Bosanquet's contribution to J. H. Muirhead (ed.), *Contemporary British Philosophy*, 1st series (London, 1924), p. 71.

[75] See, e.g., R. E. Stedman, 'Bosanquet's Account of Religion', *Hibbert Journal*, 29 (1930–1), 465 ff. For Bosanquet's own view that the 'religion of the Absolute is not mere Pantheism' see his article 'The Evolution of Religion', *IJE* 5 (1895), 443.

[76] Broad, *Five Types of Ethical Theory*, pp. 99 ff., 180, 273 ff.

[77] J. M. E. McTaggart, 'The Conception of Society as an Organism', *IJE* 7 (1897). This article was later incorporated into a chapter 'On the Supreme Good and the Moral Criterion' in his *Studies in Hegelian Cosmology* (Cambridge, 1901).

philosophy can abate the presumption, and leave the ground clear for genuine appeals to fact.[78]

This seemed to restrict the sphere of philosophy to correcting deductions from bad philosophy, rather than to claim it had a positive contribution to make concerning practical social reform.

Later on, pursuing further his reply to McTaggart, Bosanquet produced his most elaborated attack on hedonistic Utilitarianism.[79] He could not be convinced that it was possible, except in evaluating the more facile satisfactions, to make a 'calculus' of pleasures and pains. The higher satisfactions were usually attended with the pains of such exertion and difficulty that the person who was seeking them 'would often possess greater pleasure if he were cultivating his garden'.[80] The attempt to employ a calculus of pleasure in social decisions tended therefore to give priority to the 'easy' pleasures. Important decisions ought to rest, and usually did rest, on the acceptance of some hierarchy among the activities of life. The test was what we *really* wanted, which brought in the idea of the main aim or design of life. Bosanquet conceded it would not be the idea of the ultimate metaphysical Absolute that at any particular moment guided the decision, but the moralist could discern in each practical problem a meeting of universal forces and principles, with the actors seeking the satisfaction of achieving some goal just in advance of where they stood. The satisfaction might or might not bring pleasure as a consequence: 'Some solutions may bring pleasure; others intellectual repose; others "the approval of conscience"; others the tranquillity or endurance of completed tragedy.'[81] Needless to say, Bosanquet's reply did not silence critics, who continued to find his views too vague. Whether they were any vaguer than those of other moral theorists remains, perhaps, a moot point.

To return to Bosanquet's argument in *The Philosophical Theory of the State*: up to this stage, he appeared to be arguing in a strongly Collectivist spirit, emphasizing the importance of the community or the State in the individual—State relationship. Moreover, he made no sharp distinction between community and

---

[78] B. Bosanquet, 'Hegel's Theory of the Political Organism', *Mind*, NS 7 (1898), 13.

[79] B. Bosanquet, 'Hedonism among Idealists', *Mind*, NS 12 (1903), 202 ff., and 303 ff.

[80] Ibid., p. 222.   [81] Ibid., p. 312.

State[82] The community (or society) *was* the State, and the powers of community and State differed only in degree. The State was simply the community in its capacity as a legal and administrative unit, recognized by its members as rightfully exercising sovereignty and compulsion over them through physical power. It was the 'ultimate arbiter and regulator, maintainer of mechanical routine, and source of authoritative suggestion, a character which is one with the right to exercise force in the last resort'.[83] This was in accord with an earlier article on 'Liberty and Legislation' Bosanquet had written,[84] in which he seemed to go as far as any Idealist, including D. G. Ritchie (who had become a Fabian),[85] in denouncing *laissez-faire* and declaring that liberty did not depend on the absence of social compulsion, but on the range of positive freedom and the quality of civilized life society offered.

But having granted with one hand so formidable an extension of State power, Bosanquet proceeded, in Chapter 8 of *The Philosophical Theory of the State*, to take it back, or at least impose severe limits on it, with the other. His prestidigitation was accomplished by summoning a Liberal principle of Kant and T. H. Green to modify Hegel's fuller commitment to the State.[86] This was the principle that the State cannot, by force, make its citizens moral; it can only force outward compliance. If the State sought to go beyond the 'general will' by force, it would degrade any attempt it was making to secure a better life, and it could ultimately 'lead us straight to a machine-made Utopia',[87] faced with the constant dangers attending disobedience, rebellion, and repression. Certainly, the State could at times take the lead in appealing by reasoning and persuasion to the general will for an advance in collective thinking and character, and it should continue to do that. But that was something apart from the State's essential function of exercising power. In its distinctive capacity, the State could only enforce or prohibit external actions; and in any decently ordered State the use of actual

[82] B. Bosanquet, *The Philosophical Theory of the State* (1925 edn.), pp. 172 ff.

[83] Ibid., p. 273.

[84] It became ch. 11 of B. Bosanquet, *The Civilization of Christendom and Other Studies* (London, 1893).

[85] Ritchie had joined the Fabian Society in 1889; he resigned in 1893, as a result of disagreement with Webb and Shaw's attack on the Liberal Party in their 'To Your Tents, Oh Israel!' article.

[86] B. Bosanquet, *The Philosophical Theory of the State* (1925 edn.), pp. 177–80.

[87] Ibid., p. 178.

physical force ought to be kept to a minimum. The power of the State should therefore be limited to three functions: first, legislating, administering, and enforcing measures approved by the general will; secondly, enforcing 'such acts (or omissions) . . . as it is better should take place from any motive whatever than not take place at all',[88] and thirdly, 'forcibly hinder[ing] a hindrance to the best life or common good'.[89] Bosanquet did not give an example of his second category of acts, but one might suppose that traffic rules would belong to that type. He did, however, give examples in illustration of his third category. Such proposed Liberal social reforms as compulsory education and municipalizing the liquor traffic he approved as hindering illiteracy and intemperance. Bosanquet realized that his critics would quickly ask why not hinder unemployment by State provision of employment and overcrowding by State house-building? His answer was that the fine but necessary distinction between hindering a hindrance and attempting direct promotion of the common good by force had to be discovered by asking of any proposed social measure if it 'liberates resources of character and intelligence greater beyond all question than the encroachment which it involves'.[90] This principle was intended to provide the rainbow-bridge between down-to-earth COS policy and the Idealist Valhalla.

His critics thought his rainbow-bridge was flimsy. Bosanquet himself recognized the apparent contradiction between the Hegelian collectivism of his doctrine of the general will and his attempt to set limits to state action. In face of it, he resorted to bold dialectic: 'But this *prima facie* contradiction is really a proof of the vitality of our principle'.[91] The State's role was to create the opportunities for its citizens' 'real wills' to be realized, 'forcing them to be free' only if their 'actual wills' were 'recalcitrant through rebellion, indolence, incompetence or ignorance'.[92] Thus was the 'paradox of self-government' to be resolved. But even if Bosanquet's critics were willing to go along with that argument, they were able to rejoin that the methods he suggested for discovering the general will and the real will (except in historical retrospect) remained vague.[93]

The limitations on State action for social reform which Bosanquet

---

[88] Ibid., p. 180. (This was taken from T. H. Green.)
[89] Ibid., p. 178.   [90] Ibid., p. 180.
[91] Ibid., p. 186.   [92] Ibid., p. 187.
[93] See discussion in ch. 5 above, p. 129.

imposed seemed to his Fabian opponents to be very restrictive of anything lying much beyond standard reform projects accepted by the Liberal Party of the later Gladstonian era. This raises the question of the conservatism (with a small 'c') of Bosanquet's social views. Did his acceptance of Bradley's notion of 'My Station and its Duties' mean that he accepted some rigidly hierarchical social structure?[94] The answer must be no in Bosanquet's case, as in Webb's. Class structures which defined class in terms of birth or of special privileges based on property-holding, he declared roundly, became 'ossified'.[95] But class structure was essential in any developed society, Bosanquet believed: classless societies existed only in primitive, peasant communities[96]—or in the dreams of Utopian visionaries. It was, however, essential to a modern, lively, organic society that classes allow mobility and be based on social function.[97] Occupation would necessarily remain a main determinant of class, because a person's vocation—the service or function rendered through it both to family and to society—moulded the individual's life and personality.[98] But here again, it was important that occupation should not be the only determinant of class in a democratic community, allowing talent, character, and behaviour to play their roles in the ranking individuals might achieve in the world. Any attempt to set up an ideal of equality would be to 'divorce our sense of justice from our sense of the best'.[99] In a lecture on the use of the terms 'Ladies and Gentlemen', Bosanquet approved of the use of these terms as a mark of respect from the lower classes for those more accomplished in social politeness and cultivation.[100] His ideal was a society class-divided but harmonious, where people participated according to their capacity: 'The servant who sweeps a minister's study, having respect for his office, shares in his spiritual work, and is the better even for that amount of sharing in it. The minister, of course . . . has also to learn from the servant.'[1]

---

[94] In fairness to Bradley, it must be remarked that this common interpretation of his 'My Station and its Duties' is probably incorrect, in spite of his Conservatism. But our concern here is not Bradley, but Bosanquet.

[95] Ibid., p. 294.

[96] Ibid., p. 293 (citing Dicey's *The Peasant State*).

[97] Ibid., p. 289.   [98] Ibid., pp. 289–91.

[99] Quoted in an article by R. F. A. Hoernlé, 'On Bosanquet's Idealism', *Philosophical Review*, 32 (1923), 567ff.

[100] B. Bosanquet, 'Ladies and Gentlemen', *IJE* 10 (1900), 317–18.

[1] B. Bosanquet, 'The Place of Leisure in Life', *IJE* 21 (1911), 162.

Helen Bosanquet agreed with her husband that the existence of classes was natural,[2] that classes ought to be based on social function,[3] that different class standards were necessary and beneficial, but there ought to be no inseparable chasms preventing social mobility.[4] She was specially emphatic concerning the need for and the social benefits of co-operation between the classes,[5] and stern in her attack on Marxist ideas of 'class conflict' as applied to England. *Klassenkampf* was a simple slogan of Continental Socialists; in England the policies and compromise and consensus prevailed, because class division was more complicated in England's more advanced economy. Wage-earners through savings were acquiring a share in property and capital; the aristocracy and gentry had learnt to share in and not to despise industrial enterprise. The extremes of the scale, the 'residuum' (the only real 'proletariat' in England) and the idle rich were 'relics of the old feudal system of patronage and dependence' and diminishing quantities in the modern capitalist society. The old stratification of classes was being replaced by a structure of infinitely subtle variations, and the old-style industrial conflict between workman and capitalist by a recognition that profits were not an indefinitely expansive territory on which the workman might encroach.[6]

Unlike the Webbs, the Bosanquets did not become attracted by the politics of the Liberal Imperialist faction in the later 1890s and the first years of the twentieth century. Although they were friendly with Haldane, and in substantial accord with him in their philosophic views, the Bosanquets kept well clear of involvement with the Roseberyites, no doubt, like Sir Henry Campbell-Bannerman, regarding Lord Rosebery's policy of 'National Efficiency' as 'a mere *réchauffé* of Sidney Webb'.[7] As for the Conservatives, the Chamberlain 'Tariff Reformers' were totally antipathetic to the Bosanquets, who were staunch Free Traders; and Arthur Balfour had little appeal for them either as politician or philosopher. Although Balfour managed to keep up a friendly relationship with Haldane, discussing with

[2] H. Bosanquet, *Rich and Poor* (London, 1896), p. 141.

[3] H. Bosanquet, *The Standard of Life and Other Studies* (London, 1906), p. 7.

[4] Ibid., pp. 12–15.

[5] H. Bosanquet, *Rich and Poor*, pp. 141–2.

[6] H. Bosanquet, chs. 3 ('Klassenkampf') and 4 ('The Lines of Industrial Conflict') in *The Standard of Life and Other Studies* (London, 1898).

[7] Quoted by E. Halévy, *A History of the English People in the 19th Century*, vol. v, *Imperialism and the Rise of Labour* (London, 1965), p. 105.

him in correspondence some finer points of Hegelian doctrine,[8] Bernard Bosanquet estranged himself by a savage review of Balfour's *The Foundations of Belief* in which he said it showed Balfour to be 'incapable of getting beyond [Naturalism] by fair means. . . . Those who attempt to discredit reason convict themselves more and more clearly of not knowing what reason means.'[9]

This repudiation of both the Conservatives and the Liberal Imperialists, however, did not win Bosanquet favour in the eyes of Radicals of a New Liberal persuasion, such as L. T. Hobhouse and J. A. Hobson. In spite of the evidence to the contrary, they continued to regard the Bosanquets as crypto-Imperialists, on the strength of the Hegelian views of the State's nature and role in international affairs which Bosanquet made in the concluding chapter of *The Philosophical Theory of the State*. There Bosanquet argued that each nation-state had a purpose to fulfil in world history ('we might say a mission, were not the word too narrow and too aggressive')[10] and that its achievement of this could only be judged by the tribunal of history. The State should not be judged in terms of universalistic notions of humanity, treating 'all individual human beings as members of an identical community having identical capacities and rights'.[11] Indeed, the State in its public actions could not be judged by the same moral criteria as applied to private individuals, and the State *as such* could not be held responsible for the immoral acts of its agents. All this was Hegelianism of purest 1821 vintage,[12] and Bosanquet was almost certainly innocent of any intention to justify imperialism in general; but he did not allow enough space to argue out these highly debatable propositions in a way that might have convinced disbelievers. These views did not cause much stir at the time (except for the unspecific protest against the general influence of Hegelianism by Hobhouse),[13] but they were to be featured more prominently by the rancours stirred up during the First World War.

[8] Balfour to Haldane, 30 Dec. 1899; Haldane to Balfour, 3 Jan. 1900. Balfour Papers, Add. MS 49724.

[9] B. Bosanquet, *IJE* vol. 5 (1895), 508.

[10] B. Bosanquet, *The Philosophical Theory of the State* (1925 edn.), p. 298.

[11] Ibid., pp. 308–9.

[12] 1821 was the date of publication of Hegel's *Grundlinien der Philosophie des Rechts*, in which these doctrines were expressed.

[13] See ch. 3 above, pp. 80–1.

The acceptance of Rousseau by the Bosanquets as their precursor did not involve the accepting of 'participatory democracy' in any sense of primitive mass decision-making. The referendum was not rejected outright, but it was confined to a narrow place within a constitutional system: 'It can only work within a well organised constitution, and could not be used to re-make the whole constitution—the forms and conditions of sovereignty—at a blow.'[14] The general will was, in Hegelian fashion, identified with the customs and institutions of the community,[15] and the right of rebellion denied in any State in which law could be altered by constitutional process.[16] The function of the electorate was to decide on policy in general terms and to vote in favour of the persons capable of carrying it out. Public opinion combined both 'actual will' and 'real will', both truth and falsity, and the vehemence with which an opinion was expressed was no test of the points on which the public was really in earnest. Only the true statesman could divine what was really wanted. Everyone should be allowed to contribute an opinion, so that, when things were done, the individual citizen would 'feel he has thrown in some element or criticism' and could happily acquiesce in the result.[17] But it was the function of the legislative assembly and the government to work out policy in its detailed application.[18] Government departments had an important role to play, because 'the mass of organised knowledge necessary to initiate legislation in a complex society can hardly be found outside the gathered experience of an office which has continuity in dealing with the same problems'.[19] The general will needed to be 'drafted by the help of immense piles of experience, which the general mind does not possess, and could not deal with, but which, nevertheless, enable its typical wish and intention to be embodied in effective form'.[20] There was little doubt that the Bosanquets, too, accepted the representative system that had emerged in England, and the expert Civil-Service bureaucracy that went along with it.

Certain similarities in the styles of the Bosanquets and the Webbs should now be clear enough. Both partners had hankerings after a new 'sociology', but settled for something less—for studies which

[14] B. Bosanquet, *The Philosophical Theory of the State*, (1925 edn.) pp. 98, 108 ff.
[15] Ibid., pp. 114–15. [16] Ibid., p. 199. [17] Ibid., pp. 266–7.
[18] Ibid., p. 287. [19] Ibid., p. 265. [20] Ibid.

(to use Bernard Bosanquet's phrase) did not 'attach themselves to the peculiar method and language of sociological writers'[21]—even though Bernard Bosanquet believed that he had some useful critical comments to offer to sociologists, and the Webbs believed that the sociology of the future would find its empirical foundations in an accumulation of studies in the style of their own research. At the lower level, they both wished to pioneer a 'social economics', and both offered interesting particular contributions; but in neither case were these systematic enough to appear as an effective substitute for Marshallian neo-classical economics. Their disagreements in this matter were more apparent at the lower rather than the higher level of their aspirations. In the case of their views on political philosophy, the situation appeared reversed. They set out from what seemed to be utterly opposed philosophical positions—the Benthamite-cum-Positivist tradition on one side, and the Rousseau-Hegelian tradition on the other. Yet when they descended the steps from the high philosophical gallery they appeared to have more in common than one would have imagined. Both approved of 'collectivism' as against 'individualism'; both subscribed to an 'organic' idea of society; both seemed to want to get away from a 'hedonistic' ethical criterion to a more socially qualitative one; both identified the representative democratic State with society itself; both upheld the role of the 'statesman' and the expert civil servant against demands for 'direct' democracy; their opinions on social structure endorsed a qualified version of the 'station and its duties' doctrine and questioned the continuing validity of class divisions as defined by the classical economists and by Marx (without managing quite to get away from these); both were accused (not really justly) of being 'Imperialist' in international outlook. Yet, as they stepped into the court for their great match, they were aware of the difference rather than the likeness of their styles, and each side was determined to win.

[21] See p. 147 above.

7

Arrangements for the Big Match

ESTABLISHING THE ROYAL COMMISSION ON THE POOR LAWS AND ITS PROCEDURE

Setting up the Royal Commission

ON 28 November 1905 the Conservative Prime Minister, Mr Arthur Balfour, had attended a select luncheon party at the Webbs' house at 41 Grosvenor Road, and afterwards he and Beatrice Webb drove in a victoria, which had formerly belonged to her old friend and tutor, Herbert Spencer, to the Royal Court Theatre in Sloane Square to see a matinée performance of Bernard Shaw's new play, *Major Barbara*. On the way there, Balfour remarked: 'George Hamilton is not the fool he looks', an observation intended to set at rest her doubts about the Chairman he had chosen for the Royal Commission to inquire into the Poor Laws, established as almost the last gesture of his government.[1] What a genial age the Edwardian period seems, at least at this level, when the Conservative Prime Minister could discuss matters of social policy over lunch with the leading intellectual Socialists of Britain, when he and Beatrice could then go off together to see Shaw's latest daring composition, and both be amused yet disturbed by the spectacle of righteousness according to Victorian standards being trampled underfoot by the money and guns of the twentieth century.

In their carriage, Mr Balfour went on to tell Beatrice Webb of the difficulties he had had in appointing the Commission and in deciding who should be Chairman, but she did not record these observations in her Diary, beyond his statement that he had refused to have any active[2] politicians as Commissioners. Balfour also did

---

[1] B.W.D. 29 Nov. 1908: *Our Partnership*, ed. B. Drake and M. Cole (London, 1948), pp., 313–14. Balfour had decided, before this luncheon took place, to hand in his resignation as Prime Minister.

[2] According to B.W.D., Balfour said he refused to have any politicians; but, as Lord George Hamilton and the O'Conor Don, both retired politicians, were members, he must have meant active politicians.

not tell her—or if he did she did not set down—his reasons for deciding to promote this large-scale inquiry. In the absence of direct evidence, Balfour's and the Conservative government's action has been interpreted in a number of different ways. Mrs Bosanquet attributed it to the government's recognition of a long-standing demand by the Charity Organisation Society for a full scale inquiry.[3] Mrs M. A. Hamilton has suggested (although with no convincing evidence) that it was the result of the Webbs' Fabian 'permeation' of the Balfour household.[4] The Webbs themselves believed that the move was inspired by the officials of the Poor Law Division of the Local Government Board, who felt that the administration of the Poor Law, under the influence of sentimental philanthropic and Socialist ideas, had drifted far from its moorings in the stern principles of the 1834 Act, and who wanted to return to those strict principles.[5] George Lansbury's opinion was that the setting up of the Royal Commission represented a bargain by the government to enable the Unemployed Workman's Act of 1905 to pass without serious opposition.[6] Lansbury's biographer, Raymond Postgate, however, has taken the view that it was an attempt by the Tory government to rescue itself from the unpopularity of a number of Balfour's and Chamberlain's programmes by presenting itself to the electorate as mindful of the welfare of the poorer classes.[7] One recent historian has attributed it to the influence of the Tory squire, Walter Long, a former President of the Local Government Board,[8] and another to an attempt to appease the agitations of unemployed men.[9]

Most of these explanations have some plausibility; and they are not necessarily incompatible with each other. The government's motives are likely to have been mixed. There appears to have been

---

[3] H. Bosanquet, *Social Work in London 1869–1912: A History of the Charity Organisation Society* (London, 1914), pp. 275–6.

[4] M. A. Hamilton, *Sidney and Beatrice Webb: A Study in Contemporary Biography* (London, 1932), p. 188.

[5] B. Webb, *Our Partnership*, p. 322.

[6] Article in the *Labour Leader* (19 Feb. 1909) by G. Lansbury. This seems partly verified by a letter A. J. Balfour wrote to the Clerk of Poplar Borough Council 20 Oct. 1905. Lansbury Papers.

[7] R. Postgate, *The Life of George Lansbury* (London, 1951), p. 72.

[8] J. Brown, 'The Appointment of the 1905 Poor Law Commission', *Bulletin of the Institute of Historical Research*, 42 (1969), 239 ff.

[9] K. D. Brown, 'The Appointment of the 1905 Poor Law Commission—a Rejoinder', ibid., 44 (1971), 315 ff.

an element of genuine puzzlement in the government's thinking about the proper treatment of poverty and unemployment. Since the passing of the Second Parliamentary Reform Act in 1867, the Conservative Party had not been notably more hostile to social reform than the Liberal Party: in general terms, the Tories from Disraeli to Balfour could claim to have promoted as much social legislation as the Liberals from Gladstone to Rosebery. It was true that the Conservative Party's record in social reform in the 1880s and 1890s was disappointing when compared with its achievements in the 1870s; but the same was true of the Liberal Party's. The Conservative Party was slowly changing in character as it drew more and more business interests into its ranks, notably those concerned with railways, brewing, and finance, and as it was consolidating itself on the mass basis of the 'villa Toryism' of surburbia, but there is no reason to suppose that these new interests dictated its social policies: so long as the 'Hotel Cecil' remained at the ruling centre of Conservatism, the new interests were subordinate to a traditional élite, and what Arthur and his brother Gerald Balfour thought about social policy was likely to be a decisive (or in this case an indecisive) factor. On the specific matter of the Poor Law, the Balfours were cautious, conservative, but willing to learn.[10] Their most powerful competitor for power in the Conservative Party, Joseph Chamberlain, had not lost his reputation as a social reformer, in spite of his abandonment of the cause of old-age pensions, and of the fact that his share in softening the rigours of the Poor Law belonged to his Radical days before he had linked his fortune with the Conservatives. In any case, the 'reforming' policy in Poor Law affairs, which Chamberlain had initiated, had been continued by Walter Long, as true-blue a Tory squire as might be wished, when he was President of the Local Government Board in 1900–5.[11]

Gerald Balfour succeeded Walter Long as President of the Local Government Board in March 1905; his response to the demand from his officials for a rethinking of Poor Law policy was to

---

[10] Their interest in the Webbs is an indication of this. For their initially very cautious views, however, see A. Balfour to W. Long, 23 Dec. 1904. Add. MS 49776; G. Balfour to A. Balfour, 18 Nov. 1905 and 23 Oct. 1908. Add. MS 49831; A. Balfour to Lord Mount Stephen, 15 Nov. 1905. Balfour Papers, Add. MS 49858.

[11] W. Long had been instrumental in establishing the CUB.

recognize the complexity of the problem and the need for a systematic inquiry.[12] When Arthur Balfour, replying to a pre-arranged question, announced the appointment of the Royal Commission to the House of Commons, he remarked significantly that there had been no inquiry of such scope since the great Royal Commission of 1832–4.[13] The Balfours decided on a large Commission, and intended to appoint as Commissioners persons noted for their interest in social work and social thought. It was concerning these appointments that Arthur Balfour spoke to Beatrice Webb on 28 November 1905; he had invited her to become a member of it a week earlier.[14] The Webbs had not been responsible for suggesting the establishment of the Royal Commission or (except perhaps in the case of Charles Booth, and even that is doubtful)[15] the names of any of the other Commissioners; but Beatrice Webb attributed her own appointment to the friendship which had grown up between the Webbs and the Balfours.[16] A strange association it was, between these hard-working municipal Socialists and those fastidious aristocrats, whose chief concerns were with high-level political and intellectual problems. The link between them had been forged at the time of the passing of the Education Acts of 1902–3, when Sidney Webb's expertise had proved serviceable to a cause which Arthur Balfour had deeply at heart. Beatrice Webb was captivated by Arthur Balfour's social charm and intellectual distinction; and she was strongly attracted by Lady Betty Balfour, the wife of Gerald, who seemed less aloof than the others from Beatrice's social commitments. On the other side, the secret of the Balfours' interest in Beatrice lay in her ability to raise the dull matters of economic and social affairs, for which in their raw state Arthur Balfour hardly concealed his boredom and distaste, to the level of an intellectual challenge.

The Balfour brothers, in conjunction with John S. Sandars, Private Secretary to the Prime Minister, chose seventeen of the original eighteen Commissioners. For Chairman, they considered,

[12] B. Webb, *Our Partnership*, p. 317.
[13] *Parliamentary Debates*, 4th series, vol. cl, cols. 1347–1350 (2 Aug. 1905); B. Webb, *Our Partnership*, p. 317.
[14] Ibid., p. 313.
[15] Ibid. But see the letter of J. Sandars, Private Secretary to Arthur Balfour, to his chief: Sandars to Balfour, 5 Sept. 1905. Balfour Papers, Add. MS 49763, vol. lxxxi.
[16] B.W.D., 23 Nov. 1905; *Our Partnership*, p. 313.

and turned down for various reasons, C. T. Ritchie,[17] Leonard Courtenay, Lord Rosebery, Sir Henry Fowler,[18] and Gerald Balfour himself[19]; the Duke of Devonshire was approached but declined.[20] They finally yielded to Sandars's advice in selecting Lord George Hamilton[21] a veteran of Conservative politics who had carried his free-trade convictions to the point of resigning his portfolio as Secretary of State for India and retiring from active political life in September 1903. Sandars thought Hamilton should do something 'to earn his first-class pension'.[22] By the time the Commission had ended in 1909, Lord George was to feel that he had earned it in the hardest possible way.[23]

Lord George was in his sixtieth year in 1905. He was an experienced parliamentarian and administrator, having served successively as Under-Secretary for India in 1874–6, Vice President of the Council and Minister for Education in 1880, First Lord of the Admiralty in 1885, and Secretary of State for India from 1895 to 1903. During his service as Secretary of State for India he had had to cope with a severe Indian famine, and he believed that this experience had some relevance for the Poor Law inquiry.[24] He also had a connection with the Charity Organisation Society, having been a subscribing member from its earliest days, though he had not taken any active part in its work. Service as Chairman of the London School Board in 1894 had also given him some experience of local government. Lord George was a gracious *grand seigneur* who lived simply and unpretentiously.[25] His political and social inclinations, reinforced by his Indian experience, were 'Tory paternalistic', with a distinct military-authoritarian note. He was an admirer of Prince Bismarck, and believed 'we can greatly

[17] Sandars to Balfour, 5 Sept. 1905 and 30 Sept. 1905. Balfour Papers, Add. MS 49763, vol. lxxxi. Lord George Hamilton was mistaken in attributing his appointment to Ritchie's death: Lord George Hamilton, *Parliamentary Reminiscences and Reflections 1886–1906* (London, 1922) ii, 329.

[18] Sandars to Balfour, 9 Oct. 1905. Balfour papers, Add. MS 49764, vol. lxxxii.

[19] Sandars to Balfour, 5 Sept. 1905 and 30 Sept. 1905, Balfour Papers, Add. MS 49763, vol. lxxxi.

[20] Balfour to Sandars, 10 Oct. 1905. Balfour Papers, Add. MS 49764, vol. lxxxii.

[21] Sandars to Balfour, 9 Oct. 1905, ibid.

[22] Ibid.

[23] Lord George Hamilton, *Parliamentary Reminiscences and Reflections 1885–1906*, ii. 329.

[24] He submitted a paper to the Commission about it.

[25] B. Webb contrasted his style of living with that of Asquith. B. W. D., 15 Apr. 1906, *Our Partnership*, pp. 337–8.

improve our own position by imitating Germany in many respects, but not by becoming Protectionists'.[26]

Amongst the other Commissioners appointed, high officials responsible for the administration of the Poor Law in England, Scotland, and Ireland formed a strong contingent. Four of them served as Commissioners, while two others occupied strategic posts as Secretary and Assistant-Secretary to the Commission. Amongst the four were the Permanent Head of the Local Government Board for England, and the Vice-Presidents of the LGB for Scotland and Ireland. By a coincidence, this trio represented not only the best sort of Edwardian conservative civil servants, but also the national stereotypes—a formal Englishman, a charming Irishman, and a dour Scotsman.

Sir Samuel Butler Provis was the third Permanent Head of the LGB since its foundation in 1871. *The Times* later declared him to be not as distinguished as his two predecessors in that office; but it acknowledged that, although he was reserved and not much known outside official circles, he was a man to be reckoned with in his own field of administration.[27] Born in 1845, he became a barrister of the Middle Temple, and joined the LGB as Legal Assistant in 1872; he rose to be Head of the Department after twenty-seven years of service. Sir Samuel was correct, formal, and courteous in his manners to a degree reckoned old-fashioned even in Edwardian times; John Burns, after he became President of the LGB in 1905, called him a 'fossil'; but Burns was to discover, to his irritation, that Provis's formality did not involve the deference to his ministerial chief which Burns's soul craved. Shrewd and untiringly devoted to his work, Provis had made himself a master of the detail of the Poor Law. His sympathies were with the 'strict' school of administration.

The Irish official was Sir Henry Augustus Robinson, scion of one of the Anglo-Irish families of the 'garrison', which had supplied the British Empire with so many army and navy officers, governors, and administrators. He was forty-eight at the time of his appointment to the Commission, and had distinguished himself by his administrative work concerning taxation, poor relief, and lunacy laws in Ireland. His report on the famine in Galway in 1879 led to his appointment as inspector to supervise relief there and in Mayo, and he rose in the service to be appointed Vice-President of the Irish LGB in 1898, just

[26] Hamilton to H. Bosanquet, 26 Aug. 1907. Bosanquet Papers.
[27] *The Times*, 13 July 1926.

in time to confront the major task of reorganizing local government in Ireland under the provisions of the Act of that year. This was probably his greatest single achievement as administrator, and he received a knighthood in recognition of these services in 1902. Sir Henry's political sympathies were Conservative and Unionist; he was prepared to work loyally with any Chief Secretary for Ireland whether Conservative or Liberal, but he made no secret of his preference. The Irish Nationalists regarded him as one of their most adroit and formidable antagonists, and he was to come under constant political attack by Sinn Fein. But even his Irish enemies found it difficult to dislike him personally. He had a deep love of Ireland, and a knowledge of every part of the country; and when King Edward VII made a tour of Ireland, Sir Henry was the obvious choice as cicerone. His gay humour, witty conversation, inexhaustible fund of amusing Irish stories, his talent for mimicry, and his easy, tolerant attitude to life made him a pleasant companion. He was the despair of earnest reformers who were politically or socially committed. When Beatrice Webb tried to search out his social ideals, he replied that his one aim in life was to keep his Chief Secretaries out of trouble.[28] As he was to serve twenty of them up to the time his career ended with the establishment of the Irish Free State, perhaps he was justified in regarding it as task enough.

Sir James Patten-MacDougall, the chief Scottish official, was born in 1849, the son of John Patten, Writer to the Signet; his mother was a MacDougall of Gallanach, and he adopted his second surname on succeeding her in 1891. He had joined the LGB for Scotland as legal officer in 1894 and rose to be Vice-President of it ten years later. As befitted a Scottish Whig, Patten-MacDougall's views on Poor Law reform were conservative: he was an acknowledged expert on the working of Scottish local government and joint-author of a text book on the subject,[29] and he had also revised *Skelton's Handbook of Public Health* (1898), which in turn had secured his appointment as Chairman of the Departmental Committee on Poor Law Medical Relief in Scotland (1902).

The other high official amongst the Commissioners was Dr Arthur Henry Downes, the Senior Medical Inspector of the English

[28] B.W.D., 3 May 1908; Our Partnership, p. 408.
[29] *The Parish Council Guide for Scotland* (Edinburgh, 1894).

Poor Law.[30] After a brilliant career as a medical student at London, Aberdeen, and Cambridge Universities, and as a research worker on bacteria causing putrefaction and disease, he served as Medical Officer of Health in his home county of Shropshire and later in Essex, and joined the LGB as Inspector in 1889. His services had been called upon by many departmental committees in matters of public health, and it was this experience which ensured his appointment, at the age of fifty-four, to the 1905 Royal Commission. A gentle, scholarly man, with a somewhat vague manner, Downes had become more 'orthodox' in his opinions of Poor Law reform with advancing years; a member of the Workhouse Nursing Association described his evolution unkindly as one from 'an energetic Inspector in country parts' to a 'Senior Inspector wrapped round by Cotton Wool and Red Tape'.[31] Although for official reasons he was not a member of the COS, he had proclaimed his support for the principles upheld by the COS 'old guard' for several years before the Royal Commission was established.[32]

The younger officials who acted as Secretaries to the Commission, and who therefore played an active role as intermediaries and framers of documents, were Robert Harold Ambrose Gordon Duff and John Jeffrey. Both were born in 1871, and Duff was later to have a distinguished career in the English Civil Service, Jeffrey in the Scottish; Duff was Private Secretary to the President of the LGB at the time of the inquiry, and Jeffrey had already had experience as secretary to Scottish departmental investigations. Both of them were shrewd and clever, and both young men were inclined to be more 'advanced' in their opinions than their departmental seniors— Jeffrey more so than Duff. While Duff was loquacious and often went as far as an adroit civil servant may go, even to the verge of indiscretion, Jeffrey was more guarded in expressing his views.[33]

After the officials, the largest and more prominent group amongst the Commissioners were six men and women who were known to be active and leading members of the Charity Organisation

---

[30] He was knighted in 1910.

[31] J. Wilson Chings to B. Webb (n.d. ?1909). Webb Local Government Collection, vol. 286a.

[32] *COR* 12 (Apr. 1896), 177.

[33] Hamilton to H. Bosanquet, 28 May 1908; Jeffrey, who became very friendly with Beatrice Webb, once made the Freudian mistake of addressing a letter to Helen Bosanquet 'Mrs Sidney Webb, The Heath Cottage, Oxshott, Surrey'! Jeffrey to H. Bosanquet 10 May 1909. Bosanquet Papers.

Society. Octavia Hill was the veteran philanthropist of this group, and by 1905 her sixty-seven years had made her somewhat less formidable in manner, if no less inflexible in her opinions. Charles Stewart Loch, then aged fifty-six, and Helen Bosanquet, then forty-five, were the two best-known theorists of the COS 'old guard'. Loch was a veteran of Royal Commissions: he had served on the Royal Commission on the Aged Poor in 1893–5, and he was serving on the Royal Commission on the Feeble Minded 1904–8 immediately before and concurrently with that on the Poor Laws. At the same time, he held the Tooke Professorship of Economic Science and Statistics at King's College, London; he was editor of the *Charity Organisation Review*, and also Secretary of the COS. The combination was to prove a serious strain of his health before the Royal Commission on the Poor Laws ended.

The other three COS members might be regarded as representatives of its 'younger guard'. They were three 'university settlement' men from the older Universities, and all of them had come into contact with Canon Barnett. Thomas Hancock Nunn (born 1859) and Thory Gage Gardiner (born 1857) were two of the young men who had been impressed by speeches made by Barnett—Nunn at Cambridge, Gardiner at Oxford—at the time of the founding of Toynbee Hall, and both of them came down to help with the enterprise. Gardiner took Holy Orders and became a curate in Whitechapel and sub-Warden of Toynbee Hall; Nunn followed his family in being religious but not orthodox, and, having a small private income, was able to devote himself entirely to charitable work. Both these young disciples were deeply influenced by Barnett's belief that religious dedication, philanthropy, understanding, and sympathy were necessary for the reconciling of classes and the avoiding of class conflict and class war. Gardiner gave this belief practical expression in his work for the co-operative movement in the East End of London. Nunn followed Barnett into even closer connections with the Labour movement: he had a close association with the Barge Builders Trade Union, and in the great dock strike of 1889 he acted as an assistant to Ben Tillett; he also was interested in experiments for providing work or training for the unemployed arising from the Mansion House Fund, and served as a member of the London County Council Committee on the Want of Employment in 1903 and of the Central Unemployed Body set up by the Unemployed Workmen Act in 1905; he was a member of Stepney

Board of Guardians and later of the Borough Council and Board of Guardians at Hampstead. These two men were closer to Canon Barnett than the other younger COS commissioner, the Reverend Lancelot Ridley Phelps, Fellow of Oriel College, who taught Classics and Political Economy.

Unlike Gardiner and Nunn, who were unassuming and un-ambitious, Phelps was a man of handsome and imposing presence, clearly destined to be a power in Oxford College politics.[34] He was aged fifty-two at the time of his appointment to the Royal Commission, and it came just when he had been disappointed in his hope of being elected Provost of Oriel (he had to wait another nine years for that honour). Phelps approved the University settlement movement, but he did not really follow Canon Barnett far in his more radical proposals. In later years, he talked as if he had had an ultra-radical youth that was worth regretting, but when he then went on to make the same points that he had made in a pamphlet written when he was in his early thirties, one suspects the rhetorician's tricks.[35] In fact, Phelps's views extended beyond 'orthodox' COS doctrine only in three matters: in his approval of University settlements (about which other members of the COS old guard had some doubts);[36] in his demand for 'instruction' and 'rational employment instead of stone-breaking for all able-bodied persons in the workhouses;[37] and in what he called the 'drastic step' of turning all bodies providing institutional treatment for the sick into State hospitals—that is, taking all institutional medical relief outside the Poor Law and treating it 'from the point of view of health, not of poverty'.[38]

The 'radicalism' of these three men was tested when the Barnetts finally broke with the COS. None of them followed the Barnetts' example. Phelps took pride in the fact that the Oxford COS, of which he was a leading member, upheld 'strict' principles. Gardiner, who had become by that time secretary of the COS District Committee at Newington in Kent, retained his post quietly. Nunn, though remaining a member of the COS, took over Barnett's

---

[34] There is a striking portrait of him in Oriel College, Oxford, by Briton Riviere.
[35] Contrast, e.g., his talk 'Poor Relief and Charity' in the *Proceedings of Poor Law Conferences 1901–2* with his *Poor Law and Charity*, a paper read in the Common Room of Keble College 9 Mar. 1887 (Oxford, n.d.).
[36] B. Bosanquet (ed.), *Aspects of the Social Problem* (London, 1895), pp. 23–6.
[37] Phelps, *Poor Law and Charity*, p. 5.
[38] *Proceedings of Poor Law Conferences 1906–7*, pp. 414–21.

former position as 'leader of the opposition' within it. His close association with labour leaders made him aware of the unpopularity of the COS amongst the working class, and he hoped for reforms initiated from within the Society to overcome it. These broadly amounted to a modification of the COS's sterner doctrines concerning involuntary unemployment, a change of name of the society through its sinking its identity in wider-based 'Social Welfare Councils', and its concentration on practical social work, abstaining from collective pronouncements on debatable matters of public policy. Nunn took the initiative in organizing the Social Welfare Council in Hampstead which (as Mrs Bosanquet remarked) 'played the part of Jonah's whale, and the Charity Organisation Society [of that district] vanished within it, sacrificed to an access of dread of unpopularity'.[39] These proceedings were anathema to the old guard, and Nunn was more than a little estranged from his COS colleagues by 1905.

Closely linked with the COS group, though not actually members of the Society, were two other Commissioners, Frank Holesworth Bentham and Professor William Smart. Bentham was a Bradford businessman, the founder and director of a firm of textile comb makers. He was aged forty-seven in 1905, and was a staunch Liberal free trader; he owed his appointment to the Commission to his position as member of the Central Committee of Poor Law Conferences and to his Chairmanship since 1898 of the Bradford Board of Guardians, which was considered to be a model of an enterprising provincial Board.[40] Frank Bentham was a man of thoughtfulness and ingenuity of mind, deeply concerned with problems of Poor Law policy, but as he recognized he had difficulties in expressing himself clearly and effectively in speech and writing, and as a result his contributions were inclined to be underrated by his more socially aggressive and verbally dextrous colleagues. Speeches he made at the 1904 and 1905 Poor Law Conferences left little doubt that his sympathies lay, by and large, with COS doctrines; but he was attracted by some of Canon Barnett's ideas for helping the 'genuinely unemployed' through

[39] H. Bosanquet, *Social Work in London 1869–1912*, p. 92.
[40] There is an obituary notice of Bentham in the *Bradford Telegraph and Argus*, 8 Apr. 1931 and an article about his work in the *Bradford Weekly Telegraph*, 30 Dec. 1910. (I am indebted for this information to Mr David James, Archivist of the Central Library, Bradford.)

training schools and public works; he was prepared to contemplate treatment for the children, the sick, and the aged outside the Poor Law; and he wanted closer organizational links between Poor Law Guardians and voluntary charity.[41]

Professor William Smart was Adam Smith Professor of Political Economy at Glasgow University at the time of his appointment as Commissioner, and like Frank Bentham, he was prepared to temper the rigour of orthodox COS doctrine with some less doctrinaire benevolence. Aged fifty-two at the time he became a Commissioner, Smart in his early days had been a disciple of Thomas Carlyle and John Ruskin and a member of Ruskin's Guild of St George, but he had fallen out with his master when he failed in his attempt to reconcile Ruskin to political economy and political economists.[42] Smart later went on to become the chief proponent of the ideas of the Austrian 'marginal utility' school of economists in England, and translator and editor of works by Böhm-Bawerk and Wieser. Nevertheless the moral commitment, which had originally drawn him to Ruskin, always remained a prominent feature of his writings, even when he became (what would have been anathema to Ruskin) an outspoken defender of free-trade capitalism:[43] he was always explicit in stating his ethical preferences, and never resorted to the disingenuous trick of criticizing alternative systems and leaving his approval of the *status quo* unspoken. With suitable academic detachment, Smart approved COS work in Glasgow, and shared its criticisms of the 'crude experiments' to relieve unemployment outside the work of the Board of Guardians which in Glasgow, he said, had been 'allowed to go much too far—led . . . by a lot of people who are avowed Socialists'.[44] But his was not at all a

[41] His papers, recorded in *Proceedings of Poor Law Conferences 1904–5* and *1905–6*, give an impression of his style and his opinions; the Minutes of Indoor Relief Committee of the RC on the 1905–9 preserved in Webb Local Government Collection Vol. 286b. reveal the active part he took in making suggestions.

[42] W. Smart, *A Disciple of Plato: A Critical Study of John Ruskin* (Glasgow, 1883). Ruskin, in a note added at the end of this essay, showed that he was not placated by Smart's distinctions between 'mercantile' and 'social' economics. He wrote: '. . . I would like to add that, while I admit there is such a thing as mercantile economy, distinguished from social, I have always said also that neither Mill, Fawcett, nor Bastiat knew the contemptible science they professed to teach', p. 48.

[43] W. Smart, *The Distribution of Income* (London, 1899 and 1912); *The Return to Protection* (London, 1906); *The Single Tax* (Glasgow, 1905) (This last, a criticism of Henry George, was replied to by W. R. Lester, *Professor Smart and the Single Tax: A Rejoinder* (Glasgow, 1905).

[44] Smart to H. Bosanquet, 18 July 1908. Bosanquet Papers.

dogmatic or closed mind;[45] his humanity shines through his writings, and showed itself particularly in his arguments to the Commission that the 1834 Poor Law had been intended to apply only to the able-bodied paupers, not to the sick, the aged, or the children.[46] Professor Smart was an amiable man, reserved, scholarly, concerned with the things that really matter, but his mind perhaps lacked that sharp analytical edge which is the hallmark of the top-ranking economist.

An unpredictable element in the Commission at first was the 'unofficial Irishman', who was put on as a makeweight against the 'official' Irishman, Sir Henry Robinson. The Balfours had chosen Charles Owen O'Conor, who was known as the O'Conor Don, a senior member of an old Irish family. He had sat from Roscommon first as a Liberal and then as an Irish Nationalist MP of Isaac Butt's party, but his parliamentary career had come to an end at the election of 1880 after he had rejected Parnell's party pledge. He was appointed a member of the Irish Privy Council and Lord Lieutenant of Roscommon, and his services were enlisted by British governments on many Commissions of Inquiry dealing with economic, social, religious, and local government affairs in Ireland. The O'Conor Don was considered to be a spokesman of moderate Irish opinion, and a shrewd and entertaining character. He was a student of Irish customs and folklore, a noted antiquarian, and a member of the Irish Language Society. One of his fellow Commissioners found him 'racy of the Irish soil' and 'full of fun'.[47] Unfortunately, the O'Conor Don hardly figured in the history of the Poor Law Commission. He was already ill at the time of his appointment, and he died in 1906, aged sixty-eight, before he was able to attend many of its meetings. The selection of a person to replace him fell to James Bryce, the Secretary of State for Ireland in the Liberal government which had just come to power,[48] and he chose a member of the Roman Catholic hierarchy in Ireland, Dr Denis Kelly, who had been appointed Bishop of Ross in 1897, when he was aged forty-five. Those who expected the Bishop to bring any unusual religious view of the Poor Law into the discussion were

[45] Smart to H. Bosanquet, 30 May 1914, where he says he is returning 'to my old Ruskin and Carlyle faith. I wonder if it is a sign of age—or growth!'
[46] Cd. 4983, Min. of Ev., Appendix vol. xii, pp. 40–3.
[47] Phelps to Boyce, 17 Dec. 1905. Phelps Papers.
[48] John Burns's Diary, 12 Oct. 1906. Burns Papers, vol. xliv.

soon disappointed. The sins of the 1834 Poor Law had been absolved by its sufferance in Ireland even by Daniel O'Connell of blessed memory; and Pope Leo XIII, in his encyclical *Rerum Novarum* had detected, like the COS, the smell of brimstone about Socialists' views on the family. The Bishop's tendency to side with the COS was confirmed by his finding in Dr Phelps a colleague who enjoyed with him the exchange of lively conversation.[49]

The remaining five Commissioners, according to Helen Bosanquet, were 'convinced Socialists'.[50] Obviously she included Charles Booth, on the strength of his advocacy of old-age pensions and his well-known statement: 'My idea is to make the dual system, Socialism in the arms of Individualism, under which we already live, more efficient by extending somewhat the sphere of the former [i.e. the sphere of Socialism] . . .' [51] But in fact, Booth was no Socialist in any modern meaning of the term.[52] Politically, he had by 1905 become a member of the Conservative Party, having moved steadily to the right from the Liberal-Radicalism of his youth through Liberal-Unionism to Conservatism. A successful shipowner, always fascinated by the intricacies of the business world, he remained, to the last words he penned, an enthusiastic admirer of the capitalist system.[53] When his pioneering statistical study of London life and labour had revealed to him that the extent of poverty in the metropolis was even greater than the Socialists had claimed, he courageously accepted the conclusion that a bold measure of State interference to remedy poverty was necessary. But he emphasized that his kind of 'Socialism' was designed merely to provide a minimum floor-level above which private enterprise could operate efficiently, free of the dangers arising from desperate poverty: 'Thorough interference on the part of the State with the lives of a small fraction of the population would make it possible, ultimately, to dispense with any Socialistic interference in the lives of all the rest.'[54] His major remedy, for which he was still campaigning at the time of the establishing of the Poor Law Commission, was non-contributory old-age pensions. He saw

[49] Phelps to Boyce, 10 Dec. 1908.

[50] H. Bosanquet, *Social Work in London 1869–1912*, p. 276.

[51] C. Booth, *Labour and Life of the People* (London, 1891), i. 167.

[52] See my discussion of this in 'Charles Booth and the Royal Commission on the Poor Laws 1905–9, *Historical Studies* (Melbourne University), 15. 61 (1973).

[53] M. Booth, *Charles Booth: A Memoir* (London, 1918), pp. 170–1.

[54] C. Booth, *Labour and Life of the People*, i. 167.

poverty resulting from old age as the chief problem, and he had come to believe that, if the elderly were removed from the Poor Law, it might be possible to work a modified and updated version of the 1834 system, combined with voluntary charity, to deal with the rest. Charles Booth's reputation as social investigator and statistician made it certain that he would be considered for appointment to the Commission. Beatrice Webb credited herself with having suggested his name to Balfour, but it was independently suggested by Sandars, who wrote that he was sure Balfour would wish to have him on it 'from the public point of view'.[55] Booth's work had won him election to the Royal Society in 1899, and he had been appointed a Privy Councillor in 1904. He had already had experience of Commissions of Inquiry: he had been a member of the Aberdare Royal Commission on Old Age Pensions in 1893–5, and he sat also on the Tariff Commission set up by Joseph Chamberlain in 1903–4.[56] Sandars's only doubt concerned the state of Booth's health. Booth was never a robust man; he was aged sixty-five in 1905, and was recuperating from a severe illness; but Sandars thought him to be sufficiently recovered to serve. As it turned out, Booth's deteriorating health made it necessary for him to retire from the Commission in January 1908, a whole year before it completed its labours.

The Very Revd Dr Henry Russell Wakefield would also have denied Mrs Bosanquet's claim that he was a Socialist,[57] although he was quite willing to allow himself to be called an 'aggressive Radical'.[58] He said he was 'prepared at any moment to accept, from those who may have Socialistic ideas, anything which I believe to be for the good of the country to which I belong'.[59] Dr Wakefield (who was later to become Dean of Norwich and Bishop of Birmingham) was in 1905, at the age of fifty-one, Rector of one of the most fashionable churches in London, St Mary's Bryanston Square, a living which had been offered him by Lord Rosebery in 1894. Lord

---

[55] Sandars to Balfour, 5 Sept. 1905. Balfour Papers, Add. MS 49763, vol. lxxxi.
[56] During his service on this Commission, Booth became a Protectionist: B. W. D. 20 Dec. 1907; Booth to Marshall, 21 Apr. 1907. Booth Papers I/1915; B. Russell, 'Mr Charles Booth's Proposals for Fiscal Reform', *Contemporary Review*, 35 (1904).
[57] H. R. Wakefield, *Poor Law Reform* (an address to the National Liberal Club, 29 Nov. 1908), p. 2.
[58] Leeds, *Norwich Cathedral Past and Present, with a Biographical Sketch of the Dean of Norwich* (London, 1910), p. 112.
[59] Wakefield, *Poor Law Reform*, p. 2.

George Hamilton was a churchwarden of St Mary's, and he did not approve of Wakefield's politics at all; but the Rector believed in 'keeping politics out of the pulpit'[60] to ensure that 'the Church is the Church of England, not of any section',[61] though he equally insisted on his full personal freedom in political matters when not in the pulpit. Russell Wakefield came of a well-connected family,[62] and he had received his higher education at the University of Bonn. His 'Broad Church' views and his opposition to 'High Church extravagances' he derived from Charles Kingsley and F. D. Maurice.[63] From 1877 he held a number of Church offices in and around London, and wherever he went he had taken an active part in municipal administration, considering that kind of activity to be part of a clergyman's duty. He served on Boards of Guardians and the London School Board, and, after being a Progressive Alderman on the Marylebone Borough Council, he became in 1903 Mayor of Marylebone and the first clergyman to be a mayor in London. About the same time he occupied the post of Vice-Chairman of the London Unemployed Committee, which led on to his appointment as Chairman of the Central Unemployed Body for London when it was established under the Unemployed Workmen Act of 1905. Dr Wakefield's views and activities brought him into close touch with Fabian Socialists and Labour leaders. Like his friend Canon Barnett, he regretted and sought to rectify the notion commonly held by working men that the Church was a dispenser of charity from on high and detached from the life of the people. He roundly declared that the task of the nation's religion was to help mankind win a better and happier life here on earth, and that the Church should concern itself with such sins as the evils arising from luxury and capitalism, the gap between rich and poor, and the strains arising from modern living conditions. He saw a chance of a great development of Christian brotherhood in a more Collectivist society.[64] And, again like Barnett, he felt estranged from the leaders of the COS, believing their approach and methods to be too rigid, too old-fashioned, and cold. Although not himself a member of the

[60] Leeds, *Norwich Cathedral Past and Present*, p. 115

[61] H. R. Wakefield, *Pastoral Address and Report for the Year 1907–8*, St Mary's, Bryanston Square, p. 8.

[62] His grandfather was Gilbert Wakefield, scholar and controversialist of the 18th century, and friend of C. J. Fox.

[63] Leeds, *Norwich Cathedral Past and Present*, p. 109.

[64] Leeds, *Norwich Cathedral Past and Present*, pp. 116–17.

COS, he gave encouragement to his friends within it,[65] who were trying to make its policy more flexible and humane.[66]

George Lansbury, by contrast, was certainly a 'convinced Socialist'. In 1905 he had recently exchanged his membership of the SDF for membership of the ILP, and had resumed his faith as an ardent Christian Socialist. Indeed, as a great joiner of organizations, he also happened to be a member of the COS but his membership of that society was expressly for the purpose of battling with its spokesmen and leaders. Lansbury was a fighter, a crusader against injustice, a campaigner for the rights of the unprivileged. He 'lets his bleeding heart run away with his bloody head', was the upstaging remark made of him by a witty Liberal.[67] But it was only partly true; Lansbury's sympathetic heart was matched by a fairly strong head, except in moments of strong emotion. On the matter of the Poor Law, he certainly had powerful feelings, reinforced by personal experiences of poverty in his youth. These predisposed him accept Socialist criticisms of the capitalist system; but he was never unwilling to listen to explanations—even when arguments for 'letting things alone' or for a 'strict' treatment of the poor galled him into feeling that the better-off ought to be at least kind and experimental in their efforts at charity. By 1905, when he was forty-six, George Lansbury had built up a small but successful timber business in the East End of London; and during the previous decade he and his friend Will Crooks had achieved fame or notoriety in and outside the metropolitan borough of Poplar by persuading its Board of Guardians to adopt a 'Labour' (or, the COS spokesmen said, a lax) policy in Poor Law administration. Their experiments were greatly assisted by the financial help of an American philanthropist, Joseph Fels; but they led, shortly after the Commission began its labours, to an embittered dispute with the officials of the Local Government Board.[68] If a representative of 'Labour' Guardians was to be placed on the Commission, Lansbury was the obvious choice: he had become their spokesman at Poor Law Conferences for some years, and he had been appointed to the Central Unemployed Body for London when it was set up in 1905,

---

[66] Especially the Marylebone honorary secretary, F. Morris.

[66] *Pastoral Address 1907–8*, pp. 7–8.

[67] Attributed to Augustine Birrell: W. Kent, *John Burns: Labour's Lost Leader* (London, 1950), p. 280.

[68] Postgate, *Life of George Lansbury*, pp. 77–87.

becoming Chairman of its Working Colonies Committee and chief advocate of labour colonies schemes for the unemployed.

Lansbury's Labour colleague on the Commission, however, was not a member of any Socialist organization, according to Lansbury;[69] he was generally reckoned as a 'Lib-Lab' in politics. Francis William Chandler had not been included in the original Royal Warrant appointing the Royal Commission; he was added to it in February 1906, after the Trades Union Congress had pressed its demand to the new Liberal government that it should be represented. So Chandler had in fact been chosen by the Parliamentary Committee of the TUC, of which he was a member. He was a woodworker, aged fifty-seven in 1906, the General Secretary of the Amalgamated Society of Carpenters and Joiners. Although Chandler was a shrewd trade union man, who took an effective part in cross-examination and discussion where technical matters of working-class conditions were involved, he was somewhat overwhelmed by the higher fliers in abstract discussions of general policy, and, on the whole, he was willing to take his cues from Lansbury and back him staunchly.

Beatrice Webb was the middle-class Socialist on the Commission, owing her appointment to friendship with the Balfours, and to the authoritative position the Webbs had won as writers and experts on labour and administrative affairs. Even if the Balfours had reflected more deeply on the matter than they probably did, they might well have considered that, on or off this Commission, the Webbs were bound to have a finger in the pie, and that the experience of three earlier Royal Commissions, with which the Webbs had had something to do, suggested that it was safer to have a representative of the Webb partnership on rather than off.[70] The appointment of Beatrice rather than Sidney no doubt had a good deal to do with the fact that the Poor Law was regarded as belonging to the 'domestic' as opposed to the 'masculine' side of politics, in which women for a long while had been encouraged to take a share.[71] Sidney Webb

---

[69] Draft of a letter (n.d. [?1909]) to an unidentified journal in reply to a letter from Mr C. H. Norman. Lansbury Papers, vol. 29a.

[70] Sidney Webb had less influence when he had served as Commissioner on the RC on Trade Union Law 1904–6 than he had had when, not a Commissioner, he had drafted Minority Reports for Tom Mann and James Mawdsley during the RC on Labour 1894 and for Henry Broadhurst in the RC on the Aged Poor in 1895.

[71] The Boards of Guardians were the first public bodies in which women were permitted to vote. The whole question of 'separate spheres' has been well discussed

also wished Beatrice to have her turn at this kind of activity; and he could hardly have failed to have been aware at this time that Beatrice would be more acceptable as a 'Labour' representative, because his own compromises over Balfour's education acts, and his equivocal stand concerning the Taff Vale decision as a member of the Royal Commission on Trade Union Law in 1904–6, had put him temporarily out of favour with many Liberal trade unionists and Labour Party men.

The selection of Commissioners was generally applauded in the press when the names were announced. *The Times* hoped that it was a Commission designed for 'practical action' rather than for lengthy theoretical discussion, and claimed it was for this reason that the government had given the Unemployed Workmen Act of 1905 a life of three years only, not ten. It added that 'the names, in their range and variety, are a sufficient guarantee that no partisan or political bias will impair the value of the Commission's labours'.[72] Nevertheless, the selection did not go uncriticized by some of the Commissioners themselves. At the outset, Lord George Hamilton tried to have 'Russell Wakefield or Lansbury or both' excluded and replaced by a 'Conservative P. L. Guardian or country gentleman' and either Sir Henry Robinson or the O'Conor Don replaced by an 'R. C. Guardian or philanthropist'.[73] Some of the COS members, both at the time and later, thought it was a mistake for the government to 'yield . . . to the suggestion, which might seem to it to have some plausible advantages, that it should put the principal rival controversialists on the Commission and allow them to wrangle . . . '[74] Beatrice Webb considered that too many officials had been appointed as Commissioners, and that the Commission would have functioned better under the chairmanship of an eminent lawyer with firm and clear ideas about procedure and evidence.[75]

To the modern historian, it must at first sight appear surprising that the very large representation of the COS on the Commission

by E. Halévy in Book ii of *The Rule of Democracy*, vol. vi of his *History of the English People in the 19th Century*, and by B. Harrison, *Separate Spheres: The Opposition to Women's Suffrage in Britain* (London, 1978).

[72] *The Times*, 29 Nov. 1905.
[73] Undated note Hamilton to Sandars, with 'c. Oct. 1905' added in pencil. Balfour Papers, Add. MS 49778.
[74] COR, NS 18 (1905), 142; H. Bosanquet, *Social Work in London*, p. 276.
[75] B. Webb, *Our Partnership*, pp. 221–2.

was not the subject of critical comment. With six leading members of the Society as Commissioners, together with the sympathy of the Chairman, as shown by his nominal membership of it, and the expressions of sympathy with its principles made by at least two of the officials on the Commission (Downes and Provis) and by two of the other Commissioners (Bentham and Smart), one might have expected the accusation to be made that this was a 'stacked' inquiry, designed to arrive at a predetermined conclusion. The absence of such an accusation was a sign of the wide acceptance of basic COS views in informed circles in Edwardian times; indeed, it is probable that those views were widely accepted without being thought of as being the peculiar property of the COS—they were thought to be 'common-sense'. Anyone of that time in Arthur and Gerald Balfour's place, faced with the task of choosing persons with experience and expertise in Poor Law matters, could hardly have failed to have selected some such number of COS members. The COS had attracted to itself a large part of the talent in the field. Admittedly there were divergent opinions held both within and without the COS; but then those minorities were allowed spokesmen—as minorities, naturally—on the Commission. In fact, the historian must ask himself who could have been chosen who would have been more eligible than the Commissioners actually appointed? Even with the benefit of historical hindsight, alternative names do not spring readily to mind. Canon Barnett seems a notable omission, but he was invited and declined to serve.[76] W. H. Beveridge made a great name for himself later in the field of social policy, but he was too young in 1905, and was more properly called as a witness. Beatrice Webb may have been right in thinking that an eminent jurist would have added strength (in spite of the fact that two of the officials on the Commission were lawyers); but whether his particular talents would have accomplished more as chairman than Lord George's patrician genial 'muddling through' with that difficult collection of individuals is open to doubt. Seebohm Rowntree might have been a valuable addition as social investigator, as Charles Booth's health proved so frail; but that was not certain in 1905 and Booth had the senior claim to appointment. Possibly an economist of a more theoretical and analytical turn of mind than either the Revd Lancelot Phelps or Professor Smart

[76] H. Barnett, *Canon Barnett: His Life, Work and Friends* (London, 1921), ii. 285.

would have assisted the Commission on a side where it was notably weak; but it is not easy to think of a suitable candidate. J. A. Hobson was regarded as too unorthodox to have been considered; A. C. Pigou's rising star had not yet fixed itself; Alfred Marshall, on the verge of retiring, would have been unlikely to have accepted; only A. L. Bowley and F. Y. Edgeworth might have seemed better choices.

Manœuvring for Positions

When the sessions of the Poor Law Commission began, both Beatrice Webb and Helen Bosanquet scented danger—but it was danger from quite different directions. Helen Bosanquet feared that Beatrice Webb, apparently in league once again with her cousin-in-law Charles Booth,[77] would try to run or dominate the methods of inquiry. Beatrice, however, saw the danger initially as coming not from the COS, but from the officials of the Local Government Board. After a preliminary personal interview with J. S. Davy, the Assistant-Secretary of the LGB and one of the most assertive of its officials, she got the impression that he and other officials on and off the Commission had decided beforehand on the rules of the game, and its result:

We were to be spoon-fed by evidence carefully selected and prepared [*she noted in her Diary*;] they [the officials] were to draft the circular to the boards of guardians; they were to select the inspectors who were to give evidence; they were virtually to select the guardians to be called in support of this evidence. Assistant commissioners were to be appointed who were to collect evidence illustrative of these theories. And above all we were to be given *opinions* and not *facts*.

The aim of the exercise was 'to stem the tide of philanthropic

---

[77] Charles and Mary Booth never seem to have overcome their dislike of Sidney Webb, whom they considered to be a very unsuitable match for their socially eligible cousin, an attitude which caused many years of estrangement between them and Beatrice Webb in the 1890s. Their personal aversion to Sidney was strengthened by an ill-founded belief by the Booth family that it was his influence which had been responsible for Beatrice's decision to 'desert' Charles Booth as a helper in his great London survey (see the comments by Charles Booth's son in the Booth Papers). Charles Booth also had a strong distaste for Sidney Webb's special brand of Fabian 'permeation', particularly his writing of Minority Reports for the Labour men on the RC on Labour 1891–4 (see C. Booth to A. Marshall, 25 May 1894, Booth Papers 1/1352) and on the RC on the Aged Poor, 1894–5. As a machinator of Minority Reports, Sidney Webb was to be blamed again for Beatrice's tactics in the RC on the Poor Laws.

impulse' which was threatening to sweep away the deterrent Poor Law by getting a recommendation for the 'reversion to the principles of 1834 as regards policy', and suggestions for reform of Poor Law machinery to put that policy into force.[78] Although she realized that such a conclusion would be welcomed by the COS members, she felt she could rely on their claims to scientific sociological expertise in appealing to them to resist any such officially 'cooked' inquiry. At this point, her initial suspicions were confirmed when Lord George Hamilton, without consulting the other members of the Commission, issued a questionnaire to Chairmen of Boards of Guardians which had been prepared by the officials, and which Beatrice considered to be quite unsatisfactory. She lost no time in setting down her own ideas for a proper inquiry and procedure on paper,[79] and sent a copy, not only to Charles Booth (with whom she had had preliminary consultation and agreement on the matter) but also to several other members of the Commission. She accompanied it by letters to Helen Bosanquet and Professor Smart inviting them to pay a visit to 41 Grosvenor Road.[80]

Helen Bosanquet replied, declining the invitation briskly[81]—in contrast with Professor Smart's polite but vague and indefinite acceptance.[82] Neither of them wished to walk into 'The Webb'. To Beatrice Webb's main suggestion, that the Commission should appoint a Procedure Committee to make suggestions about the kinds of inquiry to be pursued, the methods to be employed, and the division of work amongst members, Mrs Bosanquet answered that she disagreed with the idea. She felt that procedure should be worked out by the Commission as a whole. On the other hand she fulfilled Beatrice's expectation by saying that 'of course' it would be necessary to have a full inquiry, and satisfactory procedures. But she must have weakened her reassurance in Beatrice's eyes by apparently approving of Mr Davy's choice of Inspectors to give evidence, and making light of Lord George's action in sending out

---

[78] B.W.D. 2 Dec. 1905; *Our Partnership*, p. 322. MacKenzie, *Diary*, iii, 15.

[79] Webb Local Government Collection, vol. 286b; Hamilton to B. Webb, 14 Dec. 1905, and B. Webb to Hamilton, 15 Dec. 1905, ibid.

[80] B. Webb to H. Bosanquet, n.d. Bosanquet Papers. The invitation to Smart is deduced from his reply (see footnote 82).

[81] H. Bosanquet to B. Webb, 26 Dec. 1905. Webb Local Government Collection, vol. 286.

[82] Smart to B. Webb, 27 Dec. 1905, ibid.

the questionnaire—saying that she thought little would come of it. As things turned out, it would have been more diplomatic of Beatrice Webb not to have been so vehement in protesting at the danger of domination of the inquiry by the Chairman and the officials. The majority of the Commissioners were already on their guard against it.[83] Charles Booth tried to warn her not to be unnecessarily aggressive: approving her suggestions on procedure, he 'hope[d] our Chairman will see their reasonableness and value, so as to adopt them himself more or less'.[84] But she was not convinced; she thought Booth was being too feeble and gentlemanly,[85] and feared that as a woman she would be ignored and overruled unless she was insistent if necessary to the point of appearing disagreeable. So she carried on her protest, not only at the first meetings of the Commission, but also by private complaint to the Secretary, R. G. Duff, of the Chairman's 'high-handed' methods, reinforced by threats of documenting and publishing her dissatisfaction.[86] Then she took the further step of insisting that the Chairman circulate a lengthier memorandum of procedure, the draft of which was didactic in tone and clearly a product of the Beatrice-and-Sidney partnership. This had the fatal effect of switching the other Commissioners' fears from the danger of being manipulated by the officials to the danger of being manipulated from outside by Sidney Webb, then at the height of his reputation as the *éminence grise* of social politics. These fears were intensified by the appearance of Sidney's hand, literally, in the draft memorandum.

The misunderstandings on both sides were by this time reaching comic proportions. The procedure followed by Lord George Hamilton at the outset, and presumably suggested to him by his secretary-officials, was almost certainly inept rather than sinister.[87] As soon as he sensed the opposition of other Commissioners, Lord George, with all the adroitness of an experienced politician, and the

[83] B. Webb, *Our Partnership*, pp. 322–4.
[84] Booth to B. Webb, 23 Dec. 1905. Webb Local Government Collection, vol. 286.
[85] B. Webb to Mary Playne, undated (?21 Jan. 1906]. Passfield Papers. See also *Our Partnership*, p. 329 and B.W.D. 15 Dec. 1905, where, after the passage published in *Our Partnership*, pp. 323–7 comes the remark: 'Charles Booth, I fear, is too wellbred and too feeble in health to be much good. But we shall see.'
[86] B. Webb, *Our Partnership*, p. 324; B. Webb to Hamilton, 15 Dec. 1905. Webb Local Government Collection, vol. 286b.
[87] Hamilton to B. Webb, 18 Dec. 1905, ibid.

mildest of protests at the surrender of his (nominal) personal leadership, was prepared to put the question of procedure to the vote of the Commission as a whole.[88] The Webbs, on their side, in the lengthier memorandum, had been sincerely trying to place the fruits of their experience as skilled investigators and historians at the service of the Commission. Their memorandum contained much information about methods of interviewing and of handling documentary evidence of the kind which was later published in their book *Methods of Social Study* and which has proved valuable for many generations of research students. But Helen Bosanquet and other Commissioners found the document tedious and patronizing. After all, they reckoned themselves to be social investigators too, with their own training: who were these Socialists to lecture them about methodology? And what were the Webbs really up to? Could it be that their suggestion, that the Commission should divide itself into small subcommittees which would employ expert investigators, was meant to take decisions or supervision of detailed research out of the hands of the Commission as a whole?

Lord George Hamilton, after circulating Beatrice Webb's memorandum, sensibly tipped the problem back to the whole Commission, by calling for memoranda on procedure from all the rest of its members.[89] Ten of them responded.[90] There were two main organizational questions: first, whether there should be a Procedure Committee, and second, what other committees should be created. On the first question, Helen Bosanquet and Beatrice Webb were at opposite poles. Beatrice wanted a small Procedure Committee to make recommendations to the Commission as a whole. Helen Bosanquet insisted that the Commission as a whole should decide on procedure.[91] When it was put to the vote neither of them won. The compromise decision was in favour of a Procedure Committee, but a large one. Its composition was settled by appointing as

---

[88] B. Webb, *Our Partnership*, pp. 326–7.

[89] B.W.D., 5 Feb. 1906; *Our Partnership*, p. 329.

[90] Bentham, Booth, Bosanquet, Downes, Loch, Nunn, Patten-MacDougall, Phelps, Robinson, Smart. Lansbury sent private letters to B. Webb giving his views, but he did not forward them to the Chairman because he was late in replying, and because, he said, 'you had all written more than enough on the subject'. Lansbury to B. Webb, 7 Feb. 1906 and 15 Feb. 1906. Webb Local Government Collection, vol. 286. The memoranda are ibid., vol. 286b.

[91] B. Webb's Memo on Procedure, ibid.; H. Bosanquet to B. Webb, 26 Dec. 1906, ibid., vol. 286.

members of it all those who had submitted memoranda, but it was reduced to nine (the Chairman, Bentham, Booth, Bosanquet, Downes, Loch, Phelps, Smart, Webb), following the withdrawal of Hancock Nunn, Robinson, and Patten-MacDougall who were unable to attend regularly.

This Procedure Committee then had to decide what other committees should be created. Once again, Beatrice Webb and Helen Bosanquet disagreed. Beatrice, hoping for a number of small expert committees, proposed beginning with three: a Statistical Committee with 'a competent young statistician' as adviser to it, a Central Authority Committee for investigating the history and policy of the Poor Law, and a Local Administrative Committee for investigating the ways in which this policy had been carried out by Boards of Guardians and other local authorities.[92] Helen Bosanquet, who had not given up her objections to the idea of small committees, proposed that there should be none but *ad hoc* and temporary committees.[93] In the end, the Procedure Committee approved a suggestion from Lord George Hamilton that there should be a Statistical Committee made up entirely of the Commission's own members, a Documents Committee which would digest information concerning foreign systems as well as all British documentary material, and an Evidence Committee, to make recommendations to the Commission as a whole concerning the evidence to be taken and the methods of taking it. Commissioners were to be assigned to one or other of these Committees by the Chairman; but any Commissioner interested in any particular proposal would be entitled to attend any Committee dealing with it, and the Chairman was to be ex officio a member of all.[94] Beatrice Webb was abandoned by Charles Booth, who was keen to become

---

[92] B. Webb's Memo on Procedure, and Suggestions to the Procedure Committee, ibid., vol. 286b. The 'competent young statistician' whom Beatrice Webb wanted was A. L. Bowley of the LSE; the suggestion was naturally not pleasing to Charles Booth, who assumed he would be in charge of the statistical research.

[93] B.W.D., 12 Feb. 1906; *Our Partnership*, p. 331.

[94] Chairman's Memo on Devolution of Work, confirmed at meeting of the Commission on 26 Feb. 1906. The membership of the three Committees was settled as follows:

(1) *Statistical Committee*: Booth (Chairman); Bentham; Downes; Loch; Robinson.
(2) *Documents Committee*: Smart (Chairman); O'Conor Don; Patten-Mac-Dougall; Provis; Wakefield; Webb.
(3) *Evidence Committee*: Phelps (Chairman); Bosanquet; Chandler; Gardiner; Hill; Lansbury; Nunn. Webb Local Government Collection, vol. 286b.

Chairman of the Statistical Committee, a position that could hardly be denied him if it were composed of Commission members, and he felt that Procedure and Statistical Committees were enough for the time being.[95] She was also abandoned by George Lansbury (although he was not a member of the Procedure Committee) because he disliked the idea of expert committees; he wrote to her: 'It may be sheer ignorance on my part, but, in my judgment, experts are not always people who arrive at true conclusions'.[96] Ironically, two of her supporters on the issue of small committees happened to be the official members Sir Henry Robinson and James Patten-MacDougall, and their self-exclusion from the Procedure Committee meant she lacked their influential voices. Another official, the Secretary R. G. Duff, wrote to her after her defeat, sending her a copy of recommendations which he had made to the Chairman (and which had been ignored) for 'the initial small committees into which I hoped the Commission would divide', agreeing with her that the larger committees actually set up had proved inefficient and time-wasting.[97]

Beatrice Webb had no doubts that this would be the consequence. In July 1906 she wrote to her sister, Mary Playne, commenting on 'the waste of time and energy and the amazing extravagance in money, brought about by having no fixed procedure and no trained person in any position of responsibility'. The result was that individual Commissioners were undertaking investigations which happened to interest them on their own responsibility. Charles Booth, she noted with wry amusement, had 'scampered off with *all* the statistics and [was] elaborating tables with the aid of 16 persons paid by himself'.[98] Helen Bosanquet was investigating outdoor relief and women's wages. So Beatrice decided to rescue herself from her tactical defeat by seizing the chance to put in hand several investigations of her own. Mrs Bernard Shaw agreed to give money to help her pay research assistants, and later a special fund was established through gifts from wealthy Fabians and Fabian sympathizers for the same purpose. Beatrice was determined also to enlist the

---

[95] C. Booth's Memo on Procedure, ibid., and B. Webb, *Our Partnership*, p. 331.
[96] Lansbury to B. Webb, 15 Feb. 1906, Webb Local Government Collection, vol. 286.
[97] Duff to B. Webb, 11 Oct. [1906], ibid., vol. 286b
[98] B. Webb to M. Playne 29 July [1906] Passfield Papers; included in N. MacKenzie (ed.), *The Letters of Sidney and Beatrice Webb*, vol. ii. *Partnership: 1892–1912* (Cambridge, 1978), p. 233.

unpaid help of Sidney Webb and other members of the Fabian Society.

These private investigations were to be additional to work she agreed to undertake for the newly established Documents Committee. Here again she had begun by suggesting that this Committee should employ trained researchers under the supervision of John Jeffrey, the Assistant Secretary of the Commission, to take notes on Blue Books, circulars, Acts, and other documents according to the special Webb method of note-taking, for later examination and interpretation by the Committee; and she got one of her own private research assistants to make some notes on the Acts of 1834, 1835, 1837, and 1878 and on the great Report of 1834 to demonstrate how it should be done.[99] But Professor Smart, as Chairman of the Documents Committee, did not care for her proposal at all: like many old-fashioned academics, he distrusted the employment of research assistants, and felt that members of the Committee should do their own research: 'It seems to me that, as responsible members of a Royal Commission we have much more to do than mere checking of other people's labour.'[1] He insisted upon dividing up the work amongst members of the Committee. He and the Revd Dr Wakefield between them would make a digest of parliamentary reports and papers; the O'Conor Don was to study the material on the Irish Poor Law and Mr Patten-MacDougall the Scottish; Beatrice Webb, helped by Patten-MacDougall, was to undertake research on orders and circulars concerning the policy of the central authority; Sir Samuel Provis was to help all round. 'Some of the work may, in time, be deputed', Professor Smart allowed, but he declared firmly that any early delegation of it was to be distrusted. Beatrice Webb predicted, when the Documents Committee accepted Professor Smart's proposals and rejected hers, that a great deal of the documentary research would never get done. She decided to press on with her share, making use of her own research assistants, and getting what help she could from Patten-MacDougall and Provis—occasionally, indeed, quarrelling with them or going behind their backs to get material she needed.[2] By the

[99] Suggestions of B. Webb to Documents Committee [dated in pencil 2 Mar. 1906]. Webb Local Government Collection, vol. 286b.

[1] Suggestions of Prof. Smart to Documents Committee 5 Mar. 1906, ibid.

[2] B.W.D., 12 Feb. 1906 and 1 Mar. 1906; *Our Partnership*, pp. 331, 334; MacKenzie, *Letters*, ii. 231.

third meeting of the Documents Committee she had already made substantial progress with her Report on the policy of the central authority from 1834 to 1847,[3] and by the eighth meeting in October 1906 it was ready to be submitted to the Commission as a whole. Her private investigations (to be described later) were soon proceeding apace. Beatrice Webb's efficiency in pushing her own barrow was soon to be another cause for alarm on the part of some of her fellow-Commissioners.

At this point, in June-July 1906, Charles Booth made an attempt to bring the discordant factions of the Commission together on the basis of a common programme. Remarking that he felt himself well placed for giving a lead in this, because he held 'a middle position between what I believe to be the opposing schools of thought on poor law questions',[4] he circulated a memorandum to the other Commissioners setting out his tentative general ideas on reform. The primary assumption of his proposals was that the Government would soon introduce old-age pensions for all at 70 years of age. He believed that if the elderly, the largest group amongst the pauper class, and those whose claim to generous treatment was strongest, could be removed from the Poor Law, then a return to the 'principles of 1834' might be possible. A good deal of terminological dexterity was needed to make a modern interpretation of the 'principles of 1834' acceptable on these conditions to both the COS and the Socialist members of the Commission, as Booth realized; but he undertook to supply it.

Booth's main objective was to abolish outdoor Poor Law relief as far as possible, and to provide only indoor relief (to be renamed 'institutional treatment') on a standardized pattern through a centralized system, which would co-operate with private charity. In fact, private charity was to be allowed a large role in handling the 'curable' cases (Booth proposed the word 'curable' instead of 'deserving' or 'helpable' poor, looking upon pauperism as a 'social disease'). Some whole sections of the poor, such as widows and deserted wives, could be dealt with mainly by charitable assistance. And he thought extensive use should be made of other agencies, such as voluntary insurance societies and labour exchanges to bring

---

[3] Minutes of the Documents Committee, 14 May 1906, Webb Local Government Collection. vol. 286b.

[4] C. Booth, 'Notes for a New Poor Law'. Webb Local Government Collection, vol. 286.

'all possible means to bear before resort is had to the . . . assistance provided by the Poor Law'. Pauper children should be excluded from workhouses, and be boarded out or sent to scattered homes or grouped cottage homes or special residential Poor Law schools;[5] but they should remain within the scope of the Poor Law and not be given over-generous treatment which would excite the envy or resentment of the thrifty workman and his wife scraping to provide education for their own children. Similarly the sick poor should be treated within the Poor Law system, or rather within the existing related systems of Public Health, Poor Law, and voluntary charity which had grown up over the years and could work in 'harmonious co-ordination' in spite of some overlapping. The able-bodied should receive only 'institutional treatment'. But the name 'work-house' should be dropped. There was no need for the new institutions to be 'organised like prison[s], nor indeed the internal treatment to be in itself deterrent'. The 'less eligibility' principle of the 1834 Poor Law could be interpreted to mean the surrendering of one's economic independence and being placed for a fixed term under 'national tutelage'. A whole series of institutions should be provided which would be 'based on progressive discipline, which would bring with it more laborious work and less comfort, both within each institution and comparing one grade of institution with another'. Good behaviour would result in less severe discipline; bad behaviour in more severe. Work would no longer be confined to such low-grade activities as stone-breaking or cross-cut sawing. 'The greatest possible variety of employment would be provided, [and, hopefully] made the means of training the individual and fitting him for a return to self-supporting life . . .' On the matter of machinery for his reformed Poor Law, Booth (though he later changed his mind about this[6]) at first proposed that the existing Poor Law Guardians be abolished and their functions handed over to local Poor Law Boards appointed by county or county borough councils, with representation on them ex officio of representatives of the Local Government Board. The central control of the LGB was also to be increased by giving it full control over finance,

[5] Ibid. See also C. Booth, Memo A: Poor Law Unions, England and Wales, Abstract of Statistics with Remarks, Cd. 4983, Min. of Ev. of RC on Poor Laws 1905–9, Appendix vol. xii, p. 355, and Booth's later Address to Poor Law Conference, Feb. 1912. Booth Papers 11/43.

[6] On Booth's change of opinion Jan. 1907 see my article 'Charles Booth and the Royal Commission on the Poor Laws 1905–9', especially note at p. 728.

allowing it to appoint an 'assessor' who would act with the local authorities in administrative matters, and making it responsible for choosing paid officials to control local institutions from a list of names supplied by the county councils.

Charles Booth's attempt to bring about a compromise or reconciliation proved a disastrous failure for a number of reasons. In the first place, his effort was premature. He knew that old-age pensions really were on the Cabinet's agenda;[7] but many of the other Commissioners did not know this till several months after he circulated his first memorandum; they still had not accepted the idea, and felt that they were being hoodwinked into giving their approval to this 'socialist' scheme. Old suspicions of Booth as a crypto-Socialist stood in the way of acceptance of his olive branch by his old opponents, Loch, Octavia Hill, and Helen Bosanquet. In the second place, Lord George Hamilton resented Booth's initiative, as an attempt to usurp his leadership as Chairman. He replied testily that these suggestions 'anticipate[d] the principles of the Report' too far ahead of the evidence.[8] Third, Beatrice Webb had deeper disagreements with some of Booth's proposals than he seemed to appreciate, although she expressed them in an open and friendly way in marginal notes on a copy of his memorandum which she returned to him.[9] Her disagreements were firmly enough stated, but they were offset or masked by those long paragraphs of the memorandum where she had graced the margin with a cordial 'agreed'.

She approved of larger areas, and was happy to accept his proposal that counties or county boroughs should become the units. She favoured his plan for increased centralization, though she was not sure about some of his methods of attaining it. Her eye was captured by the proposal for an 'assessor' to work with the local authorities: she underlined the word 'assessor' and commented: 'Yes the more *judicial* this part of the machinery is the better.' (Here perhaps was the origin of the judicial 'Registrar of Public Assistance' in the Minority Report). Her agreement with the idea of

[7] C. Booth to M. Booth, 12 Feb. 1907. Booth Papers 1/1705.

[8] Lord George Hamilton's Suggestions on Procedure, 1 July 1906. Webb Local Government Collection, vol. 286b; C. Booth to B. Webb, 10 Sept. 1906, ibid., vol. 286.

[9] Booth to B. Webb, 12 June 1906, ibid. He realized she was intending to go 'farther and faster than [he] should', but he hoped that 'we at any rate go a long way together'.

abolishing or diminishing outdoor relief was, however, tempered by remarks showing her unwillingness to yield an inch to COS views: she objected to the withdrawal of State assistance so that private charity might take its place; she wanted the replacement of outdoor relief by the expansion of State social services, removed from the sphere of the Poor Law. She objected to old-age pensions administered through the Poor Law: she wanted them administered through the Post Office, as in New Zealand; and she entirely rejected his notion that children should still remain under the Poor Law, under however stretched a definition: she wanted their care transferred to the county Education Committees.

Although Beatrice Webb had not yet fully worked out a plan for the 'break-up of the Poor Law', her comments on Booth's memorandum already indicated the direction in which her thoughts were running. They had already moved beyond the machinery of a county Poor Law Board (which Sidney Webb had approved of in the 1890s), and she suggested that it would be 'better to make it a statutory committee of the County Council with co-optation of outsiders'. Booth's plan for having paid officers managing Poor Law institutions subject to the direct control of the LGB also received the comment: 'This takes the institutions out of the hands of the County authority? This goes dead against modern tendency of greater autonomy of County & County Borough action & cd. not be carried & wd. I think be bad if it were.'

Three months later Charles Booth wrote to Beatrice Webb about the failure of his initiative, remarking that it seemed 'almost impossible to lift [the Commission] out of the rut in which I fear the Chairman prefers it to remain'.[10] But at that very moment, Lord George Hamilton, having rebuffed Booth, decided to reassert his leadership by launching a memorandum of his own on 'provisional working ideas'.[11] His ideas were much more general than Booth's, but not dissimilar, except on one main item. He proposed larger Poor Law areas, a new type of Poor Law authority (leaving open the question of what type), an increase in power for the central authority, and compulsory detention for certain classes of pauper. His disagreement was over outdoor relief, where he protested against what he believed to be the view of many members of the

[10] C. Booth to B. Webb, 10 Sept. 1906, ibid.
[11] Suggestions for some Provisional Working Ideas, 21 Sept. 1906, ibid., vol. 286b.

Commission who favoured its abolition. He feared abolition might 'result in something like a rebellion in the rural districts', and he pointed out that the cost of institutional relief was high compared with outdoor relief. The time had now come, he suggested, for setting up a number of small discussion committees in the Commission, and he recommended five of these: a Transfer of Functions Committee, to consider whether to transfer the Guardians' powers to other authorities; an Areas Committee to discuss Poor Law areas; a Central Authority Committee to concern itself with problems of centralization and uniformity; a Detention Committee to debate compulsory powers; and a Prevention Committee to explore methods of 'the prevention of pauperism'.[12]

Lord George's suggestions provoked another, and, as far as Beatrice Webb was concerned, the final procedural squabble on the Commission. Helen Bosanquet once again rallied her supporters to oppose the division of the Commission into small committees, and by a majority decision it was resolved to have only two large committees to be called the 'Outdoor Relief Committee' and the 'Indoor Relief Committee'. For Beatrice Webb, who had continued to advocate small committees, and who had supported the Chairman's latest proposal[13], this seemed to show the determination of the COS members to keep the inquiry operating within their own framework of ideas. At the meeting where the two new committees were set up she announced that she would not attend either of them, and reinforced her announcement by a letter to the Chairman. She declared her feeling

that such views as I have are quite irrelevant to any distinction between 'Indoor' and 'Outdoor' Relief. Whether any particular person . . . is to be given institutional or domiciliary *treatment* ought to depend not on any generalised principle distinguishing 'outdoor' from 'indoor' relief, but upon expert opinion whether for his case, at the particular period of his illness or of his failure to earn a livelihood, institutional or domiciliary treatment is most likely to cure him. . . . We have first to decide whether we wish to increase or decrease the amount or the area of collective provision or curative treatment. With regard to the aged, the sick and the children, at any rate, I wish to enormously *increase* the area and the efficiency of the provision . . . of the curative treatment provided by the State . . . With

[12] Draft Scheme of Committees based on the Chairman's Memo of 21 Sept. 1906, ibid., vol. 286.
[13] B. Webb's reply to the Chairman's suggestions, n.d. [?Sept. 1906], ibid.

regard to the able-bodied, I have not yet formulated in my own mind any working hypothesis except a negative one. The Workhouse Test has broken down, and must, in my opinion be dismissed as no longer practicable or even desirable. How far we can invent a curative treatment for the unemployed, I do not know; but I am not at all inclined to assume that even in the case of the able-bodied there is any relevant distinction between 'outdoor' and 'indoor' relief. . . . Here again, we must get the best brains to work on the problem without being in any way shackled by the old formulas, or by any presumption in favour of institutional treatment over domiciliary treatment. . . . I have jotted down these somewhat vague working ideas to show you how hopelessly out of gear my present thoughts are with any notion of drawing a line between 'outdoor' and 'indoor' relief; and how useless my presence would be on either of these Committees . . . [14]

Lord George Hamilton replied to her regretting her 'secession', but hardly expressing any surprise: '. . . whilst not agreeing with you in many things I feel that your opinions are helpful and always a tonic; but I am afraid that Collectivism & Individualism cannot cooperate together'.[15] She knew that there was an undisguised sense of relief on the part of the COS members at her withdrawal. They had certainly made no concession to tempt her to stay; but, given Beatrice's aggressive manner, it did look as if she was in the wrong in deciding to sulk in her tent. Charles Booth certainly thought so: he was aggrieved by her conduct, thinking not only that she was wilful and mistaken in her tactics, but also that she was letting him down by failing to give him the weight of her support. He still had not fully realized, as Beatrice already had, that an unbridgeable gulf had opened between his views and hers. It was not till later that she realized how much she had offended him.[16] But Beatrice's withdrawal came just when Booth's reconciliation tactics seemed to him likeliest to succeed. By the end of 1906 the Chairman and the COS members got the message that old-age pensions really were on the political *tapis*—a thing that they had been steadfastly refusing to believe up to that point.[17] Precisely at

[14] B. Webb to Lord George Hamilton 10 Oct. 1906. Lansbury Papers, vol. 29a. (B. Webb sent a copy of her letter to Lansbury).
[15] Hamilton to B. Webb 19 Dec. 1906. Webb Local Government Collection, vol. 286.
[16] B.W.D., 29 Oct. 1908 (the passage is not printed in *Our Partnership*).
[17] As late as 21 Sept. 1906 the Chairman was maintaining that no scheme of old-age pensions that had been proposed was practicable and would not 'destroy individual thrift'. Lord George Hamilton's Suggestions for some Provisional Working Ideas, Webb Local Government Collection, vol. 286b.

the moment when the way seemed open for discussion on Booth's initial premise, his tactics were wrecked by this withdrawal of co-operation on the left.

Beatrice Webb has been blamed, not only at the time, but also by historians[18] for wrecking any chance of a united Report from the Royal Commission, and one can understand why. But a great deal of the criticism of her tactics has been based on two quite untenable assumptions: first, that there ever was any likelihood of a united report; and second, that her colleagues on the Commission were a kindly, gentle lot, amenable to instruction from an intellectual Socialist. Beatrice Webb, from a tactical point of view, should perhaps have played along with hopes of a consensus for longer than she did; but, given the deep divisions between her point of view and those of the COS supporters, no united Report seems at all probable. The other Commissioners also came to their task with their own firm convictions, and most of them had plenty of weight of their own to throw around. There was an assertion of authority by many of them which was not easily shaken. George Lansbury, by no means an unaggressive character, complained about this to Beatrice Webb when he wrote 'Men like Phelps are so very learned and have such an uncommon good opinion of themselves that for a person like me to try to instruct them is not worth the attempt.'[19] It was necessary for the Socialist cause that Beatrice Webb's confidence in her own superiority could outface even a Phelps. Helen Bosanquet and her friends, C. S. Loch and Octavia Hill, also knew very well how to assert themselves, and under Helen Bosanquet's leadership, they had won the battle of tactics. Beatrice Webb had to choose whether to play the game according to their rules. She chose not to do so.

[18] U. Cormack, *The Welfare State, the Formative Years 1905–9*, Loch Memorial Lecture, London, 1953.

[19] Lansbury to B. Webb, 23 Apr. 1907. Webb Local Government Collection, vol. 286.

8

Attack in Depth

BEATRICE WEBB'S RESEARCH INITIATIVES AND THE RESPONSE OF THE COMMISSION

BEATRICE Webb was quite right in anticipating that the evidence of the Inspectors of the Poor Law Division of the Local Government Board, which was taken first, would be hostile to her point of view. She was anxious that all fourteen should be called[1] because she hoped that at least one of them would disagree with the LGB 'line', and that differences would appear between others which could be exploited in cross-examination. It soon emerged, however, that only minor points could be scored by that method of attack, and its total impact would be trivial. The COS members of the Commission were well able to afford the fullest concessions, because all the Inspectors showed themselves to be keen disciples of the general doctrines of the COS, though some felt that these 'principles' needed to be applied with some latitude in particular areas, while others preferred to give them a harder bureaucratic edge.[2] The general tone of the official case was set at the beginning by the able evidence of the stern Chief Inspector, James Stewart Davy, and Beatrice Webb observed the skilful way in which the ball was tossed between him and the COS members in his cross-examination. Davy spoke favourably of the co-operation which had grown up between the COS and Poor Law officials; he quoted with approval books and pamphlets written by prominent COS theorists; and he agreed to a number of central formulas and definitions as phrased and put to him by some of the COS members.[3] This does not mean that Davy was a weak man led along by COS theorists. On the contrary, he was a man of emphatic and outspoken opinions, who found

---

[1] B.W.D., 2 Dec. 1905; *Our Partnership*, ed. B. Drake and M. Cole (London, 1948), pp. 322–3.

[2] Contrast, e.g., the evidence of F. T. Bircham (Q. 5340) with that of Baldwyn Fleming (Q. 9121), Cd. 4625, Min. of Ev., Appendix vol. i.

[3] Ibid., Qq. 2130–3, 2405–6, 2411, 2419, 2428, 2536, 2971, 3264, 3429.

himself in whole-hearted agreement with the kind of principles the COS was expounding, and he expressed these views crisply and confidently as truths, bolstered by his wealth of administrative experience, which ought to be accepted generally.

Beatrice Webb decided that, in due course, she would use her influence to call witnesses who would present a different case. In the mean time, the best tactics for penetrating the solid defensive front seemed to her to be to go behind the accepted responses to immediate administrative problems through an investigation in depth of a number of crucial issues. During 1906 she initiated five major research projects. The first of these was an investigation of the history of Poor Law policy since 1834, with the help of Sidney Webb and two private research assistants, Miss Mary Longman, a Cambridge Fabian, and Mrs F. H. Spencer (formerly Amy Harrison), a graduate of the LSE. As a supplement to this large-scale project, Mrs Spencer also had in hand a second investigation into the history of the policies actually adopted by selected Boards of Guardians since 1834, and Beatrice Webb had persuaded F. H. Bentham, as Chairman of the Bradford Board, and George Lansbury, as Chairman of the Poplar Board, to make available the records of these two apparently different Boards for comparison. Beatrice Webb's third project was an investigation into applications for outdoor relief in certain Poor Law Unions during a given period, noting—over six months—the effects on the applicants and their families of a grant or a refusal of relief. The research worker was Miss G. Harlock. The fourth major investigation was begun some months later than the first three, when in July 1906, in the course of cross-examination of some COS witnesses who advocated the restriction of medical relief, the idea suddenly struck Beatrice Webb to play up the contrast between the attitude of Poor Law and Public Health authorities to medical services. She suggested to the Commission that the question should be investigated, but when it delayed action, she decided to start her own inquiry, with the help of a group of progressive medical men and women, whose work was organized by Dr Louisa Woodcock.[4] The fifth major inquiry planned by Beatrice Webb was an investigation of the circumstances of children who were being maintained on outdoor relief, and of

---

[4] Dr Woodcock joined the Fabian Society in 1907. N. MacKenzie, *The Letters of Sidney and Beatrice Webb*, vol. ii, *Partnership 1892–1912* (Cambridge, 1978), p. 252.

the adequacy of the relief given them. This research was being carried out by Mary Longman, a social worker, and Marion Phillips, a young Australian historian who was reading for a doctorate at the LSE, both of them members of the Fabian Society. They were studying a sample of a thousand cases selected from the 200,000 children supported on outdoor relief.

At first Beatrice Webb did not encounter much resistance to her private research projects. Little method had been used in settling the kind of special investigations the Commission would undertake, and several Commissioners were pursuing lines of their own. Initially Sir Samuel Provis made some difficulties about giving Beatrice Webb's assistants access to LGB files for their historical research into the policy of the central Poor Law authority. He did not want, he said, 'a poking enquiry into LGB policy'.[5] But after some discussion and an invitation to a carefully arranged dinner-party at 41 Grosvenor Road, he was persuaded of the scientific validity of the investigation[6] and ended not only by assisting the work but also by contributing personally to the appendices of the resulting survey. Another Commissioner, Frank Bentham, was also drawn in to help in the final revision of a supplementary appendix on the policy of his own Poor Law Union in Bradford. When Beatrice Webb presented the first results of her researches on policy for the period from 1834 to 1871 to the Documents Committee of the Commission, she was invited to continue her good work.[7] In fact, she could claim, and did claim later with some plausibility, that four of her five investigations had 'either been undertaken at the express request of the Commission as a whole, or of its Documents Committee; or have received its sanction'.[8]

Rumblings of hostility to her private researches began over her medical services inquiry. In December 1906 she sent out a letter, drafted by Sidney, to 600 local Medical Officers of Health asking for their confidential opinions about the advisability of uniting the medical services provided by the Poor Law and the Public Health Department. The letter was sent through the Medical Officers of Health Society, on her own authority, without consulting her

[5] B.W.D. 12 Feb. 1906; *Our Partnership*, p. 331. The word is given as 'picking' in transcriptions, but appears to be 'poking' in the MS.

[6] B.W.D., 1 Mar. 1906; *Our Partnership*, p. 324.

[7] Documents Committee Minutes, 15 May 1906. Webb Local Government Collection, vol. 286b.

[8] B. Webb to Hamilton, 12 Feb. 1907. Ibid., vol. 286.

colleagues, but mentioning her membership of the Commission. The 'old guard' of COS members quickly got wind of it, and C. S. Loch protested to Lord George Hamilton about this unauthorized gathering of evidence.[9] But nothing was done about it immediately beyond a letter from Lord George Hamilton notifying Beatrice Webb that the Commission was also appointing its own medical investigator.[10] So she simply went ahead with her inquiries. In any case, the official medical investigator turned out to be Dr J. C. McVail, one of her friends. Beatrice Webb confided to her Diary: 'I should not have dared to suggest [his appointment]: it is *almost* sufficiently unfair to the other side to make me protest'.[11] He had been nominated by the Assistant-Secretary of the Commission, John Jeffrey, the closest friend of the Webbs amongst the officials. The gentle and indecisive Dr Downes, the only Commissioner whose knowledge of the medical world was any match for the knowledge of it that Beatrice Webb was quickly acquiring, did not even try to resist her assertiveness, so she found no difficulty at all in getting the Evidence Committee to accept her list of nine medical witnesses, chosen from her advisers and helpers, to be invited to give oral or written evidence.[12] As some of them presented their statements or gave evidence before her medical memorandum was completed, she was able to deploy their material as well.

The real storm began early in 1907, and arose over the investigation of children on outdoor relief. This inquiry invaded one of Helen Bosanquet's particular fields of interest, and, unlike the others, no claim could be made that it had been authorized by the Commission in any way. Helen Bosanquet therefore raised a protest about these unauthorized proceedings at a meeting of the Evidence Committee on 11 February 1907. Beatrice Webb was not a member of the Evidence Committee, and had not attended this meeting as observer, but after discussing the problem the Committee by a majority voted that individual Commissioners should not undertake investigations on a large scale or collect evidence without its consent or the consent of the Commission as a whole, and asked

[9] B.W.D., 18 Dec. 1906; *Our Partnership*, p. 368.
[10] Hamilton to B. Webb, 19 Dec. 1906. Webb Local Government Collection, vol. 286.
[11] B.W.D., 28 Jan. 1907; *Our Partnership*, p. 370.
[12] Minutes of Evidence Committee, 11 Feb. 1907. Webb Local Government Collection, vol. 286b. The names were: Drs Newsholme, Newman, McCleary, Richards, Bond, Davies, Millard, Butler, and Pattin.

Lord George Hamilton to speak to Mrs Webb about it.[13] Instead of
speaking directly to her, Lord George wrote a fairly stern note
telling her of the Evidence Committee's views and saying '. . . I
think it [B. W.'s conduct] is contrary to the almost universal
practice of Commissioners. The Commission as a whole must judge
and decide upon the evidence it intends to collect and use . . .'[14]

The Chairman got no meek response to his rebuke. Beatrice
Webb sent back a letter the next day expressing surprise that her
colleagues should have condemned her conduct without notifying
her that it was under discussion or hearing her defence. She
admitted that the inquiry about children had not been authorized
by the Commission as a whole, or by its Documents or Statistical
Committees as her other investigations had been. She declared,
however, that she had pressed the Commission to undertake such
an inquiry itself. When it had not seemed interested she decided to
put her own researchers on to it, because she felt she could not
make a report without this information. She pointed out that other
Commissioners were making their own similar inquiries, mentioning
Mrs Bosanquet in particular; and she observed that on this and
other Royal Commissions, individual Commissioners had used
their own subordinate investigators. Then she concluded:

This . . . opens up the question of the right of individual Commissioners to
pursue their own enquiries. I entirely accept your view that 'the
Commission as a whole must judge and decide upon the evidence it intends
to collect and use'. For this reason, feeling myself in a minority, I have
never resisted the determination of the Commission as a whole to pursue
certain lines of enquiry, and to ignore others. But it is plain that if, along
with this view, we had to accept the corollary that no individual
Commissioner was at liberty to supplement the official investigations by his
own examination of the facts, and his own enquiries, the majority of any
Royal Commission could not only decide the Majority Report, but could,
by selecting for exploration only those parts of the field which yielded
results favourable to their underlying assumptions, and by refusing to
explore other portions of the field which they thought unimportant,
control even the possible conclusions of the Minority. I venture to suggest
that any member of a Royal Commission is authorised, and indeed bound,

[13] Ibid. The members of the committee were Phelps (in chair), Hamilton,
Bosanquet, Nunn, Gardiner, Hill, and the Bishop of Ross, with Bentham, Booth, and
Downes also attending.
[14] Hamilton to B. Webb, 11 Feb. 1907. Webb Local Government Collection, vol.
286.

to make whatever enquiries, and collect whatever evidence, he considers necessary to enable him to report upon any part of the reference—a reference which is addressed to him individually, as well as collectively to the Commission as a whole . . .

I fully recognise that the position of a member of the Commission entails two special obligations to his colleagues. He must not, by his investigations, obstruct or impair the investigations of the Commission as a whole; or even interfere with those of individual colleagues. I have throughout been scrupulously careful in this respect . . . The more practical obligation upon every Commissioner is to place at the disposal of the Commission all his knowledge and information relevant to the reference, including all his material and other evidence. This . . . I intend to do.[15]

This brought a more placatory reply from Lord George, asking her to tone down some of the sharper passages of her letter before it was submitted to the Evidence Committee. But he reiterated his own and the Evidence Committee's view that independent investigations could forestall or impair the action of the Commission as a whole, and be an embarrassment, because they had 'a tendency to shape themselves according to the idiosyncracy of those running the investigation'; if accepted, they were too often unchecked, if rejected, this action appeared to be a slur on their author.[16] Beatrice Webb agreed to tone down her letter a bit, but she stood her ground:

My position on the Commission is not an altogether pleasant one & I am afraid that I must necessarily rouse some antagonism. Few Majorities willingly concede belligerent rights to a weak Minority. That does not relieve the Minority from its duty of patiently insisting on its rights even at the cost of some unpopularity . . .

If after reading the letter there remains any doubt on the right of individual Commissioners to make at their own expense subject to the two conditions stated in my letter any investigations which they deem necessary in supplement of those which the Commission as a whole chooses to undertake, I think we had better take the opinion of one or perhaps two eminent constitutional lawyers. Should the matter be raised again I shall formally propose this course . . .[17]

She sent a copy of her letter to her friend R. B. Haldane, who replied with male jocularity:

[15] B. Webb to Hamilton, 12 Feb. 1907, ibid.
[16] Hamilton to B. Webb, 13 Feb. 1907, ibid.
[17] B. Webb to Hamilton, n.d. [?13 Feb. 1907. Draft by B. Webb with emendations by S. Webb], ibid.

My dear Mrs Webb,

Splendid—the adversary will not be in a hurry to encounter you again. You have routed him as completely as the police routed the suffragettes.

Sidney, whom I met in the street, told me that Ld. George had hastily retired. He had no alternative in the face of this artillery.

Ever yours,
R. B. Haldane.[18]

In fact, Lord George Hamilton and Beatrice Webb came to a 'fair working compromise' on a memorandum to be put before the Evidence Committee.[19] In it, the Commission was to express its indebtedness to her for the trouble she had been to in carrying out research she had been asked to do. But the particular investigation relating to outdoor relief of children was to be taken over by the Commission, employing the same research workers, but put under a new superintendent, Dr Ethel Williams of Newcastle. (Beatrice Webb remarked in a letter to Edward Pease, the Secretary of the Fabian Society, that this meant that her former researchers would now get a considerably increased salary, and that Dr Williams was an 'old acquaintance' who was 'coming to stay with me next week'.[20]) On the general question, the memorandum laid down that the authority of individual Commissioners and the Commission as a whole should be *kept apart*, and that if individual Commissioners wished to obtain information at their own expense and trouble

the authority of the Commission should not be used or named in connection with such enquiries unless sanction be expressly given. If evidence so collected be offered to the Commission it must reserve to itself full discretion as to whether or not such information be printed.

So things remained for a time. Beatrice Webb's own researchers of course went on with the inquiry into the effects of the refusal of outdoor relief; and she immediately began to think of starting new ones. She wrote to Edward Pease about the prospect of beginning an inquiry into the effect of dead-end jobs for boys in causing their later unemployment,[21] and she sent another letter to R. C. K.

---

[18] Haldane to B. Webb, 14 Feb. 1907, ibid.
[19] Hamilton to B. Webb, 28 Feb. 1907 and Memo of 10 Mar. 1907, ibid.
[20] MacKenzie, *Letters*, ii. 252; see also B. Webb to Mary Playne, 19 Mar. 1907, Passfield Papers, and *Our Partnership*, pp. 376, 378.
[21] B. Webb to Pease, 18 Apr. [1907], MacKenzie, *Letters*, ii. 252.

Ensor, the Oxford historian and Fabian, asking him to organize investigations into all experiments for dealing with able-bodied unemployed.[22] She was not satisfied with the Commission's attitude to the problem of unemployment, nor with the report on relief works which had been done for it by the Revd John Pringle, a young COS man, and Cyril Jackson, a Toynbee Hall man more favourable to the Webbs. She wrote to Ensor:

. . . Messrs Pringle and Jackson's investigation did little else but discredit relief work and suggested no alternative ways of dealing with the unemployed. Moreover their investigation was limited by their reference *to the working of the Unemployed Acts* and they were not asked to enquire or report into the working of the Poor Law alternatives of the Workhouse test, and the Labour Yard. These alternatives have also been ruled out of our enquiry next autumn, as it is assumed that we have dealt with them in our general enquiry into Poor Law Administration which is now practically concluded. That is not the case, and these alternatives therefore hold the field if we arrive at an unfavourable verdict on relief work. What I wanted (but was over-ruled) was an enquiry into *all ways of dealing with the Ablebodied or persons assumed to be Ablebodied*, including even the Casual Ward, and therefore Vagrancy. Only in that way shall we get a statesmanlike grip of the question. The Charity Organisation Society policy, on the other hand, is to break the subject up into little bits and get a negative conclusion on each division so as to fall back on the 'Non Possumus' attitude.

Now what I should like would be some help both in suggestions as to possible reforms and actual investigation into facts. Would it be possible to form a little Committee to take each way of dealing with the Ablebodied into consideration, getting all evidence together on each point, and looking at each by the light of the others? If then we could get a secretary (for a small salary to do the clerk's work and possibly some additional investigation) we might draw up a report of our own which the progressive members of the Commission might circulate as a memorandum . . .[23]

Early in the Commission, Beatrice Webb had told Lord George Hamilton that she had 'not yet formulated in [her] own mind any working hypothesis' concerning the able-bodied.[24] Now, in April 1907, she set about formulating some, in her characteristic way. She and Sidney began by making an index of 'all the expedients that have been tried since 1834, with the evidence we need for coming to

---

[22] B. Webb to Ensor, 4 May 1907, ibid., p. 253.
[23] Ibid.
[24] B. Webb to Hamilton, 10 Oct. 1906. Lansbury Papers, vol. 29a.

a conclusion about them'.[25] From this, they then drew up an analysis and set of tentative conclusions.[26] She then submitted a 'Memo on Lines of Inquiry and Evidence about the Unemployed' to the Commission on 17 April 1907. This opened on a beguiling note that she knew would appeal even to the more conservatively disposed of her colleagues, by declaring that what stood out in the mass of statistics and evidence before them was 'the *total and universal failure of relief works for the unemployed [her italics]* . . . whether conceived in the spirit of Mr Chamberlain's Circular of 1886, or under the conditions of Employment of Workmen Act, 1905'. If this conclusion were accepted, she went on, it would 'somewhat startle Parliament and public opinion'. In order to substantiate it, a number of the arguments that had been advanced in its support would need to be backed up by 'irrefutable evidence'. For example the argument that relief works caused an increase in unemployment, advanced by the Commission's investigators, Jackson and Pringle, would need support for its three main hypotheses: first, that relief works diverted men from ordinary employment; second, that they encouraged employers to discharge their workmen in slack periods; and third, that they encouraged men to throw up their jobs lightly. She suggested that these hypotheses might be tested by asking the Charity Organisation Society to furnish evidence, obtained perhaps from the Chief Officer of the Parks Department of the London County Council, or from foremen in the neighbourhood of relief works. Opponents of relief works also claimed that they were costly to the public, that the unemployed did not give a fair return for the public expenditure upon them. Supporters of relief works, however, made an opposite claim. These competing claims would need to be tested by a proper statistical survey. The argument had also been advanced that relief works caused moral harm to the men employed, in that they deliberately shirked their assignment of work. This would involve taking evidence from the managers of relief works.

Quite apart from criticism of relief works that had been attempted, she declared, the Commission would need to come up

---

[25] B.W.D. 10 Apr. 1907; *Our Partnership*, p. 375.
[26] *Our Partnership*, p. 375, and Memo on the Lines of Enquiry and Evidence about the Unemployed 17 Apr. 1907, Para. 1(c), Webb Local Government Collection, vol. 286c.

with some practical proposals for alternative remedies. Beatrice Webb argued that the Commission's official investigators had so far not provided any answers, except for some vague references to labour exchanges, emigration, farm colonies, and industrial schools. Obviously the first step was to get as reliable statistics as possible about the extent of unemployment. She suggested that this might be supplied by Arthur Wilson-Fox, the Comptroller of the Statistical Department of the Board of Trade, and A. L. Bowley, Professor of Statistics at the London School of Economics. Then there was the question of increasing the mobility of labour, and on this she suggested hearing evidence from William Henry Beveridge, a young member of the Central Unemployed Body for London, who had made a special study of labour exchanges. On the matter of regularizing public employment by government bodies distributing their normal orders in such a way as to provide more work in slack times, she again advised calling Professor A. L. Bowley, who was an advocate of that policy. But some local authorities objected to it as contrary to the organization of a permanent 'Works Department', so she suggested Will Crooks of Poplar be invited to put their point of view. Above all, Beatrice Webb stressed the importance of casual labour. So long as a large casual labour force existed, it would swamp all attempts to relieve unemployment. Unless the casual labour problem were dealt with at its source, no solution to the unemployment problem could be permanent: 'If . . . we could get rid of the whole of the unemployed and the whole of the adult male paupers and vagrants of today—*there would be, in a very few years, an exactly similar class reproduced, practically as numerous*' (*her italics*). On decasualization, she proposed that William Beveridge should be heard about experiments at the docks, and some railway managers about those in their industry. The Commission would also need to consider the raising of the school age and the provision of half-time technical training by employers of boys between 14 and 18 years of age. Sidney Webb and representatives of some big firms employing boys would be useful witnesses on that topic. Beatrice concluded her memorandum by declaring bluntly that so far as 'institutional treatment' went, the workhouse had already proved a failure; attention should be turned to farm colonies and industrial retraining schools as alternative methods, and a comprehensive survey of experiments in those directions should be made. She did not conceal her scepticism of farm colonies and her belief that industrial schools would be a better and more practicable answer.

This memorandum of suggestions was, as it happened, quite well received by her colleagues on the Commission. The reason was that it proffered more questions and suggestions for going about answering them than would-be solutions. As she confessed in an entry to her Diary at the time: '. . . I am blest if I know yet what to do with the able-bodied!'[27] Her colleagues were equally perplexed, and Professor Smart also submitted a memorandum proposing the investigation of much the same topics. She thought that either Professor Smart's or her proposals would have been 'a business-like basis' for the Commission's preliminary discussion of unemployment, but the Chairman spoiled the meeting by 'making up, out of ours, [an agenda] of his own which sprawled over the subject without sequence or order'.[28] However, most of the topics for inquiry and the more important witnesses she had suggested were accepted. There was some unwillingness to call Sidney Webb, but the two labour members—Lansbury and Chandler—insisted upon it,[29] and the proposal was agreed to. The strongest criticism of Beatrice's memorandum came, in the event, not from her opponents but from her supporter George Lansbury. He did not put these forward at the meeting, but in two private letters to her. These show that he was not simply a passive supporter of Beatrice's ideas; he had interesting suggestions to make, some of which she later incorporated into her plans for reform as she elaborated them.[30]

Lansbury thought that the social causes, rather than individual moral causes, of unemployment should have been more strongly emphasized, in particular that while moral or physical defects might determine which persons were sacked first, they did not determine the volume of unemployment. This led him to the conclusion that 'the idea that unemployment exchanges or labour bureaus are going to extend the area of employment . . . is . . . quite nonsensical . . . and the only utility of the exchanges is to register people who are unemployed'. He approved her observation that if all the unemployed could be removed, they would be recreated if industrial conditions remained the same, but added: 'You will

[27] B.W.D., 23 Apr. 1907; *Our Partnership*, p. 378.   [28] Ibid.
[29] B. Webb to Mary Playne, 2 Feb. 1908; MacKenzie, *Letters*, ii. 281.
[30] Lansbury to B. Webb, 23 and 24 Apr. 1907. Webb Local Government Collection, vol. 286.

excuse me for saying it, but if we adopted all your suggestions, the same thing would happen.' In his opinion, the provision of work for the unemployed had to be administered by a central government department, 'which could be called a Public Works or a Labour Department'. It could not be left to the localities. Parliament should vote each year a sum for public works, and if these benefited a particular locality, it might be required to make a contribution. Lansbury then returned to his hobby-horse of labour colonies, although he was 'aware, of course, that you are opposed to them'; he announced his intention of fighting to include in the Commission's report a scheme of labour colonies in three grades. These were: (1) for vagrants ('The proposal to hand over the tramp to the police will meet with my very strenuous opposition, even if I am alone on the Commission in taking that line of action'); (2) for ordinary able-bodied paupers regularly applying for relief; and (3) for the ordinary unemployed . . . 'the hope for the first 2 being that they will eventually work their way into the third, and the hope for those in the third being that one day that they will work their way on to the land of England or in the Colonies'.

Lansbury's criticisms were a warning to Beatrice Webb that it might be dangerous for her to go too far in appeasing her other colleagues, and that the Labour members had some strong views of their own, which they were at this time presenting in their 'Right to Work' Bill to Parliament. Though Beatrice Webb remained unconvinced by Lansbury's plea for labour colonies, she was able to find a place for a central labour department and a graded set of retraining centres—including farm-training centres—in her later plans. In any case, she soon discovered that the acceptance of her proposals by other members of the Commission had strict limits, and had been determined more by their perplexity on the question of unemployment than by any real willingness to accept her ideas. On 8 April 1908 she offered to the Commission the analysis and set of conclusions which she and Sidney Webb had made of all the experiments, past and present, by Poor Law and municipal authorities and voluntary charitable agencies in relief of the able-bodied. Her offer got an enthusiastic reception at first from Dr Phelps, who wrote to say that he was 'pretty confident that [the Evidence Committee] will not let your paper slip'.[31] But four days

[31] Phelps to B. Webb, 9 Apr. 1908. Webb Local Government Collection, vol. 286a.

later he was obliged to write: 'No! the Commission thought on the whole that yr. paper had better appear independently . . .'.[32] Lord George Hamilton and the majority of the Evidence Committee had vetoed its acceptance on the ground that the investigation had not been previously authorized, and was based on evidence not before the Commission.[33]

In the mean time, Beatrice and Sidney Webb had been threshing out their general ideas about the future of the Poor Law. The full conception of the 'break-up of the Poor Law' was developing gradually in her mind from April 1907. It represented the drawing together of the trend of policy she had been suggesting in each particular field of Poor Law activity and combining this with the notion of abolishing the Guardians, handing over their functions in each of the fields to committees of the county and county borough councils. At first she thought of getting this policy adopted by the Fabian method of one reform at a time, as she recorded in her Diary entry for 10 April 1907:

Suddenly it occurred to me that it would ease matters if I did not propose abolishing Boards of Guardians straight away and creating a new authority [*She said to Sidney*:] 'The majority will flounder about seeking for a new bottle for the old wine. Why not leave the old thing standing and take the stuff out drop by drop—the sick first, and place them under the sanitary authority—then the children, placed under the education authority—then the aged—pensions—perhaps the unemployed and the vagrants. The Boards of Guardians could be steadily reduced in functions—institutions and officials could be slowly handed over and at the last the remnant might be taken over by the Borough Council or County Council'. 'That is a brilliant idea', chuckled Sidney.[34]

Sidney Webb tried to encourage her to pursue those 'Fabian' tactics, which as a shrewd committee manipulator he would have adopted himself if he had been on the Commission. Beatrice Webb might have had more success if she had been able to do so: she would certainly have carried more of her colleagues a long way further with her. But there were two difficulties. She foresaw one of them: that the majority of the Commissioners would refuse to postpone discussion about the nature of the new authority to be set up until the question of the transfer of the different classes of

[32] Phelps to B. Webb, 13 Apr. 1908, ibid.
[33] Hamilton to B. Webb, 9 Apr. 1908, ibid.
[34] This passage is not included in *Our Partnership*.

paupers was settled.[35] What she did not foresee was something about herself: that when she had got a bright general idea into her head she could not refrain from communicating it. Unlike her husband, she was not a natural Fabian tactician; she had to be taking the lead, whether her colleagues liked it or not. It was not long before her general report on the 'Break-up of the Poor Law' was being composed.

The general substance of Beatrice Webb's memoranda, and their reception by the Commission needs to be traced, and for this purpose each memorandum will be considered in the order in which it arrived in completed form before the Commission as a whole.

1. *The Report on the Policy of the Central Authority 1834–1907, (with Appendices on the Administration of the Bradford and Poplar Boards of Guardians 1837/8–1906).*[36]

The brilliant 'Memorandum on the Policy of the Central Authority from 1834 to 1907', which later became the basis of the Webbs' book on *English Poor Law Policy*, advanced an ingenious and sophisticated argument. It began by accepting that the 1834 Poor Law Report embodied three principles: (1) that the treatment of paupers should be nationally uniform, (2) that their condition should be made 'less eligible' (i.e. less desirable) than that of the lowest-paid worker in independent employment, and (3) that the 'outdoor relief' (i.e. relief in the paupers' own homes) should be reduced as far as possible, and relief should be given 'indoors' (i.e. in a workhouse). Beatrice Webb then proceeded to point out the deviations from these 'principles', both in theory and in practice, that were allowed even at the very outset of their proclamation.

Those 'principles' were primarily intended by the 1834 Commissioners to apply to able-bodied male paupers and their families, although no clear definition of 'able-bodied' was given in the Report or the subsequent legislation. There was certainly no clear indication that this treatment was to replace the existing system of outdoor relief generally for the non-able-bodied—the sick and the aged and infirm, or orphaned and deserted children. It was not even clear if it was to apply to able-bodied unmarried women, widows,

---

[35] B.W.D., 10 Apr. 1907.
[36] RC on the Poor Laws 1905–9, Cd. 4983, Min. of Ev., Appendix. vol. xii, pp. 109–260.

or deserted wives who were destitute: there was no phrase excluding them from the category of 'able-bodied', but the term usually referred to men only. In the cases where non-able-bodied paupers were obliged to be given 'indoor treatment' (because they had nowhere else to go or no one to look after them) the Commissioners of 1834 envisaged that they should be classified separately and accommodated in institutions separate from the workhouse for the able-bodied: the children were to be educated by a qualified schoolmaster; the aged were to have a separate building and be allowed 'to enjoy their indulgences'; no mention of indoor treatment of the sick was made, and the assumption was that the existing practice of outdoor relief would continue, except for special separate institutions for lunatics and the blind. Where the able-bodied were concerned, the workhouse was not intended to be a prison or place of compulsory confinement. The inmates were to be free to go whenever they pleased, but so long as they remained their conditions were to be 'less eligible'. This was to be achieved not by making them perform 'fictitious, artificial or useless labour'. Their labour was supposed to be useful, especially in producing articles for use in workhouses and prisons. Their 'less eligibility' was to consist in their receiving less food, inferior clothing, and worse accommodation than they would have enjoyed in private employment (to encourage them to leave and get it).

Beatrice Webb traced the development of policy in the three periods 1834–47, 1847–71, and 1871–1907, corresponding to the times when the Poor Law Commissioners, the Poor Law Board, and the Local Government Board were the central authority. Up to 1847, she found that little had been done to attain national uniformity, even in regard to able-bodied men, and it was altogether disregarded in the treatment of the non-able-bodied. There was a wide diversity of practices, and local Boards of Guardians largely devised their own policies. Outdoor relief was widespread (especially for relief of the non-able-bodied) and the few measures that the Commissioners took to reduce it were ineffectual. In 144 Poor Law Unions (one-fifth of the whole number) the 'workhouse test' was not used, and as a substitute the practice had grown up of making able-bodied male paupers break stones in stone-yards as a test of the genuineness of their claim for relief. Within the workhouses, the Commissioners had abandoned as impossible the task of achieving 'less eligibility' by less food, inferior clothing, and worse accommodation than those enjoyed by the lowest class of independent workers, and were attempting to secure it instead by monotonous and not very useful toil, lack of recreation and mental stimulus for the inmates, and confinement of them within the workhouse. In response to the relatively loose rein of the Commissioners, there was developing amongst some self-appointed intellectual theorists on Poor Law affairs, and some of the subordinate officers of the Commissioners, a tendency to advocate 'stern' policies and to interpret 'less eligibility' more rigorously than the original 1834 theorists did, as applicable to all paupers, not merely to the able-bodied. That line of thinking had not, however, affected the policy of the Commissioners by 1847.

In the second period, that of the Poor Law Board of 1847–71, Beatrice Webb argued that no greater attempt was made to bring general policy into conformity with the recommendation of the Report of 1834. There was no further endeavour to secure national uniformity. Outdoor relief was indeed allowed to increase. The main characteristic of the period was 'a slow and almost unself-conscious development of a supplementary policy in respect to certain favoured classes of paupers, notably children and the sick'[37]—giving training and treatment which placed them at an advantage as compared with the lowest class of independent labourer. The advances in public education at the end of this period solved a difficulty for the Poor Law authorities in the treatment of children:

By this beginning of the communistic provision of education for the whole population . . . the Poor Law authorities were enabled to escape . . . from the embarrassing dilemma of either placing the pauper child in a position of vantage, or of deliberately bringing up the quarter of a million pauper children in a state of ignorance similar to that of the children of the poorest independent labourer prior to 1870.[38]

The Poor Law Board was encouraged to aim at the removal of children from workhouses to special schools. The progress of the public health movement similarly encouraged the central authority to urge 'apathetic or parsimonious Boards of Guardians' to spend more on medical relief, without troubling their heads about whether it was contradicting the 'less eligibility' principle. During the Lancashire Cotton Famine in 1863–6, when many respectable

---

[37] Ibid., p. 158.   [38] Ibid., p. 167.

and skilled cotton workers were thrown out of employment, some remarkably successful experiments in providing unemployed relief works were sanctioned. There was even a movement, during the later 1860s, towards the improvement of workhouses. The central authority did not go so far as to abandon 'mixed' General Workhouses and establish the separate institutions for separate categories of pauper which the 1834 Commissioners had recommended. But many minor improvements were achieved. Buildings were more substantial; separate dormitories, dayrooms, and yards (but not dining-rooms) were provided for separate categories; better dietaries were prescribed. These were not enforced by General Order, and so were dependent upon 'the slow and haphazard discretion of the 600 Boards of Guardians', but the central authority's urging had some effect, and it did represent a vast advance on earlier policy. At the end of the period, the Poor Law Board began to place emphasis on co-operation between the Poor Law and organized voluntary charity, which became more prominent a feature of the next phase.

The regime of the Local Government Board from 1871 did not mark any official change in Poor Law policy. But two distinct influences on policy emerged. The first was produced by a 'new school of unofficial Poor Law experts [*meaning the COS*] who were in favour of the "logical development" of the "principles of 1834" '[39]—of developing them in ways 'which went beyond any proposals of the 1834 Report, or any policy embodied in the documents of the Central Authority of 1834–47'. Their ideas were taken up by 'the able, zealous and somewhat doctrinaire [Poor Law] inspectorate, especially between 1871 and 1885'. This new policy involved a steady pressure exercised through the Inspectors to reduce outdoor relief, not only to the able-bodied but to the non-able-bodied as well. There was an increased emphasis on 'testing' destitution, on vigilant inquiry into applicants' *bona fides*, and on reducing the burden on the rates. The 'offer of the House' was seen as an appropriate objective test. As far as the able-bodied were concerned, the policy was to make the workhouse exclusively disciplinary, and the General Workhouse came in for criticism as not being disciplinary enough: the setting up of special 'Test Workhouses' for the able-bodied was advocated. But 'offer of the

[39] Ibid., p. 189.

House' in general was proposed as a way of preventing the aged and the sick from expecting outdoor relief, and forcing their families and friends to help them. For the first time, outdoor relief to women was discouraged, especially to single able-bodied women without children and to widows with no children or only one child. The policy of taking the children of widows into the workhouse was also advocated, not as appropriate treatment for the children but as a test for the mother. Beatrice Webb noted, with scarcely veiled sarcasm, that there could be little doubt that the policy was effective in reducing greatly the number of women and children receiving outdoor relief. The assumption of this 'stern' treatment was that 'deserving' cases would be looked after by voluntary charity—'assumed . . . to be always at hand whenever required'.

The other, and contradictory, influence on policy of the period after 1871—and particularly after 1885—was what

some might term a sentimental, others an enlightened, humanitarianism with regard to particular sections [of paupers]—the unemployed, the decayed members of friendly societies, the 'deserving and poor' generally. This humanitarianism was certainly in direct contradiction of the 'Principles of 1834'. How far it may be said to have embodied, perhaps unconsciously, other principles will subsequently appear.[40]

For the non-able-bodied poor on 'indoor' relief, the policy was a continuation and an extension of an earlier one. The idea continued to grow that children, so far as possible, should be removed from the workhouses, and ordinary education, not merely education for menial occupations, should be provided for them. In 1904, the inspection of Poor Law schools was transferred to the Board of Education. The provision for the sick was expanded so far that the researcher had to note the 'remarkable spectacle' of the Poor Law authorities 'annually congratulating themselves' on attracting cases to their 'expensive Poor Law institutions'. In the treatment of the aged, there was a further development in favour of the policy recommended by the 1834 report that the old might be allowed to enjoy their indulgences. After 1892, tobacco was provided; from 1894, the ingredients for making tea were allowed to women; in 1896 coffee or cocoa could be had by both sexes. Separate rooms or cubicles were furnished; well-behaved old people were allowed to go out for walks or be visited by friends; the respectable were

---

[40] Ibid., p. 187.

separated from others; special foods were given if needed; libraries and books allowed and even, occasionally, pianos.

But the revolutionary breakthrough came in February 1886 with the Circular of Joseph Chamberlain (then President of the Local Government Board) which 'may be said to have, for good or evil, begun a new era as regards the treatment of such of the able-bodied as were classed as "the unemployed" '.[41] The unemployed were to be provided with work by the municipalities, with assistance towards the cost by Poor Law authorities. It was a revival of the expedient adopted during the Lancashire Cotton Famine of 1863–6, under less carefully controlled conditions. Later presidents of the LGB—Ritchie, Fowler, Shaw-Lefevre, and Walter Long—extended the Chamberlain system, until the situation of 1905 was reached, where many devices were used to aid the unemployed—assisted emigration or internal migration, temporary employment, and labour exchanges at the expense of municipal rates, with relief or wages paid for by voluntary subscription or subventions from the national Exchequer. Experiments in farm colonies were pioneered by the Guardians of Poplar and Bradford, and by voluntary organizations such as the Salvation Army and the Church Army.

The position that had been reached by 1907, Beatrice Webb concluded, was that the 'principles of 1834' had become obsolete. The principle of 'national uniformity' had been in practice abandoned, except for vagrants. There was no uniform policy concerning other able-bodied paupers, and with regard to the non-able-bodied (four-fifths of the whole) 'the precisely opposite principle has been adopted, that of permitting experimental variation by the 646 boards of guardians'.[42] The principle of less eligibility also was applied unreservedly only to vagrants. The standards for other able-bodied paupers were now subject to all sorts of experimental departures. Even the 'stigma' of electoral disqualification remained only as a vestige, and had been removed from the unemployed coming under the Unemployed Workmen Act of 1905. Less eligibility had been found to be inappropriate, and had been virtually abandoned over large areas of treatment of the non-able-bodied. The principle of the 'workhouse system' had never been recommended even by the 1834 Report for any but the able-bodied. Attempts to extend it were based on a misconception;

[41] Ibid., p. 195.   [42] Ibid., p. 241.

and alternative methods had become available even for the able-bodied.

New principles, unknown in 1834, had gradually emerged, and were already discernible in 1907. First, the principle of curative treatment—the direct opposite of the principle of less eligibility; second, the principle of universal provision of services designed to achieve certain universal minimum living standards; and third, the principle of compulsion by which the State required that citizens did not neglect the opportunities it provided for securing a better life for themselves and their families. Beatrice Webb maintained that the three principles, both the old and the new, hung together to form aspects of a single philosophy of life. The three principles of 1834 spelt *laissez-faire*: the non-responsibility of the community for anything beyond keeping the destitute alive; the reliance on economic pressure resulting from letting alone to force the unfortunate to conform. The three 'principles of 1907', on the contrary, embodied the doctrine of mutual obligation between the community and the individual, an obligation on both sides to maintain a certain minimum of civilized life—an obligation unknown in the world of *laissez-faire*. But the new principles still needed clear recognition and clear working out in their practical application.

Beatrice Webb remarked, immediately after the submission of her memorandum to the Commission as a whole that it 'was (to say the least of it) coldly received'.[43] That was putting it mildly. Only Lord George Hamilton and Professor William Smart wrote to her appreciating the amount of work that had gone into it, and they both reserved their judgements about its conclusions.[44] The 'old guard' of the Charity Organisation Society found no difficulty in forbearing to cheer. If Beatrice Webb's interpretation of the development of Poor Law policy were correct, the COS's own historical interpretation of the beneficent principles of 1834 broadening down to the policy advocated by the COS in the present was false. Indeed, it suggested that 'strict' Poor Law policies misunderstood the original 1834 principles and contradicted the

[43] Minutes of the Documents Committee, 19 Nov. 1907 (at which a letter from B. Webb was read). Webb Local Government Collection, vol. 286b.
[44] Smart to B. Webb, 4 July 1907, Hamilton to B. Webb, 17 Sept. 1907, ibid., vol. 286. Booth and Robinson, however, had commended the first draft of the memo (up to 1847) earlier—Booth to Webb, 10 Sept. 1906, Robinson to B. Webb, 26 Sept. 1906, ibid.

evolution of Poor Law practice. Helen Bosanquet therefore denounced the Webb interpretation roundly as 'propaganda'.

She declared that the whole direction of the research was misguided: Poor Law policy was not made at the level of the central authority, upon whose records the Webbs' depended; it was made at the level of the 646 Boards of Guardians. All the central authority's records would tell was the principal direction in which the Guardians' work was thought, at one time or another, to require criticism and stimulation. The Webbs' approach thus allowed them to convey a false impression of dramatic breaks and changes of policy. In fact, there were no such sudden changes—merely a gradual development in an attempt to adapt the 1834 principles to local conditions. Mrs Bosanquet also attacked the Webbs' research methods in getting their research assistants to note 'facts' on identically sized slips of paper. It was too easy with such a method to divorce excerpts from their context, and to let some of the slips of paper fall under the table whenever it was convenient for the interpreter to make 'false omissions'. The principle of national uniformity was never abandoned as a principle, whatever deviation occurred in practice. Nor was the principle of less eligibility abandoned, in spite of the Webbs' claim. The Webbs, she pointed out, admitted that there was no 'explicit statement' of its abandonment by the central authority; but they were supposed to be dealing with 'explicit statements', not moving from intentions to policy as it was actually carried out as it happened to suit their argument. The 'workhouse system' was not a *principle* at all: it was a *means* of applying the less eligibility principle.

Helen Bosanquet then turned her attention to the alleged 'new principles' of 1907. She claimed that the principle of curative treatment was actually embodied in the principles of 1834 and the practices that developed from them—quite explicitly in the case of the sick and children, but implicitly also in the treatment of the able-bodied in inducing them to restore themselves to independence. As for the principle of compulsion, while this was involved in the nature of the large, modern State, it would be better for those who respected liberty to go much more slowly and less far in that direction than the Webbs seemed to be proposing. The principle of universal provision had no place at all in the Poor Law—no more place in the Poor Law of 1907 than it ever had. The Webbs were trying to foist that principle on to it, 'purposely confusing the issue', trying to get in 'the thin end of the Communist wedge'. There ought to be a clear distinction between those social services where the State provided 'something for all' and the Poor Law where it provided 'all for some'.[45]

The younger members of the COS (Hancock Nunn, T. G. Gardiner, and L. R. Phelps) and those who might have thought of themselves as belonging to a 'centre group' as Charles Booth did (it also included F. H. Bentham, Professor Smart, and possibly Lord George Hamilton) were wary of Beatrice Webb's interpretation of Poor Law policy, but by no means so vociferous against it as Mrs Bosanquet. There was one aspect of it indeed which rather appealed to them: the notion that the original 1834 recommendations were more generous than they had been represented to be by the 'stern' school of Poor Law interpreters on one side and by some Socialist critics on the other. This gave the policy of 'getting back to the principles of 1834' a less harsh meaning than it might otherwise have seemed to convey. Professor Smart presented a rival memorandum to the Commission on Poor Law principles and policy from 1832 to 1877. It was a dull chronological summary lacking all of Beatrice Webb's organizing capacity and interpretative sparkle, but Smart too was concerned to argue that the 1834 principles had been intended to apply only to the able-bodied, not to the sick, the aged, or the pauper children.[46] Charles Booth also believed that it was possible to return to the true principles of 1834, removing the accretion of obsolete 'hallowed phrases' which had become associated with them.[47] It does not seem likely that this was quite the effect that the Webbs had intended. On 14 November 1907 Beatrice Webb wrote a letter to Professor Smart, as Chairman of the Documents Committee, asking to be relieved of her promise to write a report on policy pursued by Guardians between 1834 and 1907 (which was to supplement her report on the policy of the Central Authority), for she no longer thought that such a report would be welcomed by the Committee.[48] To this, Professor Smart

---

[45] These criticisms, which were made at the time, were later consolidated systematically in H. Bosanquet's review of the Webbs' *English Poor Law Policy* in the *Ec. J.* 20 (1910), 182–3.

[46] Cd. 4983, Min. of Ev., Appendix vol. xii, pp. 40–3.

[47] See my article 'Charles Booth and the Royal Commission on the Poor Laws 1905–9', *Historical Studies* (Melbourne University), 15. 61 (1973), pp. 726–7.

[48] Draft of Letter to Smart (in Sidney Webb's handwriting) dated 14 Nov. 1907, Webb Local Government Collection, vol. 286.

replied smoothly that he was sure that her 'health and presence at the Commission are much more valuable than any document you could undertake',[49] and Lord George Hamilton, regretting her decision, added 'but I cannot say that I think you are wrong in the course you have taken'.[50]

2. *The Report on the Medical Services of the Poor Law and the Public Health Department*

Beatrice Webb quickly followed up her memorandum with her next one entitled 'The Medical Services of the Poor Law and the Public Health Departments of English Local Government, in their relation to each other, to the Public, and to the Prevention and Cure of Disease'. It was delivered to the Royal Commission on 7 September 1907.[51] This investigation traced the history of the two medical services, showing how they had become separated although they had sprung from the one source—'the prevalence of disease amongst the pauper class, and the economy of diminishing it'—and the interest of Edwin Chadwick in both.

The division of functions between municipalities and Poor Law Guardians had been largely the results of the chaotic state of English local government when the Public Health movement began in the 1840s. When the Local Government Board was established in 1871 the unity it achieved was little more than nominal: the Poor Law and Public Health sections were connected only through the departmental heads of the Local Government Board (and here and there in some local areas by the same medical practitioner being both Medical Officer of Health and District Medical Officer); each section went ahead with its own very different practices and principles. In 1907 England and Wales was divided, for public health purposes, into 'something like 1,800 areas', and served by 'approximately 1,380 separate medical officers of health' (all qualified doctors) having under their control 'several thousand sanitary inspectors' and 'several hundred isolation hospitals and other institutions'.[52] For Poor Law purposes, England and Wales was divided into 646 areas, seldom coinciding with the public

---

[49] Smart to B. Webb, 15 Nov. 1907, ibid.
[50] Hamilton to B. Webb, 15 Nov. 1907, ibid.
[51] Ibid., vol. 286c; the report was printed in Cd. 4983, Min. of Ev., vol. xii, pp. 261–311.
[52] Cd. 4983, Min. of Ev., vol. xii, p. 264.

health ones, served by 3,713 district medical officers. In addition, the Poor Law provided workhouse sick wards, dispensaries, infirmaries, and hospitals, of greatly varying standards, but the best of them in London and the larger towns were as efficient as most voluntary hospitals, and acted, to all intents and purposes, as general hospitals for their districts.

The memorandum then contrasted the medical services provided by the Public Health Department and by the Poor Law in considerable detail, greatly to the credit of the Public Health system and to the discredit of the Poor Law system in terms of general efficiency. The one aimed at full curative treatment, the complete prevention of disease, at early diagnosis, extending to the searching out of cases needing attention, the provision of a better environment and education in health matters for patients. The other merely provided essential medicine and treatment for those already, often seriously, ill. Its work had little bearing on prevention, and the treatment provided was subject to the capriciousness of a decentralized and ill-organized system in which 'good administration' was often taken to mean the cutting down of medical expenses. The existence of two overlapping medical services, working on different principles, resulted in 'chaos, almost ludicrous in its paradoxes', many examples of which were provided. A large amount of illness was still left untreated by either, and even more left unprevented. It was idle to pretend that voluntary agencies or private medical practice could fill the gap. A considerable proportion of the working class could not provide for their medical treatment at their own expense; even a modicum of provision was not possible for casual labourers and women workers. Provident clubs and friendly societies, even if universal, would be inadequate, as 'club practice' was useless for prevention. Charity hospitals were for the most part confined to London and to sixty or seventy provincial towns.

Beatrice Webb concluded that the Public Health and Poor Law medical services should be brought together into a united and systematically organized service, which should have prevention as its aim. 'Deterrence' was inconsistent with the very object of such a service. But she left open for discussion several questions: whether such a service should be free, or fees be charged upon some basis of principle; whether it was desirable to limit the public medical service to advice, medicine, and institutional treatment, leaving home maintenance to the patient, provident agencies, or organized charity; and whether the public medical service should be centrally organized or left to local sanitary authorities supported by an Exchequer 'grant-in-aid' and central inspection. She insisted that it would be quite possible to organize a unified public health service without interfering adversely with private medical practice, voluntary hospitals, medical research, or existing arrangements for medical education.

If Beatrice Webb's first memorandum had been received with coldness by the other Commissioners, this one had sufficient impact to be a 'cause of irritation'[53] to the COS 'old guard'. When it was discussed by the Commission in October 1907, the idea of taking medical relief out of the Poor Law and handing it over to the Public Health authority won the favour not only of Beatrice Webb's usual supporters—Lansbury, Chandler, and Dr Wakefield—but also of Dr Phelps and Professor Smart and, with some reservations, Lord George Hamilton and Hancock Nunn.[54] Dr McVail's draft report, supporting Beatrice Webb's, seemed to put her policy within reach of gaining a majority on the Commission, if she could win the two Irishmen (who were not present) as she confidently hoped to do. The 'old guard' COS had cause for anxiety. It seemed that the two reports might be reflecting a general view of MOHs in favour of the reform, as it was known that Beatrice Webb had sent out letters to them asking their opinions.

Beatrice Webb in her memorandum had been careful not to feature the result of her inquiries of the MOHs. But shortly after this meeting of the Commission, Helen Bosanquet received information that their replies were certainly not overwhelmingly in favour of the change. She therefore demanded that Beatrice Webb's correspondence with them be tabled. It was a shrewd stroke, which put Beatrice Webb in an extremely awkward position as she had accepted the principle that Commissioners should make all their information available to their colleagues. She could hardly refuse, even on the plea that the replies were confidential, without reneguing and being insulting to her fellow Commissioners. Yet the fact was that the majority of the replies, as was perhaps to be

---

[53] Minutes of the Documents Committee, 19 Nov. 1907. Webb Local Government Collection, vol. 286b.

[54] B.W. to M. Playne, n.d. [?Oct. 1907]. B.W. wrote: 'The Medical Investigator (who was put on to look after me) has completely "out Heroded" me in his complaints. "He corroborates Mrs. Webb" said the Chairman sadly "and I think we must accept their conclusions".' Passfield Papers.

expected from the medical profession, was conservative and opposed to change. She needed to put as good face on it as possible, and agree to make the correspondence available to the Commission. But while sorting the letters she made a fateful decision. She thought that a number of the letters from her friends including those from two members of the Commission (Provis and Downes) were too 'compromising to the authors', so she withheld these and also 'a due proportion of stupid conservative ones'.[55] What did she mean by 'a due proportion'? As many as the 'compromising' ones to keep the balance, or more? She did not say, but it must have been more, because she seems not to have sent on nearly one-third of all the letters she received. But however many she kept back, she could not alter the fact that a majority of MOHs was opposed to the reform she had recommended. When the letters she tabled were checked by F. H. Bentham, he reported 25 in favour of merging Poor Law and Public Health services, 49 against, and 30 offering no opinion.[56] Helen Bosanquet could not fail to suspect that many letters had not been forwarded, and drew the conclusion, which she had been convinced of earlier anyway, that Beatrice Webb was intellectually unscrupulous and deliberately suppressing material evidence. In any event, the result was clear, and Mrs Bosanquet followed up her advantage by getting the Evidence Committee to ask that the letters be printed.[57]

At this point, Sidney Webb had to intervene. Beatrice Webb was stricken with an attack of remorse and conscience at what she had done and the shame of its exposure, and this, added to the exhaustion of overwork, brought her to a state of nervous collapse. She had to go away for some weeks' holiday to Beachy Head to recover. Sidney Webb took charge of the situation, and drafted notes for her to send refusing publication of the letters on the ground that they were confidential, but allowing two or three copies to be typewritten for passing around, in confidence, to her fellow Commissioners with a prefatory statement saying that these letters formed 'only a tiny fraction of her material' for her

[55] *Our Partnership*, p. 392.
[56] Webb Local Government Collection, vol. 286c. Sidney Webb in his letter of 13 Nov. 1909 quoted below says there were 150 letters altogether.
[57] Report of Minute of Discussion at Evidence Committee, n.d. Webb Local Government Collection, vol. 286. *Our Partnership*, p. 393.

memorandum.[58] He also had to cope with Lord George Hamilton, and described his meeting with him in a letter to her:

My own dearest,

Instead of going to the Educ. Ctte., I have spent the afternoon with Lord George! I went there at 2.30, & found Duff out. I went again at 3 p.m. & found him with Ld. George—to whom I was presently shown in.

He was very pleasant, but very troubled, & very persistent. I was equally so, and with all politeness held my own—or rather your own.

He first began about your preamble to the M.O.H. letters, which he said was aggressive, & would raise no end of trouble. He had drafted a very brief statement, to much the same effect as yours, but more loosely. I said you were most anxious not to cause trouble—so I reinserted in his brief formula all the *gist* of yours, making his longer and more precise—and then authorized him to substitute it for yours. I think my version is all right. Then & there I looked through your Med. Report, & on the strength of the absence of references to the letters, I inserted a sentence 'They have not been quoted in her Report'—which is either quite true, or true barring one out of 150 letters. This took the wind out of his sails! He had been assuming that the Report was full of quotations from them . . .

I ought to add that Duff had procured for him a copy of your Circular to M.O.H., which we read together. He had thought it biassed, but I made him see that it was a quite fairly balanced document. (It reads quite excellently). He did not intend to produce this: & said he would get his revised preamble through the Evidence Comtte. on Monday—he said it was your 'proposal', but I stopped him, & said it was your *condition*, without which you could not allow your private letters to be copied . . .

We were throughout on the most friendly terms—I protesting your earnest desire to accommodate yourself, he explaining what a difficult team he had to drive . . . I found I had been more than an hour with him . . .[59]

In this exchange, Beatrice Webb lost a great deal of the credit and support which her memorandum had won. As Helen Bosanquet had shrewdly calculated, the inference that a majority of MOHs was not in favour of a transfer of the Poor Law medical services won back the waverers.

A few months later, in February 1908, Helen Bosanquet tried to follow up her advantage by proposing the establishment of a scheme of provident dispensaries to which all workers below a certain wage limit would contribute and thus provide for their own medical services. Unfortunately, it has not been possible to trace

[58] Webb Local Government Collection, vol. 286.
[59] Ibid., S. Webb to B. Webb, 13 Nov. 1907.

details of her original scheme, and only the mocking references to it in Beatrice Webb's *Diary* appear to survive.[60] This proposal was put before three meetings of the Commission on 17 February, and 9 and 10 March 1908. After some rather acrimonious discussions, there was an agreement that these provident dispensaries were desirable, but could not be made generally available to the poorest classes without compulsion to belong to them and subsidies from the rates, neither of which was acceptable; however, a majority of the Commissioners approved of them as supplementary to Poor Law and Public Health medical services. In general, the majority reached three decisions: that there should be 'greater co-operation' between the Poor Law and Public Health; that Poor Law medical relief should not be dissociated from other forms of relief; and that it was not desirable to make medical relief gratuitous or uncon-ditional, though the penalty of disfranchisement should not be attached to any form of medical relief.[61] Helen Bosanquet had not won, but Beatrice Webb had certainly lost this round of the contest in a disastrous way, just as she appeared to be on the edge of victory.

3. *The 'Break-up of the Poor Law'.*

Some months before the controversy about the Medical Services Report had arisen in late 1907, Beatrice Webb had been working out her ideas of 'breaking up' the Poor Law. Sidney Webb put them together for her into draft form early in May 1907, and as soon as she had them in this form Beatrice could not resist circulating the draft 'in strict confidence' to selected members of the Commission. The selected members did not include Helen Bosanquet or any others of the COS 'old guard'. But in addition to her supporters Wakefield, Lansbury, and Chandler, she sent it to Charles Booth, Professor Smart, Sir Henry Robinson, Dr Phelps, Hancock Nunn, Thory Gardiner, and Lord George Hamilton. It went, in effect, to all the Commissioners she thought she had some chance of persuading to accept her views, and she also sanguinely hoped later on to win over the Bishop of Ross.[62] But she was not content with

---

[60] B.W.D., 17 Mar. 1908; *Our Partnership*, pp. 404–5.
[61] Copy of Resolution as to Medical Relief agreed to by the Commission at meetings on 17 Feb., 9 Mar., and 10 Mar. 1908. Webb Local Government Collection, vol. 286d.
[62] B.W.D., 15 May 1907; *Our Partnership*, p. 381.

this audience, and only a few weeks elapsed before she was sending the draft also to a number of influential persons outside the Commission. It went to several politicians: Gerald Balfour, Lord Fitzalan, Walter Long, and Alfred Cripps on the Conservative side of the House, the Liberal–Unionist Henry Hobhouse, and R. B. Haldane on the Liberal side. Several churchmen, Canon Barnett, Bishop Cosmo Lang and the Revd Percy Dearmer got copies. F. A. Hyett, Chairman of Quarter Sessions, and Sir Robert Morant, the Permanent Secretary to the Board of Education whom the Webbs were hoping would succeed Sir Samuel Provis at the Local Government Board, and several of Beatrice's MOH friends also received it.[63] By that time, the new scheme was unlikely to remain a well-kept secret for much longer.

It is unnecessary to outline at this stage the details of Beatrice Webb's proposals for the 'break-up of the Poor Law', as they were essentially those embodied in her Minority Report. In general, the Boards of Guardians were to be swept away, and their functions divided up and handed over to separate committees of county and county borough councils—the Education Committee, the Public Health Committee, the Asylums Committee, the Pension Committee. Their activities were to be co-ordinated and recorded by a stipendiary officer (later called Registrar of Public Assistance). The Registrar was to keep a 'common register' of cases, to check whether regulations had been complied with in treatment of the case, to make any necessary inquiries into the pecuniary resources of applicants for assistance, and to decide how far the services provided should be charged for or free.

The first draft of this scheme was received rather gingerly by many of the people to whom she sent it. Charles Booth wrote to his wife: 'I enclose a letter from Beatrice with its enclosure which you will be interested to see. It seems quite impracticable and even wild to me. I have replied very circumspectly'.[64] Haldane hoped to discuss it with Asquith, and thought that in substance he himself was in agreement with her, though he doubted if she made enough 'of the huge amount of voluntary help that can be obtained if the

---

[63] B.W.D., 4 and 11 June, 5 and 9 July 1907. *Our Partnership*, pp. 381, 384. See also letters of reply in Webb Local Government Collection, vol. 286.

[64] C. Booth to M. Booth, 10 Dec. 1907, Booth Papers 1/1764 (Booth had not been able to attend to it earlier, because of illness).

right steps are taken'.[65] Walter Long sent no more than an acknowledgement. Gerald Balfour was on the whole encouraging, and liked the proposal for a stipendiary.[66] F. A. Hyett considered the scheme would 'work smoothly', but he suggested that more care was needed in defining the relation of the stipendiary to the Council.[67] Russell Wakefield, though in general agreement, was to confess later that he had been 'perplexed' by her stipendiary suggestion: '. . . somehow or other it appears to me *undemocratic* & a little *inhuman*'.[68] Bishop Cosmo Lang, described as 'a wily ecclesiastic' in Beatrice Webb's Diary, was encouraging but cautious,[69] Morant and Dearmer, however, were whole-hearted supporters, Morant arranging to have extra copies of the draft made, and Dearmer offering to circulate the scheme as a Christian Social Union pamphlet.[70] Lord George Hamilton wrote to say of it 'like all your schemes it is very thorough and drastic', but there would be 'no use putting forward a scheme which no Government will venture to propose to Parliament'. In particular, her plan for the stipendiary 'would arouse so much opposition that any scheme that was founded upon it would not proceed far in any House of Commons. My own view [*he went on*], so far as I have gone, is that we cannot dispense with an *ad hoc* authority for Poor Law purposes.'[71]

The main result of the circulation of this draft was its effect in stimulating Lord George Hamilton into preparing a similar 'skeleton report' of his own. He announced that he was thinking of doing this in his reply to Beatrice Webb, but he was urged forward by another manœuvre of hers. She suggested to Russell Wakefield that he should circulate as his own proposal a modified version of her scheme, and attempt to get the support of Smart and Phelps. He agreed, and, as she recorded in her Diary: '. . . Sidney and I drafted

[65] Haldane to B. Webb, 6 Oct. 1907. Webb Local Government Collection, vol. 286.

[66] B.W.D., 11 June 1907; *Our Partnership*, pp. 381–2.

[67] Hyett to B. Webb, 21 Nov. 1907. Webb Local Government Collection, vol. 286.

[68] Wakefield to B. Webb, 24 Aug. 1908. Ibid., vol. 286a.

[69] B.W.D., 5 July 1907; *Our Partnership*, p. 384.

[70] Ibid.; Morant to B. Webb 27 Apr. 1908, B. Webb to R. G. Duff, n.d. (? 15 Aug. 1908) both in Webb Local Government Collection, vol. 286a; MacKenzie, *Letters*, ii. 301–2.

[71] Hamilton to B. Webb, 10 May 1907. Webb Local Government Collection, vol. 286.

a series of propositions beginning piano and ending piano, with the substance in the middle, and I sent three copies of these to Wakefield . . .'[72] He replied: 'I have modified your suggestions somewhat and in some ways have made more vague proposals. I have also treated the matter for the moment as an individual effort purposing to ask for support or at any rate for counsel gradually.'[73] Whereupon she recorded:

Russell Wakefield has circulated the memorandum which I drew up for him (with one or two tiny alterations) as his own: he clearly did not want to share the glory of the new idea with Smart and Phelps. 'Jeffrey tells me that it will be a bomb', he said to Lansbury. 'That's splendid', I rejoined sympathetically, 'I only hope we shall be able to agree with it.' Oh! the vanity of men! How far is it wrong to play with it?[74]

The manœuvre did not deceive Lord George Hamilton, however. Presently he wrote to Beatrice Webb:

Russell Wakefield had a talk of some length with me the other night. He was emphatic as to the necessity of an 'ad hoc' authority. Two days later he issues his memo. Who was the Circe who metamorphosed him? I have my suspicions.[75]

Until November 1907 Lord George Hamilton and the 'old guard' of the COS had been in favour of the retention of an *ad hoc* authority in control of the Poor Law, although Lord George and Mrs Bosanquet had accepted the decision of the Indoor Relief Committee of the Commission (of which Beatrice Webb was not a member) that the administrative area should no longer be the Poor Law Union but should be identified as far as possible with that of the county or county borough.[76] This decision, taken as early as 19 November 1906, had divided the Commissioners. Octavia Hill, Patten-MacDougall, Downes, and Charles Booth (who had changed his mind on the subject)[77] opposed the decision and preferred to

[72] B.W.D., 8 Oct. 1907; *Our Partnership*, p. 391.
[73] Wakefield to Webb, 18 Oct. 1907. Webb Local Government Collection, vol. 286.
[74] B.W.D., 22 Oct. 1907; *Our Partnership*, p. 392.
[75] Hamilton to B. Webb, 27 Oct. 1907. Webb Local Government Collection, vol. 286.
[76] Minutes of the Indoor Relief Committee, 19 Nov. 1906, and 26 Nov. 1906. Webb Local Government Collection, vol. 286b.
[77] See my article, 'Charles Booth and the Royal Commission on the Poor Laws 1905–9', p. 728.

maintain the status quo. Loch, Nunn, and Wakefield (until Beatrice Webb persuaded him to her point of view) were undecided. Lord George Hamilton and Helen Bosanquet favoured a new directly elected *ad hoc* body for the new county areas. Bentham proposed a new *ad hoc* authority for the counties but with its members indirectly elected by the county councils and district councils, with some nominated or co-opted members. Phelps, Smart, and Robinson as well as Beatrice Webb, Lansbury, and Chandler took the view that a logical consequence of the change in area was the transfer in some way of Poor Law administration to the county councils.[78] This division of opinion, although it had revealed itself to some extent in earlier discussions of the Indoor Relief Committee, came fully to the surface in a discussion by the full Commission on 8 October 1907.[79] Russell Wakefield's conversion and action in circulating his memorandum therefore seemed dangerous to Lord George, in case Beatrice Webb should manage to persuade the other five to accept her view on the 'break-up of the Poor Law'. She was confident—over-confident—of being able to do this; and Lord George was fearful of a disastrous three-way split of the Commission with three competing reports emerging as a result.[80]

Lord George revealed himself as an experienced administrative tactician. In consultation with Helen Bosanquet, he worked out a compromise in which he and she would drop the notion of an *ad hoc* authority, and placate their opponents by transferring the Poor Law functions *en bloc* to a statutory committee of the county and county borough councils.[81] This manœuvre would probably have been successful in any case; but presented, as it was, to the Commission immediately after the exposure of Beatrice Webb's duplicity in the handling of Medical Officers' letters, it could hardly fail to gain acceptance by the majority of the Commission. Beatrice Webb was encouraged to make her memorandum on the 'Break-up of the Poor Law' available to the Commission as a whole; then Lord George introduced his scheme, claiming it to be 'more

---

[78] B.W.D., 8 Oct. 1907; *Our Partnership*, p. 390. Robinson made his general approval clear in a letter to B. Webb, 22 Nov. 1907. Webb Local Government Collection, vol. 286. Provis and the Bishop of Ross also agreed.

[79] B.W.D., 8 Oct. 1907; *Our Partnership*, p. 390.

[80] Hamilton to B. Webb, 24 Oct. 1907. Webb Local Government Collection, vol. 286.

[81] Hamilton to B. Webb, 5 Dec. 1907, ibid.

democratic and less autocratic' than hers.[82] The result, as Sidney
Webb observed to Haldane,

was like the bark of the shepherd's dog. It drove [the Commissioners]
helter-skelter into the Chairman's fold! Sinking their differences they have
provisionally adopted—rather than accept anything from her—a blurred
outline which may not unlikely work out to the same thing: viz. abolition
of all Boards of Guardians, adoption of the County and County Borough
area, County and County Borough Council to be the supreme authority for
Poor Law, some sort of stipendiary officer to sit with nominated local
committees to hear applications, etc.[83]

Beatrice Webb now had definitely to decide whether to compromise with the majority or to go ahead with a separate Minority
Report. She did not hesitate. In spite of a hard-eyed look at the
strength of her support at the time—'I shall lose Phelps and,
perhaps, Wakefield and not gain any others'—she decided to throw
down the gage.[84] She kept her spirits buoyant by underestimating
the capacity and cohesion of her fellow-Commissioners:

. . . it is doubtful if the chairman's party will hold together.[85]

I cannot make out what the majority are doing—no one seems to feel any
responsibility for the result except Lord George who really is light-headed
in his lack of appreciation of the gravity of the task of coming to
conclusions and setting them before the public in an efficient and dignified
way. My only hope is that he and his majority will get so sick of the whole
business that they may, after much troubling, hand the whole thing over to
me.[86]

The Chairman, Mrs Bosanquet and some others have settled that the report
is to be out in August [1908]! But unless I am very much mistaken, we shall
still be floundering in the morass six months hence. 'Mrs Webb comes here
to drive wedges between us' said Mrs Bosanquet angrily. So I shall take the
hint and stay away.[87]

Once again, the Webbs had lost another game in the match. But
Helen Bosanquet had been obliged to abandon the original base-
line position of the COS and take up a centre position to win.
Beatrice Webb has been criticized for her refusal to accept the

[82] Ibid.
[83] S. Webb to Haldane, 12 Dec. 1907. MacKenzie, *Letters*, ii. 276–7.
[84] B.W.D., 9 Dec. 1907; *Our Partnership*, p. 397.
[85] B.W.D., 12 Dec. 1907; *Our Partnership*, p. 398. MacKenzie, *Diary*, iii, 83.
[86] B. Webb to M. Playne, 2 Feb. 1908. MacKenzie, *Letters*, ii. 281.
[87] B.W.D., 13 Jan. 1908 (this passage is not included in *Our Partnership*).

compromise which the Chairman proposed;[88] but it is unlikely that she would have got any further if she had done so. The majority was determined to have nothing to do with her proposals for breaking up the poor law. An accommodating Fabian might have accepted the compromise as the likeliest practicable step on the road to a long-range objective, but Beatrice was not a Fabian in that sense: she was determined to fight on.

4. *The Report on Poor Law Children*

As we saw earlier,[89] Beatrice Webb had been obliged to surrender the private investigation she had launched into the condition of pauper children. By arrangement, the Commission itself took over this inquiry, employing the same research workers, Mary Longman and Marion Phillips, but placing them under the superintendance of a new chief investigator appointed by the Commission, Dr Ethel Williams.[90] The transfer was quite satisfactory to Beatrice Webb, because she knew Dr Williams and she realized that the financing of the research by the Commission could widen the scope of the inquiry. In the six months before 6 May 1907, the date on which Dr Williams took over, Marion Phillips and Mary Longman had already carried out investigations into the condition of the children of widows in receipt of poor relief in the Poor Law Unions of Derby and Paddington. This material was made available to Dr Williams, who extended the inquiry on the same lines into twelve other Poor Law Unions, and in her own capacity as a medical woman was able to make a more thorough investigation of the physical condition of the children. As a result, the sample included three London Unions (Paddington, Lambeth, and St George's Hanover Square), eight other urban Unions (Bradford, Derby, the Parish of Liverpool, Merthyr Tydfil, Newcastle upon Tyne, Rochdale, West Derby, and York) and three rural Unions (Warwick, Mitford, and Launditch). Altogether this represented a study of 1,137 cases, involving 3,375 children out of a total of 171,497 children classed as in receipt of outdoor relief in England and Wales.[91]

[88] U. Cormack, *The Welfare State, the Formative Years 1905–9*, Loch Memorial Lecture (London, 1953), pp. 30–1.

[89] See above, p. 215.

[90] Dr Ethel Williams later became President of the British Federation of Medical Women and treasurer of the Socialist Medical League.

[91] Of the total number of Poor Law children (234,004), 73% were on outdoor relief.

The report which was eventually submitted was a comprehensive document of 122 pages with another 163 pages of appendices. It discussed the causes of chargeability, and the administration of outdoor relief regarding children; it described the general character of the Unions studied, with special attention to housing and overcrowding, and extended this to a particular description of the environment of the dwellings inhabited by the pauper children; it then assessed the income and expenditure of the families of the children, the comfort of their homes as regards furniture and cleanliness, the character, intelligence, health, and employment of their parent or parents; and it arrived at conclusions about the condition of the children themselves in terms of cleanliness and clothing, education and intelligence, and employment. In Parts II to IV of the report comparisons were made between the condition of the children on outdoor relief with those who were boarded out, those who were housed in separate Poor Law establishments, and those who had been kept in workhouses and workhouse infirmaries. Finally, in Part V, a description was given of the physical condition of these pauper children. The report was notable as one of the first efforts to use modern sampling techniques. An attempt was made, by the use of proportional multipliers, to extend the results hypothetically to England and Wales as a whole.[92]

Dr Williams's general conclusions were that there were large numbers of children on outdoor relief who were suffering, physically and mentally, from the conditions under which they were living. Outdoor relief was the only form of relief which enabled pauper children to preserve their home ties, and Dr Williams stated her view with an emphasis which overrode her regard for pronouns:

I take it, what every child wants, and what every home which is reasonably good gives, is a certain stability in life, a sense that there is one place, one little group, to which it stands in a unique relation, and who regard it as they regard no one else, a point to which, under any circumstances, it can turn.

She admitted that some Poor Law institutions could be 'excellent places': 'Both at Pentland and Bradford and also at Warwick, the life in the Homes was vigorous and bright, just the very thing for children.' But the head of a Poor Law school or the foster-mother of

[92] Cd. 5037, p. 9.

a set of children, however wise and devoted, could not provide what a satisfactory home could give. She conceded that there were bad mothers: some were women of actively bad character, quite unfit to have the charge of children, but there was a much larger group of mothers of a 'negatively bad type, people without a standard, whining, colourless people, often in poor health'. In her opinion, outdoor relief should never be given to the actively bad parent; but she considered that the negatively bad parent could as a rule be guided and stimulated by kindly and wise supervision of a sort that could be, but was not yet, provided. So she recommended that those responsible for granting outdoor relief should supervise the recipients more closely, not only by employing women sanitary inspectors and using the voluntary help of women visitors but also by the members of the outdoor relief committee of the Poor Law Guardians themselves playing their part in visiting.

Relief, according to Dr Williams, should be taken to the homes of the recipients, to ensure frequent visits and to prevent children being sent to make 'a very undesirable acquaintance with the Relief Station' to collect it. Guardians should not give outdoor relief merely because they thought it cheaper than indoor relief: in most cases it would not be cheaper if it were adequate and well administered. Dr Williams gave an example of the attitude she considered wholly misguided:

In talking to the Superintendent Relieving Officer of one of the large Urban Unions investigated, I asked him whether he thought the incomes of the Out-Relief families adequate for their needs. 'Yes', he said, 'I don't know how they manage, but they do it somehow, so it must be enough and certainly they are ready to go on with it'. This is the doctrine which is at the root of the evil. We give relief without knowing whether the recipients can manage on it, we go on giving it without knowing how they are managing on it.

The Guardians should make sure that relief was adequate; and if the mother was in employment but not able to make arrangements for the children while she was away, they should provide enough out-relief for her to give up her job and live at home. The Guardians should also regard it as part of their duty to see that the living quarters of the children were sanitary, to provide regular medical inspection for them, to make sure that they had adequate education, and to give them guidance in their choice of work.

No Board of Guardians, so far as my investigations go, takes any interest whatever about the placing and starting in life of boys who have had Out Relief, nor does it try to help them to any technical training. In some Unions the women Guardians help to place the girls in domestic service, and the Board generally tries to persuade mothers to send their girls to service. For a boy, Out-Relief stops at 14, and he turns to the first job at which he can earn. Most likely this job will be one that will lead to nothing.

Neither Beatrice Webb nor Helen Bosanquet could feel pleased with the conclusions of Dr Williams's report. Beatrice Webb approved the research done by Mary Longman and Marion Phillips, but she considered that Ethel Williams had abandoned methodical investigation for sentimental exhortation.[93] The notion of a change of practice without a change of system must have seemed to her to be a piece of woolly thinking. Helen Bosanquet, much as she might have liked the notion of closer supervision and guidance by visitors, felt that this was the business of charitable endeavour and not of the Guardians, especially when it would result in an increase in outdoor relief. As a result, when a similar investigation was later made into the treatment of children in Scotland, Mary Longman and Marion Phillips were re-engaged for the task, but Beatrice Webb made no protest when Dr C. T. Parsons, medical superintendent of the Fulham Infirmary and Workhouse, was put in charge of it instead of Dr Williams, although she knew that Dr Parsons was not one of her supporters.[94]

The Scottish inquiry was, in any case, merely an application of the methods that had been developed earlier, because it had to be done at speed, in two months. It involved 1,060 children in the parishes of Glasgow, Govan Combination, Edinburgh, Dundee Combination, and Lanark. The same kind of detailed statistical and descriptive information was furnished by the two assistant investigators; but Dr Parsons's general conclusions were taken up with the medical results of the study and were extremely chary of recommendations about general policy compared with Dr Williams's. He observed that the physique of Poor Law children compared badly with the average standard, though it was better than that of children from the poorest quarters of Glasgow. There was no really marked difference in the physique of children in workhouses, and those boarded out, or on outdoor relief, though that of the outdoor relief

[93] B.W.D., 28 Sept. 1907; *Our Partnership*, p. 388.
[94] MacKenzie, *Letters*, ii. 244.

children was slightly better. He was shocked by the amount of dental and eye trouble in the children, and recommended that dental and optical services should be provided as part of an improved system of medical examination and observation. He favoured more variety in the diets provided for the children in Poor Law institutions, but in general he considered that boarding out was better for children than institutional life. However, he warned that foster-parents of boarded-out children should be prohibited from making a profit out of young children by sending them to work at 9, 10, or 11 years of age. There was a faint note of pessimism in his conclusions, for he believed that the fact that the cause of the children's pauperism was the death or illness of the father in over 76 per cent of cases (incidentally, this matched the 73 per cent for England and Wales) showed that there was in general some hereditary defect on that side of the family.

The reports of the supervising investigators of the two inquiries into the conditions of Poor Law children gave advantage, then, neither to Beatrice Webb nor to Helen Bosanquet. But Mary Longman and Marion Phillips had piled up a vast amount of particular information and statistics which they could, and did, draw upon when they were writing their own final reports.

5. *The Report on the Effects of a Refusal of Outdoor Relief*

Miss Harlock's inquiry into the effects of refusal of outdoor relief was conducted in two stages. A preliminary investigation was first made in one Poor Law Union—Bradford—of 41 cases, the names having been supplied by the clerk to the Bradford Board of Guardians. Miss Harlock interviewed these families and cross-checked the results of her interviews with the local Guild of Help and Charity Organisation Society and the official Visitor of the Bradford Board. On this occasion no attempt was made to investigate the causes of the victims' poverty: Miss Harlock concentrated on the consequences of refusal of outdoor relief to them. She visited the families some time after they had been refused outdoor relief, and presented her report mainly in the form of detailed case-papers describing what had happened to them. She was able to contact 39 out of the 41 cases (two had disappeared without trace). In her opinion, in 17 of those 39 cases a grant of outdoor relief would have been an unsuitable method of treatment and 3 other cases were doubtful, but in 19 of the cases she concluded that a grant of outdoor relief would have been appropriate, and its refusal had involved the applicants in suffering, either mental or physical or both. She was 'particularly struck with the hardship of women with children, who are expected to be at the same time both the breadwinner and the housewife of their families ... These women so often go under in their struggle to perform this impossible task, dragging their children down with them.' Only one woman had 'risen superior to the refusal of relief' but she had been in an exceptionally good position: 'She was a capable, competent woman, and in addition had friends who were able to help her with money, work, advice and encouragement.' In general, out of her 39 cases, Miss Harlock found that 15 had survived economically: 9 had found work of some sort, and 6 were living with relatives in reasonable quarters. Of the rest, 6 had gone to the workhouse, 8 had later been granted out-relief, 7 were still living in their own dwellings in distressed circumstances, one was living with a son who had a large family and was himself out of work, one was ill in lodgings without any source of income, and one was in prison.

This preliminary investigation was followed up by another survey with a wider scope partly because Mr Frank Bentham had objected that many of her final 19 cases were also not cases in which outdoor relief was appropriate,[95] and partly because Miss Harlock acknowledged that her first attempt was too narrow to allow any wide-ranging conclusions to be safely drawn. In the second attempt, 49 cases were taken from a random selection of Unions: Paddington (11 cases) and Hackney (12 cases) in London, the Township of Manchester (15 cases), Atcham Union in Shropshire (6 cases), Helston Union in Cornwall (4 cases), and Thame Union in Oxfordshire (1 case). The information was again cross-checked with charitable agencies, Poor Law, and health officials; but on this occasion the interviewer made two visits, the second after an interval of six to eight weeks. She also attempted to give an analysis of the causes of poverty, finding that in 16 of the cases the cause was unemployment, in 11 cases the cause was the loss of the chief wage-earner through death, desertion, or imprisonment, and in 22 cases the cause was incapacity through illness or old age. The last-mentioned cause (old age, i.e. over 65 years) accounted for 18 cases; and in the unemployment category Miss

[95] F. H. Bentham to B. Webb dated 'Sept' [?1907]. Webb Local Government Collection, vol. 286a.

Harlock reckoned 9 of the cases to be attributable to *bona fide* lack
of work, or to the seasonal or casual nature of the work, as against
7 whose plight was caused by drink or habitual laziness.

After a full inquiry, carefully documented in detailed case-papers,
Miss Harlock had a number of important conclusions to offer. She
found that in no case was support by relatives increased through
refusal of outdoor relief. In practically all cases the relatives
themselves were so poor they could offer no assistance. In no case
had any voluntary charitable agency done anything effective to
provide help, apart from the spasmodic gift. The applicants had not
been stimulated to greater efforts of their own through refusal of
outdoor relief; they had been discouraged and disheartened by it.
Only two of the applicants had found work, and the employment of
one of them was not likely to be more than temporary. Six had
entered workhouses, two had died, and six were missing by the
time of the second interview. In a majority of the cases the refusal of
outdoor relief had led to a disposal of furniture and clothes and to
'unmistakable signs of marked physical deterioration of the
members of the families, owing to lack of food, warmth and proper
clothing'. Miss Harlock's investigation could still be claimed to be
too narrow in scope to shake the faith of the COS representatives in
some of their cherished articles of faith: but it did at least raise some
doubts, which the Webbs were able to deploy with effect in their
Report.

The Outcome of the Attack in Depth.

Our focus in this account has been upon Beatrice Webb's initiatives
and the response of Helen Bosanquet and the other Commissioners
to them. Helen Bosanquet did not succeed in matching Beatrice
Webb's onslaught in depth with any similar counter-attack of her
own, in spite of the private investigations she had begun. No doubt
that was due to illness—she suffered her breakdown in health in the
spring of 1908; but her defensive game had been fairly effective
against the most dangerous of Beatrice Webb's drives. By ironical
fortune, the COS team proved more successful in warding off
Beatrice Webb's attacks in depth than it was in mounting its own.
The main one was the Special Investigation (which has been
mentioned earlier) conducted by Cyril Jackson and John C. Pringle.
These men were appointed, at the initiative of the COS Commis-

sioners, to inquire into 'the effects of employment or assistance given to the unemployed since 1886 as a means of relieving distress outside the Poor Law'. The enterprise turned out to be as little satisfactory for the COS as Beatrice Webb considered it to be from her point of view. The researchers were given six months to rush into largely uncharted territory of social investigation and return with answers to an unreasonably long list of questions. They accumulated a vast mass of material, and tried manfully to cope with the task, but they were obliged to protest at its difficulty in the preface to their report. They concluded (as was expected) that relief works established since Chamberlain's 1885 Circular had been a complete failure, and that any solution to the unemployment problem did not lie along the lines of the Unemployed Workmen's Act of 1905, and they threw in gratuitously (it did not come within their brief) their opinion that a larger national programme of public works would not be effective either. After considering a long and eclectic list of causes of unemployment, which included sickness, faults in character, casual and seasonal labour, over-specialization, the effects of introducing new methods and new machinery, dead-end jobs for juvenile workers, inefficient business methods, distortions of trade caused by 'wars, tariffs, strikes and the like', cyclical trade depressions, and seasonal variations in trades, they finally expressed their opinion: 'We believe that the unemployed problem as it appears today is largely due to the want of organisation of casual unskilled labour.' The remedies they proposed were only very modestly innovative. 'The solution', they wrote, 'lies in a better organistion of the workers and more consideration from the employers.' Trade unions and employers needed to get together to regularize labour. Government departments and local councils ought to arrange to carry out ordinary public works that were not urgent at times of slack trade. Better housing and wages would improve the lot of the poorer classes. Training should be provided in schools to fit children for regular work and check their drift into the ranks of the unskilled. (Cyril Jackson later furnished a separate report on Boy Labour.) Labour exchanges, not successful so far, might work if organized on a larger scale. Emigration, assisted and encouraged, could help to relieve the pressure. A thorough classification in the Poor Law was needed, and drastic measures, in the shape of penal colonies, to check vagrancy. These remedies amounted to old COS prescriptions modified by a tinge of new doctrine; but social causes of unemployment appeared to have taken precedence.

The COS fared even less happily with the reports of other Special Investigators appointed by the Commission. Dr McVail's report on 'the methods and results of the present system of administering Indoor and Outdoor Poor Law Medical Relief in certain Unions in England and Wales' upheld Beatrice Webb's criticisms of the Poor Law medical system and favoured her proposal for its absorption by Public Health. Miss Norah Roberts, a COS worker, appointed to investigate 'the overlapping of the work of the Voluntary Hospitals with that of Poor Law Medical Relief', reported from her study of three London hospitals that about eleven per cent of the patients receiving outdoor treatment at the hospitals were also receiving medical relief from the Poor Law. Another piece of massive research, to report on 'the relation of industrial and sanitary conditions to pauperism', had as its Special Investigators Arthur Steel-Maitland and Rose Squire. In this case, Beatrice Webb claimed that she had been 'practically permitted . . . to select them', and, indeed, both were members of the Webbs' entourage; but they were choices readily acceptable to the whole Commission: Steel-Maitland was a brilliant Balliol man, who had been Private Secretary to the two last Conservative Chancellors of the Exchequer, and Rose Squire was a senior Factory Inspector. In their two very able and well-written reports, involving extensive inquiries in London, Liverpool, and Bristol, the chief manufacturing towns of England, and some other places, the researchers arrived at the firm conclusion that casual and irregular employment was by far the chief cause of poverty. Seasonal fluctuations in trade were causes only to the extent that they added to the problem of casual labour. Bad housing conditions, unhealthy trades and work-places, low wages, and dangerous trades all had a contributory effect, but they were in no way so important. Moral shortcomings, such as drunkenness and slack habits, were considered likely to be consequences rather than causes.

The most shattering blow to some cherished COS beliefs came, however, from the report on 'the effects of Outdoor Relief on wages and conditions of employment'. This research was carried out by Constance Williams, a COS social worker, and Thomas Jones, a lecturer in Professor William Smart's department of Political Economy at Glasgow University, who also happened to be a Fabian. They were set to test, by inquiry into a large number of Poor Law Unions all over England, several propositions crucial to the COS belief that outdoor relief was an evil which ought to be reduced as much as possible. The investigators found that very little outdoor relief was given to able-bodied men; almost all the recipients were aged, sick, or women, and a high percentage of the women were in distress because they needed to support young children through widowhood or the disablement of their husbands or desertion. They discovered there was almost no evidence of out-relief acting as a rate-in-aid of wages. Its effect on men's wages was negligible; even in rural areas, outdoor relief was not given with the intention of 'tiding over' seasonal slack periods to retain labourers on the farms. Even though most women paupers were obliged to take casual and in most cases (where they had to look after their children) irregular work, in order to eke out their meagre outdoor relief, there was no evidence that their rates of pay were reduced because they were in receipt of relief. The number of paupers employed compared with the total supply of women workers was too small to affect the general level of women's wages, and the only result of the withdrawal of outdoor relief would be to deprive poor women of that little assistance they badly needed. The Special Investigators could also find little evidence of migration of unskilled labour from 'strict' districts to districts where outdoor relief was freely given, or the attraction of 'sweated' or irregular industries to districts 'lax' about outdoor relief, or of industries being subsidized by outdoor relief or kept alive when they would have perished without such Poor Law help. The conclusion was that outdoor relief could not easily be dispensed with, and the main trouble with it was its haphazard administration. And once again casual and irregular labour was diagnosed as the underlying social problem. Perhaps the Commission's own Special Investigations scored more points for the Webbs than Beatrice Webb had been able to achieve herself?

9

Cross-Court Play

EVIDENCE OF EDWARDIAN ECONOMISTS TO THE COMMISSION

HELEN Bosanquet and Beatrice Webb both took an active part in cross-examination of witnesses, as indeed did most of the other Royal Commissioners. The procedure of cross-examination was subject to no firm legal control or guidance, and Lord George Hamilton in general allowed it to take its course; consequently there were complaints by the Commissioners to each other, and to the Chairman, that formal rules of questioning were being disregarded, and witnesses were being 'led' or otherwise cajoled.[1] An extensive reading of the evidence reveals that the Commissioners were by no means guiltless of these attempts, and that the Commissioners making complaints were usually no holier than their colleagues; but, in the main, witnesses were well able to stand up for their own opinions in the face of quite severe questioning.

Beatrice Webb became notorious for a style of cross-examination that was aggressive and persistent. In another age, she might have become an eminent barrister; and she showed she could match any of the other Commissioners, including the formidable C. S. Loch and Octavia Hill, in the vigour of her questioning. Helen Bosanquet's style was quite different: she seldom indulged in sustained attacking cross-examination. She had little need to, as she could always rely on one of the other COS Commissioners to fulfil that role. She could, and did, play a quiet part, getting in the shrewd shot or two occasionally. Hers was not the style of which myths were made; Beatrice's was. Sir Henry Robinson, noted for his witty but unreliable anecdotes, told in his memoirs a story of the one

---

[1] B.W.D., 1 Mar. 1906, *Our Partnership*, ed. B. Drake and M. Cole (London, 1948), pp. 335–6; B.W.D., 10 Apr. 1906, *Our Partnership*, p. 377; B.W.D., 22 May 1906, *Our Partnership*, p. 341; Hamilton to B. Webb, 24 Oct. 1907. Webb Local Government Collection, vol. 286.

occasion in which Beatrice Webb was baffled by a witness. After paying graceful tribute to Mrs Webb's skill as cross-examiner, and her way of confusing witnesses by subtle deductions from their own theories, he declared:

The only time I ever saw her floored was by an obstinate old Yorkshire farmer, a chairman of Poor Law guardians, who was convinced that any opinions he held must be infallible, and that anyone who differed from him was sincerely to be pitied. Mrs Webb proceeded to draw him upon the principles on which he gave outdoor relief.

'We do it this way', he said. 'If a man's a drunken chap, say, we'd only give him maybe half a crown, but if he was a decent fellow, a thrifty sort of chap, why then we'd give him more, say three-and-six. Oh, yes, we discriminate right enough, we do that'.

Mrs Webb was on to him like a shot. 'Oh, of course, Mr Hodge—most reasonable; I quite understand. And following out your principle, if he was a *very* thrifty chap and had money in the bank, I suppose you'd give him five shillings?'

'Haw, haw, haw!' roared Mr Hodge. 'Eh, but that's good. Money in the bank. Five shillings. Oh these ladies, these ladies!' And he shook his fat sides with laughter, winking at the other members of the commission, and kept leaning over the table and explaining to them. 'She'd give them five shillings with money in the bank, she would'. Then, when he managed to bottle down his laughter, he turned round to Mrs Webb: 'Now do go on, Miss; I'm a-listening to you'. But Mrs Webb was so disconcerted at this method of meeting her logic that she blushed and dried up, and left the old fellow shaking his head from side to side with laughter and ejaculating, 'Oh the ladies, the ladies!' and then confidentially to Lord George as he left the witness chair, 'I expect you has a heap of fun from them, my Lord'.[2]

The absence of any such Yorkshire farmer from the very detailed minutes of evidence of the Royal Commission on the Poor Laws suggests that Sir Henry's anti-feminist story was apocryphal; but it may nevertheless be a tribute to Beatrice Webb's formidable presence in the court-room, which has been attested by more dependable sources.[3]

The task of selecting evidence from the massive volumes of minutes of the Royal Commission to illustrate its complicated cross-court play is rather a teaser when so much is offering. Most of the witnesses who appeared for examination were Poor Law

[2] Rt. Hon. Sir Henry Robinson, *Memories: Wise and Otherwise* (London, 1923), pp. 213–14.
[3] See, e.g., A. G. Gardiner, *Pillars of Society* (London, 1913), pp. 204–6.

Administrators, Guardians, social workers, employers—practical men and women who usually had firm views about what was what. But we have chosen, for our illustration of the whole court in action with a larger range of players, the testimony of economists on the more speculative problem of the treatment of the able-bodied poor. On this subject, the Commission felt a need to appeal to economic theorists. Most of the Commissioners recognized that the issue of unemployment was a central and most difficult question. Certainly Beatrice Webb did: 'The difficulty of solving the question oppresses me [*she wrote in her Diary*]. I dream of it at night, I pray for light in the early morning. I grind, grind, grind all the hours of the working day to get a solution'.[4]

In 1907 the Commission was persuaded—mainly by Professor Smart—that it needed some advice from economists. He wrote to Professor Alfred Marshall asking for his help.[5] Marshall was regarded with awe by most of the other economists of his age, as the 'father-figure' of neo-classical economics.[6] Even Sidney Webb, who in his brasher days as a young Socialist was not quite so respectful, had been somewhat subdued by a severe verbal encounter with Marshall in 1892.[7] Marshall was a veteran of several Royal Commissions, and his views on the Poor Law were fairly well known, although, like those of all oracles, they were capable of being 'interpreted' in various ways. On this occasion, Marshall did not respond with an offer of any direct assistance to the Royal Commission; he left to his favourite pupil, Arthur Cecil Pigou[8] (who was to be appointed his successor in the following year, 1908, as Professor of Political Economy at Cambridge), the task of presenting to it a 'Marshallian' analysis of a number of Poor Law problems. In 1907, however, Marshall had published a

---

[4] B.W.D., 15 Nov. 1908; *Our Partnership*, p. 419; MacKenzie, *Diary*, iii, 103.

[5] Smart to B. Webb, undated [?c.Apr. 1907]. Webb Local Government Collection, vol. 286a.

[6] *DNB* 1922–30; J. M. Keynes, 'Alfred Marshall 1842–1924' in A. C. Pigou (ed.), *Memorials of Alfred Marshall* (London, 1925), reprinted in his *Essays in Biography* (London, 1933); G. F. Shove, 'The Place of Marshall's *Principles* in the Development of Economic Theory', *Ec.J.* 52 (1942).

[7] Cross-examination of Webb by Marshall, Royal Commission on Labour, 17 Nov. 1892, C. 7063–1, Min. of Ev., vol. xxxix, Pt. 1, Qq. 4069–169. Webb stuck valiantly to his Socialist guns, but had the worse of the exchange on the history of economic doctrine. He later took his revenge by drafting the Minority Report for the Labour members, to the annoyance of Marshall. Booth to Marshall, 25 May 1894. Booth Papers 1/1352, MS 797.

[8] *DNB* 1951–60.

famous article, 'The Social Possibilities of Economic Chivalry',[9] in which he expressed a guarded optimism about the progress of Britain's economy, as providing the means for a judicious measure of social reform: '. . . there is a margin of at least one or two hundred million [a year] which might be diverted to social uses without causing any great distress to those from whom it was taken . . .'[10]

A new 'economic chivalry' could soften and ennoble capitalism, as an earlier chivalry had softened and ennobled feudalism, Marshall believed. But moderation and caution should be the keynote of social reforms. In urging the claims of 'economic chivalry' economists had a duty to remember that its basis was further improvement in production and an increase of the National Dividend. 'Ill-considered measures of reform by Utopian schemers',[11] involving large-scale redistributions of wealth, could slacken the springs of productive energy; and nothing but damage, Marshall felt, would come of any attempt to shackle entrepreneurs with the bonds of collectivism and bureaucracy: '. . . every great step in the direction of collectivism is a grave menace to the maintenance even of our present moderate rate of progress'.[12] The State had a duty to ameliorate the condition of the people, but it could do that best by promoting a sense of economic chivalry and associating individuals and voluntary associations with it in charitable and educational work to enlarge the welfare of the poorer classes. Marshall's article of 1907 was confined to the statement of very general principles. But it attracted considerable attention at the time, including the attention of some of the Royal Commissioners on the Poor Law. Charles Booth wrote to Marshall soon after its publication praising it for its 'profoundly true' utterances.[13] However, the task of translating these principles into precise recommendations concerning the Poor Law was left to A. C. Pigou.

The 'Memorandum on some Economic Aspect and Effects of Poor Law Relief', which was submitted by Pigou to the Royal

---

[9] This was first delivered as a lecture to the Royal Economic Society in Jan. 1907; it was reprinted as an article in *Ec.J.* 17 (1907), and reproduced in *Memorials of Alfred Marshall*, ed. Pigou (London, 1925; New York 1966). The references to quotations from it which follow are to the latest reprint of the *Memorials* as the most readily available text.

[10] Pigou, *Memorials of Alfred Marshall*, p. 325.

[11] Ibid., p. 328.   [12] Ibid., p. 342.

[13] Booth to Marshall, 21 Apr. 1907. Booth Papers 1/1715, MS 797.

Commission in 1907,[14] was attached as an Appendix to the volumes of Evidence of the Royal Commission. Pigou was not called to give evidence personally. He was still young and relatively unknown as an economist in 1907, and his paper merely reiterated some Marshallian views with which the Commissioners were already familiar. It might be described as mainly a cost–benefit analysis of the policies of the existing Poor Law. He did not, in this paper, address himself at all to the problems that were to concern him so deeply in later years—the problems of the causes and remedies for general unemployment. He defined his inquiry strictly in terms of the relief of the destitute, and saw his task as attempting to assess the economic merits (or demerits) of various methods of providing relief. Whether these methods were administered by public functionaries—the Poor Law Guardians—or by voluntary charitable agencies did not greatly concern him. He considered the Guardians and voluntary charitable agencies as to a considerable extent complementary, and he referred the Commissioners to a detailed scheme for combining Charity Organisation and Poor Law activities that had been put forward by Professor Marshall to the Royal Commission on the Aged Poor in 1892.[15]

Pigou gave some cogent reasons for dismissing attempts to establish the economic merits of different policies pursued by different Poor Law Unions by calculating the numbers of paupers in each district. This was an unwelcome comment from the sideline, coming from a disciple of Marshall, to Charles Booth and his statistical assistants who had begun with high hopes of thus 'testing policies by results'.[16] The proper criterion to employ, Pigou announced in strong Marshallian terms, was the likely effect of different policies on the National Dividend. In taking this view, Pigou was concerned to explain that it did not mean that economists were unaware that social policies had ends other than economic ones to serve, but, like most economists from Adam Smith to Marshall (and beyond), he believed that the size of the National Dividend was the necessary foundation of all other social benefits. The effect of Poor Law policy was to transfer money from the rich to the poor; the central economic question was, then, to

[14] Cd. 5068, Min. of Ev., Appendix vol. ix, pp. 981–1000.
[15] Ibid., p. 984.
[16] Ibid., pp. 984–6 and C. Booth, Memo on Procedure. Webb Local Government Collection, vol. 286b.

determine whether or not these transfers (of various kinds) had the consequence of reducing incentives and output of productive energy and therefore of reducing the National Dividend. In general, Pigou was prepared to agree that the 'principle of the 1834 Poor Law'—that the condition of the pauper should not be made more comfortable (or 'eligible') by State assistance than the condition of the lowest class of labourer who fended for himself—still had a great deal to be said for it. If the poor were encouraged to believe that assistance would be forthcoming they would be less inclined to provide for themselves, and the National Dividend would be diminished to the extent of the contribution they might have made. But he went on to make qualifications. 'The principle', he said, 'is not, however, either sacred or eternal, and it is necessary to guard against exaggerated applications of it that are often made in modern Poor Law literature.'[17]

He argued that the 1834 principle of less eligibility was formulated at a time when unskilled labourers formed the majority of the workforce, and when that class made a very substantial contribution to the National Dividend. Since 1834 economic progress had given more importance to the more skilled and better paid occupations. Consequently to allow the minimum provision to be superior to that of the lowest unskilled worker would no longer be so injurious to the National Dividend. 'We can, therefore, as Professor Marshall has observed,' Pigou declared, 'do a great deal more for paupers in 1907 . . . than it was possible to do in 1834.'[18]

Furthermore, it was a mistake to think that the 1834 principle could be extended unreservedly to categories of the poor other than the able-bodied. Distinctions needed to be made. While too-generous assistance might tempt able-bodied paupers to prefer idleness, and encourage poor persons in slight sickness to neglect to make their own insurance provision, the case was different with those gravely ill or with the aged. Unskilled labourers did not, and mostly were not able to, make provision for their own support against serious illness and old age. A harsh Poor Law policy towards them would do nothing to increase the National Dividend. 'Whether the very poor "ought" or could "reasonably be expected" to forearm themselves against these severer strokes of fortune, has nothing to do with the matter,' declared Pigou. 'The ground is cut

[17] Cd. 5086, Min. of Ev., Appendix vol. ix, p. 992.
[18] Ibid., p. 993.

from under the principle of 1834 by the consideration that, as a matter of fact, they would not so forearm themselves'.[19] The other category of Poor Law provision—the education of Poor Law children—he conceded to be a more difficult problem. If the Poor Law children were given an education better than the one which the independent labourer could afford, it would cause resentment, and might discourage labourers from educating their children at their own expense. On the other hand, the provision of good education for the pauper children might have benefits in making them more useful and productive citizens in the future. Poor Law administrators would have to try to weigh the considerable evils here against the possible great future benefits.

In general, then, Pigou followed his master, Professor Marshall, in making a cautious advance upon 'orthodox' Poor Law principles of the time. For instance, he did not go as far as Charles Booth in advocating universal old-age pensions financed by general taxation; he recommended that old-age pensions should be confined to the working class and financed by some form of compulsory or voluntary insurance. In conclusion, he quoted from Professor Marshall a statement in which he had recommended that a condition of a generous Poor Law provision might be that a person should have 'saved during the years in which his earnings were high and his family expenses not yet large' an amount 'standing in some reasonable relation to his wages'.[20]

Neither Pigou nor Marshall had any specific help to give the Commission on the problem of unemployment.[21] In 1907 they were both, apparently, still inhibited in their approach to that subject by Marshall's belief that 'unemployment of capable energetic workers' had been exaggerated—that it was 'not increasing, but rather diminishing',[22] and that it would diminish more as capitalists became aware of the hazards of trade fluctuations and

---

[19] Ibid.   [20] Ibid., p. 1000.

[21] T. W. Hutchinson, *A Review of Economic Doctrines 1870–1929* (Oxford, 1953), p. 416 dates Pigou's interest in public works as a counter-cycle policy to relieve unemployment to his Inaugural Lecture as Professor of Political Economy at Cambridge in 1908. The evidence at my disposal does not allow me to decide whether he had this interest earlier, but believed it was not relevant to his submission to the Commission, or whether his interest was aroused by what he had heard of the submissions of other economists to the Commission. Probably the latter was the case.

[22] Marshall to Percy Alden 28 Jan. 1903, Pigou, *Memorials of Alfred Marshall*, p. 446.

trade unionists became aware of the need for wages to be flexible to economic conditions. This relegated that kind of unemployment to a temporary problem of adjustment and 'understanding'. They took the view that most unemployment was of another kind— namely, that 'caused by the existence of large numbers of people who will not work or can not work steadily and strongly enough to make it possible that they should be employed regularly'.[23] Such 'permanent' or 'systematic' unemployment was a problem for the Poor Law and private charity. Furthermore, the Marshall school saw economic fluctuations as caused by lack of 'confidence' amongst business men.[24] Depressions and booms could hardly be eradicated from a system which was dynamic and progressive. The hopes for their diminution in the future, and the remedy for them when they occurred lay in the maintenance or restoration of business confidence. In economic terms, the study of causes and remedies of trade cycles should be pursued in the realm of organization of production and credit. Maladjustments of consumption were only minor or contributory causes of depressions, and 'a remedy is not to be got by a study of consumption, as has been alleged by some hasty writers'.[25] In general, Marshallians saw the economic system as substantially self-adjusting.

The theorists who were thus dismissed as 'hasty writers' were J. A. Hobson[26] and his disciple, J. M. Robertson.[27] A third edition of Hobson's *The Problem of the Unemployed: An Enquiry and an Economic Policy*, appeared in November 1906 and a fourth edition in December 1908. 'Poverty: Its Causes and Cures', which gave a succinct popular account of the ideas he had put forward during two decades, was published in his book, *The Crisis of Liberalism* (1909). He apparently had not offered to put his views to the Royal Commission and he certainly was not invited to present them. It was difficult to ignore so indefatigable a publicist as Hobson, though the academic and official world tried its best to do so, until,

---

[23] Ibid.
[24] A. Marshall, *Principles of Economics* (London, 9th (Variorum) edn., 1961), pp. 709–11.
[25] Ibid., p. 712 n.
[26] *DNB* 1931–40; *Ec.J.* 50 (1940); J. A. Hobson, *Confessions of an Economic Heretic* (London, 1938); H. Brailsford, *The Life Work of J. A. Hobson* (Oxford, 1948); M. Freeden, 'J. A. Hobson as a New Liberal Theorist: Some aspects of his Social Thought until 1914', *Journal of the History of Ideas*, 34 (1973).
[27] *DNB* 1931–40.

very belatedly, he won recognition as a forerunner by Keynes in the 1930s.[28] But his presence did not go altogether unnoticed (as we shall see) even by the Royal Commission on the Poor Laws.

If the Commission received no direct assistance on the problem of unemployment from the three economists whom a later generation would come to regard as the most distinguished theorists of their time, it did not lack other able economists to turn to for advice. There were ten other men who might be called political economists who presented evidence either in writing or verbally to the Royal Commission. They were (listed alphabetically): Professor William Ashley[29] of the University of Birmingham; William Henry Beveridge,[30] then a member of the Central Unemployed Body for London; Dr James Bonar,[31] the President of the School of Social Economics, at that time an adjunct of the Charity Organisation Society; Arthur Lyon Bowley,[32] Professor of Statistics at the London School of Economics; Edwin Cannan,[33] Professor of Economic Theory at the London School of Economics; Sydney John Chapman,[34] Professor of Political Economy in the University of Manchester; Arthur Wilson Fox,[35] Comptroller-General of the Statistical Department of the Board of Trade; Seebohm Rowntree,[36] the social investigator of York; Richard Henry Tawney,[37] then Research Assistant to Professor Smart at Glasgow; and Sidney Webb, at that time Chairman of the Board of

[28] J. M. Keynes, *The General Theory of Employment, Interest and Money* (London, 1951 repr.), pp. 364–70. The criticism of Hobson's theoretical position which Keynes made briefly in these pages is developed in E. E. Nemmers, *Hobson and Underconsumption* (Amsterdam, 1956). See also P. Clarke, *Liberals and Social Democrats* (Cambridge, 1978), ch. 7.

[29] DNB 1922–30; Ec.J. 37 (1927); A. Ashley, *William James Ashley* (London, 1932).

[30] Lord Beveridge, *Power and Influence* (London, 1953); J. Harris, *William Beveridge: A Biography* (Oxford, 1977).

[31] DNB 1941–50; Ec.J. 51 (1941); *Proceedings of the British Academy*, 27 (1941).

[32] DNB 1951–60.

[33] DNB 1931–40; Ec.J. 45 (1935).   [34] DNB 1951–60.

[35] *The Times*, 22 Jan. 1909 (obituary).

[36] DNB 1951–60; A. Briggs, *A Study of the Work of Seebohm Rowntree: Social Thought and Social Action* (London, 1961).

[37] *Proceedings of the British Academy*, 48 (1962); J. R. Williams, R. Titmuss, and F. J. Fisher, *R. H. Tawney: A Portrait by Several Hands* (London, 1960); J. M. Winter, *Socialism and the Challenge of War: Ideas and Politics in Britain 1912–18* (London, 1974); R. Terrill, *R. H. Tawney and his Times: Socialism as Fellowship* (Cambridge, Mass., 1973).

Studies in Economics and Political Science at the University of London. Altogether, it seems a fairly representative roll-call of Edwardian economic talent. Six of these experts were summoned to give advice by a questionnaire sent to them by the Commission (Ashley, Bowley, Cannan, Chapman, Rowntree, and Webb), the choice having been made by agreement between Professor Smart and Beatrice Webb; the younger men were called in as experts in special fields (Beveridge on account of his experience in the London Central Unemployed Body as administrator of Labour Exchanges, Wilson Fox as a Board of Trade statistician handling unemployment figures, and Tawney because of his researches on juvenile employment in Glasgow); Dr Bonar was invited as COS economic expert to traverse the whole field of Poor Law policy.

The form of the questionnaire[38] which the Commission sent out is interesting. Broadly speaking, what the Commissioners wanted to know was: what the effect was of increased use of machinery on the demand for labour as a whole; whether machinery reduced the total demand for labour permanently or temporarily; and whether machinery led to the displacement of older men by women and young persons and skilled workers by unskilled. On the matter of remedies for unemployment, the Commissioners wanted opinions concerning the need for increasing mobility of labour and the methods of achieving it; they asked for guidance about whether some new public organization was necessary for dealing with the unemployed. There appeared to be rather heavy stress on the effects of machinery; and there was no open-ended question about the causes of unemployment.

It is possible that the questionnaire had been framed, to some extent, with reference to a challenging statement presented to the Commission by the English Marxist organization at that time, the Social Democratic Federation. That statement embodied a number of popular beliefs thought to be characteristic of Socialist and Labour thinking, which most of the Commissioners were anxious to disprove. The SDF's statement[39] to the Royal Commission had been presented by Harry Quelch,[40] who was only an amateur economist. Quelch was that familiar Marxist figure, the theoretician

---

[38] Cd. 5072, Min. of Ev., Appendix vol. xi, p. 2.
[39] Cd. 4755, Min. of Ev., Appendix vol. iii, pp. 61–4.
[40] E. B. Bax, *Harry Quelch: Literary Remains* (with a biographical introduction) (London, 1914).

rather than the theorist. He was one of those remarkable, self-educated working men who played so active a role as propagandist and as active political worker in the socialist movement of the later Victorian age. Quelch cheerfully acknowledged, when asked about it, that he had not written the paper which he presented at the Commission. It was the collective view of the Social Democratic Federation, and he subscribed to it and was prepared to defend it.[41]

Both in the statement and the cross-examination, fundamental questions were raised about the causes of poverty, and to those questions, Quelch and the SDF returned some answers which they thought were Marxist, but which to a later eye seem unsophisticated to the point of heresy. The Industrial Revolution had caused a deterioration in the conditions of the working class. 'I think that poverty, so far from having diminished, has rather increased, that is, the number of poor people has increased,'[42] said Quelch. This was a result, so the SDF statement affirmed, of the introduction of machinery.

The universal introduction of machinery has been a very great factor in throwing the worker out of employment, and thereby rendering him an applicant for Poor Law relief . . . constant improvements render a less number of human workers necessary. A great deal of machinery is automatic, and, once set going, needs scarcely any looking after. This tendency is rendering the craftsman in many industries a thing of the past; unskilled labourers—mere tenders of machinery—replace skilled workers . . . The 'drive' of modern industry, that is the higher pressure at which work is now carried on, also ages men more quickly, and once their early manhood is gone, employers are not anxious to employ them.[43]

Furthermore, the labour of adult men was replaced by the employment of women and young people in their stead.[44]

The SDF's proposals for solution of the Poor Law problem were equally terse and straightforward. The problem of the Poor Law was basically the problem of poverty, and that could not be solved until Socialism was established.[45] But something in the mean time could be done by way of 'palliatives'. Workhouses as penal institutions should be abolished.[46] Pauper children should be given

[41] Cd. 4755, Min. of Ev., Appendix vol. iii, p. 65 (Qq. 25790–1).
[42] Ibid., p. 70 (Q. 25929).
[43] Ibid., p. 62.   [44] Ibid., p. 63.   [45] Ibid., p. 64.
[46] Ibid., pp. 61–3 and pp. 66–7 (Q. 25832).

the best living conditions and education possible.[47] Old people should receive honourable pensions, instead of pauper relief. The sick poor should be given separate treatment in their own homes.[48] The able-bodied poor should be provided with work, either in undertakings of national importance, such as afforestation, the making of national main roads, or the reclamation of foreshores; or they should be trained for agriculture in State farms, with the intention of setting them up as tenants of land taken over by the State (though care should be taken in selection to avoid 'the difficulty of trying to make agriculturalists out of worn-out town dwellers').[49] Finally, State or municipal manufactories should be established to employ craftsmen, and it might be possible to arrange an exchange between the products of the State farms and State manufactories so that the products of neither came on to the ordinary competitive market.[50]

Two things are worth noticing about the SDF's evidence. In the first place, it relied entirely for its explanation on Marx's general theory of the deterioration of working-class conditions. Not until Quelch was nudged in cross-examination by George Lansbury and Charles Booth, did he hastily acknowledge casual employment and cyclical depressions as additional causes of distress.[51] The absence of any mention of the trade cycle in the statement was surprising, in view of Marx's contribution to the recognition of its importance, and the prominence accorded it in the *Communist Manifesto*. Perhaps the SDF simply had taken it for granted. The second thing is that the SDF in its remedies was more interested in gaining improved conditions for the poor and removing the stigma of pauperism than it was in abolishing the Poor Law altogether. The Social Democrats did not think that the abolition of the Poor Law was essential to the gaining of better conditions and the removal of the stigma. When Quelch was asked directly: '. . . you have no objection to the Poor Law as a method of dealing with poor people, providing that there are adequate institutions, and that the method of dealing with the poor is changed on the lines you indicate as being a change for the better?' he replied: 'Yes, that is so'.[52]

[47] Ibid., p. 64.   [48] Ibid.   [49] Ibid.
[50] Ibid.   [51] Ibid., pp. 74–5 (Qq. 26052–4, 26096).
[52] Ibid., p. 68 (Q. 25876). This was no spur-of-the-moment response. See the *Social-Democrat*, 14 (1910) for an article by H. Quelch, 'The Prevention of Destitution', attacking the proposals of the Minority Report.

It does seem likely that the evidence from the SDF, with its encapsulation of a number of popular beliefs—its echoes of Ruskin and William Morris as well as of Marx—may have prompted some of those questions the Commissioners sent out. But, alas, not all of our economists who gave evidence replied to them in direct terms. The great economic historian, Professor William Ashley, of the University of Birmingham, gave them the shortest shrift. He replied: '. . . there does not yet exist the information concerning industrial conditions which is necessary before one can safely arrive at large conclusions on the subject'; and he 'hoped that the Royal Commission will institute such investigations as will in some measure supply the defect'.[53] With that generous cheerio, he bowed out. Of course, Ashley was quite right about the paucity of statistics; but that did not make him any more helpful.

In an attempt to bring some order into the discussion, the views of these economists will be presented under two headings: (1) the contributions they had to make in diagnosing the causes of unemployment, including in this section what they had to say about the claim that the use of machinery had caused a deterioration in the conditions of the working class; (2) the remedies that the economists themselves had to offer for unemployment.

1. *The Economists' Views of the Causes of Unemployment*

First, in the matter of the causes of unemployment, the question arises whether these economists lent any support to the SDF's views of the consequences of industrial evolution. Although only eight out of eleven of them gave a direct answer to the question in writing or in verbal answer to cross-examination, it seems clear that the SDF found no support at all for its belief that there had been a general decline in working-class standards. Here are some examples of the generally optimistic outlook. Beveridge cross-examined by Phelps:

The standard of living of the working classes has improved very much in the last fifty years, and that has implied a considerable increase in the production of wealth? Yes. You do not see signs that the standard is beginning to falter? I see no signs.[54]

Bonar cross-examined by Mrs Bosanquet:

---

[53] Cd. 5066, Min. of Ev., Appendix vol. iii, p. 504.
[54] Ibid., p. 31 (Qq. 78059, 78061).

We have had it put to us that the working man is now poorer than he was before and cannot make provision for himself, and we are anxious to get some evidence from economists as to how far that is the case. . . . My own impression is that there has been a very steady progress in the right direction, but very slow . . .[55] I would not admit that there were less unemployed in those [former] days than there are now; from all one hears there were far more; and if you look at the Report on the unemployed given ten years ago (1896) you will find the distress then was as great as now at least. I do not know that we are worse than we were, but we are not so much better as we would like to be. I think that is what it comes to.[56]

Dr Bonar was convinced that conditions had improved for the working classes generally—that over the last two or three decades wages had risen, and prices (except rent) had fallen.[57] Professor Cannan also was convinced of improvement. He declared:

General observations alone must be relied on [here], and the conclusion arrived at will vary with the personal bias of the observer. For my own part I seem to observe an enormous proportionate increase in the upper ranks of labour. The poorest class of house and the worst clothes seem to me to be becoming an obviously smaller proportion of the whole; the rise of the 'lower middle-class' seems sufficiently notorious and proclaims itself to anyone who will contemplate our modern towns.[58]

The increase of production per head of population was taken to establish improving conditions. The only economist to query this at all was Sidney Webb, who dared to point out that 'there may be more work and more wealth, and yet theoretically fewer labourers employed to do it'. But he quickly added: 'I do not think that this is the actual result statistically [at present]'.[59]

The same kind of optimism was shown by the economists about the long-term effects of machinery on employment. Every one of the economists who replied directly to the questions rejected the notion which had been put forward by the SDF, that machinery decreased the demand for labour generally and in the long run. Bowley answered brusquely that the general effect of the spread of machinery and more highly industrialized processes on 'the demand for labour as a whole and in the long run is *nil*'. Both experience and theory demonstated that the available labour force of the

[55] Cd. 4755, Min. of Ev., Appendix vol. iii, p. 217 (Q. 29556).
[56] Ibid., p. 221 (Q. 29673).   [57] Ibid., p. 217 (Qq. 29556-7).
[58] Cd. 5072, Min. of Ev., Appendix vol. xi, p. 6.
[59] Cd. 5068, Min. of Ev., Appendix vol. ix, p. 203 (Q. 93300).

country is, 'apart from temporary congestions and want of adjustment' employed.[60] Edwin Cannan took the same view. The total number employed was determined by population, by the age structure of the population, and by arrangements of the society about property. Machinery entered as a factor influencing the quantity of labour only in so far as it affected population.[61] That appeared also to be the view of others. However, Sidney Webb again sounded a note of caution. He warned that statistical studies of total employment were not adequate. He thought that there had been, as he put it, a 'considerable substitution of intelligent machine-minding for mere mechanical effort'. This must have had the result of raising the 'minimum capacity [of persons] considered [to be] worth employing'; and this in turn might 'afford some explanation of the apparent surplus of common unskilled labour in the great towns'. There did not seem to be 'any automatic absorption of this surplus'.[62]

All of our economists allowed, however, that the introduction of new machinery could cause temporary distress and unemployment. Rowntree gave examples from his own factory where machinery had replaced human labour. Some previously skilled workers were thrown by technological change on to the unskilled labour market.[63] The chief difference between the economists lay in the note of optimism or pessimism which they struck concerning the length of time 'adjustments' to technological changes would take, and whether the capitalist system could cope automatically with dislocation or needed a bit of a shove from the government. In general, the economists did not see technological change as a chief problem, in the way the SDF had done. A. L. Bowley's view here was perhaps typical. He said that in the earlier days of the Industrial Revolution technological change had produced major social and economic crises, as with the displacement of the hand-loom weavers. But he thought that there had been no catastrophe of that magnitude in recent times. Asked by Professor Smart if the displacement of hand bootmakers by machine bootmaking that had occurred in the previous ten years was not a similar case, Bowley

---

[60] Cd. 5066, Min. of Ev., Appendix vol. viii, p. 463.
[61] Cd. 5072, Min. of Ev., Appendix vol. xi, p. 5.
[62] Cd. 5068, Min. of Ev., Appendix vol. ix, p. 183.
[63] Cd. 5072, Min. of Ev., Appendix vol. xi, p. 12.

said he did not imagine the distress was nearly so serious.[64] It emerged that he considered that the industrial state, as it became more advanced, was more capable of absorbing technological changes. Nevertheless, all the economists allowed that technological change did help to create an unemployment problem.

The next item faced by the economists who answered the questionnaire arose from the claims that there had been a replacement of skilled labour by unskilled, of older men by younger workers, and a replacement of adult men by women and young persons in industry. Several of the economists[65] began by declaring that there were no adequate statistics to settle these questions reliably; but that did not stop them giving their opinions. Bonar thought skilled workers had been replaced by unskilled.[66] But Webb, Bowley, and Pigou considered there had been an increase in the proportion of skilled.[67] Professor Cannan pointed out neatly some of the difficulties of defining the terms 'skilled' and 'unskilled' when comparing, say, manual production with machine-minding.[68] Professor Sydney Chapman, whose special study was the cotton trade, saw development in these terms:

The tendency of machinery is always to cause a substitution of 'intelligence' for dexterity, the person who was in effect a machine by reasons of his dexterity giving place to one who could understand and direct a mechanical process. Incidentally a number of monotonous operations are created, but these . . . afterwards tend to be reduced [by the invention of new machinery], and it is not certain that they are always more monotonous than the hand operations abolished, though they may require less dexterity.

And he concluded:

I incline to believe . . . that it could not be shown that such developments have caused absolute damage to any one class of labour. In considering this question, the higher real wages caused by machinery must not be left out of account.[69]

---

[64] Cd. 5066, Min. of Ev., Appendix vol. viii, pp. 464, 472 (Qq. 88136, 88321-2).

[65] Bowley, Cannan, Webb.

[66] Cd. 4755, Min. of Ev., Appendix vol. iii, p. 224 (Q. 29751).

[67] Cd. 5068, p. 183 (Webb); Cd. 5066, p. 463 (Bowley); Cd. 5086, p. 992 (Pigou).

[68] Cd. 5072, Min. of Ev., Appendix vol. xi, p. 6.

[69] Cd. 5066, Min. of Ev., Appendix vol. viii, p. 334.

On the question of the replacement of older men by younger
workers, or adult men by women and children, there was some
division of opinion. Bonar thought that this had taken place.[70]
Rowntree confessed that he did not know.[71] Cannan was sceptical:
he thought that if this had been the case, it should be revealed in
larger percentages of adult and older men in unemployment
statistics. 'I know of no statistics which show this', he said, 'and do
not believe it is patent to common observation'.[72] Sidney Webb
went further, declaring that in recent years there had actually been
a decline in the industrial employment of women and children
relative to men.[73] Webb was supported in this view by Wilson Fox
who produced some figures.[74]

The major contentions of the SDF statement clearly had won
little support from the Edwardian economists. One of them,
Professor Sydney Chapman, carried the battle further. He sailed in
to attack the Marxists' notion that public ownership could be a
remedy for poverty and unemployment. Public ownership would
not be a remedy, he claimed, unless it involved a regimentation of
labour regardless of economic criteria and economic progress.[75]
Sidney Webb, in cross-examination, agreed with Chapman on this:

. . . the problem [of unemployment] has nothing to do with individualism
or collectivism. I hold that there would be fluctuations of employment and
changes of industry, and therefore men dropping out even if you had all the
industries of the country worked by collectivist organisations.[76]

So having rejected the SDF's views, it was up to the economists to
provide alternative diagnoses. Before we come to these directly, let
us pause to consider a problem that was not raised in the
questionnaire, but which haunted the whole proceedings of the
Commission like Banquo's ghost: the notion that pauperism and
unemployment were the outcome of personal failings on the part of
individuals who were poor. The problem kept cropping up
repeatedly in cross-examination. Here is an example: the young
Richard Tawney cross-examined by the old Octavia Hill. Miss Hill

<hr/>

[70] Cd. 4755, Min. of Ev., Appendix vol. iii, p. 224 (Q. 29751).
[71] Cd. 5072, Min. of Ev., Appendix vol. xi, p. 12.
[72] Cd. 5072, Min. of Ev., Appendix vol xi, p. 6.
[73] Cd. 5068, Min. of Ev., Appendix vol. ix, p. 183.
[74] Ibid., p. 455 (Qq. 99030–3).
[75] Cd. 5066, Min. of Ev., Appendix vol. viii, p. 332.
[76] Cd. 5068, Min. of Ev., Appendix vol. ix, p. 203 (Q. 93303).

was questioning Tawney's claim that boys ended up as shiftless applicants to distress committees because of industrial reasons and not because of their inherent defects of character:

[The boy] leaves a place because he is tired of the job, or because he could not get on with the foreman or because he wanted more money? Certainly. The employer offers him work of a kind that is absolutely uneducative, and done under purely monotonous and mechanical conditions. It is often the best boys and not the worst who leave jobs because they are [more] enterprising.

Is it not very often the want of discipline in the boy? It may be increased by the system, but surely it is the want of steady work very often that prevents them from rising into better places? The majority of them cannot rise in the industries I am speaking of, because the number of better places is so small that all the boys are not wanted to recruit them, as my figures show. You cannot expect boys to rise above the average boy nature.

But you cannot say it is not personal, can you? It seems to me that it is due to the personal characteristics of the boy, even if he cannot be very much to blame for that? It no doubt depends upon that, which boy is the first to go and which boy suffers most. The general system degrades the whole class of boys, and puts an incentive in the way of all boys, good and bad, to make a mess of their lives . . .

If we had a loyal boy, a punctual boy, an obedient boy, a good tempered boy and an industrious boy, he would get on? Certainly, but I say the present conditions of work-shop life tend to produce precisely the opposite type.[77]

We can see emerging there the line of attack on the old COS argument which was developed more effectively by Beveridge and Webb during their cross-examination. They did not deny that in the ranks of unemployed would be found a considerable number of loafers, drunks, and incompetents. But the reason for this, they maintained, was that these kind of people were likeliest to be dismissed in bad economic conditions. Moral shortcomings might determine which individuals went first to the wall; but they were not a primary cause of unemployment. Even if everyone were industrious and fit, industrial dislocation would cause some persons to be unemployed. And the condition of being unemployed could

---

[77] Cd. 5068, Min. of Ev., Appendix vol. ix, p. 346 (Qq. 96841–3, 96845).

lead to moral failings: these personal failings were as likely, or more likely, to be a consequence as a cause of unemployment.[78]

It was really this question of the causal emphasis to be given to personal or social factors that was at stake. None of our economists affirmed the complete irrelevance of personal failings, and even the most advanced reformers among them retained a bit of steel *au fond* in dealing with loafers. But not one of the economists who addressed himself directly to the causes of unemployment thought that moral failing was the major cause. Professor Sydney Chapman, who was possibly somewhere to the right of centre on this issue, put moral defects at the head of his list of causes of unemployment, but his later discussion left little doubt he thought that at least one of his social causes (casual labour) was more important.[79] Even Dr Bonar, the COS's own economist, proved to be a weak reed if the older COS members were relying on his help. He agreed that 'the unemployed are very many of them very respectable men who have been trade unionists' and he considered that they did not deserve to be treated in the same way as able-bodied paupers.[80]

Another supposed general cause of unemployment was raised only to be dismissed by every one of the economists who considered it. That was the old Malthusian argument about overpopulation. The declining rate of population growth, the increase of production per head, and the growth of capital accumulation all seemed decisive against it. The Malthusian bogy seemed at least temporarily dead.

To what social factors, then, did the economists attribute unemployment? Their first item has already been mentioned: unemployment caused by industrial changes (what we now call technological unemployment). They extended it to cover not only unemployment caused by the introduction of new machinery and new methods, but also to unemployment caused by the decay of particular industries, or the removal of industry from one geographical area to another. The general attitude taken by the economists was that this could produce sad results for individual workers, who might have to move, at an advanced, not easily adaptable age, to new occupations. But it was a necessary condition

---

[78] Beveridge: Cd. 5066, Min. of Ev., Appendix vol. viii, pp. 10, 22 (Qq. 77844–5); Webb: Cd. 5068, Min. of Ev., Appendix vol. ix, p. 204 (Qq. 93312–21).
[79] Cd. 5066, Min. of Ev., Appendix vol. viii, pp. 330–1.
[80] Cd. 4755, Min. of Ev., Appendix vol. iii, p. 226 (Qq. 29805, 29819).

of social progress and, they hoped, adjustment would be achieved in the long run.

The second cause which occupied a lot of attention was what Professor Chapman called 'the system of casual labour', and for which Beveridge coined the term 'underemployment'. Beveridge, Chapman, and Webb all developed the argument at some length that there was a tendency, particularly in unskilled or semi-skilled trades, for an overstocking of the trade with labour, owing to a lack of organization of the demand for that labour and the inability of the labourer to move easily to other types of work. Sidney Webb presented the most vivid description of this industrial evil to the Commission, making suitable acknowledgement to Beveridge. He declared:

. . . (as Mr. Beveridge has shown) reliance by individual employers on casual labour creates little crowds of surplus labour at each dock gate, by each wharf, even around each builder's foreman—each crowd waiting wholly or mainly for jobs from that particular source. It is to the interest of each such employer to have waiting for his jobs a crowd large enough to get through the maximum amount of work at any moment that he is ever likely to need to get done. Thus there are now collected on the Thames and the Mersey, at Bristol and at Newcastle, at Glasgow and at Hull, not merely enough casual labourers to supply the maximum needs of the busiest day of the port as a whole, if all the needs were combined, but enough to supply the aggregate total of the separate maxima that the several employers may, on many different days, individually require. And what is true of dock and wharf labour is true to a greater or less extent of the slightly specialised manual labour employed by the builders, and the contractors for engineering works, of the workers in practically all the seasonal trades, of the outworkers in the clothing and furniture trades, and, in fact, in all industries in which there is not a definite regular staff, filling permanent situations, but in which labour is 'casually' employed. The result of this excess is that the casual employment is rendered even more intermittent and 'casual' than it need be.[81]

Behind the emphasis that all these men placed on the problem of casual labour we discern the results of much sociological work of the late nineteenth and early twentieth centuries: sociological inquiries of the sort inspired by Charles Booth's great survey, by research done in connection with investigations into sweated industries, and by social workers interested in poverty and its

[81] Cd. 5068, Min. of Ev., Appendix vol. ix, pp. 185–6.

treatment. There had been a heavy concentration of interest in areas where casual employment was most common.[82] Beveridge's work at Toynbee Hall in the East End, on the Stepney Distress Committee, as a member of the Mansion House Fund, and on the Central Unemployed Body for London had been the basis of his insight.[83] A major extra contribution to the discussion of casual labour made by some of the economists was the stress they laid on the self-recruiting nature of the casual labour force. Beveridge said:

. . . casual employment, by maintaining a large number of families in chronic poverty, forces the elder children into the first and best-paid job that offers, irrespective of the future. The casual labourers of today are largely the children of the casual labourers of yesterday.[84]

Sidney Webb added:

At present it is scarcely too much to say we re-create every eight or ten years our whole army of paupers. If, by some miracle, we could get rid of the present million of paupers, we should, if we made no other change, simply have an equal number on our hands within a decade.[85]

R. H. Tawney weighed in to demonstrate how dead-end jobs for boys in Glasgow inevitably swelled the ranks of casual labour in that city.[86]

The third major cause of unemployment recognized by the economists was fluctuations of industrial activity, either seasonal or cyclical. Beveridge, Bowley, Chapman, Wilson Fox, and Webb all discerned the importance of these fluctuations. But the statisticians, Bowley and Wilson Fox, took the lead in the discussion of cyclical fluctuations.

It is interesting to observe how the economists who addressed themselves to the causal problem distributed their emphasis amongst these three major factors: technological unemployment, casual labour, and economic fluctuations. Although all of them mentioned all these factors, Dr Bonar seemed most concerned with technological unemployment; Beveridge, Webb, Sydney Chapman, and Tawney focused on casual labour as the central problem; while Bowley and Wilson Fox were engaged primarily with cyclical fluctuations. Their distribution of emphasis was sometimes explicit,

---

[82] G. Stedman Jones, *Outcast London* (Oxford, 1971), pp. 52 ff.
[83] Harris, *William Beveridge: A Biography*, pp. 108 ff.
[84] Cd. 5066, Min. of Ev., Appendix vol. viii, p. 10.
[85] Cd. 5068, Min. of Ev., Appendix vol. ix, p. 183.   [86] Ibid., p. 311.

sometimes it came out indirectly. For example, Professor Chapman de-emphasized technological unemployment by taking the hopeful view that, as the industrial system matured, these changes would take place gradually, and that the drop in wages that would occur when the demand for a particular class of labour was reduced would check entry into the trade, causing it to dwindle automatically without many operatives having to be dismissed. Chapman also was inclined to think that the intensity of trade cycles might be expected to diminish in future. So, for him, casual labour was the real problem.[87] Professor Bowley took the same view as Chapman about technological unemployment, but he thought that surplus casual labour needed to be removed from the market by 'philanthropic, colonising, and emigration agencies'. So the central problem for him was periodic fluctuations which bore so hard on the willing and able workmen.[88] Of course, the economists learnt from each other in the course of the inquiry. Beatrice Webb's cross-examination of Bowley marks the point where the Webbs picked up his ideas and incorporated them in their own.[89] If genius consists in an infinite capacity for picking brains, the Webbs certainly had it. But they could do even better: they could combine the ideas they had picked with ideas of their own.

Altogether, the Edwardian economists who presented their analyses of unemployment to the Royal Commission managed, between them, to confront the Commissioners with a rich and complex set of social explanations. But only one of the economists in his submission made any attempt to pursue the causes of unemployment into higher levels of theory than the immediate or phenomenal level. Professor Sydney Chapman sallied into theory in order to do battle with J. A. Hobson's doctrines of 'underconsumption' and the disequilibrium of savings and investment. He rejected Hobson's explanations on grounds already put forward by Marshall—because they involved a denial that demand was a continuous function of price and that savings were to be identified with investment in the long run.[90] Actually, we know from other evidence[91] (but not from the evidence given to this Royal

---

[87] Cd. 5066, Min. of Ev., Appendix vol. viii, pp. 330–1.
[88] Ibid., pp. 466–8.   [89] Ibid., pp. 469–71 (Qq. 88245–65).
[90] Cd. 5066, Min. of Ev., Appendix vol. viii, pp. 331–2.
[91] See, for example, W. Smart, 'The Dislocations of Industry', *Contemporary Review*, 53 (1888); E. Cannan, review of Hobson in *Ec.J.* 7, (1897); *Fabian News* (May 1895) (review of Hobson's *Evolution of Modern Capitalism*).

Commission) that the other economists rejected Hobson on these grounds too.

2. The Economists' Views of Remedies for Unemployment

What remedies for unemployment did these economists have to offer? The form in which the question was put to them was: what public organization, if any, was necessary to supplement the Poor Law? Three distinct kinds of answer were given to this question. The first answer was yes—that some additional, supplementary organization or organizations should be created. Dr James Bonar, William Beveridge, and Professor Bowley took that line. The second answer was no—that nothing outside the Poor Law was really required. Professor Edwin Cannan upheld that point of view. The third answer was that the Poor Law should be swept away entirely and the functions it performed handed over to other authorities. Sidney Webb was the spokesman for this third attitude.

Dr James Bonar was one of those who felt that some organization outside the Poor Law was necessary, although his approach was extremely cautious. As we have seen Bonar was a COS man who had come to believe that a distinction could definitely be made between the respectable men who fell temporarily into unemployment and the able-bodied destitute poor who were permanently out of work. While the Poor Law workhouse with its hard labour, social stigma, and penalty of disfranchisement was, in Bonar's view, a suitable treatment for the able-bodied pauper, he was willing to approve of experiments outside the Poor Law altogether in providing for the temporarily unemployed. He was not sanguine in his hopes of these experiments and he thought they should be on a small scale and not draw too heavily on public funds—if possible, they should be financed by voluntary charitable contributions. These experiments should take the form of public works programmes of a type that had already been tried in London by the Central Unemployed Body.[92] Bonar was not a great innovator, but he showed that the younger generation of COS people were willing, however timidly, to move beyond the confines of earlier COS thought.

William Henry Beveridge's approach was different. He had been a member of the CUB and was not at all happy with its experiments

[92] Cd. 4755, Min. of Ev. Appendix vol. iii, pp. 220–1, 224, 226 (Qq. 29656, 29670, 29677, 29681, 29753–4, 29815).

in 'making work for the unemployed'. These experiments had failed because the underemployed had flooded out the class of men they were designed to help—those temporarily unemployed through exceptional causes beyond their control. The remedy for underemployment which Beveridge proposed was the organization of the labour market through labour exchanges, designed (in the later famous phrase of Winston Churchill) 'to find jobs for men and men for jobs'. Labour exchanges would try to find new work for those displaced by technological changes, and supplementary work for the unemployed and seasonal workers; at the same time the worker's willingness to present himself at a labour exchange could act as a test of his willingness to work. It was essential that labour exchanges should be separate institutions—quite distinct from any organizations giving direct relief or identified by public opinion with relief. 'The name "unemployed" is enough to ruin [any labour exchange]', said Beveridge. They were to become a permanent industrial organization under some public authority of nation-wide scope, such as the Board of Trade. They were to be staffed by expert administrators representing both employers and employed. Beveridge wanted these labour exchanges to be developed at least at the outset by the encouragement of voluntary co-operation between employers and workmen. He was convinced that both employers and trade unions would soon come to see their advantages.[93]

Beveridge foresaw that one problem would remain even when the labour market was organized in this way: unemployment caused by cyclical fluctuations. As a separate remedy for this he proposed, first, the encouragement of insurance against unemployment through trade unions and perhaps through labour exchanges, fostered by government grants to assist unemployed pay in times of depression; and second, the shortening of working hours in times of depression and the increasing of hours in times of expansion in order to create more or less jobs.[94] But Beveridge realized the difficulties of unemployment insurance and the regulation of hours. The Poor Law would survive for those who would not or could not be helped in these ways.[95]

Bowley also wanted organization outside the Poor Law, but,

---

[93] Cd. 5055, Min. of Ev., Appendix vol. viii, pp. 15–16, 26 (Q. 77941 for the quotation).
[94] Ibid., pp. 17–18.
[95] Ibid., pp. 26, 28, 32 (Qq. 77945, 77991, 78093).

because his main attention was directed to cyclical fluctuations, he had a different slant from Beveridge. He allowed that labour exchanges might help to promote mobility if they were linked in a national system, but he was inclined to think that means of communication and travel had so improved that information about jobs could be adequately provided whether or not labour exchanges were set up, so long as persons choosing jobs for young people would take note of the information and make provision for workers to travel in search of jobs.[96] Bowley's main argument was that the government should give thought to staggering its public works programme, particularly of works not needing to be done at any particular time—such as the building of docks, schools, parks, and roads—in order that these works should be undertaken at times when cyclical unemployment was anticipated. He suggested that they should be launched when the unemployment index reached 4 per cent. Such a scheme needed no extra expenditure; it required only thought and foresight. It was intended to be of the nature of prevention rather than cure, and he felt that if its scale of operation was sufficient it could remove a principal cause of the dissatisfaction of the genuine workman with industrial conditions.[97] The Poor Law of course would remain to deal with the non-genuine.[98] These three were the most striking contributions from the economists to the notion of supplementing the Poor Law.

Edwin Cannan, however, took quite a different view. He said bluntly, 'for the relief of distress I consider that the long-established organisation, usually known as the Poor Law, is necessary, and that no other organisation, public or private, should be set up alongside it'. He very much doubted whether labour exchanges, even if they were organized on a national scale, would meet any existing need. He pointed out that in some occupations, especially in domestic service, private labour exchanges called registries had been set up by co-operation between employers and employed—if there were a demand for them in other trades they would similarly be set up without government intervention. As for providing work, this could be done through the Poor Law and did not require any outside agency either. Anybody who could not support himself or his family should get relief from the Poor Law with whatever conditions 'such as work, abstinence from drink and so forth that

---

[96] Ibid., pp. 464–5 (Q. 88145).　　　　[97] Ibid., pp. 467–8.
[98] Ibid., pp. 469–70 (Qq. 88242, 88264).

the State may decide to enforce'. There should be no stigma
associated with public relief, and the belief that private charity was
superior to or more honourable than Poor Law assistance he
thought a lot of nonsense.

As a matter of fact people are much more demoralized by the fitful
operations of private benevolence than by any tolerably well-regulated
Poor Law. I should rejoice to see the operations of the Poor Law
considerably extended, if by that expansion the operations of private
benevolence were reduced.[99]

Sidney Webb's suggestions for solving the unemployment problem
were presented after Beatrice and he had already decided that the
Poor Law needed to be 'broken up'—in effect abolished, and its
different functions handed over to local government committees
already in existence or to be created. The Poor Law children were
to be put in charge of the Education Committees of the local
councils; the sick poor were to be handled by the Public Health
authorities; old people by Pension Committees, and so on. In the
case of unemployment, Webb first of all took over (with suitable
acknowledgments) Beveridge's scheme for labour exchanges. But
he thought it would be necessary to make them government
agencies and to introduce a measure of compulsion. It should be
made legally necessary for employers either to guarantee to the
workman a minimum period of employment (of, say, a month) or
to hire the labour they wanted, whether for a job, a day, or a week,
exclusively through the public labour exchange. This would not
prevent voluntary labour exchanges, but they would be forbidden
to hire workers for less than a month. The public labour exchanges
would be controlled by a new Ministry of Labour. The labourers
for whom work could not be found by the labour exchanges would
be given full maintenance in return for undergoing a course of
industrial retraining. These retraining centres, also under the
general care of the Ministry of Labour, would take several forms:
central labour depots for the best of the surplus labourers giving
technical classes; day industrial schools providing less advanced
training; farm colonies for various sorts of agricultural training;
various institutions run by religious and philanthropic organizations
(subject to State inspection); and finally a penal settlement for the
recalcitrant, providing disciplinary treatment of a curative nature,

[99] Cd. 5072, Min. of Ev., Appendix vol. xi, p. 7.

calculated 'to raise and stimulate, never to depress'. Webb took up Beveridge's idea of State aid to provident and trade union insurance against unemployment. He also adopted Bowley's notions of the staggering of government works. This was to be an additional matter for the watchful attention of the Minister of Labour.[1]

The economists, between them, had managed to present a wide range of suggestions to the Royal Commission. Various though they were, all of them broke away from old fashioned Poor Law thinking. None of them was 'reactionary', or wanted a return to a really harsh Poor Law system. Even those who were, in some ways, closest to the old stance, wished for some softening of Poor Law policy. Cannan wanted any notion of a stigma attaching to Poor Law relief to be rejected with derision. Pigou at this time, like his master Alfred Marshall, thought that England was now wealthy enough to allow, with due regard for the continued growth of the National Dividend, a measure of 'economic chivalry' to soften the harsher features of capitalism. The others wanted some organization of the labour market outside the Poor Law, whether the experiments proposed were very cautious, like Bonar's, or larger but voluntary, such as those of Beveridge and Chapman, or bolder and more bureaucratic like those of the Webbs.

The general 'progressiveness' of the economists who were called to testify might seem to have represented a victory for the Webbs' side in this cross-court exchange. But we must not exaggerate their progressiveness. While they were all more advanced than the stern policy of the 'old guard' of the COS and the Poor Law officials, their views were not incompatible with a softer interpretation of COS doctrine. They rejected schematic criticisms of the existing system, as put forward either by the Marxists, or by Hobson. Most of them were content with the neo-classical theoretical framework, as restated by Marshall. Its doctrines—concerning the virtues of private enterprise and thrift, the equation of investment with savings through flexible interest rates, the equation of consumption and production through flexible prices, and the maintenance of full employment through flexible wages—formed the links in a chain of reasoning that proved hard to break. Even the Socialists, Webb and Tawney, who doubted the strength of some of these links, declined to follow the example of Hobson in his bid to create a system of

[1] Cd. 5068, Min. of Ev., Appendix vol. ix, pp. 186–90.

counter-doctrine. They hoped to outflank the 'Great Boyg' of theory by attacking on a practical, empirical level. Sidney Webb, who had respect neither for the efficiency nor the justice of the capitalist system, thought of his remedies for unemployment as separate from his central ethical criticism of capitalism. This prevented their being dismissed, as the Marxists' and Hobson's were, as the doctrinaire ideas of 'impractical theorists'. On the other hand, it made them vulnerable to being bypassed by the more moderate proposals of progressive Liberals, such as Beveridge and Pigou, who (though they were to advance to more radical proposals later) believed at this time that the radical remedies of the Webbs were not needed.

10

The Scramble for Victory

BY 1908, everyone on the Commission was beginning to realize that time was passing, and speed would be needed to win the contest. Beatrice Webb had organized herself more efficiently than her opponents for this final spurt. Once she had decided that she would need to put in a separate minority report, she was confident that she and Sidney, with their experience as writers of history and social analysis, could get their drafting done in good time. Her only concern was whether she could persuade any of the Commissioners into signing her report apart from the Labour men, Lansbury and Chandler. At her most forlorn moment, she doubted it; but she was determined to press on with her separate report all the same. She bolstered her confidence with her contempt for the apparently bumbling methods of her opponents, relying on their making a mess of their report through lack of co-operation. For her own part, she was determined to 'draw up a rattling good report, vivid in statement of fact, and closely reasoned with a logical conclusion and immediately practicable proposals of a moderate character'.[1] Knowing how much work she and Sidney had already put into their preparation, she sneered at Lord George Hamilton's optimism that he could get his main report drafted by July 1908 and settled in August.[2]

Beatrice Webb's scepticism at the time seemed well based. A great deal of confusion reigned in the camp of her opponents in 1908. Charles Booth had been obliged to resign from the Commission in January, because of a severe attack of angina; and

---

[1] B.W.D., 15 May 1907; *Our Partnership*, ed. B. Drake and M. Cole (London, 1948), p. 381; MacKenzie, *Diary*, iii, 74.
[2] B. Webb to S. Webb, 26 Apr. 1908, N. MacKenzie (ed.), *The Letters of Sidney and Beatrice Webb*, vol. ii. *Partnership 1892–1912* (Cambridge, 1978), p. 303.

in any case he, together with Dr Downes and to a lesser extent
Octavia Hill, had been alienated by the decision of the majority to
abolish the Boards of Guardians and transfer their functions to the
county councils.[3] The accusation made by Helen Bosanquet, that
Beatrice Webb was trying to 'drive wedges' into the majority to add
to their confusion,[4] seems to be justified, for Beatrice Webb tried to
persuade Dr Downes to put in a separate 'status quo report'.[5] He
confessed, however, that he did not feel capable of taking on such a
heavy task of writing, although he and Octavia Hill did eventually
append particular reservations to the Majority Report. Charles
Stewart Loch and Helen Bosanquet, although not put out of action,
were temporarily obliged to rest for health reasons: he was
threatened with a stroke and she had an incipient heart weakness.
Lord George had come to regard both Thory Gardiner and
Hancock Nunn as too unreliable and quirky to be entrusted with
any central task of drafting. Bentham had proved useful in making
suggestions, but he could not write effectively. Provis, on the verge
of retirement, was willing to give his advice, but not to throw
himself into the major task of drafting. Patten-MacDougall was
interested only in the Scottish section of the report; Robinson and
the Bishop of Ross only in the Irish part. Wakefield, along with
Lansbury and Chandler, was regarded by Lord George as a
potential supporter of the Webbs (as, indeed, it turned out). Phelps,
who had a good style and later gave valuable service in an editorial
capacity,[6] was unprepared to undertake the rigours of heavy
scholarship in preliminary drafting; and Lord George Hamilton,
although in his letters he tried to magnify his share in the
preparation of the Report, was also mainly concerned with
organization and editing.

[3] Booth, who had begun by favouring the adoption of the counties and county
boroughs as the areas for a reformed Poor Law ('Notes for a New Poor Law', July
1906, Webb Local Government Collection, vol. 286), later changed his mind about
this ('Memorandum A', Dec. 1907, ibid.) and decided in favour of the retention of
existing Unions with a flexible plan for their combination into larger areas. The local
authority in both of his schemes was to be a Poor Law Board; in the first proposal it
was to be appointed by the county or county borough council, in the later proposal it
was to be an *ad hoc* Board elected by ratepayers with some LGB nominees. Although
the proposal adopted by the Majority was very like his first plan, he came to regard it
as a capitulation to the Webbs' ideas.
[4] B.W.D., 13 Jan. 1908 (Extract not included in *Our Partnership*).
[5] B. Webb to S. Webb, 25 Apr., 1908. MacKenzie, *Letters*, ii. 300.
[6] Hamilton to Phelps, 26 May 1909. Phelps Papers.

Three persons were responsible for rescuing the Majority from what must have seemed (and, to Beatrice Webb, did seem) to be a hopeless situation. These three were Helen Bosanquet, Professor William Smart, and the Secretary of the Commission, Robert Duff. Chief credit must go to Helen Bosanquet, who, ill though she was, forced herself or perhaps allowed herself to be forced by the slave-driving Chairman, to shoulder the main burden not only of drafting the largest share of the Report, but also of revising most of it. Professor Smart had second place: as originator of its historical and economics sections, he helped to give the Majority Report a more radical slant than it might otherwise have taken. Robert Duff, the well-informed and compliant Secretary, was made responsible for the drafts of sections concerning legal and administrative matters, and he appears to have handled this task quite well, in spite of the Chairman's complaints: 'Poor Duff, with all his merits is a very bad writer. I have had to rewrite the whole of some of his sections, others I have patched up, but they are patchwork, & bad patchwork.'[7] This, however, was a familiar prelude to Lord George Hamilton's constant plea to Helen Bosanquet: 'From a literary point of view your apt pen might like to improve the style . . .'[8]

The sections of the Majority Report for which particular commissioners were responsible can be discovered from surviving correspondence. Duff and the Chairman were mainly responsible for Part I, dealing with the procedure adopted in the Commission's enquiries. Professor Smart (with help provided by LGB officials and by Charles Booth's secretary, Mr Jesse Argyle) drafted Part II, the statistical survey of Poor Law problems; and Professor Smart also wrote Part III, the historical sketch of the Poor Laws down to 1834, as well as the introductory section to Part IV, describing the historical development and present condition of the various branches of the Poor Law. Helen Bosanquet then took over as drafter of descriptive chapters 1 to 8 of Part IV—the chapters which dealt with the development and the existing powers of the Central Authority, the Local Authorities, the Officers of the Local Authority, the Administrative Areas, the administration of Indoor and Outdoor Relief, the treatment of the Aged and the Poor Law Children. Professor Smart and she then collaborated in the final two chapters (9 and 10) of Part IV, concerning the treatment of the

---

[7] Hamilton to H. Bosanquet, 17 Sept. 1908. Bosanquet Papers.
[8] Ibid.

able-bodied under the Poor Law and the Causes of Pauperism. Lord George Hamilton also had a finger in the pie in altering the drafting of that last chapter. Helen Bosanquet began the drafting of Part V on Medical Relief, but when she was forced to protest that she had been given too much to handle, Lord George Hamilton persuaded the reluctant Dr Downes to take it off her hands,[9] in spite of the fact that Downes thought the Majority's decisions rash and much too radical—as he made clear in his addendum to the Report later on. Helen Bosanquet, however, was responsible for the special section on medical relief to children.[10] Professor Smart did the original drafting of all of Part VI on the problem of the Unemployed and Unemployment,[11] with some assistance from Hancock Nunn on the provision of public works for the unemployed by Distress Committees, although the bulk of Nunn's 'reminiscences' (as the Chairman contemptuously labelled them)[12] were relegated to his special memorandum as appendix to the Report. Helen Bosanquet was called upon to revise the whole of this Part VI.[13] Charles Stewart Loch, who was 'driving to distraction' both Professor Smart and the Chairman with pedantic amendments,[14] was allowed to draft Part VII on Charities and the Relief of Distress on his own. Helen Bosanquet contributed two sections, Chapter 1 on Invalidity Insurance and Chapter 2 on Settlement and Removal to the 'Miscellaneous' Part VIII of the Report; the rest of Part VIII was drafted by Duff. The final summing up in Part IX, the Review of Existing Conditions and Proposed Changes, was written jointly by Helen Bosanquet and the Chairman assisted by Duff: it appears to be mainly her work, except for the patriotic Conclusion, in which Lord George's fist is clearly visible.[15]

Altogether, Professor Smart's remark to Helen Bosanquet in a letter to her in the early stages of the assignment of the drafting, that their colleagues would find out 'what is submitted to them is to a large extent your work and mine',[16] proved to be justified. Lord

---

[9] Hamilton to H. Bosanquet, 22 May 1908, ibid.
[10] Hamilton to H. Bosanquet, 12 Aug. 1908, ibid.
[11] Smart to H. Bosanquet (undated). ibid.
[12] Hamilton to H. Bosanquet, 12 Feb. 1909, ibid.
[13] Hamilton to H. Bosanquet, 30 Aug. 1908, ibid.
[14] Smart to H. Bosanquet, (undated), ibid. Hamilton to Phelps, 12 Dec. 1908. Phelps Papers.
[15] Hamilton to H. Bosanquet, 30 Aug. 1908, 17 Sept. 1908, 27 Feb. 1909. Bosanquet Papers.   [16] Smart to H. Bosanquet, 7 July 1908, ibid.

George Hamilton praised Helen Bosanquet as his 'mainstay';[17] he described her in a Circular to his other colleagues as having

by far the clearest head on the Commission; her information is very great; her judgment very sound, and, in addition, she wields by far the ablest pen of anyone on the Commission. I also found her most pleasant and agreeable to work with, for she is so very reliable;[18]

and in letters to her he said:

I am greatly indebted to you for what you are doing and have done. You have throughout this enquiry been my right hand.[19]

I cannot tell you what help and guidance you have been to me in this heavy task.[20]

My other helps are not as rapid and thorough a worker [*sic*] as you are.[21]

These remarks were not intended merely as flattery to persuade the ill and overworked Helen Bosanquet to keep increasing her stint; he obviously meant them. By contrast, he was critical of the literary ability both of Duff and Professor Smart.[22] He found Smart too long-windedly 'historical', too verbose, and rather inflexible about permitting alterations to what he had written. Sir Henry Robinson in his memoirs endorsed the major part played by Helen Bosanquet in writing the English Majority Report, even if he overlooked Professor Smart's and Duff's contributions:

I thought that Mrs. Bosanquet, a quiet, delicate woman, who spoke very little, provided the best-balanced mind of the whole lot of us, and Lord George Hamilton probably thought the same, for the preparation of the first draft of the Majority Report for submission to the commission was, I believe, nearly altogether the work of these two.[23]

Helen Bosanquet was invited also to take a major part in drafting the Scottish report, which she declined[24] (as also did Professor

[17] Hamilton to H. Bosanquet, 19 Feb. 1908, ibid.
[18] Circular by Hamilton to the other Majority Commissioners, 2 June 1908, ibid.
[19] Hamilton to H. Bosanquet, 2 July 1908, ibid.
[20] Hamilton to H. Bosanquet, 14 [?] Aug. 1908, ibid.
[21] Hamilton to H. Bosanquet, 27 Aug. 1908, ibid.
[22] Smart to H. Bosanquet, 9 Oct. 1908; Hamilton to H. Bosanquet, 22 May 1908, 28 May 1908, 23 July 1908, 17 Sept. 1908, 19 Sept. 1908, ibid. Hamilton to Phelps, 19 Sept. 1908. Phelps Papers.
[23] Sir Henry Robinson, *Memories: Wise and Otherwise* (London, 1923), p. 213.
[24] Patten-MacDougall to H. Bosanquet, 13 May 1909, Jeffrey to H. Bosanquet, 20 May 1909. Bosanquet Papers.

Smart); but she agreed to draft the charities section of it, and did so, to the great satisfaction of her colleagues.[25] The rest of the Scottish Report was finally drafted by the Assistant-Secretary to the Commission, John Jeffrey, and Patten-MacDougall,[26] under the general editorship, once again, of Phelps and Lord George Hamilton, who, as Phelps quipped, had 'been commissioned to put the Scottish Report into English'.[27] The Irish Report was the work of Sir Henry Robinson and the Bishop of Ross, with some assistance from Thory Gage Gardiner.[28] Concerning this Report, Lord George Hamilton made the terse remark: 'It is Irish',[29] which Duff elaborated into: 'The Irish Report has several emerald patches: because the Irish will only swallow green.'[30] Both Helen Bosanquet and Professor Smart read the whole of these reports, and submitted comments on them.[31]

It is not certain what share, if any, Bernard Bosanquet had in assisting his wife with the composition of her sections of the Report. Their general ideas were in harmony, and he must have read her work and discussed it. But it is unlikely that he would have been concerned with the detail, or that their co-operation was a veritable 'partnership' like the Webbs'. The scant evidence in the Bosanquet papers is contradictory. In a letter to Helen Bosanquet, Thory Gage Gardiner wrote indignantly about a reference to Bernard Bosanquet in the Webbs' Scottish Report: 'The "author"! of the Minority argues: You say my husband wrote my Report: Mr.Bosanquet wrote the Majority; Because my husband did her husband must have!" I agree it is rather sickening especially to those who sympathise with a proper recognition of and use of women's capacity & power.'[32] But Helen Bosanquet's niece, Ellen P. Bosanquet, remarked: 'Uncle Bernard was good enough to tell us how much of *you* there is in it [the Majority Report], & I think also that there must be a good deal of him.'[33]

Beatrice Webb, in the mean time, was also feeling the strain of

[25] Hamilton to H. Bosanquet, 17 May 1909, Jeffrey to H. Bosanquet, 24 Mar. 1909 and 26 Apr. 1909, ibid.
[26] Jeffrey to H. Bosanquet, 20 May 1909, ibid.
[27] Phelps to Boyce, 7 Aug. 1909. Phelps Papers.
[28] Bishop of Ross to H. Bosanquet, 26 Jan. 1909. Bosanquet Papers.
[29] Hamilton to H. Bosanquet, 11 Mar. 1909, ibid.
[30] Duff to H. Bosanquet, 9 Mar. 1909, ibid.
[31] Ibid., and Jeffrey to H. Bosanquet 5 June 1909, ibid.
[32] Gardiner to H. Bosanquet, 31 Aug. 1909, ibid.
[33] E. P. Bosanquet to H. Bosanquet, 19 Feb. 1909, ibid.

the final rush. In spite of the preparatory research and writing that she and Sidney had done, they had not started on their real draft of the Report any earlier than their opponents. Work on it had been delayed when, from the middle of April to the beginning of May 1908, she became a member of a team of the Commissioners who made a tour of inspection of workhouses in Ireland. Her companions on this expedition were Lord George Hamilton, Bentham, Duff, Downes, Patten-MacDougall, Nunn, Phelps, Robinson, the Bishop of Ross, and Smart. Her attempts in discussion to persuade them to her point of view, and foment disagreements between them, do not appear to have been successful, even in her own account of it: 'The chairman did literally run away and the Bishop was absolutely silent. Downes made little half-humorous remarks. He was the most friendly, except Phelps . . .'[34] Beatrice finally fell out with Professor Smart on the journey. She gave a scathing account of him in her Diary:

Professor Smart has maintained throughout the little trip what Robinson calls 'a mad dog' habit of wandering off by himself, jotting down little facts about the countryside—the number of public houses in a village street, the character of the crops on the wayside, and every other morsel of disjointed fact that he can pick up—in the intervals of heavy eating. He is a dull fellow without intellectual purpose—and with precious little intelligence, with all the less attractive qualities of the Scotchman.[35]

But he gave an equally scathing picture of her in a letter to Helen Bosanquet of the same time:

Mrs. Webb tried hard to keep me up to the collar—talking shop without a break from her breakfastless morning to her vegetarian nights—but she gave me up as a hopeless ass and settled down to conquer Sir Henry, and I wandered all day among the peasants trying to understand them and their ways of looking at things. But I was very much irritated by her incessant 'pumping'—in particular to find out what *our* relations were.[36]

Sidney Webb, at least until late in April 1908, maintained a rather more optimistic view than Beatrice of her chances of winning over some of her colleagues:

I think it is quite impossible to forecast how your Commission will finally

---

[34] B. Webb to S. Webb, 25 Apr. 1908. MacKenzie, *Letters*, ii. 301.
[35] B.W.D., 5 May 1908; *Our Partnership*, p. 410.
[36] Smart to H. Bosanquet, 27 May 1908. Bosanquet Papers.

divide up. If Robinson can carry Provis, as I should think he could easily if he tried seriously, those two could control a majority—because they could arrange to give you enough to secure the adhesion of your group; and at the same time convince the Chairman and Phelps that only in that way could they be in a *good* majority—thus also carrying Wakefield, Smart, and Bishop and doubtless Bentham = Eleven, besides MacDougall, Gardiner and Nunn, who *might* eventually fall in.

On the other hand, Loch and Mrs. Bosanquet will certainly make it impossible for the Centre Party as a whole, if it attempts to form at first on that nucleus; and the outcome might conceivably be 5 reports; viz. Chairman (counting about 7 or 8), your 3 or 4, Loch's 3 or 4, Downes 2 or 3, and Nunn by himself. It may come to this; or develop into this before a final struggle for rival coalitions. After all, I cannot believe that Loch would, in the end, not be prepared to compromise with the Centre Party; and thus the Chairman may probably win, and come through with something like his present majority . . . Anyhow, your course is clear, viz. to have your Report ready as though you had a majority.[37]

The Webbs' attention was also distracted at this time by the bid made by H. G. Wells to take over control in the Fabian Society.

As soon as Beatrice returned from Ireland, the Webbs settled down to drafting their Report. She had sent ahead some preliminary ideas to Sidney:

. . . I am longing to get to work on my Report . . . With seeming impartiality and moderation every word of that Report has to fall in the direction of Breaking-up the Poor Law, the argument has to be repeated in any conceivable form so that the reader cannot escape from it. It must be a real work of Art; we can dismiss Science! It will be High Jinks doing it and we will get to work at once. The more saturated it is with argument the less they will be able to adopt any part of it without the conclusions—but the argument must be cunningly wrought—so as to seem a mere recital of facts. The Wood shall absorb the Trees.[38]

In order to find the retirement and the leisure to do the writing, the Webbs accepted an invitation of Sir Julius Wernher to holiday at 'The Hermitage', a cottage in the grounds of his large country house, Luton Hoo. Sidney Webb had become friendly with the millionaire South African industrialist (of Wernher, Beit, and Co.) in his days as a reformer of technical education in London, when Wernher had put half a million at his disposal which was used to

[37] S. Webb to B. Webb, 27 Apr. 1908. MacKenzie, *Letters*, ii. 306.
[38] B. Webb to S. Webb, 2 May 1908. MacKenzie, *Letters*, ii. 313.

organize the Imperial Technical Institute. The Webbs appreciated the ironical side of composing their 'collectivist document' in such an environment; but it was an ideal retreat, at a time when the 'great mansion stood, closed and silent, in the closed and silent park—no one coming or going except the retinue of servants'— '54 gardeners, 10 electricians, 20 or 30 house servants and endless labourers'.[39]

The Webbs divided their Report into two Parts, one dealing with the non-able-bodied poor and the other dealing with the able-bodied and the unemployed. They completed the draft of the first, and longer, Part while the Commission was in summer recess. Beatrice Webb decided there was no point in attending regularly the meetings of the other Commissioners when they resumed at the beginning of October 1908, for these meetings were concerned to get approval of the drafts of the Majority Report—at least, what was hoped *would* be a Majority Report. All Lord George Hamilton's resources of authority and diplomacy were needed to hold the rest of the Commissioners together. A general fear of the Webbs helped in this. Beatrice recognized their fear clearly enough, but was constitutionally incapable of mollifying it. She left Lansbury and Chandler to conduct any guerilla warfare that might be necessary at these meetings, visiting only occasionally, but giving vivid sketches of the other Commissioners at work when she did:

. . . Robinson and Phelps rather glum; Bentham, Loch and Provis quite affairé; Downes pulling back towards the *status quo*, but always being over-ruled; the Bishop assenting to everything; Mrs. Bosanquet poor lady looking deadly ill; Miss Hill not intervening; Gardiner and Nunn occasionally coming in as lone handers.[40]

Lord George forced the pace by guillotining the time for submission of amendments and their discussion in stages.[41]

On the completion of the first Part of the Minority draft report, Beatrice Webb made several tactical moves which had the effect of uniting the opposition to her and inflaming hostility. At the end of July 1908, she allowed herself to be persuaded by the Secretaries of the Commission, Duff and Jeffrey, to submit her draft, as far as it

[39] B.W.D., 27 July 1908; *Our Partnership*, p. 413. MacKenzie, *Diary*, iii, 96.
[40] B.W.D., 16 Oct. 1908. [This passage was omitted from *Our Partnership*.]
[41] B.W.D., 7 Oct. 1908. [Omitted from *Our Partnership*.]

had gone, for printing.[42] At first she hesitated about this; but she was tempted by the idea of seeing it in print; then she found that Duff had supplied a copy to the Chairman, and, in any case, looking over the printed copy she was very pleased with it, and began to circulate it herself to other Commissioners. Its quality put the Majority on its mettle. Carried away by her pride in the draft, Beatrice Webb next showed it to Leo Amery, who was then a journalist on *The Times* and one of the few young Conservatives who had become members of the Fabian Society. Amery saw the possibilities of a journalistic scoop in a series of special articles, and the Webbs allowed him to use their draft as the basis of these.[43]

It is not quite certain how far the Webbs actually instigated this journalistic venture. Later they claimed that they had permitted Amery to use their ideas, but had told him that he was not to mention their names or the Royal Commission.[44] If this was so, he stuck only to part of that compact, for he went on to outline their whole scheme, mentioned that these ideas were before the Royal Commission, and quoted some passages verbatim from the Webbs' draft. Maybe Amery had to some extent abused the Webbs' confidence, but Beatrice Webb had shown, as she had done earlier and was to do again very soon, that she was not a respecter of Commission confidentiality when it served her turn. Most of the other Commissioners were outraged at this breach of confidence and the attempt to steal a march. Even the faithful Lansbury protested. Lord George wrote to Helen Bosanquet: 'Lansbury came to see Duff & expressed great annoyance at Mrs. W's proceedings. Duff thinks that we could detach him. However is it worth while?'[45] Duff no doubt overestimated Lansbury's detachability; but in any case the others did not bother to try. Beatrice Webb herself had an attack of remorse, analysed perceptively enough in a passage in her Diary which admitted substantial responsibility: '. . . the worst of my temperament is, that I have far more audacity than I have passive courage—I do this thing with splendid dash and then tremble with fear afterwards. All of which means nervous strain.'[46] Sidney consoled her with the thought that her ideas about the

---

[42] Duff to H. Bosanquet, 16 Aug. 1908 and Duff to H. Bosanquet [undated]. Bosanquet Papers.
[43] *The Times*, 11, 14, and 15 Aug. 1908.
[44] B.W.D., 15 Sept. 1908; *Our Partnership*, p. 413.
[45] Hamilton to H. Bosanquet [n.d.]. Bosanquet Papers.
[46] B.W.D., 15 Sept. 1908; *Our Partnership*, p. 414; MacKenzie, *Diary*, iii, 97.

breaking up of the Poor Law had been promoted by the publicity, even if the Webbs were in disgrace with her colleagues. Certainly *The Times* articles attracted plenty of attention, especially when they were repudiated and denounced in vigorous letters to the editor by Lord George Hamilton as representing only one point of view before the Commission.[47] But whether this *ballon d'essai* (as Duff called it in correspondence with Helen Bosanquet) in fact proved useful to the Webbs, or resulted merely (as Duff thought) 'in the puncture of the balloon',[48] is debatable.

Beatrice Webb's attack of remorse did not mean that she changed her ways of behaviour. Towards the end of October, Mr Asquith wrote to Lord George asking to be supplied with copies of the Minutes of Evidence taken by the Commission, for the use of Cabinet. Lord George refused, but offered to send the sections of the Majority Report to Cabinet piecemeal as soon as they were agreed to by the Commission. When Lansbury asked him if the Minority might send its conclusions also, Lord George replied testily: 'There is no reason for anyone to protect the Minority, they are far better able to look after themselves than the Majority of the Commission.'[49] He finally declared that the Minority's proposals would be sent on by the Secretary Duff, but only after they had been considered by the Commission as a whole.[50] Beatrice Webb took the view that the Chairman's attitude to the Prime Minister and Cabinet was silly, and that his attitude to the Minority was dangerous, because the Majority would be placed in a position to hold up the forwarding of the Minority's opinions indefinitely. She and Sidney had in any case already talked with considerable freedom to some Cabinet Ministers, notably Haldane, Winston Churchill, and Lloyd George, and to their secretaries about particular problems, and she hardly needed Haldane to remind her that Cabinet could get the material from John Burns, who had been supplied with copies.[51] She suspected, probably rightly, that Lord George Hamilton had not been as discreet with his political cronies in the recesses of clubland as his formal stand suggested, and, perhaps less warrantably, that some other Commissioners had not preserved secrecy. So she agreed to furnish Haldane with whatever

[47] *The Times*, 12 and 17 Aug. 1908.
[48] Duff to H. Bosanquet, 25 Aug. 1908. Bosanquet Papers.
[49] B.W.D., 29 Oct. 1908. [Omitted from *Our Partnership*.]
[50] B.W.D., 15 Nov. 1908; *Our Partnership*, p. 418.   [51] Ibid.

material he needed for Cabinet use that was in her own or in Lansbury's possession. It does appear that Mr Asquith was being supplied with material by Duff from December 1908, if not before,[52] but whether this was a consequence of Beatrice Webb's disclosures or not is hard to tell.

From August the scramble for the completion of the two reports had begun in earnest. Lord George cracked the editorial whip—gently perhaps, but very noticeably. Professor Smart had already complained that it was ridiculous to work under such pressure.[53] Helen Bosanquet, strained and overtired, was forced, reluctantly, to desert her husband and the peace of St Andrews and return to Oxshott, where she was available for regular consultations; C. S. Loch's health became unsteadier;[54] even Beatrice Webb complained of the 'terribly high pressure' and the 'state of complete exhaustion' which the struggle to complete the work produced.[55] With all his driving, Lord George was forced to abandon anything like his original schedules; he was exhilarated enough—'Shouting hurrah like a schoolboy'—when the first draft of the Report was completed just after mid-September 1908.[56] Discussion and revision dragged on the final version of the English Report until mid-January 1909. The Webbs had finished only a fortnight earlier, on New Year's Day 1909.[57]

The two reports were both of massive length, running, in the official edition, to 908 pages for the Majority Report and 716 pages for the Minority Report. The Revd Lancelot Phelps, who was certainly in a position to judge, admitted with handsome generosity to the other side that 'The Minority Report is much abler in many ways than ours and better written. The Webbs are masters of that kind of thing e.g. the drafting of ideas. She supplies the one & he does the other—reading between the lines.'[58] Some of his modesty might have been induced by the sour aftermath of sub-editing. But it must be agreed that the Minority Report has a tightness of organization, a force and energy of argument, and an integrated theme well hammered home, that makes the Majority Report seem

[52] Duff to H. Bosanquet, 24 Dec. 1908. Bosanquet Papers.
[53] Smart to H. Bosanquet, 7 July 1908, ibid.
[54] Duff to H. Bosanquet, 25 Aug. 1908, ibid.
[55] B.W.D., 15 Nov. 1908, 1 Jan. 1909; *Our Partnership*, pp. 419–20.
[56] Hamilton to H. Bosanquet, 17 Sept. 1908. Bosanquet Papers.
[57] B.W.D., 1 Jan. 1909; *Our Partnership*, p. 420.
[58] Phelps to Boyce, 16 Mar. 1909. Phelps Papers.

comparatively pedestrian. The Majority Report is more formal and 'official', slower moving. This is not to say, however, that it is unclear or difficult to read. Helen Bosanquet and Phelps had performed an admirable feat of revision and editing to draw the composite work into a coherent whole. Beatrice Webb had grossly underestimated the organizational and literary talent of her opponents. In any case, the Majority Report, in that it was the chief Report from which the Webbs were dissenting, had to carry more formally descriptive material about the procedures of the Commission, statistics, and historical sketches; the Webbs were in a position to omit or to absorb their observations about such things into the overall drive of their argument.

The Webbs were able to begin with a stirring assault on the evils of the General Mixed Workhouse, still to be found in every one of the Poor Law Unions of England, Wales, and Ireland and in large numbers of parishes or combinations of parishes in Scotland. In spite of the attempts which had been made to provide schooling in separate institutions and separate infirmaries for the sick, over one-third of the indoor pauper children in England and Scotland, and 8,000 out of 9,000 indoor child paupers in Ireland were housed in General Mixed Workhouses;[59] two-thirds of sick and infirm indoor paupers; and all but a small proportion of the aged indoor paupers. In these establishments the non-able-bodied poor mixed with the able-bodied who had been obliged to resort to the workhouse. The Webbs carefully noted that the Commissioners had discovered most of these workhouses clean, with sufficient warmth and food, and in some cases governed with zeal and devotion. But they found 'promiscuity' a word to conjure with in describing them, and their eye for striking instances from the evidence could make life in the General Mixed Workhouse seem, at times, positively sensational. They summed up the 'evil reputation' of the General Mixed Workhouse amongst the 'respectable poor' in the words of the Commission's medical investigator, Dr McVail, as

partly traditional or historical, and partly due to the curious and objectionable agglomeration of purposes which it now serves. It is a home for imbeciles, an almshouse for the destitute poor, a refuge for deserted children, a lying-in hospital for dissolute women, a winter resort for the ill-

[59] Cd. 4499, Minority Report, pp. 8–9.

behaved casual labourer or summer beggar, a lodging for tramps and vagrants as well as a hospital for the sick.[60]

The Webbs pointed out that, with the best will in the world, the unspecialized management of those workhouses could not hope to cater for the needs of so many classes of inmates. They demonstrated that the Royal Commissioners of 1832–4 had no intention of perpetuating such institutions. Why then, they asked, had the General Mixed Workhouse continued to exist? The explanation, they argued, was to be found in the nature of administrative organization that was established by the 1834 Act. The care of all classes of poor in each local Poor Law Union was put in the hands of a single local authority, the Poor Law Guardians. In an age of parsimonious finance, amateur administration, and numerous small local areas, the establishment of a number of separate institutions for the different categories of poor was unviable, and once the General Mixed Workhouse was generally established, it became difficult, for reasons both of apparent economy and of prestige, to persuade the Boards of Guardians to relinquish this type of control over all classes of the destitute. Since the 1830s there had been a continuous, and in the case of the children a frustrated campaign to get special categories dealt with outside the workhouse. Only in London and the larger provincial cities had the battle on behalf of the sick poor been successful, and that imperfectly. The stubbornness of the Boards of Guardians was not to be attributed to their lack of good intentions, but to their nature as a 'destitution authority', thinking of themselves as responsible for all classes of persons because they were destitute, allowing destitution to become their dominant idea. The Webbs had cleverly developed their attack on the Guardians out of their criticisms of the General Mixed Workhouse. Fundamental reform was foreshadowed in their opening chapter.

Helen Bosanquet, in her draft of Part IV of the Majority Report, also attacked the General Workhouse in terms not dissimilar to those of the Webbs, if less vivid:

... the difficulty mainly arises out of the attempt to deal in one institution, under one master, with people requiring such different treatment as the infirm and the able-bodied, the old and the young, the feeble-minded, epileptic, insane, and those of bad character. The difficulty can only be met

---

[60] Quoted in Cd. 4499, Minority Report, Part I, Ch. 1, p. 15.

by setting apart special institutions for special classes, as was intended by the Royal Commission of 1832 . . .[61]

She accepted the view that the original idea of the 'classification of institutions' had been abandoned in favour of 'classification in [the same] institution' mainly for financial reasons, and argued that 'in view of the multiplicity of institutions now existing' the financial consideration no longer had much weight, and that attempts to carry out classification within one institution had in general failed.[62] The cause of failure, in her diagnosis, lay not in the very nature of the Boards of Guardians as 'destitution authorities' but in the fact that the areas which they administered were not large enough. Voluntary and permissive attempts to get Guardians to combine their areas had proved unsuccessful. Again her conclusion, different from that of the Webbs, was foreshadowed.

Both the Majority and Minority Reports criticized severely the existing methods of administering outdoor relief, but both agreed that it would need to continue in some form or other. They recognized that outdoor relief was the major form of aliment. As the Majority Report put it:

. . . we still have approximately half-a-million on any given day, or two outdoor paupers to one indoor. In rural or mainly rural Unions, for every one indoor pauper there were on March 31st 1906, 4.46 outdoor, while in urban or mainly urban Unions, excluding London, for every one indoor there were 2.45 outdoor. In London, however, the number of indoor paupers exceeded the number of outdoor paupers by nearly 60 per cent . . .[63]

Outdoor relief was mainly given to the aged, and to women and children. Helen Bosanquet's chapter in the Majority Report harked back nostalgically to the COS idea of strict (or as she now called it 'careful') administration of outdoor relief,[64] but she did not recommend the abolition of outdoor relief as an attainable ideal,[65] as the strictest of careful administrators had claimed it to be in evidence before the Commission. Outdoor relief was permissible, under uniform rules and more careful scrutiny of cases; it should be

[61] Cd. 4499, Majority Report, Part IV, Ch. 5, para. 194, pp. 178–9.
[62] Cd. 4499, Majority Report, Part IV, Ch. 4, paras. 153–4, p. 165.
[63] Ibid., Part IV, Ch. 6, Sect. 253, p. 195.
[64] Ibid., part IV, Ch. 6, Sects. 250–1, p. 194.
[65] Ibid., Part IV, Ch. 6, Sect. 292, p. 209.

adequate, case records should be kept, and skilled supervision provided to ensure certain conditions of behaviour and standards in the home. The Webbs, making skilful use of the report of their special investigator, Miss Harlock, pressed home their victory over the 'old-guard' COS views, claiming that the abolition of outdoor relief to the non-able-bodied poor was wholly impracticable, and even if it were possible, it would be misguided.

There are, and, in our opinion, there always will be, a large number of persons to whom public assistance must be given, who can, with most advantage to the community, continue to live at home; for instance, widows with children whose homes deserve to be maintained intact, sick persons for whom domiciliary treatment is professionally recommended, the worthy aged having relations with whom they can reside, and such of the permanently incapacitated (the crippled, the blind, etc.) as can safely be left with their friends.[66]

Voluntary charity could not be relied upon to cope with all these cases. But having made these points firmly, the Webbs agreed that the existing system of administering outdoor relief was open to grave criticism and should be remedied to ensure that certain standards were attained. They disagreed, however, with Helen Bosanquet and the Majority about the remedy for the shortcomings. Helen Bosanquet's solution was closer scrutiny of cases, to be achieved by greater co-operation between voluntary charity, given official recognition and status, and Poor Law authorities.[67] The Webbs ascribed the defects to the 'very nature' of the existing local authorities[68]—because the Guardians attempted to be at once policy-determining bodies and administrative bodies, and they tried to deal with too many different types of cases under the one umbrella of 'destitution'. The solution was to be found in separate committees, making rules and overseeing them, served by salaried administrative officers.

There was a good deal of agreement between the Minority and Majority Reports about practical matters in the way of treating the non-able-bodied poor. Both criticized severely the record of Poor Law maternity, recommended more and better medical treatment, and the fullest possible use of such voluntary agencies as rescue and

---

[66] Cd. 4499, Minority Report, Part I, Ch. II, p. 68.
[67] Cd. 4499, Majority Report, Part IV, Ch. 6, Sects. 301–3, pp. 211–12.
[68] Cd. 4499, Minority Report, Part I, Ch. II, pp. 69–70.

maternity homes, midwifery charities, and day nurseries.[69] They differed only in the question of whether such cases should be transferred from the Poor Law to the Local Health authority (although they agreed that mentally defective unmarried mothers should be looked after by prospective local authorities for the feeble-minded). The Minority and Majority Commissioners also agreed that children should be removed from the mixed workhouses. The system of 'boarding-out' children to foster-parents was approved in general by both, but they both emphasized the deficiencies of the existing system of inquiry and inspection, and made detailed suggestions for its improvement to ensure the children's welfare. The need for inspection and supervision was their principal demand for the children maintained by the Poor Law authorities in homes or schools run by voluntary philanthropic committees or paid housekeepers. In the case of workhouse schools or of separate boarding-schools established by the Poor Law authorities (there were about 100 of the latter type of school, containing just over 20,000 children in 1908),[70] the chief questions were the quality of the teaching staff, and whether it was wise to keep these children, selected so haphazardly, together in one school, or to distribute them, according to their ability, amongst the schools of the public education system. The Webbs had a clear-cut answer: the children should be taken out of the hands of the Poor Law authorities and entrusted to the Education authorities, which were in any case already providing education for many of them, and had been empowered by the Act of 1906 to provide school meals. Teachers and education authorities were in a better position than Guardians to find out destitution amongst children, and to take preventive action. Helen Bosanquet could not agree to that proposition at all. She defended the Poor Law boarding-schools in terms of their *esprit de corps*, which she compared to that of the 'great public schools'.[71] All that was necessary was to make sure that the education provided to Poor Law children was as good as that given in elementary schools, and that teachers in Poor Law boarding-schools had the same status as teachers in public

---

[69] Cd. 4499, Majority Report, Part VIII, Ch. 4, Sect. 167, p. 154; Minority Report, Part I, Ch. III, p. 109.

[70] Cd. 4499, Minority Report, Part I, Ch. IV, p. 127.

[71] Cd. 4499, Majority Report, Part IV, Ch. 8, Sect. 438, p. 257.

elementary schools.[72] Poor Law schools were better able to deal with children 'handicapped by their antecedents', and she dismissed the idea that attendance at Poor Law schools imposed a 'stigma of pauperism' on the children.[73] There should certainly be co-operation between Poor Law and Education authorities, but she declared the 1906 School Meals Act was an unwarrantable infringement of the principle that only one authority should be empowered to grant relief out of the rates; the Act ought to be 'reconsidered'.[74] Children under the Poor Law 'should not be transferred entirely to the care of the Local Educational Authorities'.

The recommendations of the Majority and the Minority Reports showed a similar balance concerning the aged and the sick poor. They both agreed that the 'aged and infirm' Poor Law category needed to be subdivided into separate classes, with special conditions provided for each, and that all of them be accorded separate treatment from other paupers. The Majority Report was rather tight-lipped about the Old Age Pensions Act of 1908, treating it as merely another, and not very satisfactory, form of outdoor relief. The Minority approved old-age pensions in principle, but recommended the lowering of pensionable age from 70 to 65 (or even 60) and the removal of the disqualification for persons who had already accepted relief from the Poor Law, or the empowering of local authorities to grant pensions to those disqualified for the national pension. Helen Bosanquet and the Webbs both recognized that, next to old age, sickness was a chief cause of pauperism—'at least one-half of the total cost of pauperism is swallowed up in direct dealing with sickness'.[75] The Webbs, of course, proposed a unified public medical service, under the control of the Public Health authorities, which would provide treatment that would not be limited by considerations of whether the patient could or should repay the cost. This did not mean, they hastened to point out, that they were recommending a free public medical service: it was to be a service open to all, but costs should be recovered, under definite rules of chargeability, from patients who could afford to pay. Helen Bosanquet's recommendations, accepted by the Majority, were for a general system of provident

[72] Ibid., Sects. 434 and 436, p. 256.
[73] Ibid., Sects. 433 and 437, pp. 255, 257.
[74] Ibid., Sects. 439 and 440, pp. 257–8.
[75] Cd. 4499, Majority Report, Part V, Ch. 3, Sect. 197, p. 372.

dispensaries to be set up with the adhesion, if possible, of existing private dispensaries and medical clubs, which would supplement and help to co-ordinate the services already offered by the Public Health and Education authorities, provident societies, and voluntary hospitals. All local medical practitioners would be invited to enrol in the panel of dispensary doctors. Subscribers to these provident dispensaries would be guaranteed medical assistance, with their choice of doctor within the panel, and would get it at a cheaper rate than they could obtain it from an ordinary medical practitioner. There should be a wage-limit for membership of provident dispensaries to prevent the well-to-do from 'abusing the system'. Persons who had not become subscribers to the dispensaries could get help subject to an investigation of their means by the Public Assistence authorities, and either action for recovery of costs or their enrolment in a provident dispensary and the payment of subscription for as long as deemed necessary by the Public Assistance authorities.

Echoes of earlier verbal scuffles in the Commission were audible in the Reports and made the differences more apparent than the agreements. They may be illustrated by the exchanges concerning the methods of dealing with the sick poor. The Webbs said, in criticism of the Majority proposals:

. . . if the labourer who has neglected to contribute to the Provident Medical Association finds himself, when illness overtakes him, with just the same privilege . . . as if he had himself contributed, it is difficult to see why anybody should be at pains of contributing at all . . . what would tend to be provided under such a system would be, not preventive or curative treatment or hygienic advice, but, in the literal sense of the word, medical *relief*, and that wholly without conditions.[76]

To which Helen Bosanquet acridly replied:

We do not pretend that the system we propose will realise the ideals of those enthusiasts who contemplate unfettered and unintermittent medical control, supervision, and treatment of every human being from the cradle to the grave. A system which thus made every human life the helpless subject of relentless and aggressive medical inspection and, to some extent, of medical experiment, might tend to encourage morbidly some of the human ills it was designed to destroy. A race of hypochondriacs might be as useless to the State as a race of any other degenerates . . . We are not

[76] Cd. 4499, Minority Report, Part I, Ch. IV, pp. 209–10.

inclined, therefore, to make medical assistance so attractive that it may become a species of honourable and gratuitous self-indulgence . . .[77]

The main tussle came in the recommendations concerning the able-bodied poor and the unemployed. The discussion of these topics occupied more than a quarter of the whole Majority Report and nearly a third of the Minority. Here again fundamental antagonisms obscured a measure of agreement on particular points. These sections of the Majority Report were drafted jointly by Helen Bosanquet and Professor William Smart, and, as Lord George Hamilton observed, they were not always quite at one in their ideas;[78] Lord George and Dr Phelps had to do some editorial ironing-out of their differences. Unfortunately, the surviving evidence does not make clear just what these differences were; but a compromise agreeable to all was eventually reached. Lord George and Phelps were rather impatient of Professor Smart's long-winded 'industrial review of the past century',[79] as Lord George called Chapter I of Part IV of the Report, but Smart insisted on most of it going in. Discursive it may be, and perhaps lacking in theoretical 'bite', but it is the work of a remarkably open-minded economic historian. Professor Smart's main theme was that the problems of pauperism and poverty were far more complicated in the early twentieth century than they had been in 1834. Moral causes of pauperism remained much as they were, he argued, but material forces affecting employment had changed in scope, and were now 'quite beyond local control'. He showed his appreciation of the arguments of his fellow economists concerning cyclical fluctuations (presenting a detailed tabular chronology of them from 1815 to 1907 in a footnote),[80] technological unemployment and the exclusion from the workforce of the less skilled through rising standards of wages and demands for greater industrial efficiency, unemployment caused by dead-end jobs, and the underemployment resulting from casual labour. All these factors, he declared, 'require a treatment more elastic and varied than the simple method which,

---

[77] Cd. 4499, Majority Report, Part V, Ch. 3, Sects. 211 and 220, pp. 377 and 379.

[78] Hamilton to H. Bosanquet, 15 July 1908 and 23 July, 1908. Bosanquet Papers.

[79] Hamilton to H. Bosanquet, 23 July 1908, Smart to H. Bosanquet, 2 Sept. 1908, ibid.

[80] Cd. 4499, Majority Report, Part VI, Ch. 1, footnote to Sect. 144, pp. 421–2.

eighty years ago, was sufficient to cope with able-bodied pauperism in agricultural districts'.[81]

The stress Professor Smart gave to new causes was viewed by Lord George Hamilton with sour apprehensiveness. He noted, in several letters to Helen Bosanquet, the differences of emphasis between the joint drafters, and declared to her his belief that 'the causes of pauperism and distress are more moral than economic'.[82] Meeting with a favourable response, he expressed his opinion more boldly to her at the final drafting stage:

> . . . I want, if possible, the moral side of the causes of unemployment to be drawn carefully and fully. I believe it is not so much material or industrial changes as deterioration in grit and self-reliance that now causes unemployment . . . London is becoming horribly like Rome. 'Panem et circenses'.[83]

As a result, the Majority Report's section on the 'Causes of Pauperism'[84] featured drink, gambling, and thriftlessness very high in its list of causes. Even old age, which could hardly be denied the premier place in the list in terms of numbers, was said 'hardly in itself to be a "cause" ' except when combined with other factors, notably intemperance and failure to save. But, COS honour satisfied, a long string of 'social causes' followed—beginning, however, with the supposed effects of the Employers' Liability Act and Workmen's Compensation Acts and trade union minimum wages as making it difficult for older men to get employment. There was a revealing exchange on that matter between Professor Smart and Helen Bosanquet, when he wrote: 'I am much relieved to hear that you do not like Trade Unions! I hate them so much that I am always too fair to them—to atone for my bias.[85] After the causes mentioned, the remainder of the list followed in this order: sickness, bad housing, casual labour, boy labour, unhealthy trades and insanitary work-places, low wages, irresponsible and un-organized charitable relief, the failure of unsound Friendly societies and clubs, the payment of pensions at long intervals, domestic ignorance and mismanagement on the part of housewives, and lax

---

[81] Ibid., Sect. 304, p. 459.
[82] Hamilton to H. Bosanquet, 15 July 1908, 23 July 1908, and 21 Aug. 1908. Bosanquet Papers.
[83] Hamilton to H. Bosanquet, 3 Sept. 1908, ibid.
[84] Cd. 4499, Majority Report, Part IV, Ch. 10.
[85] Smart to H. Bosanquet, 16 July 1908. Bosanquet Papers.

administration of the Poor Law. The Majority Report announced that it did not 'propose either to endorse or to controvert certain other causes urged by witnesses', namely '(1) Capitalism. (2) Free Trade. (3) The system of land tenure'.

The Webbs, in their Minority Report, reversed the emphasis, playing up the importance of the social causes and playing down the importance of moral causes. They did not deny that

taking the workmen as a whole and ignoring many individual cases to the contrary, the men out of work at any one time are apt to include the less efficient, the less energetic, the less strong, the less young, the less regular, the less temperate or the less docile of their class.[86]

But they declared:

We have deliberately subordinated the question of personal character, because in our view, although of vital importance to the method of treatment to be adopted with regard to the individuals in distress, it does not seem to us to be of significance with regard to the existence or the amount of Unemployment . . . the fluctuations in the volume of employment, and, therefore, the aggregate number of the Unemployed in the nation are in no way related to the existence of drunkenness or misconduct among the workmen; and the fluctuations certainly would not be any the less (though the consequent distress would be) if all the men were teetotallers and as thrifty as could be desired.[87]

It was truer that unemployment or underemployment produced moral deterioration than that moral failings caused unemployment. The Webbs stated roundly that unemployment was a constant and essential feature of 'industry and commerce as at present administered',[88] directly related to fluctuations and depressions of trade, seasonal and discontinuous employment, decay of industries, but above all to the underemployment involved in the system of casual labour. The Webbs claimed that the reports of the Special Investigators had demonstrated that underemployment was the main cause of at least two-thirds of all able-bodied pauperism, reducing to insignificance many other suggested social causes:

The outcome of these investigations was all the more impressive in that it was not what we anticipated. We do not exaggerate when we say that these enquirers—numbering, with their assistants, more than a dozen, starting

---

[86] Cd. 4499, Minority Report, Part II, Ch. IV, Sect. F, p. 628.
[87] Ibid., pp. 626–7.   [88] Ibid., Sect. H, p. 632.

on different lines of investigation, and pursuing their researches independently all over the Kingdom—came, without concert, to the same conclusion, namely, that of all the causes or conditions predisposing to pauperism the most potent, the most certain and the most intensive in its operation was the method of employment in odd jobs. Contrary to the expectations of some of our number and of some of themselves, our investigators did not find that low wages could be described, generally speaking, as a cause of pauperism. They were unable to satisfy themselves that insanitary conditions of living or excessive hours of labour could be shown to be, on any large scale, a cause of pauperism. They could find no ground for believing that Outdoor Relief, by adversely affecting wages, was itself a cause of pauperism . . .[89]

The Webbs also dismissed as causes of unemployment the alleged effects of the Employers' Liability Act, Workmen's Compensation Act, and trade union minimum standards.[90]

When we come to the proposals for reform, there is again some common ground within the boundaries of widely divergent general systems. Both favoured the establishment of labour exchanges, differing only on the questions of whether the use of the exchanges should be compulsory in certain trades where casual or discontinuous employment was rife, and whether the exchanges should be under the control of the Board of Trade or a new Ministry of Labour. Both agreed that the government should look into the problem of decasualization, and that public authorities should plan to 'stagger' some of their work in order to increase it in times when unemployment was high. The minority proposals about this were more detailed, recommending the full programme suggested by Professor A. L. Bowley be put into operation whenever the unemployment index rose above four per cent; but the Majority agreed with the principle in less specific terms. Both the Majority and Minority recommended the raising of school leaving age to 15 with provision for part-time continuation technical schooling to the age of 18. The Webbs proposed that mothers of young children whose husbands were unemployed should receive a 'Home Aliment' high enough to prevent their being driven into the work-force to the neglect of their children; and Helen Bosanquet agreed that sufficient outdoor relief should be given so that 'mothers should not be expected to earn unless satisfactory arrangements can be made for the children'. Both Reports also desired to encourage workmen

---

[89] Ibid., Sect. C vi, pp. 597–8.   [90] Ibid., Sect. E iv, v, pp. 619–25.

to insure against unemployment, discussing particularly the scheme instituted at Ghent in 1901 which had spread to many continental countries—a scheme involving state or municipal subsidies to encourage trade unions to extend out-of-work benefits. Both Reports were sceptical of any possibility of introducing general state compulsory insurance. There were similarities, also, in their plans for abolishing the workhouse and substituting for it retraining institutions, farm colonies, and (for the work-shy and refractory) detention colonies of a reformatory kind. Neither proposed the abolition of *ci-devant* outdoor relief, or as it was now termed, 'Home Aliment' or 'Home Assistance', in suitable cases.[91]

The agreement on these particular items was overshadowed by the divergence of their opinions about the machinery for dealing with unemployment. Throughout their Minority Report the Webbs had reiterated their theme of the need to get away from the notion of a special 'Destitution Authority'—a body whose special function was to supply any and every kind of 'relief' to the destitute at a level 'less eligible' than was enjoyed by the lowest class of independent labourer. They urged that the State should accept the responsibility for seeing that nobody fell below a certain National Minimum standard. What they meant by National Minimum standard was never defined precisely—it was defined only by implication (which was perhaps a weakness). But it is clear that the Webbs were wanting, as they put it, to break up the Poor Law, not simply to modify its practices and to overhaul its machinery. They did not want the functions of the Guardians to be transferred *en bloc* to a new organization which would still deal with 'the destitute' or 'the paupers' as a class. As we have seen, under their arrangement the non-able-bodied poor would be divided for services amongst different existing committees of the local county and county borough councils: thus the sick poor would be dealt with by the Public Health Committees of the existing local authorities, the pauper children by the Education Committees, the mentally deficient poor by the Asylums Committees, the aged poor by the Pensions Committees. Each of these committees would be providing services that did not necessarily apply only to the poor, so the 'stigma of the Poor Law' could be eliminated. It would be left to a judicial officer in each county or county borough known as

---

[91] Cd. 4499, Majority Report, Part VI, Ch. 4, and Part IX, *passim*; Cd. 4499, Minority Report, Part II, Ch. V, *passim*.

Registrar of Public Assistance to decide whether the services should be paid for or free, and the poor person would be receiving the same services and not specially marked off from his fellow citizens. In the case of the able-bodied unemployed, they were to be looked after by a new Ministry of Labour (which would replace the existing Local Government Board). The Ministry of Labour, created for the purpose of organizing the whole labour market, was to consist of six divisions: the National Labour Exchange, the Insurance Division, the Maintenance and Training Division, the Industrial Regulation Division, the Emigration and Immigration Division, and the Statistical Division. The function of the Ministry was to take preventive action against unemployment so far as possible and to minimize its effects where it was unavoidable, by providing maintenance freely, without disfranchisement or other stigma of 'less eligibility', but on the condition that the unemployed undertake work and training that the Ministry would offer.

The Majority, in abolishing the Guardians, had no such far-reaching changes in mind. They aimed at improvements in administration rather than changes in principle. The Poor Law was to stay, though renamed 'Public Assistance', all the services formerly provided by the Poor Law Guardians being transferred *en bloc* to new special 'Public Assistance Authorities' of the county councils and county borough councils, with the Local Government Board continuing as the central government body. The 'Public Assistance Authorities' (designed on the model of the Education Committees set up under the Balfour Education Acts of 1902–3) would have their members nominated by county councils and county borough councils, in part from amongst their own members and in part from outside 'experts', and would exercise general supervisory functions. Actual administration would be carried on by subordinate 'Public Assistance Committees', which included a certain proportion of persons nominated by the urban and rural district councils, and by Voluntary Aid Committees, set up to regularize and systematize voluntary charitable societies. In London the Majority recommended the 'Public Assistance Authority' be a committee of the London County Council, three-quarters internally appointed (but at least one-quarter from outside the LCC's own members) and the other quarter nominated by the Local Government Board. On the local 'Public Assistance Committees' for London, nominees of the Metropolitan Borough Councils replaced those of the urban and rural district councils of the more general scheme. Private charity had a special place built for it by the Majority Report into the 'Public Assistance' administration, and it was hoped that this would add a special preventive, curative, and restorative dimension to its work:

The Public Assistance Authority can help only those who are destitute or, as we prefer to call it, necessitous, it cannot help many others who are, from various causes, steadily slipping downwards in the social scale. To stop the downward progress is the special duty of charity which, if properly organised, should be an effective agent combating the incipient development of destitution and distress.[92]

A measure of deterrence survived by making any 'Home Assistance' provided by the Public Assistance Authorities less eligible not, it is true, than the condition of the lowest-paid independent class of worker, but, significantly, than the relief given by voluntary charity.[93] The penalty of disfranchisement was also retained for persons receiving Public Assistance (other than medical relief) for a period of more than three months in a year. Local authorities were allowed to provide special public works in times of exceptional distress but 'only during the early years of the reforms we suggest'.[94]

Beatrice Webb and Helen Bosanquet each had a stinging epigram to sum up the other's proposals. Beatrice's was:

What is proposed by the Majority . . . is, for all the novel terminology, essentially the present Poor Law under non-elective administration. *Plus ça change, plus c'est la même chose!*[95]

Helen's riposte was:

There was a scheme brought to our notice known as the 'Breaking up of the Poor Law' . . . It seems clear to us that the idea upon which it is founded is faulty and unworkable . . . To thrust upon these [existing educational and sanitary] Authorities, while their work is still uncomplete, the far more difficult and delicate duties of dealing with families which have already broken down, would be to court failure in both directions—that of prevention and that of cure.[96]

---

[92] Cd. 4499, Majority Report, Part IX, Sect. 23, 105, p. 223.
[93] Ibid., Part VI, Ch. 4, Recommendation 26, p. 562.
[94] Ibid., Recommendation 51, p. 565.
[95] Introduction to the Longman's 1909 edn. of the Minority Report, p. xvi.
[96] Cd. 4499, Majority Report, Part IX, Sect. 6, 12–13, pp. 196–7.

II

Appeal to the Spectators

REACTIONS OF PRESS AND POLITICIANS
AND PUBLIC CAMPAIGNS

BEATRICE Webb's anticipations of victory and her belief that the Minority Report would overwhelm the Report of her adversaries were quite disappointed, as she acknowledged honestly in her Diary. She had overestimated the Webbs' influence and capabilities, and underestimated those of the Majority. The preliminary responses of the Cabinet Ministers to whom she had given a preview of her Report might have warned her that they were 'playing safe', but the reaction of the press was a bitter disillusionment. She wrote in her Diary:

February 18th [*1909*].—The day after the reception of the reports of the Poor Law Commission. We turned out to be quite wrong as to the reception of the Majority Report. So far as the first day's reviews are concerned, the majority have got a magnificent reception. We have had a fair look in, but only in those papers which had got to know of the existence of a Minority Report before the issue late on Wednesday night. If we had not taken steps, we should have been submerged completely . . . Roughly speaking, all the Conservative papers went for the majority proposals, and all the London Liberal papers were decidedly for ours. We secured, in fact, belligerent rights, but not more than that. The majority hold the platform. Perhaps we feel a trifle foolish at having crabbed the Majority Report to our family and intimate friends, and exalted our own. That has certainly not proved to be the estimate of public opinion.[1]

In an accompanying analysis of the reasons for this public success of the majority, she acknowledged the substantial merits of the Majority Report, its proposals which '*in name at any rate*' appeared to be revolutionary, Lord George Hamilton's success in holding together so large a majority of Commissioners, and the

---

[1] B.W.D., 18 Feb. 1909; *Our Partnership*, ed. B. Drake and M. Cole (London, 1948), p. 425; MacKenzie, *Diary*, iii, 107.

weight of the names of some of the signatories.[2] Beatrice Webb did
not have reason to change her opinion of the reaction of the press in
the next few weeks, or even after her return from a much-needed
holiday in Italy on 20 April.

In that interval, Helen Bosanquet lost no time, as soon as she
had finished drafting the Majority Report, in preparing a small
book, called *The Poor Law Report of 1909: A Summary
Explaining the Defects of the Present System and the Principal
Recommendations of the Commission . . . ,*[3] which Lord George
Hamilton thought 'an excellent synopsis', that would be 'greatly
read by those who will not buy the report in its entirety'.[4] Copies of
it were quickly dispatched for review and for the information of
busy journalists, and met with an appreciative welcome. For
example, J. St. Loe Strachey, editor of the *Spectator*, wrote to Helen
Bosanquet on 5 March 1909,[5] praising her work on the Commission
and the book. He went on:

The Majority Report is I feel a really great and useful document, and
though it goes perhaps a little further than I like in one or two points and
makes rather more concessions than I think good to the enemy, I do not
mean to press those personal views in any way but to back up the Report
for all I am worth.

He feared the government's picking out a few popular ideas from
both Reports and jumbling them into ill-considered measures
which would add to its 'dreadful record of demoralising legislation',
such as the Old Age Pensions Act.

The chief support for the Webbs' Minority Report, outside
Fabian ranks, came from the group of journalists and theorists
known as 'New Liberals': Leonard Hobhouse, frequent contributor
to the *Manchester Guardian* and the weekly *Nation*; Henry W.
Massingham, editor of the *Nation*; Alfred G. Gardiner, editor of
the *Daily News*; the academics G. P. Gooch, a director and later
joint-editor of the *Contemporary Review*; Gilbert Murray and
Graham Wallas, who wrote for Liberal journals; and the freelance
writer J. A. Hobson. Many of these liberals had been estranged
from the Webbs in the 1890s and early Edwardian period, but the

[2] B.W.D., 18 Feb. 1909 and 22 Feb. 1909; *Our Partnership*, pp. 425–6 (her
italics).
[3] London, 1909.
[4] Hamilton to H. Bosanquet, 8 Mar. 1909. Bosanquet Papers.
[5] Ibid.

Minority Report as a whole (though many of them had minor criticisms of it)[6] rekindled their interest and support. In Parliament, the Webbs had whole-hearted approval for their ideas only from a minority of back-bench Radicals on the Liberal Party side. As Beatrice Webb had given the Liberal leaders several months preview of her conclusions, they had had time to decide, soon after the Reports were public, that the Minority proposals were so hot that they needed to be handled gingerly. Early in February 1909 the Prime Minister, Mr Asquith, had expressed an opinion in favour of removing the mentally defective and the sick from the Poor Law and transferring them to the Health authorities, and removing also the vagrants who were to be placed in Detention Colonies in charge of the Home Office; he also at first favoured the Majority plan of transferring all the remaining categories of paupers (including the unemployed) to statutory committees of the counties and county boroughs. He opposed the idea of establishing a Ministry of Labour on the grounds that an accepting of full State responsibility for 'organizing the labour market' would be too expensive and would involve recognition of the 'Right to Work'.[7] A few months later, he was to become doubtful if there was any need to create a new 'Public Assistance Authority' at all if certain categories of poor could be taken out of the Poor Law.[8]

John Burns, as President of the Local Government Board, was a key political figure. This former Social Democrat and leader of the unemployed and the dockers during the 1880s and early 1890s became in 1905 the first working man to be appointed to a British Cabinet. At the time of his appointment, relations between him and the Webbs were still cordial, although Burns had never really

---

[6] See M. Freeden, *The New Liberalism: An Ideology of Social Reform* (Oxford, 1978), ch. 6, concerning the general social views of New Liberals at this time. Hobhouse's reservations were expressed in his letter to Gilbert Murray of 24 May 1909: 'Understanding that one is not pledged to any detailed agreement I joined Mrs Webb's Committee. Of course she is bitterly anti-Liberal & carries him [Sidney Webb] with her & I think, furthermore, Balfour is one cleverer than she & humbugs her into believing that he will do all she wants. On the other hand it is true that Burns has become a regular stick-in-the-mud & the situation will be serious if they do not move him to another office. In sum however the Govt. seem likely to be doing rather big things next year & I doubt if they will be seriously open to attack on this flank whether Mrs Webb wishes it or not.' (Quoted from Gilbert Murray Papers, Bodleian Library, by P. P. Poirier in his edition of L. T. Hobhouse's *The Labour Movement* (Brighton, 1974), p. xxvi.)

[7] Cab. 37/97 No. 20, 12 Feb. 1909; Cab. 37/98 No. 40, 10 Mar. 1909.

[8] Memo to Cabinet, June 1909.

forgiven Sidney Webb their differences over the Boer War and Balfour's Education Acts of 1902–3.[9] They began to fall out when on 27 October 1906 Beatrice Webb over-confidently tried to press Burns to accept the early drafts of her scheme for the break-up of the Poor Law.[10] At the interview, Burns considered her ideas to be 'a little too doctrinaire', but was not yet positively hostile. As soon as he and his officials had looked over the draft his attitude hardened, and by the end of October, Beatrice Webb was recording some harsh opinions in her Diary of his vanity, his susceptibility to deference and flattery:

[His] faculty of seeing facts as they are is being overgrown by a sort of fatty complacency with the world as it is . . . He talks incessantly and never listens to anyone except the officials to whom he *must* listen, in order to accomplish the routine work of his office. Hence, he is completely in their hands and is becoming the most hidebound of departmental chiefs, gulled by an obstructive fact or reactionary argument, taken in by the most naive commonplaces of middle-class administrative routine . . . What *is* the right conduct towards such a man?[11]

Burns's own Diaries suggest that these views of him, though savage, were shrewd. Under pressure from unemployment agitation, determined to back his official James Davy in proceedings against 'lax' Guardians in West Ham and Poplar, and becoming a main spokesman against the Labour Party's Right to Work Bill (or as he called it in his picturesque cockney, 'the Bedlam Bill establishing the right to shirk'),[12] Burns was identifying himself more and more with his Department and its policies. He came to see himself a champion of public economy and as a successful Canute 'stemming the tide of Pauperisation'.[13] His attitude to the unemployed themselves was losing any trace of his former sympathy, and his feelings towards his opponents were becoming increasingly vindictive. George Lansbury and Keir Hardie as 'Kings of the Cadgers' were his two special *bêtes noires*.[14]

Beatrice Webb, in her puzzlement about how to handle such a

---

[9] See Burns's comments in margin of a letter from G. B. Shaw, 11 Sept. 1903. Burns Papers, vol. vii.

[10] B.W.D., 22 [?27] Oct. 1906; *Our Partnership*, p. 392. Burns's Diary 27 Oct. 1906. Burns Papers.

[11] B.W.D., 30 Oct. 1906; *Our Partnership*, pp. 393–4. (The official to whom Burns mainly listened was his private secretary, Walter T. Jerred.)

[12] Burns's Diary, 9 Mar. 1908. Burns Papers.

[13] Ibid., 4 Dec. 1908.   [14] Ibid., 4 Dec. 1908 and 16 Jan. 1909.

man, made a fatal move. She decided he needed an able official in his Department who would counteract the influence of such men as Davy, Downes, and Jerred. She wrote to him on 1 May 1907, mixing appeal with flattery:

> If you are thinking of carrying out any new departure you will require a really strong subordinate—a man of the type of Morant (who by the way is a great admirer of yours). I do so want your administration to stand out as constructive in the best sense. You have achieved the reputation of a strong man to *resist* foolish proposals, now you want to show yourself strong in carrying out wise ones.[15]

Unfortunately, as Robert Morant knew, Burns hated him as the official who had carried out the Balfour Education reforms.[16] The Webbs did not improve matters by continuing to scheme for the next two years—unsuccessfully—with other Liberal Ministers to get Morant into the Local Government Board, regarding his appointment as essential to their plans. When Asquith succeeded Campbell-Bannerman as Prime Minister in April 1908, their hopes were raised that Burns might be transferred to another Cabinet post (there was little hope of dropping him as some Radicals wanted, for he was a necessary feature of the government as its token 'Lib-Lab'). Churchill was invited to take over from Burns, but declined;[17] so Asquith appointed Charles Masterman, a young journalist Radical, MP for West Ham, who was friendly with both the Webbs and John Burns and in favour of a progressive social policy, as Under-Secretary to the Local Government Board. Masterman had been persuaded by the Webbs of the need to get Morant into the department. But Masterman's attempt to work with Burns and ginger up the department was a failure and lasted only a year: in June 1909 he left the LGB and joined Churchill at Home Office to work in 'an efficient and progressive Government department' for a change.[18] Burns (as he recorded in his Diary) had

---

[15] B. Webb to J. Burns, 1 May 1907. Burns Papers, vol. vii.

[16] Morant to B. Webb, 1 May 1907. Passfield Papers.

[17] K. D. Brown, *John Burns* (London, 1977), p. 137. This contains a statement of Churchill's reasons. His private secretary of that time reported (many years later) that Churchill said: 'I refuse to be shut up in a soup kitchen with Mrs. Sidney Webb': E. Marsh, *A Number of People: A Book of Reminiscences* (New York, 1939), p. 163. In his letter to Asquith, Churchill referred to the boring detail of LGB work and the prospect of his being confronted with earnest people who knew their subjects thoroughly. In the reckoning of ambitious and rising young politicians, the LGB was regarded as no more than a consolation prize.

[18] Brown, *John Burns*, p. 145.

adopted a policy of 'Patience with the moody creature of vain visions flowing sentiment and overleaping ideals':[19] Masterman proved lightweight and ineffectual against Burns's solid stonewalling.

The only minor victory that the Webbs could claim was the appointment of Dr Arthur Newsholme, their friend and supporter, to the LGB at the end of 1908, to replace the retiring medical officer; but it seems most likely that this appointment was made because Burns was impressed with Newsholme personally, rather than because of the Webbs' persuasion.[20] In any case, Newsholme was not in a position to act as a substitute for Morant. When Sir Samuel Provis finally retired as Permanent Secretary to the LGB in December 1909, Burns insisted on his replacement not by Morant but by his immediate subordinate, H. C. Monro, and on his own private secretary, W. T. Jerred, succeeding Monro as Assistant Permanent Secretary: both Monro and Jerred were thoroughly 'old-style' LGB officials. The Webbs' last hopes of reform from within the LGB faded when, in the remaking of Cabinet after the elections of 1910, Burns was still kept on as President.[21]

In his early days as a young Liberal minister, Winston Churchill had been happy to frequent the Webbs' high thinking and frugal (by Edwardian and Churchillian standards) dinners at 41 Grosvenor Road. As a clever young man he realized that he had a lot to learn from these experts; he sincerely believed that social reform was a 'big issue' for the new Liberal government, and he had a sharp eclectic eye for policy items that might make his fame. The Webbs' habit of dispensing their information freely and somewhat unguardedly, and their generous practice of fostering the careers of young men of ability, whether they were their devoted disciples or not, served Churchill well. He had picked up from them the general concept of a National Minimum, and embodied it in the Trade Boards Act of 1909. They had also brought to his attention the importance of labour exchanges, and introduced him to William Beveridge, whom he took on to his staff at the Board of Trade. Churchill found Beveridge's ideas of labour exchanges more acceptable than the Webbs' own variant of them. But there were

[19] Burns's Diary, 13 Apr. 1908. Burns Papers.
[20] Brown, *John Burns*, p. 133.
[21] The Webbs were misled by Morant into thinking that there was again a chance that Winston Churchill would accept the LGB in this reshuffle. B.W.D., 1 Dec. 1909; *Our Partnership*, p. 437.

also other ideas for social reform simmering in the minds of several talented young administrators at the Board of Trade before Churchill joined it, and Churchill's quick appreciation and development of these were to carry him away from the influence of the Webbs. The notion of social insurance was the most important.

Arthur Wilson Fox, the Comptroller-General of the Commercial, Labour, and Statistical Department of the Board of Trade, had commissioned Beveridge in August 1907 to prepare three research papers on the history of labour bureaux, on trade union insurance, and on Continental experiments with social insurance against unemployment to help his own preparation for giving evidence to the Royal Commission on the Poor Laws. Wilson Fox's assistant at the Board, W. H. Dawson, also studied German experiments. On 6 April 1908, a week before Churchill's appointment to the Board of Trade was announced, Wilson Fox outlined to the Royal Commission[22] a possible scheme of compulsory and contributory unemployment insurance combined with voluntary labour exchanges. It would be financed by a contribution of 2*d.* a week from workers, 1*d.* from employers, ½*d.* from the State, and ½*d.* from municipalities, and could be begun experimentally in particular trades. Wilson Fox was hesitant about the possibility of introducing his scheme soon: 'I do not say that you can do it on national lines now—I think it is perhaps too big a scheme, because the English people do not like big changes too suddenly.'[23] Churchill's contribution was his willingness to take the political gamble with an idea that appealed to him strongly. Wilson Fox's death in December 1908 caused his role in originating it to be forgotten.[24] Churchill, with Unemployment Insurance as his social policy, was

---

[22] Cd. 5068, Min. of Ev., Appendix vol. ix, Qq. 98930, 98340.

[23] Ibid., Q. 98930.

[24] There has been a good deal of discussion about the origins of the idea, and Wilson Fox's contribution has tended to be overlooked in the dispute concerning Lloyd George's and Churchill's respective roles. Lloyd George's claim that he gave the idea to Churchill has some slight justification in the fact that the idea was launched by Wilson Fox and his assistants while Lloyd George was still at the Board of Trade (cf. B. B. Gilbert, 'Winston Churchill versus the Webbs: The Origins of British Unemployment Insurance', *American Historical Review*, 71 (1966), 850, 852; J. Harris, *Unemployment and Politics* (Oxford, 1972), p. 276; J. R. Hay, *The Origins of the Liberal Welfare Reforms 1906–1914* (London, 1975), p. 51. E. P. Hennock in 'The Origins of British National Insurance and the German Precedent 1880–1914' in W. J. Mommsen (ed.), *The Emergence of the Welfare State in Britain and Germany 1850–1950* (London, 1981), ch. 5, has demonstrated the complexities in assessing the 'influence' of the German example.

able to follow in the footsteps of his predecessor as President of the Board of Trade, David Lloyd George, and make a name for himself by taking initiatives undreamt of in John Burns's busy administrative futility at the Local Government Board.

David Lloyd George, in moving from the Board of Trade, where he had laid the foundations of his reputation as a social reformer, to be Chancellor of the Exchequer in 1908, carried with him ideas for the more negotiable items of social policy, such as the old-age pensions and health insurance. A visit he paid to Germany in 1908 filled him with enthusiasm for the scheme of health insurance established by Prince Bismarck in 1889. Soon he had a young Treasury official, William J. Braithwaite (like Beveridge a product of Balliol College and Toynbee Hall) studying the German scheme; and it was agreed that a joint bill should be prepared, with the Treasury responsible for drawing up the health insurance part and the Board of Trade drafting the unemployment insurance section. Lloyd George's relations with the Webbs, unlike Churchill's, had never been close, so there was no question of his 'drifting away' from them. Both Ministers had decided, as Churchill put it, to 'thrust a big slice of Bismarckian tissue over the whole underside of our industrial system'.[25] They were both embarking on a line of policy that differed markedly from that of the Webbs. The moment of final separation came when, on 9 October 1908, the Webbs were invited to breakfast at 11 Downing Street for a discussion of social insurance with Lloyd George, Winston Churchill, and R. B. Haldane.[26] The Webbs refused to compromise and to endorse the government's social insurance schemes in the Minority Report, which they were then completing. They considered the government proposals not only totally inadequate, but also impracticable. Compulsory social insurance would do least for those in the deeper levels of poverty; it would do nothing in a preventive way against sickness and destitution, as it provided only an unconditional payment for a limited time after sickness and unemployment had occurred; and its contributory principle amounted to a poll tax, imposed without regard to ability to pay, and ludicrously expensive and cumbersome to collect and administer.[27] The Webbs believed

[25] Churchill to Asquith, 29 Dec. 1908. Asquith Papers, vol. ii.
[26] B.W.D., 16 Oct. 1908; *Our Partnership*, p. 417.
[27] Ibid.; The Webbs elaborated their arguments later in ch. 7 of their book, *The Prevention of Destitution* (London, 1911).

that whatever was beneficial in compulsory insurance could be achieved by State subsidies to voluntary insurance organizations and trade unions to extend their scope. They dismissed as wasteful the suggestion that the State should bring insurance companies, Friendly Societies, and trade unions into the compulsory scheme, and they were sure that the opposition of these vested interests would wreck the government's proposed bill. In the 'heated discussion' at this meeting, the Webbs burnt their boats with the Liberal ministers. Even R. B. Haldane, who up to that point had been closest to them, and had given them support and encouragement, was alienated. Shortly afterwards Masterman, who had been helping Lloyd George with the scheme, deserted them too.

The severing of the Webbs' links with the Liberal leaders did not mean their complete isolation. They had preserved their connections with the Conservatives, and from 1909 they were even speculating whether the Liberals might not lose the next election.[28] Their personal friendship with Arthur Balfour had survived, and Balfour had allowed them to understand that personally he admired the Minority Report.[29] He agreed that the Minority Report was not a 'Socialist' document, and was inspired by the worthy aims of 'raising character and individual responsibility', but he was sceptical of whether the changes it proposed would have the long-run effect of realizing those aims.[30] The Webbs had cause to be grateful for his absence of hostility;[31] but Arthur Balfour used his charming evasiveness to avoid committing either himself or his party further than that.[32] Beatrice conducted a long correspondence with Lady Betty Balfour (the wife of Gerald) who became for a while her close friend, in the course of which Lady Betty wrote:

I dont know Arthur's views on the subject of the Minority Report. Gerald's I am afraid are not practically favourable though he thinks it a profoundly interesting document and would like to see parts of the scheme experimentally tried. He is always moved to deep admiration for your husband and yourself—for your capacity, your knowledge, industry & selfless devotion to the public good. My natural instincts go more with the Minority Report than his do . . .[33]

[28] e.g. B.W.D., 20 Apr. 1909; *Our Partnership*, pp. 427–8.
[29] B.W.D., 14 Nov. 1909; *Our Partnership*, p. 436.
[30] Lady Betty Balfour to B. Webb, 25 Dec. 1910. Passfield Papers.
[31] B.W.D., 12 Apr. 1910; *Our Partnership*, p. 449.
[32] See his speech, *Parliamentary Debates*, 5th. series (1910), vol. xvi, cols. 828 ff.
[33] Lady Betty Balfour to B. Webb, 24 Apr. 1910. Passfield Papers.

Lady Betty actually got to the point of chairing a public meeting of Beatrice Webb's at Edinburgh; but she was not prepared to go further without the approval of her husband or her brother-in-law.[34]

The Webbs got a much colder reception from the Tariff Reform section of the Conservative Party. Austen Chamberlain's rejection of the Minority proposals on the grounds that they would cost about fifty million pounds[35] evoked a bitter outburst from Beatrice, who had expected some sympathy for her views from the Chamberlain family:

I was staying the other day with his [Austen Chamberlain's] aunt & found the whole atmosphere steeped in plutocratic fear for their own incomes! When one remembers the old days when I, coming from the dogmatic individualism of Herbert Spencer, broke my poor little heart quarrelling with the magnetic Jo over his demagogic utterances, it does seem strange to see the Chamberlain family as Established Capitalism![36]

Disgust with the Tariff Reform leaders led her into rueful speculations about the size of the class of 'the non-political elector—the man *without social purpose* of any kind—the reader of the *Daily Mail* and *Express*, intent on keeping all he has . . .'.[37] Amongst back-bench Conservatives, however, the Webbs found some support. The warmest upholders of the Minority Report amongst them were Sir Gilbert Parker, MP for Gravesend, and John Waller Hills, MP for Durham City;[38] but there was a group of about a dozen other Tory MPs, uncommitted to the Webbs' particular ideas, who were in favour of a substantial measure of Poor Law reform somewhere between the Majority and Minority proposals.[39] Their activities in urging changes in the Poor Law were not discouraged by Arthur Balfour.

---

[34] Ibid.
[35] A. Chamberlain, *Politics from the Inside* (London, 1936), pp. 238–9. A passage from this is quoted in a footnote to p. 450 of *Our Partnership*.
[36] B.W. to Lady Betty Balfour, n.d. [?Nov. 1910]. Passfield Papers.
[37] B.W.D., 20 Dec. 1909; *Our Partnership*, p. 438.
[38] B.W.D., 27 Sept. 1909; *Our Partnership*, p. 434.
[39] They were: Hon. Waldorf Astor, John Lawrence Baird, Charles Bathurst, Lord Henry Cavendish-Bentinck, Charles Sydney Goldman, Henry Percy Harris, George Ambrose Lloyd, Clement Anderson Montague-Barlow, Mark Sykes, Lord Alexander George Thynne, Lord Windsor. This group became members of the Unionist Social Reform Committee (see p. 343 below). The Hon. William George Arthur Ormsby-Gore has been excluded from the list, although he later became a member of the

The task of enjoining the Labour Party to take up the cause of the Minority Report vigorously was assigned to George Lansbury and Francis Chandler, and the omens, at the beginning of 1909, seemed favourable. During 1907 and 1908, spurred on by the government's inactivity in face of rising unemployment, the 'Right to Work' movement, which had had a long but intermittent history during the nineteenth century, flared up again. A national Right to Work Council,[40] established under the joint auspices of the Social Democratic Federation and the Independent Labour Party in November 1905, was galvanized into action and set up a London Right to Work Committee in October 1907. The purpose was to provide a backing of agitation for the parliamentary Labour Party's Unemployed Workmen's Bill (which soon became known as the 'Right to Work' Bill) put before the House of Commons by Ramsay MacDonald on 9 July 1907. Although the Bill seemed moderate in its practical proposals, it embodied the revolutionary principle of the 'right to work'. It provided that local authorities were to set up unemployed committees, on which representatives of trade unions were to sit, and the duty was imposed on these committees to find work for the unemployed in their areas or maintain the unemployed workmen and their families. A national unemployed committee was also to be established to advise the Local Government Board about the planning of national schemes of work for the unemployed. The Local Government Board was to remain the supreme authority with power to decide whether national or local funds should be used to provide schemes of employment, except in times of great distress, when the national Exchequer would be obliged to pay. This first 'Right to Work' Bill did not even get a second reading. The measure was reintroduced early in 1908 and reached a second reading in March, before being defeated; and it was presented once more by the Labour Party at the 1909 session, and again thrown out in the second reading. The House of Commons had emphatically rejected the notion of the 'right to work', but the slogan had become entrenched as part of the Labour Party's rhetoric and policy.

It might seem that the Minority Report arrived just at the right moment, with the third defeat of the Labour Party's measure

Unionist Reform Committee, because he utterly repudiated the Minority's recommendations, and stood perhaps slightly to the right of the Majority's.

[40] George Lansbury was its Treasurer.

looming. But there were difficulties. The Webbs were anxious to avoid connection of their proposals with the 'inadmissible'[41] notion of the right to work. As Utilitarians, they thought this claim of natural rights to be nonsense, and as Fabians they saw it to be a barrier to the acceptance of their proposals. They were somewhat unguarded in their expressions of scorn, which offended the more zealous champions of the principle. In any event, the Marxist Social Democratic Federation, which had played an active agitational role in the 'Right to Work' campaign, decided to repudiate some of the chief propositions of the Minority Report. Led by Harry Quelch, the SDF critics denounced the Minority recommendations to abolish the Guardians and transfer their functions to the county councils as an attempt to remove administration of the Poor Law further from democratic control. They rejected the office of 'Registrar of Public Assistance' as bureaucratic; and also the notion that 'the unemployed question can be solved inside the capitalist system' by labour exchanges, subsidies to insurance funds of trade unions, training establishments, and

the appointment of a Minister of Labour at Five Thousand a year, with comfortable appointments for an unlimited number of subordinate bureaucrats, whose duty it is to collect or dispense labour just as the demands of the capitalist labour market require its concentration or distribution.[42]

The Webbs were undismayed by this attack from the extreme left, reckoning that it would offset the attack on the Minority Report from the extreme right as 'Socialist', and reassure the moderate and middle-class audience which they were trying to convince. They left it to George Lansbury to answer his former associates.[43] By 1909 the association between the SDF and the ILP and Labour Party over the 'Right to Work' campaign was showing signs of tension,[44] and many ILP leaders were ready to abandon the agitation and take up something likely to be more productive of results. If Lloyd George and Winston Churchill had not begun to

---

[41] This term was Asquith's: K. D. Brown, *Labour and Unemployment 1900–1914* (Newton Abbott, 1971), p. 90. But cf. B. Webb to Lady Betty Balfour [n.d.—? Nov. 1910]: 'Some folly like the Right to Work'. Passfield Papers.
[42] 'The Prevention of Destitution', *Social-Democrat*, 14 (1910), 344–5.
[43] *Report of the Debate between G. Lansbury and H. Quelch on the Poor Law Minority Report on September 20th and 21st 1910* (London, n.d.)
[44] Brown, *Labour and Unemployment 1900–1914*, pp. 109 ff.

woo the trade unionists and moderate Labour leaders with prospects of social reform and a radical budget, the Webbs would have had a clear field. As it was, the Parliamentary Committee of the Trades Union Congress and the TUC itself gave the Minority Report a cool and cautious, though not an unfavourable, reception. The Parliamentary Committee had already committed itself to the policy of national unemployment insurance,[45] which the Minority Report condemned. Individual items of the Minority Report were approved by the TUC,[46] but not the report as a whole. The ILP leaders were, in the main, more enthusiastic. Even Ramsay MacDonald, no friend of the Webbs, gave his grudging approval, saying that the Minority Report was the ILP's 'old proposals paraphrased, brought up to date as to facts and experience, and issued at the public expense'.[47] Other ILP and Labour Party leaders who gave stronger support included Keir Hardie, Philip Snowden, G. N. Barnes, Arthur Henderson, James O'Grady, D. J. Shackleton, Fred Jowett, and W. C. Anderson. Both the ILP and the Labour Party endorsed the Minority Report at their conferences.[48]

When the Webbs returned in April 1909 from a holiday in Italy to recover from their labours of completing the Minority Report, they had decided to launch a great public campaign to influence public opinion and to force the Liberal government to accept their principles. It was to be a middle-class successor of the 'Right to Work' campaigns of 1907–8. Beatrice Webb was advised against it by Winston Churchill,[49] by the Haldanes, and by the Balfours. Elizabeth Haldane wrote:

I am not sure that your plan of knife to knife opposition is the wisest . . . I am so afraid that this crusade will make a sharp dividing line such that the real objects aimed at will not be arrived at as they are labelled as those of one party & supposed to be arrived at by submitting to one shibboleth only.[50]

Lady Betty Balfour's advice was similar:

[45] B. C. Roberts, *The Trades Union Congress 1868–1921* (London, 1958), p. 221 n. 2.
[46] e.g. the proposal to subsidize TU unemployment funds.
[47] ILP Annual Report, 1909.
[48] ILP Annual Conference Report, 1911; Labour Party Annual Reports, 1910 and 1911.
[49] B.W.D., 3 Oct. 1909; *Our Partnership*, p. 435.
[50] E. Haldane to B. Webb, dated 'Friday' [end 1909]. Passfield Papers.

There is only one thing I regret about yr campaign & that is that you have adopted a line that seems ever more & more to accentuate the differences between the two reports, & therefore to embitter the majority side more & more—whereas the more I try to understand the question the more it seems to me the differences might be bridged over, & the minority policy adopted without letting it appear it differed fundamentally from the majority! At any rate I think that would have made it easier for our party to deal with.[51]

Beatrice Webb, however, was determined on her crusade—'to *really change* the mind of the people with regard to the facts of destitution'.[52] As a first step, the Fabian Society issued a cheap edition of the Minority Report. The Treasury Solicitor (spurred on by Lord George Hamilton)[53] threatened the Fabian Society with an injunction for infringement of Crown copyright, but Sidney Webb, advised by Haldane, claimed the copyright, as the manuscript of the Report was in his handwriting, and dug up a Treasury minute of 1887 that authorized and encouraged the republication of Blue Books in the public interest. This enabled Lord George Hamilton and other opponents to say that Sidney Webb had 'thrown off the mask'[54] and stood exposed as the real author of the Report. But it was effective in getting wider circulation for both the Minority and Majority Reports for, again at Lord George's instigation,[55] the Treasury arranged to publish both reports together in a rival cheap edition. Soon five separate editions of the Minority Report, at differing prices, were in circulation. By the end of 1910 nearly 25,000 copies of the Minority Report had been sold.[56]

In April 1909, the Webbs formed a broad, all-party organization called 'The National Committee to promote the Break-up of the Poor Law'. The Revd Russell Wakefield became its Chairman and Beatrice Webb its Secretary; and by December 1909 it had enrolled over 16,000 members. For three years its campaign was conducted with all the skill that Beatrice Webb's organizing capacity and Sidney Webb's Fabian experience could devise. Its firmest base of

[51] Lady Betty Balfour to B. Webb, 4 Dec. 1909. Passfield Papers. It is mentioned in B.W.D., 10 Dec. 1909 (passage not included in *Our Partnership*).
[52] B.W.D., 3 Oct. 1909; *Our Partnership*, p. 435.
[53] B.W.D., 18 Feb. 1909; *Our Partnership*, p. 425. Hamilton to H. Bosanquet, 22 Feb. 1909 and 27 Feb. 1909. Bosanquet Papers.
[54] Hamilton to H. Bosanquet, 22 Feb. 1909. Bosanquet Papers.
[55] Hamilton to H. Bosanquet, 27 Feb. 1909. Smart to H. Bosanquet, 18 Feb. 1909, ibid.
[56] M. A. Hamilton, *Sidney and Beatrice Webb* (London, 1932), p. 197.

activists was found amongst the younger members of the Fabian Society and the Independent Labour Party, who brought to the campaign a genuine fervour and enthusiasm; but it also won an impressive amount of support from academics, literary men, and ecclesiastics. Beatrice Webb even did her best to get her literary friends to write *pièces de circonstance* directly for the campaign cause, but she met with more general expressions of goodwill from them than social realist action. Even Bernard Shaw declined gracefully, explaining with perceptive self-criticism: 'I should make Lord George Hamilton so funny that the sorrows of the poor would be forgotten . . .'[57]

The tactics employed in the Poor Law campaign were mainly those well tried in the Fabian Society: public meetings addressed by prominent men and women in different parts of the country; the organization of volunteer helpers in distributing leaflets and sending out circulars; the running of conferences; the interviewing of influential persons; the lobbying of MPs; the writing of letters to the press. Beatrice Webb took part herself, for the first time, in the public speaking, finding it a strain, and often critical of her own performances, but on the whole revelling in the excitement of the new experience. The National Committee even set up its own journal, the *Crusade against Destitution*, commonly known as the *Crusade*, efficiently edited by a young Fabian, Clifford Sharp. The general aim was to work up a public opinion which would press upon the government a Bill to give effect to the Minority Report. The Bill was drafted by Henry Schloesser, a young Fabian lawyer (later to be known as Chief Justice Sir Henry Slesser); it was called the Prevention of Destitution Bill, and was introduced in the House of Commons by the Liberal Sir Robert Price on 8 April 1910.

The initiative in appealing to the public had come from the Webbs. At first the Majority Commissioners had rested on the laurels awarded them by the Press, although they had not neglected to make contacts with prominent politicians and journalists—Lord George Hamilton with Asquith and *The Times*, Lancelot Phelps with Asquith and Bryce, Helen Bosanquet with St. Loe Strachey: 'Do I recognise your hand in the Spec[tator] today?' wrote Professor Smart to Helen Bosanquet as early as 31 January 1909.[58] But the size and efficiency of the campaign mounted by the Webbs

[57] Shaw to B. Webb, 9 Dec. 1910. Passfield Papers.
[58] Bosanquet Papers.

forced the Majority into greater exertion.[59] In February 1910 a body for advocating its point of view was formed, named The National Poor Law Reform Association, with Lord George Hamilton as its President. 'Hereafter, [*Beatrice Webb wrote*] wherever we penetrated, by word or by script, we were confronted by a powerful organisation doing likewise in an opposite direction.'[60] Helen Bosanquet was not able to take as active a part in the work of the body as she would have wished. The strain of completing the Majority Report had brought on a physical and nervous collapse: she had developed dangerous 'heart symptoms',[61] and, although she soldiered on until her part of the Scottish Report was completed at the end of June 1909, she was then ordered by her doctor to take the cure at the thermal waters of Bad-Nauheim in Hesse-Darmstadt, Germany, for these were considered to be specific in cases of heart trouble and ataxy. She found the cure to be disappointing, and remained in intermittent delicate health for the rest of her life.

Before she left for the German spa, Bernard Bosanquet was drawn into the fray. For the issue of the *Sociological Review* of April 1909, its editor invited Bernard Bosanquet and Sidney Webb to present the cases for the two reports of the Poor Law Commission. Sidney Webb reiterated, in pithy and forceful style, the main arguments of the Minority Report. He claimed that the facts presented to the Commissioners, together with the 'potent force of the spirit of the age', had changed the views of all the Commissioners. The conclusions they had arrived at destroyed the principles of 1834 and revealed the bankruptcy of the policy advocated for so many years by 'COS headquarters'. The Commission was united in its destructive criticism, agreeing on a number of basic issues: that the Boards of Guardians had failed as a system, and they and the Poor Law Union areas must be superseded by counties and county boroughs as authorities and areas; that the principles of 1834 must be abandoned and replaced by treatment both curative and restorative; that workhouses and workhouse tests be abolished and the whole terminology of the Poor Law changed to make a break with the past. Webb gave a quick historical sketch illustrating the

---

[59] See B.W.D., 23 July 1909 (*Our Partnership*, p. 432) for an account of F. Bentham's visit to the National Committee's headquarters and his reactions.

[60] *Our Partnership*, p. 440.

[61] J. H. Muirhead, *Bernard Bosanquet and his Friends* (London, 1935), p. 124; H. Bosanquet, *Bernard Bosanquet* (London, 1924), pp. 121, 124.

way the State's policy during the last seventy years had drifted away from the principles of 1834 and had come to recognize the mutual obligations of citizen and community. The gradualness of the drift had meant that the State had never brought its thinking and reform into harmony, and, as a result, great confusion of policy and overlapping of local authorities had developed.

According to Webb's version, the difference between the Majority and Minority Reports lay in their plans for reconstruction. The Majority did not face the facts of overlapping: their 'Public Assistance Authority' would perpetuate it, by leaving the other services in existence. The Minority solved the problem by abolishing the Poor Law: 'The choice, in brief, is between letting the duplication, overlapping, and confusion continue, and deliberately facing the facts with a plan calculated to reduce chaos to order. The issue can hardly be doubtful.' The Majority's 'Public Assistance Authorities' were intended to remove them from direct democratic electoral control: they were to be wholly nominated or co-opted bodies, with only a small representation of county councillors on them. The county council had no control over the Authority beyond nominating it and paying the bills: the county council could not sanction its expenditure, veto its actions, lay down policy, make by-laws, or even review its proceedings. By contrast, the Minority proposals were democratic 'simplicity itself'. The other main difference which Webb featured was their plans for the able-bodied: he contrasted the Minority's demand for a Ministry of Labour and its elaborate provisions for a counter-cycle policy, decasualization, and industrial training with what he claimed to be the absence of policy in the Majority Report:

[The Majority Commissioners] have no policy as to Vagrancy, except to go on alternately relieving and punishing the 'casual' as we have done for three hundred years. They cannot even make up their minds whether he is to be dealt with by the 'one and only one Authority' that they desiderate, or handed over to the Police and the Home Office—as, in fact, was the practice before 1834. They have no policy as to the ablebodied in the Workhouse, except that this place is to be henceforth called 'an industrial institution', and apparently converted into a place for carrying on all sorts of trades, which experience has demonstrated to be the most costly of all failures. They have no policy with regard to Unemployment, except the suggestion of Labour Exchanges to tell the men when there is work (or no work?) to be got; and a vague hope that someone will devise a plan of insurance.

Bernard Bosanquet's reply[62] attempted to raise the discussion to a higher philosophical plane. He wished to emphasize the divergence in principle between the two Reports, in spite of their agreement in some particular matters. He argued that the Majority and Minority were not agreed in rejecting the principles of 1834: the Majority saw the defects of the present system as a failure to adjust to heightened demands made possible by the *success* of earlier reforms and changes in economic and social conditions. The Majority Report did not, like the Minority, indiscriminately praise the personal character and work of the existing Guardians and indiscriminately condemn the system; it recognized that some Guardians had attained the new standard while many had not, and it wished to remove hindrances to the new advance by setting up bodies that could attain the level already reached by the best. The Majority did not depart from the 1834 (and COS) principle of 'respect for the self-maintaining character', nor abandon the notion that where there was a failure of self-maintenance there was 'a defect in the citizen character, or at least a grave danger to its integrity', nor did it cease to believe that this moral element differentiated the treatment appropriate to the destitute or necessitous from any services that ought to be offered to citizens maintaining themselves. Consequently the Majority did not abandon the notion of 'less eligibility', although the essence of this principle was now seen to lie in the surrender of one's self-management and the curative treatment necessary to restore it, not in hardship or inadequate treatment. The help given by the Majority's Public Assistance Authority, which was to be 'preventive, curative and restorative' was not a departure from fundamental Poor Law and COS principles, but an adaptation and new application of them. The officers of the new Authorities would be specially qualified and trained, not merely for the specialized administrative duties required in normal health and education services, but morally equipped for all-round therapeutics. Charity would have a special role, as an 'essential organ of civilised group life', for it had been the pioneer and inventive element in casework and social service

[62] In the same issue of the *Sociological Review*, 2 (1909). Bosanquet's article was printed before Webb's in the journal, which raises the question whether it was written as a 'reply'. While it is possible that it could have been written independently of this particular article of Webb's, on the basis of the Minority Report and other statements of Minority propagandists, it seems likely that Bosanquet had seen Webb's article and that it was indeed a reply.

methods. Charity workers would know how to diagnose the problems of a family as a whole, and not simply offer standardized treatment to this or that member of it.

Bernard Bosanquet then went on to dismiss Webb's claim that the Public Assistance structure proposed by the Majority was undemocratic. This, he said, was a 'misrepresentation of fact *plus* an error of social theory'. It was wrong in fact because the county or county borough council appointed all members of the Public Assistance Authorities, except in London where it appointed three-quarters of them, and this was at least as much public control as was exercised over Education Committees. It was wrong in theory because direct dependence of a particular body on a constituency or direct election was no necessary test of its democratic character. 'The distinction between the "general will" and the "will of all" is hard, no doubt, to apply in practice; but it is the one fundamental problem of democracy, which stands or falls by success in solving it.' A strong democracy was perfectly justified in delegating its authority, for the sake of efficiency, to independent organs of its will, such as the judiciary, administrative departments, or co-optive committees. In conclusion, Bosanquet argued that the proposals concerning unemployment in the two Reports were not as different as Webb represented them to be, except in the Minority's handing of such large powers over to a Minister of Labour, allowing him to manipulate the labour market on an enormous scale and inviting the danger that this might 'work as it is not intended to work'.

When, shortly afterwards, the Webbs were writing their Separate Report on the Scottish Poor Law,[63] they used the opportunity to make a pungently satirical rejoinder to some central arguments of Bernard Bosanquet's article in their penultimate section, entitled 'The "Moral Factor" in Destitution'.[64] They claimed that his arguments involved two assumptions, the first concerning a matter of fact, and the second, a consequence of the first, involving a recommendation about social policy. The first was that there was some moral defect—some 'failure of citizen character'—common to the whole class of paupers, which made them responsible for their condition. The second assumption was that this required a policy, not of treatment of different kinds to remedy various sorts of pauperism, but treatment by one Destitution Authority, in order

---

[63] Cd. 4922, *Reports on Scotland*, Sessional Paper, vol. xxxviii (1909).
[64] Ibid., pp. 274–81.

to deter with a 'stigma of pauperism' the moral rot from spreading to other members of society.

The Webbs declared Bosanquet's initial factual assumption to be quite false of the majority of paupers. Two-fifths of all paupers were children—and a large proportion of them were orphans. Nobody could maintain they were paupers through any moral fault of their own. The deaths of their parents were more likely to be due to physical defect or to sheer accident than to moral deficiency. No valid general inference could be made about the mothers simply from the fathers' deaths. The reasons for keeping the children within the Poor Law had nothing to do with what was best for them, and the notion of deterring others from dying as their parents had done was absurd.[65] The Webbs used similar contentions in the case of the sick and disabled. Where the aged were concerned, they scouted the notion that there could be any idea of improving their character, and declared roundly that to advocate returning them to a Destitution Authority, after that policy had been definitely rejected by the passing of the Old Age Pensions Act of 1908, would be hypocritical. As for the feeble-minded, the Webbs allowed that perhaps in some cases their condition might have been brought about by their own moral defects, but they claimed that the Poor Law was 'inherently unsuited' for their control. And they went on to point out inconsistencies in the recommendations of the Majority Commissioners: while they had followed the ideas of the Royal Commission on the Care and Control of the Feeble-minded for a separate Lunacy Authority in England and Wales, and had made no recommendation at all for Scotland, they had proposed in their Irish report that the feeble-minded be put under the Poor Law, although they were at present outside it.

Coming finally to the able-bodied poor—who, the Webbs were careful to note, represented the smallest segment of the pauper class—they argued that there was no reason for assuming that

[65] It is worth noting that the Webbs ignored one argument that had exercised the minds of some Majority Commissioners and which was later put by Charles Booth in this way: '. . . it does seem hard, and must appear monstrous to the thrifty working-man and his self-sacrificing wife, that they should see the children of scamps and wastrels enjoying luxuries and opportunities beyond anything they can procure for their own children, for whose welfare they "scorn delights and live laborious days"'; C. Booth, Address to Poor Law Conference, Feb. 1912, Booth Papers, 11/43. No doubt they would have replied that they wanted a satisfactory basic minimum standard for all children, and there was no reason for assuming that all, or even most, of the pauper children's parents were 'scamps and wastrels'.

unemployment was necessarily evidence of a defect in citizen
character. The 'relative defectiveness of the social environment'
mainly determined the amount of unemployment; but they were
prepared to allow that it might be the relative defectiveness of one
wage-earner as compared to others that determined which individuals were put out of work. They conceded that some of the 'lower
types' of workmen might prefer maintenance without sustained
effort on their part if given a chance, and something would need to
be done about that. But the Webbs declared Bosanquet's principle
applied only to the able-bodied. It followed, indeed, that there was
a need for an Authority dealing with the able-bodied separately.
But this did not mean that deterrent treatment should be meted out
to the unemployed without discovering whether they had a 'moral
defect' or not. A general deterrent policy was

futile and barbarous in its inhumanity and leads to demoralising forms of
parasitism on the labour of women and children, on begging and vagrancy,
and even on a career of crime . . . Only when a man has been definitely
proved to be unwilling to work for the maintenance of himself and his
dependents, or persists in recalcitrancy and refusal to co-operate in his own
cure

should he be committed to a Detention Colony. It was necessary to
give up assuming the existence of a moral fault where there was no
actual proof if the unemployment problem was to be tackled
sensibly.

This section of the Scottish report naturally excited extreme
anger from the Majority Commissioners, and provoked a tart
general rebuke to the Minority in an appendix to that report from
Lord George Hamilton; but he did not really attempt to counter the
Webbs' intrepid shots one by one.

At first, the Webbs regarded the Majority Report as the main
obstacle in their path. They took it for granted that the old order
was dead; indeed, they were a little surprised that 'the principles of
1834 should die so easily',[66] when no defence of the Guardians
surfaced during the initial Press reception of the two Reports. The
Webbs were mistaken; it was merely that the defenders of the status
quo took some time to organize themselves. They instinctively
rallied to the Majority's National Poor Law Reform Association, at
the beginning of the public campaign, against the Minority's

[66] B.W.D., 22 Feb. 1909; *Our Partnership*, p. 426.

National Committee for the Break-up of the Poor Law;[67] but they soon found the Majority proposals too radical for them, and the British Constitutional Association took the initiative in forming a third organization, the National Committee for Poor Law Reform. Its first spokesman was Sir William Chance, a member of the COS 'old guard', who had never wavered in his support of the *ad hoc* Poor Law authorities, and who wrote a pamphlet with the self-explanatory title *Poor Law Reform—Via Tertia—the Case for the Guardians* (1910).

Soon this new organization persuaded a number of leading Poor Law experts to withdraw their names from the Majority's association, and transfer to it. These included the former members of the Commission Charles Booth and Dr Arthur Downes, the officials James Davy and Horace Monro, and the historian of the Poor Law, Thomas Mackay. Urged on by Downes,[68] Charles Booth published an influential pamphlet *Poor Law Reform*, which incorporated many of the proposals he had put forward to the Royal Commission,[69] notably his statistical reasons for opposing the transfer of Guardians' functions to the counties and his suggestions for combining existing Poor Law areas into larger units. Booth joined with his new group of associates to lobby John Burns and the Prime Minister, and Burns was happy with these allies.[70] Their adhesion to the established order coincided with a ground swell of anger by the Guardians at the criticism of them in both the Majority and Minority Reports. Bitter complaints were uttered in the Poor Law journals and at Poor Law conferences. Both the Majority and the Minority Commissioners were accused of having made up their minds, before gathering evidence, to abolish the Boards of Guardians.[71] The editors of the *Poor Law Annual* of 1909 issued a call to battle against the campaigns of both the Minority and the Majority, pointing out that the 'members of

---

[67] *Crusade*, 1 (1910), 16, lists C. Booth and T. Mackay as members of the NPLRA; see also *Our Partnership*, p. 440 for officials.

[68] C. Booth to M. Booth, 15 Feb. 1910, 16 Feb. 1910, 30 May 1910. Booth Papers 1/1871, 1872, 1880.

[69] A. M. McBriar, 'Charles Booth and the Royal Commission on the Poor Laws 1905–9', *Historical Studies* (Melbourne University), 15 (1973).

[70] C. Booth to M. Booth, 2 June 1910, 27 Oct. 1911, 14 Nov. 1911, 16 Feb. 1912. Booth Papers, 1/1833, 1910, 1911, 1912. Burns's Diary, 2 Nov. 1911 and 6 Nov. 1911. Burns Papers, Add. MS 46333, vol. liii.

[71] *Proceedings of Poor Law Conferences 1909–10*, pp. 339 and 360; *Poor Law and Local Government Magazine*, 20 (1910), 40.

the Majority so far disagree among themselves that to speak of them as "the Majority" is a misuse of terms',[72] and that

The Reports have already received considerable examination at the hands of the Poor Law Unions' Association, Central and District Poor Law Conferences, separate Boards of Guardians, individual Guardians, Officers' Associations, and the leading members of the Service. From all these bodies and individuals comes a strong current of opinion that the more the Reports are scrutinised the more they fall to pieces . . .[73]

Opponents of reform were able to make great play with the more rhetorical flights of the spokesmen of the Majority and Minority cause against each other, such as Hancock Nunn's outburst against the Minority recommendations: 'This does spell Socialism . . . And if it spells Socialism, it spells all the bureaucratic paraphernalia of State aid by which, in the long run, the life-blood is sucked out of the nation';[74] or the Webbs' description of the Majority's Public Assistance Bodies:

What is clear is that the unconcealed purpose of constructing this elaborate and mysterious framework,

'With centric and eccentric scribbled o'er,
Cycle and epicycle, orb in orb,'

is to withdraw the whole relief of distress from popular control.[75]

Charles Booth's proposals got a better hearing from the Poor Law Guardians, as a *via media*, but even some of his ideas were regarded as too radical.[76] Eventually the annual meeting of the Association of Poor Law Unions, representing the whole Poor Law service in England and Wales, held in London in November 1910, repudiated his suggestions along with the others, and formulated its own recommendations, practically all of which involved an increase in existing Guardians' powers and a reversion to their control of functions concerning schoolchildren, the mentally defective, and the unemployed, which were being usurped by county councils. Both the Webbs and the Bosanquets could only fume at 'the chorus which has gone up from Poor Law conferences all over the country that all is for the best in the best of all possible

---

[72] *Poor Law Annual* (1910), 305.   [73] Ibid., p. 306.
[74] *Proceedings of Poor Law Conferences 1910–11*, p. 182.
[75] Quoted ibid., p. 375. The quotation is from the Minority Report, p. 394.
[76] *Proceedings of Poor Law Conferences 1910–11*, pp. 203 ff., 373 ff.

Poor Laws',[77] and 'the general complacency of the Guardians and their implacable hostility to all reform—at least to what ordinary persons would call reform. The Guardians' idea of reform of the Poor Law is extended powers for themselves'.[78] If the discovery came in the form of anger rather than as a surprise to both sets of reformers that the Guardians did not favour their abolition, it was a shock when many county councils revealed some hesitation and even some unwillingness to take over the onerous and expensive Poor Law functions. Opinion was so much divided at the annual meeting of the County Councils Association held at the Guildhall, Westminster in May 1909 that a committee was set up to go into the matter. On the committee, several strong upholders of the Minority scheme—J. W. Willis-Bund (Chairman of the Worcester County Council), A. W. Chapman (Chairman of the Surrey County Council and Vice-Chairman of the County Councils' Association), and Tonman Mosley (Chairman of the Buckinghamshire County Council)—were matched against equally strong advocates of the Majority proposals—Henry Hobhouse (Chairman of the Somerset County Council), and the Duke of Northumberland (Lord Lieutenant and Chairman of the Northumberland County Council).[79] Lord Belper (Chairman of the Nottingham County Council and Chairman of the County Councils' Association) was not a member of the committee, but he was also a supporter of the Majority Commissioners with some hesitations about the nominated membership of its Public Assistance Committees. The election of her friend, Aitken W. Chapman, as Chairman of this committee filled Beatrice Webb with hope that he would be able to carry the day. But the discussions of the committee dragged on and on. Its report was not presented to Lord Belper until the middle of the following year and did not come before the executive council of the CCA until January 1911.

In the mean time the Prevention of Destitution Bill, prepared by the National Committee to Promote the Break-up of the Poor Law, came before the House of Commons. The debate was a good one and well attended, but there was no division at its end. The Labour

[77] COR, NS 26 July–Dec. (1909), 303, editorial note to Nov. 1909 number (H. Bosanquet was then editor).

[78] *Crusade*, 2 Jan–Dec. (1911), 166 (Oct. 1911 issue).

[79] See Official Circular (No. 6 of June 1909), of CCA, pp. 82–6, for opinions of some members of the committee and p. 89 for its membership.

Party gave full support, and the Bill also had reasonable support
from the Liberal back-benchers, and a sprinkling of Conservatives.
John Burns was hostile, and raked up some scraps of his former
Marxism to assure the House that the causes of destitution were
'deep down in our social, industrial, and economic conditions' and
therefore beyond the reach of any Bill, but that the better
administration of the Poor Law could be satisfactorily attended to
by a few regulations of his own.[80] The party leaders temporized.
Arthur Balfour deprecated the tendency to exaggerate the differences
between the Majority and Minority Reports, by using labels such as
'Socialist' or 'bureaucratic', and called for a fair consideration of
each on its merits.[81] Asquith was also non-committal, but his
speech showed ominous signs that he had been impressed by the
outcry of the Guardians:

[The Reports] have both pronounced sentence of death on the Boards of
Guardians. Let us assume they are right, I think you will find the Boards of
Guardians will die very hard. They are powerful bodies. With all their
defects and shortcomings they after all represent an enormous amount of
gratuitous and public spirited service . . . we could ill spare from the sphere
of local administration. I confess I am old-fashioned in that matter.[82]

Beatrice Webb decided that next time it would be better to have 'a
litter of Bills embodying the different parts [of the Minority Report]
separately'.[83]

Behind Asquith's and the Liberal Cabinet's reluctance to imple-
ment either of the Royal Commission's Reports lay problems of
budgeting.[84] The tangled ramifications of local taxation and its
relations with national finance confronted social reformers of the
Edwardian period as an almost impenetrable maze. The Treasury
Departmental Committee, which was eventually given the task of
trying to solve some of the main puzzles, did not report until 1914.
In the circumstances it was not easy to add to the financial burdens
of the county councils. Progressive direct income taxation, first
cautiously introduced in Mr Asquith's Budget of 1907, seemed to
promise a new path of advance to social reformers, but the
traditional Gladstonian policy of financial retrenchment stood in

[80] Hansard, 5th Series, vol. xvi, cols. 842–51.
[81] Ibid., cols. 828–36.　　　　　　　　　　[82] Ibid., col. 838.
[83] B.W.D., 12 Apr. 1910; *Our Partnership*, p. 450.
[84] See Harris, *Unemployment and Politics*, pp. 267–73 for an excellent
discussion of this issue, to which I am greatly indebted.

the way of its speedy extension. This was shown by the great public outcry over the relatively small tax extensions of Lloyd George's Budget of 1909—a furore sufficient in itself to distract public attention quite away from the campaigns for the reform of the Poor Law. In any case, the new revenues raised by direct taxation were already earmarked by the Treasury for expenditure on Dreadnoughts to meet the naval challenge from Germany, on improvements to roads to make provision for the new motor-car age, and on old-age pensions. Fear of the unpopularity of raising more revenue from this source to finance greater extensions of social reform persuaded administrators and ministers to turn to the methods (and to extol the virtues) of contributory funding. This was to be the basis of the joint Insurance Act covering both health and unemployment insurance, which Lloyd George at the Treasury and Winston Churchill at the Board of Trade had been preparing since 1908. The Cabinet resolved in April 1909 that its measures against unemployment were to be concentrated on labour exchanges, compulsory national insurance, a measure to allow Education authorities to give boys and girls vocational guidance, and a Bill to set up a Development Commission to advise the Treasury when to give financial aid to 'expansive state industries' such as forestry, road-making, land reclamation, agriculture, fishery, 'rural industries', and the construction of harbours and canals. These measures were foreshadowed in Lloyd George's Budget speech of 1909. This programme enabled the government to claim that it was paying at least some attention to measures which the Royal Commission on the Poor Laws had in mind, whilst not ruling out possible further offerings in the future.

Neither the campaigners for the Minority Report nor those for the Majority Report were satisfied. Beatrice Webb in particular urged on her followers and the Fabian Society to fight the Insurance Act as inadequate, and its contributory principle as unjust because it attempted to 'mitigate the evils of poverty at the expense of the poor'.[85] But by the middle of 1910 it was becoming clear to both sets of Poor Law reformers that the 'steam was going out of' their campaigns. There were a number of reasons for this. At the fundamental level, the revival of a period of good trade from 1909 meant that the deficiencies of the Poor Law and the problem of

---

[85] A. M. McBriar, *Fabian Socialism and English Politics 1884–1918*, (Cambridge, 1962), p. 276.

unemployment were not so prominently in the public eye as they had been in the years 1905–8. The energetic but somewhat old-fashioned appeal by the Webbs and the Majority Commissioners at the hustings to enlightened public opinion at no stage gained the radical momentum either of the 'Right to Work' agitation of the earlier years or the compelling attraction of the new political issues—the 1909 Budget, the House of Lords, votes for women, syndicalism, Home Rule for Ireland—that were beginning to boil up in 1910. Lloyd George and Winston Churchill, whether by flamboyant demagogy or by skilful political manipulation, easily outmatched the Poor Law reformers on their own chosen ground. Without denying that Lloyd George and Winston Churchill may, vaguely, have had more long-range plans of social reform in view than those which they sponsored, their interest in Poor Law reform and unemployment policy was at that time short-range—essentially that of sharp-eyed and adroit politicians. Their outlook was in one way wider, and in another way narrower, than a concentration on Poor Law and unemployment policy as such. They were anxious to sponsor reforms that would be popular, or at least not too controversial, and which would build up the Liberal Party's image as the 'party of the people'. Labour exchanges, trade boards, social insurance, and the Development Act filled their bill exactly. They realized, however, there was little electoral advantage to be got from a direct challenge to the embattled Guardians, or from a deeper involvement with remedial measures against poverty and unemployment. The social insurance proposals not only diverted public attention, but also divided the Poor Law reformers themselves. Should insurance be opposed as a rival venture, or should it be accepted as an instalment of larger reform? The Majority Commissioners were more willing to take the latter view; but the Webbs' followers divided sharply. The trade unions were won over by the concessions made to them in the financing and administering of the Insurance Act. The majority of the Labour Party and even a substantial number of the ILP men, including Ramsay MacDonald, were prepared to compromise with the government. Two members of the Fabian Society's Executive Committee—Edward R. Pease and Sir Leo Chiozza Money—took the view that Fabian principles demanded the 'accepting and making the best of [a] Bill introduced by a strong government'.[86] Sidney Webb himself was inclined to

[86] E. R. Pease, *The History of the Fabian Society* (London, 1925), p. 224.

that opinion.[87] Beatrice publicly remained intransigent, but an entry in her Diary of 27 May 1910 revealed that she was beginning to have doubts about the usefulness of the campaign.[88]

Less than two months later, Beatrice was obliged to acknowledge ruefully that the Minority campaign was in retreat. Her champion on the County Councils Association Poor Law Commitee, Arthur Chapman, had been overborne by her hostile brother-in-law, Henry Hobhouse.[89] She had no recourse but to advise Chapman to make a fighting strategic withdrawal, salvaging as much of the Minority proposals as was possible in a compromise with Majority features. This task Chapman carried out with great skill. The report of the Committee he presented to Lord Belper, which was endorsed by the County Councils Association in January 1911, proposed that Poor Law areas should be assimilated with counties and county boroughs at the higher level and with urban and rural districts at the local level. Poor Law functions were to be exercised by County Poor Law Committees, consisting of a majority of county councillors or district councillors and other persons nominated by the county council, and locally by District Poor Law Boards, consisting three-quarters of county councillors or district councillors and a quarter of county council nominees.[90] So far the scheme resembled the Majority plan but with a greater weighting given to the councils' representation. Financial powers were also to be firmly in the control of the county councils. Poor Law schools were to be placed under the Education Committee of the county council; the feeble-minded were to be transferred to the central government and the unemployed were also to be handed over to a new government department. Those features were a gesture to the Minority.

Forewarned by Arthur Chapman of the County Councils Association's impending decision, Beatrice Webb suggested to the journalist J. R. Brooke of the *Morning Post*, who was one of the Conservative supporters of the Minority Report, that he might make a scoop by attending the CCA's meeting and immediately after it seeking the approval of Lord George Hamilton and his

[87] McBriar, *Fabian Socialism and English Politics 1884–1918*, p. 276 n. 1.
[88] B.W.D., 27 May 1910; *Our Partnership*, pp. 453–4.
[89] B.W.D., 12 July 1910; *Our Partnership*, p. 454; see Official Circular of CCA, 3. 8 (Aug. 1910), p. 117, for role of Chapman and Hobhouse.
[90] Official Circular of CCA, Feb. 1911.

colleagues of its report; she promised she would then give her
approval too, so that the *Morning Post* could cry 'Agreed: at last!'[91]
There could be little doubt about the success of this manœuvre, for
most of the Majority Commissioners were as disillusioned with the
prospects of their cause as the Webbs had become, and were as
ready to grasp at the compromise. Only C. S. Loch and Sir Arthur
Downes proved implacably hostile; the three former heads of
departments (Provis, Patten-MacDougall, and Robinson) and
Octavia Hill remained silent; but all remaining eleven signatories of
the Royal Commission's Reports of both persuasions gave their
general blessing to the CCA's scheme (with greater or less
individual measures of critical reservation). When Beatrice Webb
declared: 'I regard it as a very reasonable compromise between the
ideas of the Majority and Minority Reports . . .', and Helen
Bosanquet believed 'that an excellent system of administration
might be formed on the basis of the scheme in question',[92] the
conflict ought to have ended, except for recriminations about who
had started it in the first place. But, as the Editor of the *Local
Government Review* of March 1911 predicted, the debate was far
from ended, although he entertained long range hopes:

. . . we do not anticipate that the new scheme of poor law reform will
stimulate Government action, or, for some time to come, get beyond the
stage of discussion and criticism. But we are tolerably certain that when
poor law and local government reform is taken seriously in hand by the
Legislature, the settlement of the poor law side of the problem will be
mainly on the lines laid down by the County Councils Association.[93]

The Webbs had already laid plans for their own strategic retreat
before the CCA's resolutions were announced in the press, and at
the annual conference of the National Committee to promote the
Break-up of the Poor Law, held at Whitsun 1911, its name was
changed to the National Committee for the Prevention of Destitution.
The intention in altering the name was to change it from an
organization devoting itself to propaganda for the Minority Report
to an organization which could enlist wider support. As early as
August 1910 the Webbs accepted the fact that 'More effective
results might be obtained, in the long run, by promoting, through

[91] B.W.D., 31 Jan. 1911 (not included in *Our Partnership*),
[92] Official Circular of CCA, 4. 2 (Feb. 1911), pp. 13–14; B.W.D., 31 Jan. 1911.
[93] Ibid. (Apr. 1911), p. 47 (quoting *LGR* (Mar. 1911)).

an unsectarian organisation, the growth of development of the various parts of the Framework of Prevention . . .'[94] They hoped to win wider support at the annual conference in 1911 by concentrating on constructive proposals and arranging to have the conference running 'in sections—all sitting concurrently—*unemployment, public health, care of children*, etc.'[95] They were also planning their personal withdrawal from the scene, for they were intending to take a much-needed long (eleven months') holiday on a world tour from mid-1911. Meanwhile in January 1911:

We are organising the Whitsun National Conference with great care, whilst keeping our names well out of it . . . I should like, having started this Conference, to gradually transfer the whole staff and organisation of the National Committee [to Promote the Break-up of the Poor Law] to this Conference organisation. In this way we shall get a much wider circle of adherents to the policy of prevention than is possible by the Minority Report campaign. We want, in fact, to slip out of the movement, or at any rate from the leadership of it.[96]

The Webbs were successful in giving a broadly representative appearance to their Conference, which was held at Caxton Hall, London, over four days from 30 May to 2 June 1911. Its President was Sir Vesey Strong, Lord Mayor of London; Lord George Hamilton had accepted Vice-Presidency; the Chairman was the Bishop of Southwark, Dr Talbot; the main speakers were Arthur Balfour, Sir John Simon (then Liberal Solicitor-General), and Ramsay MacDonald, who between them proposed and seconded a resolution for

the formation of a National Conference of a non-party and non-sectional character, to promote the working of the various agencies for the prevention of destitution . . . as a valuable means of bringing together municipal representatives and social workers from all parts of the country.

The Chairmen of the five sections of the Conference were the eminent doctor, Sir Thomas Clifford Allbutt (Public Health), the great educationist, Professor Michael Ernest Sadler (Education), the well-known industrialist and MP, Sir Albert Mond (Unemployment), the right-wing COS theorist, Sir William Chance (Mental Deficiency),

[94] S. and B. Webb, *English Local Government*, vol. ix. *English Poor Law History*, Part II. *The Last Hundred Years* (London, 1929), p. 721.
[95] B.W.D., 19 Aug. 1910; *Our Partnership*, p. 456.
[96] B.W.D., 16 Jan. 1911; *Our Partnership*, p. 469.

and the legal luminary, Mr Justice Phillimore (Legal and Financial). The main organizers (apart from the Webbs behind the scenes) were the Conservative MP, J. W. Hills, the Liberal-Radical MP, Robert Harcourt, and the young Fabian journalist, editor of the *Crusade*, Clifford Sharp. Beatrice Webb considered the Conference to be 'a great success'.[97] It was attended by over eleven hundred delegates.[98] But opponents had divided views about its representativeness. Sir William Chance averred that it was representative of all opinions—in spite of appearances to the contrary;[99] Helen Bosanquet (who had become editor of the *Charity Organisation Review* in October 1909) had earlier denounced it in her 'Editorial Notes' column as merely a disguise for putting Minority ideas across.[1]

She was probably not far from the truth, for Beatrice Webb was at the time noting in her Diary: 'Having patented the name ["Prevention of Destitution"], and then getting it adopted as the name of a larger article of commerce than we can provide, we proceed to suggest that our patent is that larger article of commerce!'[2] Before leaving for their holiday, the Webbs were busily engaged in completing for publication the last of three works which they intended to leave as a legacy to their supporters. *English Poor Law Policy* (1910) and *The State and the Doctor* (1910) had been rewritings of two reports, concerning the history of Poor Law policy and the history of the development of the medical services of the Poor Law and the Ministry of Health which they had prepared for the Commission. *The Prevention of Destitution* (1911) was a systematic presentation of popular lectures they had delivered in this campaign on diverse subjects ranging over the whole field of Minority Report topics. Although Beatrice Webb found the task of writing it 'a tediously stale one',[3] there is no trace of her fatigue in the finished book, which is one of the liveliest and most persuasive of all their works. In addition to defending old positions, they engaged enemies both old and new, offering olive branches at the point of well-directed spears. The chapters on 'Destitution and Eugenics', 'Insurance', the 'Sphere of Voluntary Agencies', and the 'Moral Factor' discharged a shower of Parthian shafts into the heart of their opponents' camps, while at the same time promising

---

[97] B.W.D., 3 June 1911; *Our Partnership*, p. 476.
[98] COR, NS 31 (1912), 14–15.   [99] Ibid.
[1] COR, NS 29 (1911), 170.
[2] B.W.D., 21 Apr. 1911; *Our Partnership*, p. 473.   [3] Ibid.

accommodation on terms. Helen and Bernard Bosanquet were not inclined to let them get away with it. The criticisms which Helen Bosanquet had made of Beatrice Webb's account of the history of the Poor Laws during the sittings of the Royal Commission was refurbished as a review article of their *English Poor Law Policy* in the *Economic Journal* in 1910,[4] and Bernard Bosanquet contributed a criticism of it along the same lines to the *Local Government Review* of May 1910.[5] Helen Bosanquet, as editor of the *Charity Organisation Review*, also brought in T. Mackay, as still the major historian of the Poor Law at that date, to criticize *English Poor Law Policy* in a review.[6] But Mackay did not seriously challenge the Webbs (as they probably hoped he would) at the factual level. After some mocking remarks about the Webbs' claim to superior methodology in their introduction, he observed that 'the older writers . . . came nevertheless to much the same conclusions as to the facts as do Mr. and Mrs. Webb. The facts, indeed, do not seem to be in dispute.' He mainly disputed the Webbs' so arranging the facts 'as to show that the policy advocated in the Minority Report is an inevitable policy into which we are borne by a resistless stream of tendency whether we wish it or not. It reminds us, mutatis mutandis, of the prophecies of Marx.' Mackay did not deny there had been a tendency to a laxer policy in recent years, but he believed that the whole history of the Poor Law had shown oscillations towards laxer, than towards firmer policies: '. . . we are perfectly certain that the full acceptance of their plan is still very far distant, and that, as in 1834, when we apprehend the danger into which we are drifting, we shall be obliged to take measures to save the solvency of civilisation.'

A year later, Bernard Bosanquet took up again at a general philosophical level the attack on the historical methodology which he believed the Webbs espoused, in an address to the London School of Sociology and Social Economics (then still an adjunct of the COS).[7] He related his lecture to a protest that was then being made in the Sorbonne against Durkheim's influence in sociology and against the textbook of Langlois and Seignobos on historical methodology. The protest was against Positivist methods that sought to pulverize source-material into a powder of hard, atomic 'facts' which could then be recorded on slips of paper, cards, or

[4] *Ec.J.* 20 (1910), 182 ff.   [5] *LGR* 2 (1910), 5–10.
[6] *COR*, NS 27 (1910), 209–13.   [7] *COR*, NS 30 (1911), 287–302.

'fiches', to be rearranged by the historian according to presupposition of some 'scientific' method. The dangers of such a procedure were that it risked loss of the context of these 'facts'; it made easy careless or wilful omissions ('I have known the suggestions made in an English controversy', he remarked at this point, 'that some of the slips must have fallen under the table'); it could slur over, ignore, or deny such things as the genius of a nation or mind or soul of a people; and it reduced the method of history to the method of physical science. The world of known life was more difficult of access than the world of nature. History and sociology were not sciences; they belonged to the world of mind and were arts to be learnt by 'a long discipline under exponents of the great masters'. So much was orthodox Idealist criticism of Positivist social science; but elsewhere in his lecture Bosanquet made it clear that he followed his great master Hegel[8] in holding narrative (secondary) history in contempt as essentially ephemeral because soon superseded by later scholarship, the connections and interpretations made in it never being free from doubt. Those who did not share Bosanquet's view that the proper object of knowledge was a 'timeless world of pure universality' could perhaps be forgiven for not following some of his more esoteric points.[9]

By comparison, the reception given the Webbs' *The Prevention of Destitution* in the *Charity Organisation Review* was quite mild.[10] Although the usual arguments against the Minority proposals were made, and the government's Insurance Bill was defended against the Webbs,[11] some of the olive branches held out were acknowledged:

In the chapter on 'Voluntary Agencies' we note a slight divergence from the Minority Report. In that Report, voluntary charity was relegated to institutional work, and to certain departments of visiting exclusive of relief work; now it is suggested that volunteers should have a wide field of work under official guidance, and should even distribute State money.

---

[8] G. W. F. Hegel, *The Philosophy of History* trans. J. Sibree (New York, 1956), pp. 4–8.

[9] See R. G. Collingwood, *The Idea of History* (New York, 1956), p. 143 for a short but perceptive comment on Bosanquet's approach to history. See also B. Bosanquet to Miss Oakeley in Muirhead, *Bernard Bosanquet and his Friends*, pp. 147–8.

[10] *COR*, NS 30 (1911), 265–71.

[11] Not all members of the COS supported the government's Insurance Bill, however.

It was pleasant to see the Webbs now laying stress on moral factors, family life, etc., and, the review claimed, COS doctrine too was constantly developing:

Why [the Webbs] attack Professor Bernard Bosanquet, for associating destitution with defective 'citizen-character', is not clear; the individual is not necessarily blamed for the failure, any more than the doctor necessarily blames the sick man for his illness.

The blander tone was no doubt the result of the Majority supporters' belief that the Minority Report had become merely of 'speculative interest', no longer relevant to the political scene.[12] They had still not accepted the notion that their own Report had become equally 'irrelevant'.

At the time of their departure on their holiday, Beatrice Webb recorded her doubts about the future:

When we come back next spring we shall have to decide what is to be done—whether we are to close up or go on, or to divide the work between the National Conference and the Fabian Society. We shall know, too, how the insurance is going to affect us. If it is carried, it alters the whole situation and we shall have to begin a new kind of propaganda. And, even if it does not pass, the issues have been so much bigger that the Minority Report propaganda sinks into insignificance for the present. I think it will rise up as the only alternative to a hopeless muddle.[13]

When the Webbs returned to England in April 1912 they took part in the second annual conference of the National Committee for the Prevention of Destitution, but they realized that the campaign was dying, and decided to reduce the office staff and no longer make appeals for subscriptions. The monthly journal of the NCPD, the *Crusade*, appeared for the last time in March 1913. The attempts to promote items of the Minority Report by private bills in the House of Commons had not been successful: none of them had got so far as a second reading. About the same time, the Majority's National Poor Law Reform Association was disbanded. The appeal to the public by both sides had failed.

---

[12] COR, NS 29 (1911), 136.
[13] B.W.D., 3 June 1911; *Our Partnership*, pp. 476–7.

12

Aftermath

LATER ACTIVITIES OF THE BOSANQUETS AND THE WEBBS; NEVILLE CHAMBERLAIN'S LOCAL GOVERNMENT ACT 1929

AFTER their common defeat, the Bosanquets and the Webbs retreated to their bases. Both Helen and Bernard Bosanquet had extended periods of bad health after 1910,[1] and they retired to a quieter scholarly life in their cottage at Oxshott. Their main outside activity, beyond their literary work, was directed towards the Charity Organisation Society, where Helen Bosanquet had succeeded C. S. Loch as editor of its main journal in 1909,[2] and Bernard Bosanquet was Vice-Chairman of the COS Council up to 1916, when he took over as Chairman. It was a time when the affairs of the COS needed their diplomacy as well as their attention. A new generation of social workers was beginning to question some of the COS doctrines, especially after the COS was obliged by financial difficulties in July 1912 to allow its own training school of Sociology to be taken over by the London School of Economics. Even before then, however, the members of the Society were divided in their allegiance between the Majority and Minority Reports and the status quo. After a sharp exchange on the question whether the Majority Report should be regarded as a COS document in March 1909,[3] a compromise resolution was finally accepted in December 1909:

That while not unanimously agreeing with all the recommendations of the Majority Report of the Royal Commission on the Poor Laws and Relief of Distress, the Council [of COS] is of opinion that the necessary reform of

---

[1] Helen Bosanquet had not been cured at Bad-Nauheim; Bernard Bosanquet was in hospital in 1910 and again in 1912.

[2] She remained editor until 1921. The *Charity Organisation Review* was discontinued in 1922.

[3] *Reporter*, p. 10, attached to the COR, NS 25 (1909).

the Poor Laws lies rather along the lines laid down in that Report than in
those laid down in the Report of the Minority . . .[4]

As editor of the *Review*, Helen Bosanquet allowed ample space
to the debates and debaters. While the space was mainly taken up
by supporters of the Majority Report or of the status quo, more
radical ideas found vigorous expression, from time to time, by such
spokesmen as the redoubtable Colonel E. H. Bethell,[5] Mr H.
Holman (Chairman of the Bury COS),[6] and representatives of COS
from working-class suburbs of London.[7] Debates about particular
matters, such as the role of the Majority Report's Voluntary Aid
Committee, and whether they should accept subsidies from the
State, or the perennial dispute about the merits of Hancock Nunn's
Social Welfare Councils,[8] occasionally disturbed the harmony of
the COS's 'general will'. Attacks by outsiders also needed to be
fended off—notably a renewed blast by J. A. Hobson entitled 'The
Passing of Private Charity' in a journal called the *International*,[9]
and a Fabian Tract written by Mrs Emily Townshend, *The Case
against the Charity Organisation Society*.[10] Hobson claimed that
the Majority Report proposals were

an audacious attempt . . . to establish and endow with public authority and
public funds a self-elected body of charitable amateurs . . . , [and that] . . .
to empower a number of well-meaning men and women of leisure to go
down from their comfortable homes to the hovels of the poor, for the
purpose of improving the character of the latter, is a proposal as futile in its
necessary effects as it is impertinent in the methods it employs.[11]

The Fabian Society's Tract claimed that the COS's rejection of the
Minority Report derived from certain fundamental errors of
principle, for which C. S. Loch and the Bosanquets (and not the
founders of the COS, Dr Hawksley and the Revd Henry Solly) were
responsible. These errors were the limitations they imposed on
State action, their moral condemnation of the poor, and their

[4] *Reporter*, p. 4, COR, NS 26 (1909).
[5] COR, NS 29 (1911), 249–67; ibid. 32 (1912), 370–3; ibid. 35 (1914), 216–20.
[6] Ibid. 32 (1912), 21–44.
[7] *Reporter* attached to COR, NS 26 (1909).
[8] COR, NS 28 (1910), 70–1; ibid. 30 (1911), Editorial Notes, p. 115.
[9] *International*, 6 (1909). In Jan. 1910 this journal was united with *Progress*, the journal of the British Institute of Social Service.
[10] Fabian Tract 158 (1911).
[11] 'The Passing of Private Charity', *International*, 6 (1909) 3, 6–7.

emphasis on personal character as 'the condition of conditions', all of which boiled down in the last resort to

... a satisfaction with social conditions as they exist at the present time in England and a dislike to any proposed modification of them ... There is ... insidious attraction for the well-to-do in this notion that destitution is but the natural working out of human character. If the present condition of affairs suits us, much satisfaction is to be derived from the assurance that any alteration of outward conditions, any change in human laws and institutions, would be worse than useless. The theory thrives and spreads among our upper and middle classes because it strikes root into the indolence and self-satisfaction of an easy and sheltered life.[12]

Helen Bosanquet replied to J. A. Hobson, in a tone as barbed as his own, claiming the argument against character as a cause of unemployment was virtually to say, in effect: 'honesty, sobriety and skill are no use to their possessor'. She maintained character would not be a causal factor only in very exceptional cases of economic slump—such as 'depression caused by a foreign war'—and 'to teach that ... character has no effect on unemployment is about as sensible as to teach children that fire is a harmless plaything because the house might be struck by lightning'.[13] Answering the Fabian Tract, Helen Bosanquet reasserted several points: the COS had not committed itself completely to the Majority Report, but only given preference to it; the COS did not judge cases on grounds of moral desert but on considerations of whether they were helpable; and the

cardinal misapprehension, to call it by no harsher name, which pervades the whole Tract, is the assumption that because the Charity Organisation Society lays great stress upon the improvement of character as an ultimate object of charitable relief, it therefore attaches no importance to the environment as influencing character. The contrary is the case. It is because the Society realises the influence of environment on character that it insists on care and thought in the methods of administering relief.[14]

When they returned from abroad in April 1912, the Webbs likewise retreated to their base in the Fabian Society. While they were away they had time to reflect on their defeat, and they were kept informed of political developments by Clifford Sharp. They

[12] Fabian Tract 158 (1911), pp. 18–19.
[13] COR, NS 26 (1909), 248 (Editorial Notes).
[14] COR, NS 30 (1911), Correspondence Column Dec. 1911, pp. 383–8, and ibid., 31 (1912), Correspondence Column Jan. 1912, pp. 49–51.

acknowledged that their tactics of 'permeation' had failed, at least for the time being: the Liberal leaders had proved incorrigible. Sharp had written to the Webbs describing enthusiastically how he had helped to organize their handful of Conservative sympathizers into a Unionist Social Reform Committee, with a programme based on the compromise arrived at by the County Councils Association, and had won the patronage of F. E. Smith (later Lord Birkenhead) for the Committee. But this was small comfort to such experienced wire-pullers as the Webbs—especially when Sharp was obliged to inform them in a later letter that the Conservative Party had declined to promote a bill on the basis of its Reform Committee's programme, and was merely issuing its suggestions as a pamphlet.[15] Sharp also kept the Webbs informed about the development of the unrest in the labour movement, which was blowing up just when they left. He believed that the new atmosphere of militancy in the industrial and political world had thrown Socialist thought into a 'condition of flux' and that 'everybody is as it were waiting for a lead'.[16]

The Webbs were prepared to reassess their situation in these terms immediately on their return. Beatrice wrote:

... the new demand for industrial self-government brings into prominence a quite different group of considerations which are concerned with the structure of the industrial organisation rather than with the group of questions involved in the effort to break up the Poor Law.[17]

Sidney Webb took farewell of their former commitments in an article which formed a special supplement to the last issue of the *Crusade* (January 1913), 'The National Insurance Act at Work: What it is Effecting and Where it needs Amending'. This long, very detailed and persuasive piece was not an all-round attack on the Liberal measure, but an exposition of its provisions and achievements, with well-measured praise for its limited success, incisive analysis of its shortcomings, and helpful suggestions for its improvement. The article was held up as an example of the kind of

---

[15] Sharp to S. Webb, 28 Oct. 1911; Sharp to B. Webb, 31 Mar. 1912. Passfield Papers. The pamphlet was published as J. W. Hills MP and M. Woods (eds.), *Poor Law Reform, a Practical programme: The Scheme of the Unionist Social Reform Committee*, with an introduction by the Rt. Hon. F. E. Smith, KC, MP (London, 1912).
[16] J. M. Winter, *Socialism and the Challenge of War* (London, 1974), p. 30.
[17] Ibid., p. 32.

special supplement which would be issued by a forthcoming journal, the *New Statesman*, sponsored by the Webbs and edited by Sharp, destined to arise that year as a phoenix out of the ashes of the *Crusade*. The Webbs intended this supplement to be the parting shot of their Poor Law campaign, and were surprised and amused when it led to a resumption of relations with Lloyd George, who invited them to 11 Downing Street for their advice on the details.[18] By then, however, the Webbs had set out on the new path leading away from co-operation with the Liberals to a close alliance with Labour.

The first published signs of their new course had appeared as an article in the *Crusade* of August 1912, assessing the validity of Syndicalist theory, which was giving some ideological shape to unrest in the rank and file of the Labour movement. Their closest associate on the Poor Law Commission, George Lansbury, who was to become editor of the *Daily Herald* in 1913, was in the process of being converted to the Syndicalist cause, and Helen Bosanquet commented derisively on his 'new-found' anti-State and anti-bureaucracy views.[19] She could bring no such complaint against the Webbs, who thought that Lansbury had gone 'wild'.[20] Although they conceded that Syndicalists were 'trying to express what is a real and deep-seated feeling [of discontent] in millions of manual wage-earners, which cannot and ought not to be ignored',[21] the Webbs rejected the Syndicalist programme of relentless class war, a general strike, and the replacement of the State by highly organized industrial trade unions, as both impracticable and morally repugnant:

... The very foundation of the Syndicalist community is wrongly chosen ... we must reconstruct society on a basis not of interests, but of community of service, and of that 'neighbourly' feeling of which local life is made up, and of that willingness to subordinate oneself to the welfare of the whole without which national existence is impossible.[22]

This reaffirmation of their belief in municipal politics and State Collectivism did not mean that the Webbs were quite impervious to the new stirrings. They did feel these indicated the working class

[18] B.W.D., 22 Apr. 1912. M. Cole (ed.), *Beatrice Webb's Diaries 1912–1924*, (London, 1952), p. 22.
[19] COR, NS 35 (1914), 281–2.
[20] B.W.D., 11 Oct. 1912. Cole, *Beatrice Webb's Diaries*, p. 6.
[21] *Crusade*, 3 (1912), 151.   [22] Ibid., p. 150.

was needing a more radical statement of doctrine than Fabianism
had so far provided and a more radical policy than the Labour
Party was offering under the compromising and negotiating
leadership of Ramsay MacDonald. Bernard Shaw had been telling
them this ever since 1909,[23] but they had been too preoccupied
with their Poor Law agitation to take much notice, and they did not
believe there was evidence of a strong demand earlier. But they had
come now to recognize that both they and the Labour Party had
been defeated by Liberalism galvanized by Lloyd George and
Winston Churchill, and they were prepared to enter into closer
relations with the Labour Party. They were also willing to engage in
dialogue at least with the group of young intellectuals calling
themselves Guild Socialists, who were trying to find some Socialist
programme midway between the old Fabian Collectivism and the
new Syndicalism. Beatrice Webb took the step of becoming a
member of the City of London branch of the ILP on 28 November
1912.[24] She also took the lead in founding the Fabian Research
Department at the end of 1912 and beginning of 1913. Its purpose
was to defuse the quarrelsome young militant Fabians by concentrating their attention on the practical problems of 'Control of
Industry', and to furnish material for the promised Special
Supplements of the *New Statesman*. The Webbs were especially
concerned to obstruct attempts by the young firebrands to detach
the Fabian Society and the ILP from the Labour Party, and they
found this required their personal commitment to the Labour Party
to an extent which they had never conceded before. In spite of their
hankerings for retirement to a life of scholarship, the turbulence of
the labour unrest in the pre-war years, their disillusionment with
the older and their distrust of the younger Labour leaders, and their
feeling that they had a role to fulfil, kept the Webbs in political
harness.

Bernard Bosanquet, too, responded to the challenge of Syndicalism
and Guild Socialism, though rather later. His interest in their
theories was aroused by G. D. H. Cole, who read a paper to the
Aristotelian Society in February 1915 on 'Conflicting Social
Obligations', defending the Guild Socialist view that the State
should be demoted from the status of father to that of elder brother

[23] Shaw to B. Webb, 26 June 1909. Passfield Papers.
[24] Winter, *Socialism and the Challenge of War*, p. 56.

of other associations in society.[25] In 1916 Bosanquet wrote a
review of the English translation (by T. E. Hulme) of Georges
Sorel's *Reflections on Violence*.[26] It was a remarkably fair-minded
exposition of the views of the Syndicalist theorist, though Bosanquet
admitted that in many ways he was 'at the opposite pole to M.
Sorel', but it concluded with a paragraph which at first sight seemed
to be unexpectedly approving of Sorel's vitalist mythology:

> Give us, we are inclined to cry, in every class or functioning organ of the
> community, such a faith and inspiration as he claims for the workers and
> their gospel, and we could have confidence in the future, not because we
> could predict the detail of what must come, but because whatever comes,
> under the influence of such inspiration, and to a people so prepared to
> suffer and be strong, could not be other than good.

What he meant by this Delphic utterance, Bosanquet was expounding
at the same time in three lectures which he gave to the Charity
Organisation Society in 1916.[27] In Syndicalist and Guild Socialist
theory Bosanquet had discovered a splendid store of new ammunition
for attacking Socialist Collectivism—or 'popular Collectivism' as
he called it in the lectures.

He defined popular Collectivism as the idea that the State should
take over the means of production. What had made this idea
conceivable, he claimed, was the growth of large-scale industry and
the divorce between ownership of capital and its management.
Bosanquet was prepared to concede that the nationalization or
municipalization of such large enterprises (as opposed to small
businesses) was not impracticable, and he was prepared to imagine,
for argument's sake, that the system could be run as nearly in the
public interst as an honest and capable bureaucracy could plan it.
But his central contention was that even this ideal Collectivism
would merely make things worse. The 'creative spirit' in commerce
and industry was best exemplified when ownership and management were united. The divorce between ownership and management
was an evil which Collectivism would intensify. By generalizing
ownership into the hands of the public as represented by the State,

[25] *Proceedings of the Aristotelian Society*, NS 15 (1914–15), 140–63.

[26] COR, NS 40 (1916), 67–72. The review was reprinted in Bosanquet's
collection of essays, *Social and International Ideals: Being Studies in Patriotism*
(London, 1917).

[27] COR, NS 40 (1916), 9–26, 54–67, 102–18. Reprinted in *Social and
International Ideals: Being Studies in Patriotism*.

the influences of ownership in production would virtually be abolished. Political management would be placed in the seat of economic as well as political power, which would strengthen its hand *vis-à-vis* the working class and trade unions. If the new political managers used the existing system of supply and demand and pricing to make the Collectivist system work, there would be little change in the situation of labour or in the direction of capital; and it would not appear to be advantageous to abandon an automatic capitalist system for an authoritative Collectivist one to achieve so little result. If the new political managers sought to abandon the existing pricing and supply and demand system, they would be obliged to resort to autocratic direction of labour and capital. Syndicalism had made a valuable contribution to the criticism of 'popular Collectivism' in stressing the importance of the class-consciousness of the workers, and their claim to have a say in the management of production. But its weakness lay in concentrating on this single class. Every class in society should have a mind, an *ethos*, a myth, a culture, a gospel of its own, a recognition of its creative function in society. This in itself would be beneficial and not produce the bitterness of class conflict, which arose only when a sense of the *whole* social mind was missing; when a class, seeing life only from its own angle, claimed to represent the community as a whole in a superior degree to other classes.

Bosanquet acknowledged that Guild Socialism also had made a valuable contribution in stressing that classes were based on social function, not on a superficial contrast between wealth and poverty. He also found interesting the Guild Socialists' position on separating Collective ownership from management: the State in the Guild Socialist idea was to be Collective owner and representative of citizens as consumers, thus standing over against management by producers organized in National Guilds (these Guilds harmonizing entrepreneurs and industrial trade unions). Bosanquet made it clear, however, that he viewed even this form of Socialism with distrust, and he put forward some more modest proposals. First, that in the earlier and creative stages of business, where management and ownership coincided, it would be against public policy to change the system of control. Second, when businesses had reached the stage where ownership had come into the hands of (largely absentee) shareholders, the shareholding should be distributed as widely as possible and treated as mere loan capital—that is, the shareholders should be regarded as having invested their money at a settled rate of interest without any claim to control over management. Third, that in these larger business concerns, labour organizations should be allowed some share in management.

These three moderate suggestions (and the third and most important one was not worked out in detail at all) were preceded by a long disquisition on the theoretical reason why control in the political and the economic spheres should be kept separate. This rested on the fundamental difference between the 'class-minds' of those who lived and worked in the world of wealth-production (business) and those in the world of service (the professions). The former were specially equipped to deal with practical, bodily things, acquisition and material creation, the latter with problems involving a large element of theory, or requiring intellectual advice and service. It was true that politicians were drawn as representatives from both classes, but in becoming politicians those from the wealth-producing class entered the professional class and became separated from the habits of the world they represented. 'Political leadership is a function unsuited to the wealth-producing world as such, whether to its captains or rank and file'—just as direct organization of industry would be unfitting for the professional and political class. As Bosanquet freely acknowledged, this argument was derived from Plato's discussion in *The Republic* of the role of the Guardian class. In conclusion he agreed with Sorel (and Hegel) in denouncing any detailed plan or Utopia for the future:

The social progress, with which we are dealing, is too large and deep and concrete to be contained in any one's sketch of the ideal . . . The real point is, surely, that the social consciousness is being transformed *pari passu* with the emergence of new social creations; and new social creations are emerging at every point in the social world . . . our ideals will be present to us rather as a set of values, a faith, or a gospel of our function than as a clear-cut scheme of what is to be. We shall, as a great writer has said, remember 'What the world is, and what we are'. We shall try to understand it, and co-operate with it, rather than remould it . . .

In the mean time, Helen Bosanquet had been engaged in writing her last substantial book, which was to appear in 1914 under the title of *Social Work in London 1869–1912*. It was a history of the COS, written from its official records. The first half of the book chronicled the origin and internal development of the Society, and paid tribute to the work of its prominent members. The second half treated in separate chapters of the development of COS principles in the various fields of its activity—housing and sanitation, care of defectives, medical charities, assistance to children, Poor Law and local government, old-age pensions, and the handling of winter distress and unemployment. A well-documented defence of the COS and its outlook, the history is useful because of its extensive quotations from COS sources; it also possesses some of the interest of a memoir by a committed participant, although Helen Bosanquet kept her personal contributions severely out of the picture. Unfortunately the largest share of its detail was devoted to the Victorian years; the sections on the early twentieth century were very lightly sketched. Helen Bosanquet concluded her survey on a note that combined resignation, hope, and questioning:

Here we must end our history of the Society, leaving it in a world very different from that in which it had its birth, and with new problems before it which its founders could hardly have foreseen. Nor could they, perhaps, have foreseen how splendidly the principles and enthusiasm to which they gave shape and substance would maintain themselves throughout changing conditions, and prove to be as indispensable in the era of State aid as they were when voluntary workers held the field. What the future of the Society will be must be left to the younger generation to determine, as they step into the front ranks where the veterans have fallen . . .[28]

The outbreak of the First World War overwhelmed with its raucous clamour the lingering echoes of the Poor Law controversies. Both the Webbs and the Bosanquets were shocked and grieved at its eruption; they all took the view that Britain had to act as she did in the crisis and the national cause had to be supported, but they declined to sign a manifesto of British intellectuals in favour of the war; they deplored the more fanatical and unreasonable manifestations of belligerency and thought that genuine conscientious objectors should not be treated with severity.[29] Their views of the fundamental causes of the war were also remarkably similar: they discovered them to lie in the spirit of aggressive militarism (as

---

[28] H. Bosanquet, *Social Work in London 1869–1912* (London, 1914), pp. 408–9.
[29] Bernard Bosanquet to Hoernlé, 11 June 1916 (concerning Bertrand Russell). J. H. Muirhead (ed.), *Bernard Bosanquet and his Friends* (London, 1935), p. 190. Beatrice Webb's attitude was set out fully and frankly in B.W.D., 8 Apr. 1916; Cole, *Beatrice Webb's Diaries 1912–24*, pp. 59–61.

distinguished from armed defence). Sidney Webb, diagnosing this as 'the outcome of long continued national pride and ambition, coupled with a belief in irresistible power, and a willingness to use that power ruthlessly in the pursuit of national aims', put the chief blame on Germany, seeing the war as 'the clash of Germany's ambitions . . . with the very position of the British empire in the world', although he reflected parenthetically: 'How very imperfectly human nature is yet moralised, and how prone it is to take wherever it feels the power to take.'[30] Bosanquet's interpretation of the calamity gave more weight to the universal failings:

It is not the State, nor sovereignty, nor merely the Germans nor the Kaiser who made the war. It is all of us, pursuing our mingled aims, which take no account of others, and which, apart from due subordination of means to ends, must led to its collision.[31]

But elsewhere he also suggested that militarism, which he coupled with lack of democracy, made the Germans more to blame than the English.[32] The Webbs and the Bosanquets also agreed that the evil sentiment which led to war was promoted by internal faults in the nations involved.[33] Here again there was a certain agreement, at least so long as these faults were specified in general terms, such as insufficient democracy and equality,[34] regulations in restraint of trade and of free travelling and communication, and failure of devotion to the highest aspirations of humanity. When it came to saying more precisely what these meant, however, one detects a difference of emphasis: the Bosanquets looking at the matter through Liberal, the Webbs through Socialist spectacles. All the same, it was a belief which favoured the pressing on with social reform, even in wartime.

The Webbs (particularly Sidney) were far more successful in

---

[30] Winter, *Socialism and the Challenge of War*, p. 190.

[31] H. Bosanquet, *Bernard Bosanquet* (London, 1924), p. 136, quoting the 3rd ed. of *The Philosophical Theory of the State*.

[32] B. Bosanquet to Hoernlé, 24 Jan. 1915. Muirhead, *Bernard Bosanquet and his Friends*, p. 166.

[33] B. Bosanquet declared that it was failure to perfect the State that produced the elements favourable to war: 'Dissatisfied elements at home are the mainspring of cupidity abroad'. 1919 Introduction to *The Philosophical Theory of the State*, p. xlix of 1925 ed.

[34] On equality see B. Bosanquet's essay 'The Wisdom of Naaman's Servants', in his *Social and International Ideals*, p. 309. He defined inequality as 'differences between citizens for which there is no relevant social need'.

social reform activity than were the Bosanquets. Failing health (in 1915 Bernard Bosanquet developed the heart trouble which was gradually to incapacitate him) increased the Bosanquets' tendency to withdraw.[35] 'There was no "war-work" which he could do', Helen Bosanquet wrote of her husband,[36] and the same applied to her. Beatrice Webb was also incapacitated to some extent in the early years of the war by long periods of depression and nervous debility associated with thoughts of war horrors. She wrote:

I am neither doing my share of emergency work nor yet carrying forward, with sufficient steadfastness, my own work. Now and again I bolster up my conscience with the plea that I am elderly and past work—the very way to become so.[37]

Even Sidney and I are not of one mind! He is a sane British patriot . . . I only feel a quite immeasurable wretchedness about [the war].[38]

Sidney, indefatigable and imperturbable as ever, flung himself into the activity of the War Emergency Workers' National Committee, which was set up by the Labour Party and the Parliamentary Committee of the TUC immediately after the declaration of hostilities. As he quickly realized, wartime organization itself set a strong pace in the direction of public control, in spite of Liberal or Conservative hesitations, and it was essential for the Labour Party to formulate coherent views on prospective changes. Harrassed politicians and administrators were eager to conciliate Labour and were willing to listen to sensible advice. 'The government is calling to its aid innumerable Committees—everyone who has any kind of reputation as a social reformer is on some Committee or other',[39] Beatrice Webb shrewdly observed at the beginning of the war.

Sidney Webb's consummate skill as a committee-man, his detailed knowledge of the working of institutions, and his access to the world of power and influence were in demand both for reconciling his divided colleagues of the left and negotiating with the Establishment. The resignation of John Burns from the government and Ramsay MacDonald from the leadership of the Labour Party on the declaration of war removed at a stroke two of

---

[35] H. Bosanquet, *Bernard Bosanquet*, p. 132. [36] Ibid., p. 136.
[37] B.W.D., 3 Nov. 1914. Cole, *Beatrice Webb's Diaries*, p. 30; MacKenzie, *Diary*, iii, 220.
[38] B. Webb to [?Lady Betty Balfour], 30 May 1915. Passfield Papers.
[39] B.W.D., 10 Aug. 1914. Cole, *Beatrice Webb's Diaries*, p. 27.

the Webbs' obstacles. Sidney Webb's increasingly close relations with Arthur Henderson took him into the top circle of Labour Party leadership—a move confirmed when he replaced Stephen Sanders in November 1915 as Fabian representative on the Labour Party Executive[40] (this post had always been allotted by the Fabians to less exalted members of the Society in the years before the war). This, and Sidney Webb's work on the committee of the War Emergency Workers' National Committee,[41] which from May 1915 had been sitting to consider problems of post-war reconstruction, resulted in his election to the Labour Party Executive's own 'After the War' subcommittee, which eventually, in conjunction with the WEWNC and the Fabian Research Department, took into its purview the whole field of post-war social policy, the formulation of a Labour Party programme, and the reorganization of the Labour Party's constitution. In all of these affairs, from the formulation of the Labour Party's war aims in July 1917 to the drafting of the manifesto *Labour and the New Social Order*, issued at the end of war, Webb played a leading role.

Opportunities for 'permeation' of the Webbs' ideas were not confined to the Labour Party. At a time when problems of ordinary social disadvantage and distress became inextricably mixed up with distress due to the war, when the 'retrenchment' principles of Gladstonian finance were being blown sky-high, and when the government had continually to improvise more efficient methods of control, some of the Webbs' administrative and policy recommendations suddenly appeared to be moderate. And the Webbs themselves learnt to be insinuatingly 'reasonable'. The setting up of the Prince of Wales's National Relief Fund promised a new generous approach to relief, and the Webbs supplied continuous advice to the government about its working. They successfully recommended the raising of old-age pensions, but had reservations concerning the establishment of a Ministry of Pensions to deal with

[40] E. R. Pease claimed that he persuaded Sidney Webb to take on this job. A. Briggs and J. Saville (eds.), *Essays in Labour History 1886–1923* (London, 1971), ii. 244 n. 90.

[41] For full accounts of Webb's work on the War Emergency Workers' National Committee see Winter, *Socialism and the Challenge of War*, ch. 7; R. Harrison, 'The War Emergency Workers' National Committee 1914–1920' in Briggs and Saville, *Essays in Labour History 1886–1923*, ch. 9; and the generous tribute to Webb by his colleague on the Committee, J. S. Middleton, in M. Cole (ed.), *The Webbs and Their Work* (London, 1949), ch. 11.

a vast expansion of activity after the war. A Ministry of Labour, which they had advocated in the Minority Report, was brought into existence in 1916, even if it were only for war organization purposes and not with the full power they recommended.

Beatrice Webb, during this time, had not been really inactive according to anyone's definition but her own: she had launched the younger recruits of the Fabian Society into floating the *New Statesman*, into the wide-ranging inquiries of the Fabian Research Department, and (with financial sponsorship from Joseph Rowntree) into speculations, headed by Leonard Woolf, about supra-national organizations that might be brought into existence after the war.[42] Her return to the immediate governmental administrative circle began in January 1916, when she was invited by the Labour Party to become one of its three nominees to the Statutory Pensions Committee to allocate supplementary pensions to ex-soldiers. Sir Samuel Provis, her former colleague on the Poor Law, was Chairman, and she found that now she got on well with him;[43] but she confessed in her Diary that she was not much interested in the work (apart from getting trade unions direct representation on local pension committees) because, she said: 'I dont want the ex-soldier to be treated better than the civilian population; and the function of the Statutory Committee seemed to be just this differentiation. Petting the ex-soldier on the cheap is the note of all its activities.'[44] Her work with this group, however, led on to higher things: it brought her administrative capacity once again to the attention of politicians and officials. Lloyd George was currently revivifying the Reconstruction Committee, established but never properly functioning in Asquith's regime to consider long-range changes required in the war and post-war years. According to the story told by Dr Tom Jones to the Webbs, the new Prime Minister ordered his secretaries to 'bring [him] a list of persons with ideas', from which he chose fourteen, remarking: 'Yes, we will have one of

---

[42] B.W.D., 14 Feb. 1915. Cole, *Beatrice Webb's Diaries*, p. 32. Leonard Woolf's research produced his *International Government*, first published in two reports in *New Statesman* supplements, July 1915 and issued in book form in the following year.

[43] B.W.D., 20 Jan. 1916, 1 June 1916. Cole, *Beatrice Webb's Diaries*, pp. 54–5, 64–5.

[44] B.W.D., 19 Feb. 1917. Cole, *Beatrice Webb's Diaries*, p. 81; MacKenzie, *Diary*, iii, 275.

the Webbs', preferring Beatrice to Sidney.[45] The major task assigned to her was Poor Law reform, and she proposed to negotiate a compromise between the views of the Majority and Minority of the former Royal Commission and the Local Government Board (now once again under the control of Walter Long).

Beatrice Webb's working plan was the compromise arrived at before the war by the County Councils Association. This involved negotiations with Lord George Hamilton. Both of them have left accounts of the proceedings, which form an interesting comparison and contrast:

[*Beatrice Webb*:] I first approached the Local Government Board through Sir Samuel Provis, with whom I had worked with great cordiality on the Statutory Pension Committee. I pointed out to him that since the issue of the two reports the status of the L.G.B. had gone from bad to worse. The Insurance Commission had been set up and now claimed to be the main department concerned with Health; the new Ministry of Labour had taken over the function of dealing with the destitution due to unemployment; and within the last month yet another department had been set up in the Ministry of Pensions which, after the war, would be controlling the treatment, training and maintenance of millions of persons—and controlling these services through a series of Local Authorities excluded from the jurisdiction of the L.G.B. His old department was, in fact, being throttled by its connection with an obsolete and emasculated Poor Law. No Government dared to give any function to a Poor Law authority—central or local. This argument seems to have convinced the L.G.B. and they consented to the appointment of the committee and nominated Symonds— the Head of the Poor Law division—to represent them. My task with Lord George promised to be a more difficult and delicate one. An affecting interview at his house and we were reconciled. He walked all the way to Hyde Park Corner with me, chatting about the war and the Report of the Mesopotamia Enquiry of which he had been Chairman. 'You want me to serve on this Committee, Mrs Webb? Very well, I will', were his parting words. I gathered he had been converted to the break up of the Poor Law by service on the Venereal Disease Commission. But he acted with great generosity, and backed me up nobly in my duel with the wily Symonds who did not want to abolish the Poor Law but merely to change its name. The report was published soon after Xmas and, except for the protests of Boards of Guardians, was received as an overdue reform.[46]

[45] B.W.D., 22 Feb. 1917. Cole, *Beatrice Webb's Diaries*, p. 82.
[46] Later note (1918) to B.W.D., 11 Dec. 1917. Cole, *Beatrice Webb's Diaries*, p. 99 n. 1.

[*Lord George Hamilton*:] Mr [*sic*] Sidney Webb came to see me some six months back. She was in a very repentant and attractive mood. She admitted that she had made a mistake in trying to break up the family and in persistently objecting to our proposal to make for the future the Home Assistance Committee the foundation of Poor Law Relief and Poor Law Assistance. She told me that she was on a reconstruction Committee which seemed to me of a somewhat ambitious character . . .

On the Committee on which Mrs Webb sat was Sir Samuel Provis and Sir Robert Morant. At the commencement of their enquiries they were confronted by the mass of Committees which have been brought into existence by the present Government in connection with the Old Age Pension, Military Pension and Allowances, Insurance and gratuitous Health Assistance. Mrs Webb calculated that something like £60,000,000 annually of public money is now being handled by quasi-responsible Committees. She and Provis had put their heads together and thought that if a compromise could be arranged between the schemes of the Minority and the Majority Commissioners and the duties of the Poor Law Guardians were transferred to the County Councils and Borough Councils, the Home Assistance Committee which could then be established should be made the authoritative body for the disbursement from the rates of all assistance in the locality and, indirectly, of the payments made under pensions, etc, from imperial taxes.

So far we are in complete agreement. Then came the question of what should be the scheme for the execution of the existing duties of the Poor Law Guardians? Mrs Webb agreed to the establishment of a Home Assistance Committee which was to have complete control of all payments made or assistance in kind or money given to the family, and the family were [*sic*] to be treated as a whole. This is substantially the abandonment of the position taken up by the Minority Commissioners.

She then discussed with me what was to be done with institutional relief, and her proposal—and one to which Provis agreed—was to transfer the various institutions to authorities which were already in existence. For instance, all medical relief, curative or preventive, was to be in the hands of the Health Authority. The hospitals and infirmaries were to be taken over by the Borough and County Councils and would be administered by them through a branch of the Health Authority. As regards the able-bodied, it was proposed to utilise to a very much greater extent than before the Labour Exchanges, but to set up in each local administrative unit a special committee to deal with unemployment and the training for employment.

I pointed out to Mrs Webb that it would be necessary to have some deterrent or penal force behind this authority. To this she agreed, and on these conditions I consented to act on the Committee . . .

We had a very capable Committee. On it was—as I said before—Sir

Samuel Provis, Morant, Mr Currier (the L.C.C. educational representative), Mr Norman (who represented the L.C.C. on its financial side), Mr Curtis (who was Clerk to the Birmingham Board of Guardians, which I understand is now very well worked), and Mr Simmonds [*sic*], who is the Head of the Poor Law Department of the Local Government Board. The Deputy Speaker of the House of Commons, Sir Donald Maclean, was in the chair, and considering how little he knew of the matter he handled the Committee very well . . .

We had considerable difficulty in getting these proposals of ours into a compact and readable draft. However, Provis undertook to be Chairman of the Drafting Committee, and I think the work was really well done, and the scheme went on to the Minister of Health about a month back. It will be a difficult Bill to get through the House of Commons. At present the existence of the Guardian blocks the way to local reform, and the prejudice and antipathy amongst the working-classes against Poor Law administration prevents them taking any effective part as administrators either in solving or helping the many social and industrial difficulties which have arisen since the War.

I am bound to say that Mrs Webb throughout showed great ability and was absolutely straight. She stuck to her bargain, and enjoyed herself by sitting upon certain members of the Committee whom she demolished with her tongue; but we saw the best and the bright side of her, and I could not help writing to congratulate her upon the preliminary success of the Report, which I hope will become effective through legislation.[47]

Beatrice Webb remarked of herself in her activities on the Local Government and Social Services subcommittee of the Reconstruction Committee: 'I have learnt committee manners—an art in itself'.[48] Alas, for all her new-found adroitness, the Maclean Committee's Report was not regarded as one of the more urgent matters of reconstruction after the war; it was shelved for the next decade.

She served on two other wartime committees of some importance. First, the subcommittee to reorganize the machinery of central government, on which she found two of her friends: Haldane was Chairman and Morant Secretary. It had become necessary because Lloyd George's way of suddenly creating and as suddenly reorganizing or dismissing new committees or departments had thrown Whitehall into confusion. Beatrice Webb welcomed the opportunity for a glimpse into the inner workings of the bureaucracy. She considered the proceedings of the committee to be informal but

[47] Hamilton to Phelps, 17 Jan. 1918. Phelps Papers.
[48] B.W.D., 11 Dec. 1917. Cole, *Beatrice Webb's Diaries*, p. 99.

thorough, and her critical observations in her Diary on the Civil Service added up, on the whole, to a favourable estimate of its capacity.[49] The Report was unanimous in sorting out government activities into fourteen departments, and Beatrice (and Sidney) Webb's contribution was successful in helping to ensure the defeat of any attempt to establish a separate Ministry of Poor Relief or even of a separate Ministry of Local Government. One of the proposed new departments, the Ministry of Health, was established by an act of 1918, and it took over and absorbed the work of the former Local Government Board, the Board of Control of Mental Defectives, the Health Insurance Commission, and the General Register Office. Morant was appointed the first Permanent Secretary of the Ministry of Health. So the Webbs had their revenge on the LGB for its 'reactionary' policies and its earlier rejection of their closest friend and supporter in the Civil Service.

Beatrice Webb's other main wartime committee was that on the relationship of men's and women's wages, under the chairmanship of Sir James Atkin, a distinguished lawyer.[50] This committee owed its formation to women trade unionists' claim that the Treasury Agreement of March 1915 had given a pledge by the government that women doing war work would receive the same pay as men whose work they undertook. The committee was given the task of deciding this question and of laying down general principles. At the outset, Beatrice Webb acknowledged quite frankly, in her Diary, that she was not really interested in the subject. But as things turned out, she found herself to be, not the only woman, but the only 'Labour' representative on the committee, and she became deeply cynical about the likely prejudice of the committee's decision. So she resolved, as she had done on the great Poor Law Commission, to hand in a minority report.[51] She found (in opposition to her Majority colleagues) that a pledge had been made and was not being kept, and that wartime experience had demonstrated that the 'essential principle' should be that minimum standard rates, fixed by 'collective agreement between representative organisations of the employers and the employed', should no more 'differ according

[49] B.W.D., 13 July 1918, 8 Dec. 1918. Cole, *Beatrice Webb's Diaries*, pp. 126–7, 137–8.

[50] B.W.D., 1 Sept. 1918, 8 Dec. 1918; Cole, *Beatrice Webb's Diaries*, pp. 129, 138.

[51] B.W.D., 8 Dec. 1918, 11 Feb. 1919; Cole, *Beatrice Webb's Diaries*, pp. 138, 146.

to the workers' sex than according to their race, creed, height or weight'. The conclusion of her Minority Report, as published in the Fabian Society's Special Pamphlet (1920) *The Wages of Men and Women: Should they be Equal?*, took its place as one of the most formidably argued of feminist manifestos—all the more notable, perhaps, in that it was not the work of a recognized militant feminist.

During the war, Poor Law problems had sunk almost to insignificance. The demands of the war effort had provided employment for almost everybody capable of making a contribution, and indeed, as the Webbs cynically noted, of large numbers who were previously thought incapable of making any contribution at all.[52] It appeared to reveal, at least theoretically, that the ideal of full employment was not unattainable. This situation had accelerated the liberal policies which the Guardians, with the encouragement of the Local Government Board, had adopted in the years 1911–14, in response to the criticisms of them made by the Royal Commission. It also did nothing to curb their (and the LGB's) belief that, with a few administrative adjustments, all would be well with the Poor Law. 'Golden showers'[53]—in the form of extensions of health and unemployment insurance benefits, greatly increased opportunities of employment for women, allowances and war pensions, gratuities and 'out of work' pay to soldiers on demobilization, extensions of old-age, widows', and orphans' pensions—swept temporarily into limbo old notions of niggardliness and deterrence in the government's dealing with the underprivileged, and raised expectations of a more generous-spirited era after the war. But, equivocally, in this post-war euphoria (which lasted until 1920), government controls were blamed for wartime restrictions, and plans for reconstruction were relegated to an inferior place in the determination to recapture the supposed benefits of private enterprise. The whole scene and mood changed utterly a few years after the end of 1920, with the onset of a depression that introduced a percentage of unemployment undreamt of in Britain before.

The Bosanquets did not live to see the magnitude of the post-war

---

[52] S. and B. Webb, *English Local Government*, vol. ix. *English Poor Law History*, Part II. *The Last Hundred Years* (London, 1963; repr.; first published 1929), p. 668.
[53] The term was used by the Webbs, ibid., p. 825.

calamity. Bernard Bosanquet died on 8 February 1923, and Helen on 7 April 1925. Both of them had been invalids since 1921, and they had moved from Oxshott to Golders Green in 1922, to be near relatives. Helen Bosanquet resigned her editorship of the *Charity Organisation Review* in 1921, and Bernard Bosanquet had resigned his chairmanship of the COS Council in 1917, owing to ill health, although he remained as an 'additional member' of the Council until his death. They continued to uphold in their writings the views they had reached by 1909.[54] One of their final victories was to help secure the reversal of a resolution, passed by 'rebels' in the Society on 18 February 1919 to change the title of COS on the grounds that

The Society's name is undeservedly, but none the less finally, objectionable to many people, including in a notable degree the industrial classes, and that its sub-name [The Society for Organising Charity and Improving the Condition of the Poor] has a tone of patronage unsuited to modern conditions.[55]

The reversal of this resolution meant that the COS had to wait until after the Second World War (till 1946) for its new title: 'The Family Welfare Association'.

In the years 1911–23, Bernard Bosanquet devoted his talents mainly to a comprehensive restatement of his whole philosophical system, to a defence of various major points of it against an increasing brigade of critics from the Cambridge school, and to an attempt to come to terms with new allies amongst young Italian Idealist philosophers. The Gifford Lectures he gave at Edinburgh University in 1911 and 1912, which were later published in two volumes under the titles *The Principle of Individuality and Value* (1912) and *The Value and Destiny of the Individual* (1913), brought together into a complete system his views on logic, moral philosophy, and metaphysics. These lectures might be described as Bosanquet's theodicy, if he had been an orthodox religious; but, like his master Hegel, his attitude to religion always retained a certain ambiguity. In these lectures, and in others of his later

---

[54] See for example, B. Bosanquet, 'The Quest for the Real Thing', COR, NS 34 (1913), 288–302, 'The Ideal of Charity', ibid. 37 (1915), 69–82; 'Politics and Charity', ibid., 38 (1915), 380–95; 'The Philosophy of Casework', ibid., 39 (1916), 117–33, 'The Motive of Public Assistance: A Practical Ideal', *The Times*, 20 Sept. 1920, p. 6; 'The C.O.S.: A Necessary Social Function', *Spectator*, 18 Mar. 1922, p. 332.

[55] M. Rooff, *A Hundred Years of Family Welfare* (London, 1974), pp. 119–20.

writings, he had moved closer to religion than the position he had adopted in his Ethical Society days: he now found that certain essential Christian doctrines, which had seemed unacceptable to him earlier, could be interpreted to fit in with the immanence of the spirit of the Absolute. But he declined to identify God with the Absolute, as some Idealists did. God was only the popular imaginative conception of the Absolute, and therefore not wholly Real, but only 'an appearance of reality'.[56] The key to value and freedom in the universe was the 'soul-making' effort of the will towards its destiny of 'self-completion', by transcending the limitations of finite personality and achieving the standpoint of the Absolute.

Even during the Gifford lectures, Bosanquet had been obliged to turn aside from his 'plain tale' (as he called it—jestingly perhaps) to answer critics and opponents. William James was the main focus of these observations; the Cambridge philosophers, Bertrand Russell and G. E. Moore, just then emerging into prominence, were accorded only passing comment. Bosanquet's early attitude to G. E. Moore, indeed, was inclined to be patronizing. Reviewing Moore's *Principia Ethica* on its first appearance, he concluded:

I believe Mr Moore to have a real vocation as a critic in the sense of a free lance who will make the orthodox reflect and reconsider. But, as far as I can see, he . . . is not yet . . . a critic in the true sense, a critic who can take the standpoint of that which he criticises.[57]

By 1914 the gathering storm of 'refutations and Idealism' had been taken up by the younger disciples of Russell and Moore, and articles by C. D. Broad, C. E. M. Joad, and Susan Stebbing were appearing in the philosophical journals.[58] 'Monism seems to have gone out of fashion', Joad confidently announced. 'Certainly, since [1914] the Absolute has not loomed so large as heretofore in philosophical discussion'.[59] Armed with the method of Cambridge analysis, the young warriors were ready to probe all the main assumptions of speculative philosophy. In a steady stream of

---

[56] B. Bosanquet, *The Value and Destiny of the Individual* (London, 1913), p. 255; cf. Hegel: '. . . Religion is the general form in which Truth exists for *non-abstract* consciousness', *The Philosophy of History*, trans. J. Sibree (New York, 1956), p. 445.

[57] *Mind*, 13 (1904), 261.

[58] e.g. *Proceedings of the Aristotelian Society*, NS 17 (1916–17).

[59] Ibid., p. 95.

articles, year after year, Bosanquet had to defend major points of the Idealist outlook.[60]

One of the sharpest encounters (creditable to both contestants) was that with C. D. Broad in *Mind*,[61] just at the end of the war, concerning the validity of the concept of a 'general will'. Broad wrote that he found great difficulty in finding anything Bosanquet (or Rousseau) might mean when they spoke of a 'general will'. He suggested several possible interpretations, some of which he acknowledged could not be what Bosanquet had in mind. In the end, he decided that the notion of a 'general will' in Bosanquet's sense could be supported only by the contention that there were some propositions which all or nearly all citizens desired to be true. What propositions did all or nearly all Englishmen desire to be true? Broad answered:

I should be puzzled to find many besides the following: That everyone who will work should have a certain minimum of comfort, that the country should not be invaded and its government set at naught by those of other countries, that justice (variously understood) shall be administered, and that there should be *some* definite rules about the acquirement, distribution, tenure and bequest of property.

Such a 'general will' could be no more than a negative limiting condition within which infinite variations would be possible, and, Broad concluded:

That this amount of agreement in what is willed by all is enough to constitute a state I cannot for a moment believe. The real driving force of the state seems to me to be the will of the governing class; this will is sometimes good and sometimes bad, but in normal times it gets itself obeyed unless it flagrantly opposes the general will of all its subjects or of any large and powerful section of them.

Bosanquet retorted that Broad's interpretation was not his notion of a 'general will' at all. Broad's view reduced the agreement of wills to a residuum in whch no distinctions survived. 'That is the old bad business of excluding from the generic concept all properties which are differently developed in the species.' The individual willed all that was implied in his will, and his will was a particular within 'the system formed by other wills which imply it

---

[60] In *Mind, Proceedings of the Aristotelian Society*, and *Philosophical Review*.
[61] *Mind*, 28 and 29 (1919 and 1920), 502–504 and 77–81.

and are implied in it, as conditions *sine quibus non* of the truth of the propositions which it wills to be true'. If Smith willed to go to town by train, he willed the existence of the railway and the co-operation of the wills of those who operated it. A man's volitions and plans depended upon the support of other wills in the community, which need not be explicitly the same as his (indeed the parties concerned need not know of each other's individual existence), but which are essential to the accomplishment of his objectives. That is to say, the individual must enter into a system which is the 'general will' of the community. On the whole, the individual will accepts a certain system of life; and 'the fact that "on the whole" has different limits for everybody does not alter the fact that it is false of nobody'. The whole legal and social system of the State has been created and is constantly being remoulded by the wills of hundreds of thousands of devoted lives. To say that 'the governing classes' had directing power in democracy seemed to Bosanquet 'an extraordinary thing to say' unless Broad made it 'a tautology by including in them all the classes that *de facto* exercise control'. This exchange made clear that Bosanquet's meaning of 'will' included what was accepted of the social structure by its being taken for granted. As Broad implied at the beginning of his article, he would regard this as an 'unfortunate' use of the term.

The savagest attack on Bosanquet's theory came in the last year of the war, 1918, with the publication of L. T. Hobhouse's book, *The Metaphysical Theory of the State*. Hobhouse, who had long been an opponent of Hegelian Idealism,[62] did not scruple to exploit the wartime anti-German feeling against what he felt to be the wicked consequences of 'the Hegelian theory of the god-state'. His vigorous polemic was successful with a new generation in tarring Hegelian Idealism with the imputations that it was inherently reactionary, illiberal, totalitarian, and autocratic,[63] for it came at a time when Idealist theory was declining in popularity and when Bosanquet felt too old and weary to counter-attack. He wrote to his friend the Revd W. E. Plater, who had drawn his attention to a review of Hobhouse's book: 'I am interested to hear about Hobhouse's characterisation of me, or is it the reviewer's? It doesnt

---

[62] See L. T. Hobhouse, *Democracy and Reaction* (London, 1904), and review of it by G. P. Gooch in *IJE* 15 (1905), 499 ff.

[63] For a discussion of this, see S. Collini's article 'Hobhouse, Bosanquet and the State . . .', *Past and Present*, 72 (1976), 86–111.

matter. I don't think I shall read his book—I don't feel I learn much from him, and books are expensive since the war began; and time is not cheap.'[64]

Early in 1920, Bernard Bosanquet remarked to an Italian correspondent that 'in the English-speaking world of philosophy . . . 1. the Realists and Bertrand Russell's party with 2. the Pragmatists and 3. Bradley's friends divide that world into perhaps three nearly equal parties . . .'.[65] His interest in the Italian Idealist school had been aroused by his reading and criticism of Benedetto Croce's work on aesthetics, and he hoped to find amongst the younger Italian philosophers sympathy for, and a reconciliation with, Bradley's ideas and his own. In spite of a cordial initial reception, the task of settling their differences proved to be more thorny than he had expected, and he died before the reconciliation he had hoped for was in sight. Had he lived longer, the acceptance by Gentile of the Education Ministry in Mussolini's government (which was hailed as a triumph by one of Bosanquet's correspondents, Camillo Pellizzi)[66] might have introduced political as well as philosophical barriers between him and some of the Italian Idealist philosophers, for he remained staunchly Liberal-Radical, and was even willing to go so far as to accept the prospect of a 'labour government with one or two good liberals in it'[67] in Britain at the end of the war.

The Act of 1929, which abolished the Poor Law Guardians, must bring our story to its equivocal end. It was promoted by Neville Chamberlain as Minister of Health in the Conservative Baldwin government. The Webbs had no more to do with the passing of this Act directly than the deceased Bosanquets, although the Webbs were writing their *English Poor Law History* at the time. By then, the Webbs had become completely identified with the Labour Party, and had become prophets of the doom of capitalism (*The Decay of Capitalist Civilization*, 1923) and projectors of a scheme for the wholesale reorganization of the State (*A Constitution for the Socialist Commonwealth of Great Britain*, 1920). Sidney Webb had

---

[64] B. Bosanquet to Plater, 26 Jan. 1919, in Muirhead, *Bernard Bosanquet and his Friends*, p. 203. It was a pity that Bernard Bosanquet did not reply to Hobhouse because, in spite of the polemical qualities of Hobhouse's book, it was, perhaps, the most careful and detailed criticism to emerge from the anti-Idealist camp.

[65] B. Bosanquet to Vivante, 27 Mar. 1920, ibid., p. 262.

[66] Pellizzi to B. Bosanquet, 12 Nov. 1922, ibid., pp. 299–300.

[67] B. Bosanquet to Hoernlé, 14 Sept. 1919, ibid., pp. 217–18.

served his apprenticeship as Minister in charge of the Board of Trade in the first short-lived Labour government of 1924. Though he proved a capable enough administrator, he was prevented by Labour's precarious situation as a minority government from displaying much initiative, and he was never successful in 'capturing the ear of the House' as an orator in the Commons. In spite of his personal estrangement from Ramsay MacDonald, he supported him as a loyal henchman in his cautious policies, designed to demonstrate that Labour was 'fit to govern'. It is possible that Webb might have left more of a mark if he had been appointed Minister of Labour, as MacDonald originally proposed and as Webb would have preferred, instead of being elevated to the more senior post of President of the Board of Trade, which his colleagues insisted was his due. For, as Beatrice Webb observed, the Board of Trade had become

the least arduous and significant of any of the older and larger Cabinet departments: it has been hollowed out by handing all that relates to Customs, etc., to the Treasury; all that relates to employment of labour in industry to the Ministry of Labour; all that relates to mines to the nominally subordinate but really independent Department of Mines which the pushing Shinwell erected into a '*Ministry of Mines*'; all that relates to railways to the '*Ministry of Transport*'. There is little left but Bankruptcy and mercantile shipping, patents and other odds and ends—all matters of administrative routine. The President is kept occupied with interviews and deputations—a sort of buffer between pressure of outside interests on the Cabinet or the Prime Minister.[68]

Sidney Webb's parliamentary career was an almost textbook demonstration of the qualitative difference, noted by political scientists, between the virtues required of the administrator and those of the politician[69] (and his term in what was, for him, the very unsuitable post of Secretary of State for Dominion Affairs and Colonial Secretary in the second Labour government of 1929–31— which falls beyond our story—was to confirm it).[70] One is left with the feeling that Beatrice Webb might have been more successfully pushing in the politician's role.

[68] B.W.D., 6 Nov. 1924. Cole, *Beatrice Webb's Diaries 1924–1932*, (London, 1956), p. 50; MacKenzie, *Diary*, iv, 45.

[69] A. F. Davies, *Skills, Outlooks and Passions: A Psychoanalytic Contribution to the Study of Politics* (Cambridge, 1980), chs. 1–3.

[70] Sir Drummond Shiels, 'Sidney Webb as Minister', in Cole, *The Webbs and Their Work*, pp. 201–18.

Neville Chamberlain's Local Government Act of 1929 was part of the Baldwin Conservative Government's policy, after the fall of the first Labour Government in October 1924, to rationalize local administration and curb the uncoordinated policies of social relief which had prevailed since the war. Chamberlain had sketched a programme of twenty-five bills immediately after taking office as Minister of Health—twenty-one of which were to be enacted.[71] They ranged over the whole field of social provision, from the extension of the contributory principle in social insurance and pensions to local government reform. In the matter of local government and Poor Law reform, the Conservative government had several objectives. The one which attracted the attention of Labour Party supporters was the determination to bring to heel those Boards of Guardians whose policies in administering outdoor relief in times of unemployment had become especially lax or overgenerous. The number of Boards whose scales of relief had become extravagantly high, in the opinion of the Poor Law officials of the Ministry of Health, varied between a hundred and two hundred.[72] Their policy had become known as 'Poplarism', because of the defiant example set by the Poplar Board of Guardians both in the Edwardian and in the post-war period. The policy was also often attributed to 'Labour' initiative, although it was by no means confined to Boards which had majorities of Labour members.[73] In the aftermath of the breaking of the general strike in May 1926, the government armed itself with a Board of Guardians (Default) Act, which empowered the Minister of Health to replace any Board of Guardians that was not in his opinion fulfilling its functions with a Board of his own nominees. These powers were used, in 1926 and 1927, against the Guardians of West Ham in London, and against those in two mining areas, Chester-le-Street (Durham) and Bedwellty (South Wales). But such drastic action could be taken only in extreme cases; it occasioned resentment, and in fact exposed the limitations of the Minister's powers over the recalcitrant local authorities.

The Conservative Party in general and Neville Chamberlain[74] in

---

[71] K. Feiling, *The Life of Neville Chamberlain* (London, 1946), pp. 129–31, 459–62.

[72] S. and B. Webb, *English Local Government*, vol. ix. Part II, p. 852.

[73] Ibid.; P. A. Ryan, 'Poplarism 1894–1930', in P. Thane (ed.), *The Origins of British Social Policy* (London, 1978), pp. 56 ff.

[74] See D. Dilks, *Neville Chamberlain*, vol. i. *Pioneering and Reform 1869–1929*

particular had other and wider problems in view than the difficulties created by the 'misbehaviour' of a minority of Guardians. They had become entangled in what Winston Churchill called the 'Poor Law jungle'[75] through problems of local government finance. The burden of local rates on industry and agriculture, increased by post-war inflation and expenditure on unemployment, was loudly claimed by those interests to have become 'crippling' in face of foreign competition. Winston Churchill, as Chancellor of the Exchequer in Baldwin's Conservative government, was anxious to introduce, before the 1929 election, a large legislative measure to remove or to lighten substantially local rates on industry and agriculture, both as a concession to the Party's electoral supporters and also in hopes of giving an incentive to increased productivity. If such derating were to be achieved, the local authorities needed to be compensated by a large increase in funding by grants from national revenue—a centralizing consequence which in turn demanded a rationalization of the structure of local government if central grants were to be distributed efficiently and equitably. Neville Chamberlain, as Minister of Health, had been for many years an advocate of such local government reform, which his long and detailed experience of municipal affairs in his native city of Birmingham had equipped him to undertake. For this task, he armed himself with the careful research of his officials into many earlier government reports, including those of the Royal Commission on the Poor Laws of 1905–9, the Maclean Report of 1917, and the second report of the Onslow Royal Commission of 1928. So far as the Poor Law was concerned, Chamberlain decided that the Guardians would have to go, and their functions be transferred to the County Councils.

The Act of 1929 swept away the Boards of Guardians, and for that the elderly Webbs could not refrain from a moment of self-congratulation:

To be able to *make* history as well as to write it—or to be modest—to have foreseen, twenty years ago, the exact stream of tendencies which would bring your proposal to fruition, is a pleasurable thought! So the old Webbs are chuckling over their chickens![76]

(Cambridge, 1984), Part III, chs. 30, 32 and 34 for a full account of Neville Chamberlain's role in the passing of the 1929 Local Government Act.

[75] Ibid., p. 544.
[76] B.W.D., 4 Jan. 1929. Cole, *Beatrice Webb's Diaries*, p. 188; MacKenzie, *Diary*, iv, 156.

But they were not so naïve as to think that Neville Chamberlain's act embodied the principles of the 1905–9 Commission's Minority Report. Sidney Webb, in what was to be his most effective speech in the House of Commons, listened to attentively for its comprehensive grasp rather than for its delivery, criticized the Bill for failing to go the whole way in 'breaking up the Poor Law', providing a national authority to deal with unemployment, and establishing a complete framework for 'the prevention of destitution'. The 1929 Act really was, like so much English social legislation of the nineteenth and early twentieth centuries, an 'enabling act'. It left the county and county borough councils to decide how far they wished to go, one way or the other, towards 'breaking up' the Poor Law or handing it over entire (as the Majority Commissioners of 1909 wanted) to a 'Public Assistance Committee' of their councils. As it did nothing to establish a national authority for employment, it certainly left to the 'Public Assistance Committee', as a minimum residue, responsibility for the unemployed outside National Insurance, the aged and infirm and widows not provided with pensions, vagrants, and persons who needed relief on grounds of 'sudden and urgent necessity'. It almost stopped with the Majority Commissioners' proposals of 1909, though it did not bar the way to further advance after the Second World War.

13

Conclusion

A HISTORICAL ESTIMATE OF THE CONTEST

In our study, a longer-range viewpoint of the contest between the Bosanquets and the Webbs has been taken than the one adopted by many earlier commentators, in order to show that the antagonism between them—as well as the antagonism between the COS and Fabians—was long-standing, dating back to the early 1890s. It must be recognized that the Bosanquets' outlook was not accepted by all members of the COS, any more than the Webbs' outlook was accepted by all Fabians. There were factions which might be labelled 'right', 'centre', and 'left' within each of these societies. The Bosanquets and the Webbs occupied a 'centre' position in each—and this was usually the most powerful and influential position to hold. The difference was that the divisions within the COS were determined by views specifically related to Poor Law policy, because the COS's interest was concentrated on that one issue, whereas the Fabian factions were determined by differences concerning a wider range of political and social problems, leaving the Society's Poor Law policy to be formulated mainly by the Webbs. All the rival Socialist views of the Poor Law came from outside the Fabian Society.

The styles of social theorizing of both the Bosanquets and the Webbs had reached a high level of sophistication well before the Royal Commission on the Poor Laws was established in 1905. Bernard Bosanquet had developed a complete system which linked COS practice to an elaborate structure of Idealist philosophy. Just how far his wife followed him in those high-flying exploits remains unclear, but her own style, though more down to earth, was compatible with his grander theories, and she gave no indication of disapproval. Of course, no *necessary* link between Idealist philosophy and COS practice can be inferred from Bosanquet's system: other Idealist philosophers held quite different views of social policy, as we have seen. But there seems to be a perennial interest in the attempt to create links which suggest that a particular social policy can rejoice in the halo conferred by higher, more general principles. Even the Webbs, who had no heads for the altitude reached by Bernard Bosanquet, indulged in generalities about the 'collective' and 'organic' nature of society, 'evolutionary trends' in social institutions and social development, and a 'General will' (though of a more empirical 'public opinion' sort than Bosanquet's Idealist version).

The vital link in Bosanquet's chain of social thinking was his insistence on the will's primacy over circumstances. This idea linked the Idealist high-level metaphysical notion that the universe was structured by mind with the notion at the empirical level that the individual's will ought to be able to mould its external environment to its own interest. Neither proposition was *prima facie* absurd, although Realist (and Materialist) philosophers would think that the first proposition confused perception with the independent reality of the physical world, and some empirical social scientists would consider that the second proposition greatly overrated the power of the will of the ordinary individual to cope with his social environment. The Webbs, simply avoiding the first metaphysical issue, seem to have taken up a sensible compromise position on the second, empirical question. They did not challenge the Bosanquets' claim that will-power or strong character and a desire for self-help and independence were desirable social attributes; they merely questioned the validity of any deduction that the poor's condition was necessarily a consequence of the lack of them.

That the Bosanquets did make such a deduction was shown in their attitude to what they called the 'Residuum'—the sizeable class at the bottom of the social ladder which they regarded as social wreckage and abandoned to the tender mercies of the Poor Law or to extinction. But early in the 1890s the Bosanquets had led the COS away from its simple dichotomy between 'deserving' and 'undeserving' poor to a more refined distinction between 'helpable' and 'unhelpable'. Their new terminology was designed to divert social workers' attention away from the faults in character that were supposed to have led paupers into their poverty and turn their attention to discovering whether or not the paupers had qualities of character that might help them to rescue themselves from their plight. The COS 'case papers' were expected to be a repository of such judgements. This was a clever shift of emphasis, which appeared to bypass the evidence of social investigations suggesting that the causes of poverty and unemployment were due to social rather than individual failings. It meant, however, if the COS's function was merely remedial—helping to rescue those who had already demonstrated some personal capacity to survive—that it was endangering its claims to make firm pronouncements about the relative importance of moral *vis-à-vis* social causes of poverty or unemployment, or indeed about remedies for unemployment in general. That was not a consequence the COS leaders were ready to admit in a hurry, but the Bosanquets' later talk about poverty as 'a failure of citizen character' acquired a certain air of vagueness as a causal statement, and some members of the COS became more willing to play a part in experiments in remedies for unemployment during the later 1890s and the years up to 1905—though it was usually the role of sceptical participants or observers.

In any event, as we have noted earlier, the COS case for 'strict' Poor Law policies had never rested exclusively on the notion that the poor were to blame for their own condition. The COS also held to the belief that, if the Poor Law were not in some way deterrent, too many people would be willing to take advantage of it and rates would have to rise to an unacceptable height to pay for the increased relief. Such an outlook involved a certain (pessimistic) view of human moral behaviour, but it is a judgement about the moral nature of man and is something different from believing the poor's condition is their own fault. This view of the dangerous social consequences of a 'lax' administration of the Poor Law was almost certainly the more important element in COS thinking, as it was in the thinking of 'strict' Poor Law officials, such as C. S. Davy. Although the Webbs' desired economy in government spending, and recommended the establishment of a 'Registrar of Public Assistance' to administer a means test for social services on the grounds of 'efficiency' and 'economy', they did not share the COS's general pessimism about the public morals of the labouring class: they believed the unemployed wanted work, not hand-outs.

The Bosanquets' views were not out of date in the sense of being tied immovably to '1834 principles' as Fabian propaganda tried to suggest, for they had displayed considerable flexibility in adapting their ideas. But they did lay themselves open to that charge, because they liked to represent themselves as being the upholders of past truths, which emphasized their conservatism rather than their innovations. It must be acknowledged that the Bosanquets had made clear they had no objections to State regulation and action in principle, and they had supported such reforms as compulsory education, State action in housing, prison reform, legislation for the protection of children, and the provision of industrial schools; but their acceptance of State Welfare schemes was very selective. Even after the 1905 Royal Commission was established, they were still opposing reforms such as State provision of the old-age pension, meals at school for underfed children, free medical provision for the working classes, child endowment, and minimum wage legislation. So their 'progressiveness' must not be exaggerated. In comparison with the real Radicals of the 'New Liberal' team, the Bosanquets' attitude appears to be that of Whiggish reform in the tradition of Edmund Burke (with which indeed Hegel's own ideas had much affinity). Although they were cautiously progressive, they, like Burke, were outpaced in their time by the forward movement of social ideas. Stedman Jones has described late nineteenth-century philanthropists of their type as 'urban gentry',[1] and the label seems to fit Bernard Bosanquet, with his nostalgia for the patriarchal harmony of Rock Hall. Helen Bosanquet went along with those feelings to some extent, although the sentiments of her own writings showed fewer 'neo-feudal' sympathies; she preferred rather to invoke the economic virtues of the battling small independent business man, determined against all odds to succeed in a competitive free-market society. Even the Webbs were not quite immune to the idealized virtues of supposed feudal mutual social obligations,[2] but Beatrice Webb's style was rather that of the grand entrepreneur, envisaging large-scale innovation, with Sidney as her reliable adviser, adroit manager, and master of technical detail.

Historians looking at a past age often see similarities in what appeared at the time to be antagonistic characters and ideas, when those who took part in the action had been aware principally of their differences. So it seems to be in this case; and we must try to avoid exaggerating our historical hindsight. The Bosanquets and

---

[1] G. Stedman Jones, *Outcast London* (Oxford, 1971), pp. 267–8.
[2] B.W.D., 19 July 1907; *Our Partnership*, ed. B. Drake and M. Cole (London, 1948), p. 385.

the Webbs certainly shared a feeling characteristic of many intellectuals in the later Victorian age: a sense that the traditional values of earlier Victorianism no longer provided a satisfactory way of reconciling man to society and the universe. Not being either revolutionaries or deniers, they were in search of a new creed to live by, a new 'collectivism' that would restore a sense of true community to a society become divided and disharmonious. Both sets of partners felt a new 'sociology' was essential to help understand the untraditional society evolving in their modern world. They wanted a new 'social economics', which they believed the academic economic establishment was not capable of furnishing. And they gave their blessing both to the representative-democratic State emerging in Britain and to the expert bureaucracy arising to accompany it as its guardian spirit. But within those general resemblances, so visible to the long-range observer but which the contestants themselves took for granted, lurked the differences between them of which they were so vividly aware, and which we have detailed in earlier chapters. There is no point, therefore, in assuming that the Royal Commissioners of 1905 began their task in an atmosphere genial and open-mindedly reforming. The rival ideologies of the COS and Socialist representatives had been developed to a fine dogmatic point; and, at the personal level, Helen Bosanquet at the outset of the inquiry showed more hostility to Beatrice Webb than Beatrice Webb did to her and the COS contingent. Both the doctrinal and the personal antagonism continued throughout the Commission's sittings.

This is not to deny that Beatrice Webb behaved badly in some ways. As she herself admitted later, she had yet to learn 'committee manners'. Her attitude was aggressive; she undertook unauthorized investigations when it suited her, and in one of these, when trapped over her inquiry into the opinions of the Medical Officers of Health, she did try to conceal the evidence; she was no respecter of the Commission's confidentiality; and she was instrumental in dividing the Commission. The question immediately arises whether she should, or could, have pursued different and more effective tactics. Historical commentators' answers to this question have been dominated to a large extent by Canon Barnett's opinion that, if the Majority Report had been unanimous, it would have been invincible; and it is argued as a consequence that Beatrice Webb's aggressive and at times unscrupulous tactics destroyed this possibility.[3] The assumption is that she should, and could, have gone along with a Majority Report as far as she was able, and put in a particular, minor dissenting memorandum on behalf of herself and her colleagues, like the ones submitted by certain other signatories to the Majority Report, such as Hancock Nunn, Octavia Hill, Dr Downes, and Helen Bosanquet and C. S. Loch themselves.

We must, however, raise some questions about this kind of argument. In the first place, was it at all likely that a united report could have been achieved at the Royal Commission? It is true, as many commentators have pointed out,[4] that there was a considerable area of agreement in the two Reports, and furthermore, a compromise of sorts was achieved in 1911 on the basis of the County Councils Association's plan. But during the Commission and at the time when the Reports were drafted, the Majority and Minority were aware mainly of the items of fundamental disagreement between them. The County Councils Association's compromise was accepted only after the struggle between the antagonists had been fought to the finish, and both sides had been obliged to acknowledge defeat. Until that moment arrived there was no likelihood (quite independently of Beatrice Webb's personal behaviour) that the Majority would be willing to accept her more radical proposals—or, of course, that she would tone them down. Too much was at stake for her to sign a Majority Report dominated by COS ideas and merely append a dissenting memorandum stating her own. She was probably right in that, because nobody took much notice of the dissenting memoranda or their authors—at least until Octavia Hill and Dr Downes, joining forces with Charles Booth when he returned to the fray, threw in their lot with the British Constitutional Association.

---

[3] See, e.g., U. Cormack, *The Welfare State, the Formative Years 1905–9*, Loch Memorial Lecture (London, 1953), pp. 29–31.

[4] See, e.g., J. H. Muirhead, *By What Authority? The Principles in Common and at Issue in the Reports of the Poor Law Commission* (London, 2nd edn., 1909), *passim*; S. and B. Webb, *English Local Government*, vol. ix. *English Poor Law History*, Part II. *The Last Hundred Years* (London, 1929), pp. 473–6, 529–31 (it is interesting to notice that the Webbs themselves reiterated, in retrospect, their opinion that the 'guiding hand of an experienced lawyer' as chairman might have drawn the contending parties together!); Cormack, *The Welfare State*, pp. 14–19; T. H. Marshall, *Social Policy in the Twentieth Century* (London, 1975 edn.; first published in 1965), p. 46; K. Woodroofe, 'The Royal Commission on the Poor Laws 1905–9', *International Review of Social History*, 22 (1977), Part II, p. 153; and also ch. 10 above.

A second major query must also be raised: is it really so certain that the Liberal government would have been *obliged* to accept a united Majority Report, even if it had been possible to achieve one? The answer must be that this is far from certain. While the existence of two Reports enabled astute politicians to play one off against the other when they chose to do so, the government also found no difficulty in evading the main recommendation on which the Commissioners were united—the abolition of the Guardians. With memories of the fuss over the abolition of School Boards by the previous government so fresh, the Liberal leaders could see no immediate political advantage in following that example. They pursued their own ideas of reform which they believed would be more immediately attractive and safer electorally, adopting a few assimilable particular reform proposals from the Commissioners. If the social Welfare State in Britain developed in a piecemeal, haphazard fashion, the credit—or blame—must go to the caution of Asquith, the obstinacy of Burns, the improvisation of Lloyd George, and the temerity of Churchill. It had very little to do with the integrated scheme of either Report, or the differences between them. The Webbs' 'campaign' was a lost cause from the start, as the politicians were well aware. So was the counter-campaign of the Majority, submerged by the solid conservatism of the more right-wing campaign of the National Committee for Poor Law Reform. No doubt the Webbs' effort had done much to inspire the enthusiasm, and later to stir the memories, of men and women who were young radicals in those days,[5] while memories of the Majority's efforts had to be dredged up more painfully by historians; but the Webbs can hardly be held responsible for destroying the Majority's public image.

There is yet another question, not so far raised by historians, about the effectiveness of Beatrice Webb's tactics on the Commission. Should she really have bothered about the whole difficult administrative reform of abolishing the Boards of Guardians and transferring their functions to the county councils? Was that relevant to Labour and Socialist aims of obtaining more favourable treatment for the unemployed and the poor? The Social Democratic Federation thought not. Had the Webbs become so fascinated by the

---

[5] The Webbs' interpretation of the RC on the Poor Laws held the field from the 1930s to the 1950s, until enthusiasm for social reforms in a Fabian direction began to ebb.

bureaucratic reforms, which were streamlining and simplifying local government structure in the later nineteenth century, that they had lost sight of primary Socialist objectives? The Webbs' answer was that only by getting rid of a specific 'destitution authority' would it be possible to escape from the patronage, 'stigma', and humiliation associated with relief of poverty to a situation where a State with a well-developed economy would recognize its obligation to secure a minimum standard of living for all its citizens. They considered that the SDF was sacrificing this principle to the immediate advantages it enjoyed in bringing democratic pressure to bear on elected Guardians in working-class areas. In this argument, it is difficult to deny either the force of the Webbs' contention or wholly to discount the SDF's view that transferring the Guardians' functions to the county councils removed them further from popular influence. (Certainly this latter point was not lost on later Conservative governments.) The crux of the argument was whether it was possible to obtain the vital change in social ethos without at the same time getting institutional change. In this matter, the Webbs might be said to have out-Marxed the British Marxists (or, alternatively, the SDF to have out-Fabianed the Webbs). The long persistence of the idea of social welfare as a 'dole' to social 'failures' seems to give much force to the Webbs' attitude. But diplomatically (or from a 'Fabian' point of view?) perhaps it would have been more astute to have played down the institutional change somewhat —allowing the Liberal government an escape route for the time being if it did not want to face that issue, and trusting that the need for institutional change to match policy changes would make itself apparent in the long run. The Webbs, however, had deliberately woven the themes of policy change and institutional change so closely together that such flexibility was impossible for them. The Majority, with fewer radical changes to justify it, got itself into a similar fix.

Charges against both the Bosanquets and the Webbs that they were 'State worshippers' or 'bureaucrats' have been thrown around freely by commentators at the time and since. Perhaps it is understandable, given the special qualities of their social theories, that the Bosanquets have been the main victims of the former accusation and the Webbs of the latter. But such charges are seldom more than slimly based on evidence, and are hard to reconcile with the beliefs, writings, and activities of either the Bosanquets or the

Webbs. As we have seen, they were very interested in reforms of local government and the Civil Service that were taking place in Britain from the 1870s onwards, designed to adapt them to the new democratic State that was gradually emerging. Neither partnership recommended for Britain a bureaucratic structure incompatible with a modern representative democratic State. The Bosanquets fell victims to some extent of the unpopularity in England of 'Prussian' Hegelianism which grew at the time of the First World War and continued until after the Second World War. As for the Webbs, the charges against them were of a more varied sort. When the Social Democrats called them 'bureaucratic', they were using the term to mean that the Webbs did not subscribe to the SDF's ideas of 'primitive democracy'—which was true enough.[6] When contemporary Liberals accused the Webbs of being 'bureaucratic', they were often expressing their dislike of the Webbs' support for Balfour's replacement of School Boards by County Council Education Committees, or in more general terms, simply assuming that Socialism must necessarily be bureaucratic. When modern philanthropists dismiss them as 'bureaucratic',[7] they seem to mean either that they were deficient in human warmth—a debatable matter of personal opinion[8]—or that they thought in abstract categories rather than in terms of people—which is partly the same thing as the earlier proposition, but amplified by a flip *ad hominem* judgement calculated to avoid serious consideration of social theory. The main charge of bureaucracy against the Webbs from contemporary Liberal and Conservative critics of their Poor Law Report centred on the role of their 'Registrar of Public Assistance'. But if there was to be a means-testing of applicants for the kind of open social servicing they advocated, some such official and office were necessary. The outcry against them on this matter was politically effective—it did tap deep Liberal instincts—but much of it was disingenuous and revealed that the upper and middle classes were not willing to impose on themselves the tests which they never had any hesitation in imposing on the poor. The really sensible criticism came from L. T. Hobhouse, who, although he had certain Liberal prejudices against the Webbs because of their association

---

[6] See ch. 4, pp. 98–101 above.

[7] e.g., U.Cormack, *The Welfare State*, pp. 16–17, 23.

[8] In contrast with the views of U. Cormack, see M. Cole, *Beatrice Webb* (London, 1945), ch. 17 Conclusion, pp. 188–92.

with Arthur Balfour, nevertheless accepted the Registrar in principle, but considered that the Webbs should have made this official responsible to the local councils and defined his role as advisory.[9] The Webbs had missed this valuable point, not because they were 'bureaucratic' in an undemocratic sense,[10] but because they were anxious—perhaps over-anxious—to defend themselves against the inevitable accusation of being too lax with public funds.

How far were the views of the antagonists on the Commission modified in the course of proceedings? In both instances, they had begun with a large stock of opinions previously developed in the course of their membership of the Fabian Society and the COS respectively. Therefore we may take as markers the views expressed, which had their approval, by those organizations at the outset of the Commission's deliberations. Fabian Tract No. 126, *The Abolition of the Poor Law Guardians*, published in February 1906 and actually drafted by the Fabian Secretary, E. R. Pease, but with the Webbs' approval, serves in Beatrice Webb's case, and Bernard Bosanquet's *The Social Criterion or How to Judge of Proposed Social Reforms*, a paper read before the Edinburgh Charity Organisation Society and published in 1907, provides a satisfactory last-minute encapsulation of the Bosanquet's thinking. Although Beatrice Webb's views acquired an immensely sophisticated elaboration through her experience on the Commission, it seems clear that the main outlines of the Minority Report were foreshadowed in the Fabian pamphlet. Notable innovations were the elaboration of a more intricate and satisfactory machinery to supersede the Boards of Guardians, which was clearly the work of the Webbs themselves; the proposal for the unification and extension of State medical services, which showed the influence of the band of radical doctors who acted as their advisers; the adoption of the idea of national labour exchanges for which the Webbs acknowledged their immediate indebtedness to Beveridge although they modified his scheme; the acceptance of a Ministry of Labour, which derived from Labour Party sources via Lansbury; and the deeper understanding of all aspects of the problem of unemployment, its causes

---

[9] P. Clarke, *Liberals and Social Democrats* (Cambridge, 1978), p. 210.

[10] B. Webb's remark, 'no nonsense about democracy', in her Diary entry for 15 Nov. 1908 (*Our Partnership*, p. 418), which has been quoted against her by several commentators, was an expression of impatience with the Liberals' shilly-shallying and piecemeal approach to Poor Law reform. She thought if the Liberals failed, the Tories might be willing to tackle Guardians with 'no nonsense about democracy!'

and remedies, which may be said to have been the greatest collective achievement of this Commission, through its researchers and witnesses (although the Webbs had played an important part in putting forward the names of some of them). The Webbs were open to new ideas, but selective in their choice—choosing those which made a contribution to developing and enriching basic Fabian doctrine. They had the knack of putting new ideas together into a convincing system.

Mrs Bosanquet and her husband also had this ability; but in face of the aggressive tactics of Beatrice Webb, they and other COS champions had the disadvantage of appearing to be on the defensive. In his *Social Criterion* lecture, which we are using as marker of the Bosanquets' position before the Majority Report, Bernard Bosanquet represented himself as defender of the existing system (organically developed over time and capable of further cautious reform) against the brutal 'mechanical' reforming methods of doctrinaire Individualists on one side and doctrinaire Collectivists on the other. By the time of the drafting of the Majority Report, the Bosanquets had moved forward very cautiously, careful to represent each advance as a development of COS social theory. They were not opposed to interpreting the terms of reference of the Commission in a wide sense to cover unemployment (as some officials and other COS members may have been[11]); and Beatrice Webb did not think they were. Beatrice Webb had no direct persuasive influence upon Helen Bosanquet, whose important role in drafting the Majority Report (hitherto unrecognized) has been demonstrated in this study. And Beatrice Webb sacrificed whatever influence she may have had at first with other COS members (Phelps, Smart, Bentham, Nunn, and Gardiner) by her behaviour. But indirectly, Beatrice Webb occasionally provoked her opponents to put forward innovative proposals, by forcing them to find solutions to counter her ideas. Thus, Helen Bosanquet's scheme for a system of provident dispensaries for the poor established by the State to supplement voluntary dispensaries was a direct counter-move to Beatrice Webb's more radical schemes for medical provision. Hostility to Beatrice Webb's ideas also partly motivated Helen Bosanquet's acceptance of the abolition of the Guardians and the transfer of their functions to the counties. Helen Bosanquet had

---

[11] e.g., J. S. Davy and C. S. Loch.

independently decided in favour of the county boundaries as the new area for Poor Law purposes; but at first she wanted to retain a directly elected *ad hoc* administrative body. She dropped the latter idea in favour of the scheme which subsequently became the Majority proposal, because she feared at a particular moment that Beatrice Webb's alternative, the breaking up of the Poor Law, might win acceptance if she did not help the Chairman to keep a majority. As a result the administrative change, which she with the Majority accepted, turned out to be more like one that Professor Marshall or Canon Barnett might have approved, than the one with directly elected Guardians and clear distinctions between official and voluntary roles, that the Bosanquets had advocated earlier.

Unemployment policy was another field in which the Bosanquets and the Majority Commissioners made an advance on earlier COS ideas. Considering how little was really known of the problem in 1905, the work of the Commission's researchers represented a pioneering achievement, from which all the Commissioners had something to learn. As a result of their work, the Bosanquets, although they still clung to the priority of 'moral' causes of destitution in the case of the able-bodied, gave more stress than they formerly had done to 'social' causes. They had come to recognize that the COS's ambition to abolish outdoor relief altogether would never be feasible; and that a variety of new methods would be needed to deal with unemployment. They willingly accepted Beveridge's ideas for labour exchanges. Everything contributed specifically by the Webbs they rejected; but there was much new information accompanied by a general spirit of reform in the later Edwardian years (as shown by the opinions of the economists called before the Commission) to which the Bosanquets responded with caution. The only part Beatrice Webb had in this influence, was the role she played in selecting certain of the Commission's researchers and witnesses. She was able to do this because of her own and Sidney Webb's intimate knowledge of the research and the scholarly world of social science via the London School of Economics and Fabian Society.

The Webbs' crusade for the Minority Report following its publication was, from a political point of view, a failure, but effective in popularizing their ideas. There can be little doubt that the Minority Report would have slipped much more quickly into oblivion if the campaign had never been mounted. It was particularly effective in spreading the Webbs' message to the younger generation of Radicals and Socialists by engaging their enthusiasm. The Majority Report was not overshadowed in the campaign, but the Minority asserted itself sufficiently to win some points at the time of the County Councils' Association compromise, before both Reports were overwhelmed by the backlash from the Guardians, and the government's indifference. The Webbs' campaign seems unlikely to have been a cause of the eclipse of the Majority Report. In spite of the Bosanquets' illness and gradual withdrawal and the Webbs' longevity and continued action, Beatrice Webb herself, during the First World War, fell back on promoting the County Councils' Association compromise, which had awarded more points to the Majority than to the Minority. That formed the basis of the recommendations of the 1917 Maclean Committee, which in turn became the basis of Neville Chamberlain's 1929 Act. The Webbs, as usual, put an optimistic face on it in 1929, but they ended up disillusioned and soured by the experiences of the Great Depression and the Labour government's failure in 1931. Their ideas of a Welfare State, as expressed in the Minority Report, however, continued to endure, through the influential intellectual position they had attained in the Labour Party, into the Second World War and post-war years.

We return, at the end, to the tennis metaphor. The match between the Bosanquets and the Webbs had been the culmination of a long drawn-out tournament, in which both sets of players had distinguished themselves. It had been a hard-fought contest, in which feelings had risen high at times, and even moments where the play had come to the point of breaking the rules of the game. But, by and large, the contest was conducted as a high level of intelligent exchange, and was relatively free of *ad hominem* abuse. Though it was all very British and Edwardian, it offered some permanent lessons for later ages and other countries.

SELECT BIBLIOGRAPHY

OFFICIAL SOURCES

Royal Commission on the Poor Laws and Relief of Distress 1905–9:
  Majority and Minority Reports for England, Scotland, and Ireland.
  Appendix volumes of Minutes of Evidence (36 volumes).
Hansard: Parliamentary Debates.
Cabinet Papers for 1909–10.
Annual Reports of the Local Government Board.
Proceedings . . . of the Poor Law Conferences.
Official Circulars of the County Councils Association.

COLLECTIONS OF PRIVATE PAPERS

Asquith Papers (Bodleian Library).
Balfour Papers (British Museum).
Beveridge Papers (British Library of Political and Economic Science).
C. Booth Papers (University of London Library and British Library of
  Political and Economic Science).
H. Bosanquet Papers (University of Newcastle Library).
Burns Papers (British Museum).
Fabian Society Papers (Nuffield College Library, Oxford).
Family Welfare Association (COS) Collection (Goldsmiths' Library,
  University of London).
Lansbury Papers (British Library of Political and Economic Science).
Passfield Papers (British Library of Political and Economic Science).
Phelps Papers (Oriel College Library, Oxford).
G. B. Shaw Papers (British Museum).
Wallas Papers (British Library of Political and Economic Science).
Webb Local Government Collection (British Library of Political and
  Economic Science).

NEWSPAPERS AND JOURNALS

Charity Organisation Review and *Fabian News* were consulted for the
  whole period from the early 1890s to 1918; other newspapers and
  journals for selected occasions and periods (see footnote references).

AUTOBIOGRAPHIES, BIOGRAPHIES, MEMOIRS,
PUBLISHED DIARIES, AND LETTERS

Adam, R. and K. Muggeridge, *Beatrice Webb: A Life* (London, 1967).
Allen, B. M., *Sir Robert Morant: A Great Public Servant* (London, 1934).
Amery, L. S., *My Political Life* (3 vols.; London, 1953–5).
Ashley, A. *William James Ashley* (London, 1932).
Asquith, C. with J. A. Spender, *Life of Herbert Henry Asquith, Lord Oxford and Asquith* (2 vols.; London, 1932).
Asquith, H. H., *Memories and Reflections* . . . (2 vols.; London, 1928).
Ball, O. H. (ed.), *Sidney Ball: Memoirs and Impressions of 'an Ideal Don'* (Oxford, 1923).
Barnes, J. and D. Nicholson (eds.), *The Leo Amery Diaries*, vol. i. 1896–1929 (London, 1980).
Barnett, H., *Canon Barnett: His Life, Work and Friends*, (2 vols.; London, 1921).
Begbie, H., *Life of William Booth, the Founder of the Salvation Army*, (2 vols.; London, 1920).
Beveridge, W. H. (Lord), *Power and Influence* (London, 1953).
Booth, M., *Charles Booth: A Memoir* (London, 1918).
Bosanquet, H., *Bernard Bosanquet: A Short Account of his Life* (London, 1924).
Brailsford, H., *The Life Work of J. A. Hobson* (Oxford, 1948).
Briggs, A., *Social Thought and Social Action: A Study of the Work of Seebohm Rowntree* (London, 1961).
Brown, K. D., *John Burns* (London, 1977).
Bunbury, Sir Henry (ed.), *Lloyd George's Ambulance Wagon: Memoirs of W. J. Braithwaite 1911–12* (London, 1957).
Burgess, J., *John Burns: The Rise and Progress of a Right Honourable* (Glasgow, 1911).
Chamberlain, A., *Politics from the Inside* (London, 1936).
Churchill, R. S., *Winston S. Churchill*, vols. ii and iii. *Young Statesman 1901–1914* (London, 1967).
Churchill, W. S., *Great Contemporaries* (London, 1937).
Clay, A. (ed.), *A Great Ideal and its Champion* [C. S. Loch] (London, 1923).
Cole, G. D. H., *John Burns* (Fabian Biographical Tract No. 14, London, 1943).
Cole, M. *Beatrice Webb* (London, 1945).
—— (ed.), *The Webbs and their Work* (London, 1949).
—— (ed.), *Beatrice Webb's Diaries*, vol. i. 1912–1924, vol. ii. 1924–1932 (London, 1952 and 1956).
Dilks, D., *Neville Chamberlain*, vol. i. *Pioneering and Reform 1869–1929* (Cambridge, 1984).

Egremont, M., *Balfour: A Life of Arthur James Balfour* (London, 1980).

Ervine, St. J., *God's Soldier: General William Booth* (2 vols.; London, 1934).

Feiling, K., *The Life of Neville Chamberlain* (London, 1946).

Fraser, P., *Joseph Chamberlain: Radicalism and Empire 1868–1914* (London, 1966).

Gardiner, A. G., *Pillars of Society* (London, 1913).

Garvin, J. L. and J. Amery, *the Life of Joseph Chamberlain* (4 vols.; London, 1932–51).

Grigg, J., *Lloyd George, the People's Champion 1902–1911* (London, 1978).

Haldane, R. B., *An Autobiography* (London, 1929).

Hamilton, Lord George, *Parliamentary Reminiscences and Reflections*, vol. i. *1868–1885*, vol. ii. *1886–1906* (London, 1917 and 1922).

Hamilton, M. A., *Sidney and Beatrice Webb: A Study in Contemporary Biography* (London, 1932).

Harris, J., *William Beveridge: A Biography* (Oxford, 1977).

Havighurst, A. F., *Radical Journalist: H. W. Massingham* (Cambridge, 1974).

Haw, G., *From Workhouse to Westminster: The Life Story of Will Crooks, MP* (London, 1907).

Hobson, J. A., *Confessions of an Economic Heretic* (London, 1938).

—— and M. Ginsberg, *L. T. Hobhouse: His Life and Work* (London, 1931).

Hyndman, H. M., *The Record of an Adventurous Life* (London, 1911).

—— *Further Reminiscences* (London, 1912).

Jenkins, R., *Asquith* (London, 1964).

Jones, T., *Lloyd George* (Oxford, 1951).

Kent, W., *John Burns: Labour's Lost Leader* (London, 1950).

Keynes, J. M., *Essays in Biography* (London, 1961).

Koss, S. E., *Lord Haldane: Scapegoat for Liberalism* (New York, 1969).

Lansbury, G., *My Life* (London, 1928).

Latta, R. (ed.), *D. G. Ritchie's Philosophical Studies, with a Memoir* (London, 1905).

Lee, G. L., *The Story of the Bosanquets* (Canterbury, 1966).

Leeds, H., *Norwich Cathedral Past and Present, with a Biographical Sketch of the Dean of Norwich* (London, 1910).

Letwin, S., *The Pursuit of Certainty* (Cambridge, 1965). [Chapter on Beatrice Webb.]

Long, W., *Memories* (London, 1923).

Mackay, R. F., *Balfour: Intellectual Statesman* (Oxford, 1985).

MacKenzie, J., *A Victorian Courtship: The Story of Beatrice Potter and Sidney Webb* (London, 1979).

MacKenzie, N. (ed.), *The Letters of Sidney and Beatrice Webb*, vol. i. *Apprenticeships 1873–1892*, vol. ii. *Partnership 1892–1912*, vol. iii. *Pilgrimage 1912–1947* (Cambridge, 1978).

MacKenzie, N. and J. (eds.), *The Diary of Beatrice Webb*, 4 vols. (1873–1892, 1892–1905, 1905–24, 1924–43) (London, 1982–5).

McLachlan, H., *Records of a Family 1800–1933: Pioneers in Education, Social Service and Liberal Religion* [Dendy family] (Manchester, 1935).

Marquand, D., *Ramsay MacDonald* (London, 1977).

Masterman, L., *C. F. G. Masterman: A Biography* (London, 1939).

Maurice, C. E., *Life of Octavia Hill, as told in her Letters* (London, 1913).

Maurice, E. S., *Octavia Hill: Early Ideals* (London, 1928).

Maurice, Sir Frederick, *The Life of Viscount Haldane of Cloan* (2 vols.; London, 1937).

Mill, J. S., *Autobiography* (New York, 1944).

Moberly Bell, E. H. C., *Octavia Hill: A Biography* (London, 1942).

Morgan, K. O., *Keir Hardie* (London, 1975).

Muirhead, J. H. (ed.), *Bernard Bosanquet and his Friends* (London, 1935).

—— *Reflections by a Journeyman in Philosophy on the Movements of Thought and Practice in his Time* (London, 1942).

Nord, D. E., *The Apprenticeship of Beatrice Webb* (Amherst, 1985).

Nunn, F. K. H., et al., *Thomas Hancock Nunn: The Life and Work of a Social Reformer . . .* (London, 1942).

Olivier, M. (ed.), *Sidney Olivier: Letters and Selected Writings* (London, 1943).

Postgate, R., *The Life of George Lansbury* (London, 1951).

Radice, L., *Beatrice and Sidney Webb, Fabian Socialists* (London, 1984).

Robinson, Sir Henry, *Memories: Wise and Otherwise* (London, 1923).

Rowland, P., *Lloyd George* (London, 1975).

Russell, B., *Portraits from Memory and Other Studies* (London, 1956).

Simey, T. S. and M. B., *Charles Booth, Social Scientist* (London, 1960).

Spender, J. A., *The Life of the Rt. Hon. Sir Henry Campbell-Bannerman* (2 vols.; London, 1923).

Squire, R., *Thirty Years in the Public Service: An Industrial Retrospect* (London, 1927).

Tawney, R. H., *The Webbs and their Work* (Webb Memorial Lecture; London, 1947).

—— *The Webbs in Perspective* (Webb Memorial Lecture; London, 1953).

Taylor, A. J. P. (ed.), *Lloyd George: Twelve Essays* (London, 1971).

Terrill, R., *R. H. Tawney and his Times: Socialism as Fellowship* (Cambridge, Mass., 1973).

Thomas, H. P., *The Work and Play of a Government Inspector* (London, 1909).

Tsuzuki, C., *H. M. Hyndman and British Socialism* (Oxford, 1961).

Webb, B., *My Apprenticeship* (2 vols.; Harmondsworth, 1938). [First published London 1926.]
—— *Our Partnership*, ed. B. Drake and M. Cole (London, 1948).
Williams, J. R., R. Titmuss and F. J. Fisher, *R. H. Tawney: A Portrait by Several Hands* (London, 1960).
Young, K., *Arthur James Balfour* (London, 1963).

OTHER PUBLISHED BOOKS AND PAMPHLETS

Alden, P., *The Unemployed: A National Question* (London, 1905).
Allett, J., *New Liberalism: The Political Economy of J. A. Hobson* (Toronto, 1981).
Avineri, S., *Hegel's theory of the Modern State* (Cambridge, 1974).
Barnett, Canon, and H. O., *Practicable Socialism* (London, 1888).
Bax, E. B., *Harry Quelch: Literary Remains* (London, 1914).
Bealey, F. (ed.), *The Social and Political Thought of the British Labour Party* (London, 1970).
Beer, M., *A History of British Socialism*, vol. ii (London, 1953 edn.).
Beveridge, W. H., *Unemployment: A Problem of Industry* (London, 1909).
Bland, A. E., P. A. Brown and R. H. Tawney (eds.), *English Economic History: Select Documents* (London, 1914).
Booth, C., *Labour and Life of the People* (2 vols.; London, 1891).
—— *Old Age Pensions and the Aged Poor: A Proposal* (London, 1899).
—— *Poor Law Reform* (London, 1911).
Booth, W., *In Darkest England and the Way Out* (London, 1890).
Bosanquet, B., *Knowledge and Reality: A Criticism of Mr F. H. Bradley's 'Principles of Logic'* (London, 1885).
—— *Logic, or the Morphology of Knowledge* (Oxford, 1888).
—— *Essays and Addresses* (London, 1889).
—— *'In Darkest England' on the Wrong Track* (London, 1891).
—— *A History of Aesthetic* (London, 1892).
—— *The Civilization of Christendom and Other Studies* (London, 1893).
—— (ed.), *Aspects of the Social Problem* (London, 1895).
—— *The Philosophical Theory of the State* (London, 1925). [First published London, 1899.]
—— *The Social Criterion: Or How to Judge of Proposed Social Reforms* (Edinburgh, 1907).
—— *The Principle of Individuality and Value* (London, 1912).
—— *The Value and Destiny of the Individual* (London, 1913).
—— *Three Lectures on Aesthetic* (London, 1915).
—— *Social and International Ideals: Being Studies in Patriotism* (London, 1917).
—— *Some Suggestions in Ethics* (London, 1918).

Bosanquet, B., *Implication and Linear Inference* (London, 1920).
—— *What Religion Is* (London, 1920).
—— *The Meeting of Extremes in Contemporary Philosophy* (London, 1921).
—— *Science and Philosophy and Other Essays by the late Bernard Bosanquet*, ed. J. H. Muirhead and R. C. Bosanquet (London, 1927).
Bosanquet, H., *Rich and Poor* (London, 1896).
—— *The Administration of Charitable Relief* (The National Union of Women Workers of Great Britain and Ireland, Tract 6; London, 1898).
—— *The Standard of Life and Other Studies* (London, 1898).
—— *The Strength of the People: A Study in Social Economics* (London, 1902).
—— *The Family* (London, 1906).
—— *The Poor Law Report of 1909* . . . (London, 1909).
—— *Social Conditions in Provincial Towns* . . . (London, 1912).
—— *Social Work in London 1869 to 1912: A History of the Charity Organisation Society* (London, 1914).
Bradley, F. H., *Ethical Studies* (London, 1927 edn.). [First published in 1876.]
Brand, J. L., *Doctors and the State: The British Medical Profession and Government Action in Public Health 1870–1912* (London, 1965).
Briggs, A. and J. Saville (eds.), *Essays in Labour History 1886–1923*, vol. ii (London, 1971).
Britain, I., *Fabianism and Culture: A Study in British Socialism and the Arts 1884–1918* (Cambridge, 1982).
Broad, C. D., *Five Types of Ethical Theory* (London, 1967).
Brown, K. D., *Labour and Unemployment 1900–1914* (Newton Abbot, 1971).
—— (ed.), *Essays in Anti-Labour History* (London, 1974).
Bruce, M., *The Coming of the Welfare State* (London, 1968).
Caine, Sir Sydney, *The History of the Foundation of the London School of Economics and Political Science* (London, 1963).
Carlyle, T., *Essays* (2 vols.; London, 1950). ['Shooting Niagara: and After' in vol. i and 'Chartism' in vol. ii.]
Chapman, S. J. and H. M. Hallsworth, *Unemployment: The Results of an Investigation made in Lancashire* (Manchester, 1909).
Checkland, S., *British Public Policy 1776–1939: An Economic, Social and Political Perspective* (Cambridge, 1983).
Checkland, S. G. and E. D. A. (eds.), *The Poor Law Report of 1834* (Harmondsworth, 1974).
Churchill, W. S., *Liberalism and the Social Problem* (London, 1909).
Clarke, P., *Liberals and Social Democrats* (Cambridge, 1978).
Cole, M., *The Story of Fabian Socialism* (London, 1961).

Collingwood, R. G., *The Idea of History* (New York, 1956).

Collini, S., *Liberalism and Sociology: L. T. Hobhouse and Political Argument in England 1880–1914* (Cambridge, 1979).

Cormack, U., *The Welfare State, the Formative Years 1905–9*, Loch Memorial Lecture (London, 1953).

Cross, C., *The Liberals in Power 1905–14* (London, 1963).

Davies, A. F., *Skills, Outlooks and Passions: A Psychoanalytic Contribution to the Study of Politics* (Cambridge, 1980).

Emy, H. V., *Liberals, Radicals and Social Politics 1892–1914* (Cambridge, 1973).

Fabian Society, *The Government Organisation of Unemployed Labour*, printed for the information of members of the FS (London, 1886).

Fabian Society, Tracts: Those of particular relevance to the Poor Law are the following: 17 (1890); 20 (1890); 44 (1893); 47 (1893); 54 (1894); 72 (1896); 73 (1896); 89 (1899); 126 (1906); 127 (1906); 135 (1907); 158 (1911); 160 (1911); 161 (1912); 162 (1912); 176 (1914); 178 (1915); 185 (1918).

Fraser, D., *The Evolution of the British Welfare State* (London, 1973).

—— (ed.), *The New Poor Law in the Nineteenth Century* (London, 1976).

Freeden, M., *The New Liberalism: An Ideology of Social Reform* (Oxford, 1978).

Gilbert, B. B., *The Evolution of National Insurance in Great Britain* (London, 1966).

Green, T. H., *Works*, ed. R. L. Nettleship (3 vols.; London, 1885–8).

Halévy, E., *History of the English People in the 19th Century*, vols. v *Imperialism and the Rise of Labour 1895–1905*, and vi *The Rule of Democracy 1905–14* (London, 1961).

Hardie, J. K., *From Serfdom to Socialism* (London, 1907).

Harris, J., *Unemployment and Politics: A Study in English Social Policy* (Oxford, 1972).

Harrison, B., *Separate Spheres: The Opposition to Women's Suffrage in Britain* (London, 1978).

—— *Peaceable Kingdom: Stability and Change in Modern Britain* (Oxford, 1982).

Harvie, C., *The Lights of Liberalism* (London, 1976).

Hay, J. R., *The Origins of the Liberal Welfare Reforms 1906–1914* (London, 1975).

Hegel, G. W. F., *The Philosophy of History*, trans. J. Sibree (New York, 1956).

—— *Philosophy of Right*, trans. T. M. Knox (Oxford, 1952).

Hills, J. W. and M. Woods (eds.), *Poor Law Reform, a Practical Programme: The Scheme of the Unionist Social Reform Committee* (London, 1912).

Hobhouse, L. T., *The Labour Movement* (Harvester Press repr. from 3rd edn. (1912), Brighton, 1974). [Originally published London, 1893.]

—— *Democracy and Reaction*, (Harvester Press repr., Brighton, 1972). [Originally published London 1904.]

—— *Liberalism* (London, 1911).

—— *The Metaphysical Theory of the State: A Criticism* (London, 1951 repr.). [Originally published London, 1918.]

Hobson, J. A., *The Problem of the Unemployed: An Enquiry and an Economic Policy* (London, 1896).

—— *The Crisis of Liberalism: New Issues of Democracy* (London, 1909).

—— and A. F. Mummery, *The Physiology of Industry* (London, 1889).

Hutchinson, T. W., *A Review of Economic Doctrines 1870–1929* (Oxford, 1953).

Hyams, E., *The New Statesman: The History of the First Fifty Years 1913–63* (London, 1963).

Hyndman, H. M., *Commercial Crises of the Nineteenth Century* (London, 1892). [2nd edn., with a preface by J. A. Hobson, London, 1932.]

Hynes, S., *The Edwardian Turn of Mind* (London, 1968).

—— *Edwardian Occasions* (London, 1972).

Johnson, P. B., *Land Fit for Heroes: The Planning of British Reconstruction* (Chicago, 1968).

Jones, H., *The Working Faith of the Social Reformer and Other Essays* (London, 1910).

Keynes, J. M., *The General Theory of Employment, Interest and Money* (London, 1936).

Loch, C. S., *Pauperism and Old Age Pensions* [a correspondence between J. Chamberlain and C. S. Loch published in *The Times* of 28 Jan. 1892 and printed as a pamphlet] (London, n.d.).

—— (ed.), *Methods of Social Advance* (London, 1904).

—— *Charity Organisation* (London, 1890).

—— *Charity and Social Life: A Short Study of Religious and Social Thought in Relation to Charitable Methods and Institutions* (London, 1910).

McBriar, A. M., *Fabian Socialism and English Politics 1884–1918* (Cambridge, 1962).

MacKenzie, N. and J., *The First Fabians* (London, 1977).

McTaggart, J. M. E., *Studies in Hegelian Cosmology* (Cambridge, 1901).

Marshall, A., *Principles of Economics* (London, 8th edn., 1925). [First published 1890.]

Marshall, T. H., *Social Policy in the Twentieth Century* (London, 1975 edn.). [First published 1965.]

Masterman, C. G. F., *The Condition of England* (London, 1909).

Meisel, M., 'Shaw and Revolution: The Politics of the Plays', in N. Rosenblood (ed.), *Shaw: Seven Critical Essays* (Toronto, 1971).

Mill, J. S., *Essays on Some Unsettled Questions of Political Economy* (London, 1844).

—— *A System of Logic* (London, 1879). [First published in 1843.]

—— *Utilitarianism, Liberty and Representative Government* (London, 1948). [First published 1859–63.]

—— *Auguste Comte and Positivism* (London, 1865).

Mills, H. V., *Poverty and the State: or Work for All* (London, 1886).

Milne, A. J. M., *The Social Philosophy of English Idealism* (London, 1962).

Mommsen, W. J. (ed.), *The Emergence of the Welfare State in Britain and Germany 1850–1950* (London, 1981).

Morgan, K. O. (ed.), *The Age of Lloyd George: The Liberal Party and British Politics 1890–1929* (London, 1971).

Mowat, C. L., *The Charity Organisation Society 1869–1913: Its Ideas and Work* (London, 1961).

Muirhead, J. H., *By What Authority? The Principles in Common and at Issue in its Reports of the Poor Law Commission* (London, 2nd edn., 1909).

—— (ed.), *Contemporary British Philosophy: Personal Statements*, 1st series (London, 1924).

—— *The Platonic Tradition in Anglo-Saxon Philosophy: Studies in the History of Idealism in England and America* (London, 1931).

Nemmers, E. E., *Hobson and Underconsumption* (Amsterdam, 1956).

Nettleship, R. L., *Philosophical Remains* (London, 1901).

Nowell-Smith, S., *Edwardian England 1901–1914* (Oxford, 1965).

Owen, D., *English Philanthropy 1660–1960* (Cambridge, Mass., 1965).

Owen, R., *A New View of Society* (Harmondsworth, 1970 edn.). [First published 1813–14.]

Passmore, J., *A Hundred Years of Philosophy* (London, 1957).

Pateman, C., *Participation and Democratic Theory* (Cambridge, 1970).

Patten-MacDougall, J. and J. M. Dodds, *The Parish Council Guide for Scotland: A Handbook to the Local Government (Scotland) Act 1894* (Edinburgh, 1894).

Pease, E. R., *The History of the Fabian Society* (London, 1925).

Pelling, H., *Popular Politics and Society in late Victorian England* (London, 1964).

Phelps, L. R., *Poor Law and Charity* (Oxford, n.d. [?1887]).

Pfannenstill, B., *Bernard Bosanquet's Philosophy of the State: A Historical and Systematical Study* (Lund, 1936).

Picht, W., *Toynbee Hall and the English Settlement Movement* (London, 1914).

Pierson, S., *British Socialists: The Journey from Fantasy to Politics* (Cambridge, Mass., 1979).

Pigou, A. C., *Economic Science in relation to Practice* [Inaugural Lecture 30 Oct. 1908] (London, 1908).

—— *Unemployment* (London, 1913).

—— *Memorials of Alfred Marshall* (London, 1925; New York, 1966).

—— *The Theory of Unemployment* (London, 1933).

Pimlott, J. A. R., *Toynbee Hall: Fifty Years of Social Progress 1884–1934* (London, 1935).

Plant, R., *Social and Moral Theory in Casework* (London, 1970).

Poirier, P., *The Advent of the Labour Party* (London, 1958).

Popper, K., *The Open Society and Its Enemies* (London, 1945).

Pugh, P., *Educate, Agitate, Organize: 100 years of Fabian Socialism* (London, 1984).

Read, D. (ed.), *Edwardian England* (London, 1982).

Richter, M., *The Politics of Conscience: T. H. Green and his Age* (London, 1964).

Ritchie, D. G., *Darwinism and Politics* (London, 1891).

—— *The Principles of State Interference* (London, 1891).

—— *Darwin and Hegel, with other Philosophical Studies* (London, 1893).

—— *Natural Rights: A Criticism of some Political and Ethical Conceptions* (London, 1895).

—— *Studies in Political and Social Ethics* (London, 1902).

Robbins, P., *The British Hegelians 1875–1925* (New York, 1982).

Roberts, B. C., *The Trades Union Congress 1868–1921* (London, 1958).

Robertson, J. M., *The Fallacy of Saving* (London, 1892).

Rooff, M., *A Hundred Years of Family Welfare* (London, 1974).

Rose, M. E., *The English Poor Law 1780–1930* (Newton Abbot, 1971).

—— *The Relief of Poverty 1834–1914* (London, 1974).

Rowland, P., *The Last Liberal Governments* (2 vols.; London, 1971).

Rowntree, B. S. and B. Lasker, *Unemployment: A Social Study* (London, 1911).

—— *Poverty: A Study of Town Life* (London, 1914).

Russell, B., *Roads to Freedom: Socialism, Anarchism and Syndicalism* (London, 1954). [First published in 1918.]

Ryan, A., *The Philosophy of John Stuart Mill* (London, 1970).

Schäffle, A., *Quintessence of Socialism* (London, 1889).

—— *The Impossibility of Social Democracy* (London, 1892).

Schloss, D. F., *Insurance against Unemployment* (London, 1909).

Schumpeter, J. A., *Capitalism, Socialism and Democracy* (London, 1966 edn.). [First published in 1943.]

Searle, G. R., *The Quest for National Efficiency* (Oxford, 1971).

Shaw, G. B. (ed.), *Fabian Essays in Socialism* (London, 1889).

Smart, W., *A Disciple of Plato: A Critical Study of John Ruskin* (Glasgow, 1883).

—— *The Distribution of Income* (London, 1899 and 1912).

—— *The Single Tax* (Glasgow, 1905).

—— *The Return to Protection, being a Re-statement of the Case for Free Trade* (London, 1906).

—— *Second Thoughts of an Economist* (London, 1916).

Spencer, H., *Reasons for Dissenting from the Philosophy of M. Comte* (London, 1884).

—— *The Man versus the State* (Harmondsworth, 1969).

Stedman Jones, G., *Outcast London: A Study in the Relationship between Classes in Victorian Society* (Oxford, 1971).

Thane, P. (ed.), *The Origins of British Social Policy* (London, 1978).

Thompson, P., *Socialists, Liberals and Labour: The Struggle for London 1885–1914* (London, 1967).

Titmuss, R. M., *Essays on the Welfare State* (London, 1963).

Ulam, A. B., *Philosophical Foundations of English Socialism* (Cambridge, Mass., 1951).

Vincent, A. and R. Plant, *Philosophy, Politics and Citizenship: The Life and Thought of the British Idealists* (Oxford, 1984).

Wakefield, H. R., *Poor Law Reform* (London, 1908).

—— *Pastoral Address and Report for the Year 1907–8* (London [1908]).

Webb, (Potter), B., *The Co-operative Movement in Great Britain* (London, 1891).

Webb, S., 'The Relation between Wages and the Remainder of the Economic Produce' (1899), reprinted in R. L. Smyth (ed.), *Essays in the Economics of Socialism and Capitalism: Selected Papers read to Section F of the British Association for the Advancement of Science 1886–1932* (London, 1964).

—— *Socialism in England* (London, 1890).

—— *The London Programme* (London, 1891).

Webb, S. and B., *The History of Trade Unionism* (London, 1894).

—— *Industrial Democracy* (London, 1897).

—— *Problems of Modern Industry* (London, 1898).

—— *English Local Government from the Revolution to the Municipal Corporations Act*, 10 vols. (London, 1906–29).

—— *English Poor Law Policy* (London, 1910).

—— *The Prevention of Destitution* (London, 1911).

—— *A Constitution for the Socialist Commonwealth of Great Britain* (London, 1920).

—— *The Consumers' Co-operative Movement* (London, 1921).

—— *The Decay of Capitalist Civilization* (London, 1923).

—— *Methods of Social Study* (London, 1932).

Webb, S. and B., *Soviet Communism: A New Civilization?* (London, 1935).
Weiler, P., *The New Liberalism: Liberal Social Theory in Great Birtain 1889–1914* (New York, 1982).
Wiener, M. J., *Between Two Worlds: The Political Thought of Graham Wallas* (Oxford, 1971).
Wilson, T., *The Downfall of the Liberal Party 1914–1935* (London, 1968).
Winch, D., *Economics and Policy: A Historical Survey* (London, 1969).
Winter, J. M., *Socialism and the Challenge of War: Ideas and Politics in Britain 1912–1918* (London, 1974).
Wolfe, W., *From Radicalism to Socialism: Men and Ideas in the Formation of Fabian Socialist Doctrines 1881–1889* (New Haven and London, 1975).
Wollheim, R., *F. H. Bradley* (Harmondsworth, 1959).
Woodroofe, K., *From Charity to Social Work in England and the United States* (London, 1962).
Wrigley, C., *David Lloyd George and the British Labour Movement* (Hassocks, 1976).
Young, A. F. and E. T. Ashton, *British Social Work in the Nineteenth Century* (London, 1956).

ARTICLES IN JOURNALS

For the sake of brevity, some articles cited in footnotes have not been included in the following list, if they are incidental to the main theme of this work, or if they have been reprinted in collections of essays listed earlier in the book sections of this bibliography.

Ball, S., 'The Moral Aspects of Socialism', *International Journal of Ethics*, 6 (1896). (Also published as Fabian Tract 72 (1896).)
—— 'The Moral Aspects of Socialism: Concluding Note', *International Journal of Ethics*, 7 (1897).
Barnett, H., 'Passionless Reformers', *Fortnightly Review*, NS 32 (1882).
Barnett, S., 'Distress in East London', *Nineteenth Century*, 20 (1886).
—— 'A Scheme for the Unemployed', *Nineteenth Century*, 24 (1888).
—— 'Poor Law Reform', *Contemporary Review*, 63 (1893).
—— 'The Unemployed', *Fortnightly Review*, NS 54 (1893).
Beveridge, W. H., 'The Unemployed Workmen Act in 1906–7', *Sociological Review*, 1 (1908).
—— 'Public Labour Exchanges in Germany', *Economic Journal*, 18 (1908).
—— 'Unemployment and Its Cure', *Contemporary Review*, 93 (1908).
Bentham, F. H., 'The Position of the Poor Law in the Problem of Poverty', *Proceedings of Poor Law Conferences 1904–5* (London, 1905).

Bosanquet, B., 'The Communication of Moral Ideas as a Function of an Ethical Society', *International Journal of Ethics*, 1 (1890).
—— 'The Limitations of the Poor Law', *Economic Journal*, 2 (1892).
—— 'The Principles and Chief Dangers of the Administration of Charity', *International Journal of Ethics*, 3 (1893).
—— 'The Moral Aspects of Socialism', *International Journal of Ethics*, 6 (1896).
—— 'Aspects of the Social Problem: A Reply', *International Journal of Ethics*, 7 (1897).
—— 'Hegel's Theory of the Political Organism', *Mind*, NS 7 (1898).
—— 'Idealism in Social Work', *Charity Organisation Review* NS 3 (1898).
—— 'Ladies and Gentlemen', *International Journal of Ethics*, 10 (1900).
—— 'The Meaning of Social Work', *International Journal of Ethics*, 11 (1901).
—— 'Hedonism among Idealists', *Mind*, NS 12 (1903).
—— 'The Reports of the Poor Law Commission: The Majority Report', *Sociological Review*, 2 (1909).
—— 'Charity Organisation and the Majority Report', *International Journal of Ethics*, 20 (1910).
—— 'The Place of Leisure in Life', *International Journal of Ethics*, 21 (1911).
—— 'A Question of Method', *Charity Organisation Review*, NS 30 (1911).
—— 'The Notion of the General Will', *Mind*, NS 29 (1920).
—— 'The Motive of Public Assistance: A Practical Ideal', *The Times* (20 Sept. 1920).
Bosanquet, B. and H., 'Charity Organisation: A Reply', *Contemporary Review*, 71 (1897).
Bosanquet, H., 'The Farce of the Fabians', *Charity Organisation Review*, 10 (June 1894).
—— 'The Socialist Propaganda', *National Review*, 26 (1895–6).
—— 'Dr Brentano on English Trade Unionism', *Economic Journal*, 5 (1895).
—— 'Review of the Webbs' *Problems of Modern Industry*', *International Journal of Ethics*, 9 (1899).
—— 'Review of Thomas Mackay's *Public Relief of the Poor*', *International Journal of Ethics*, 12 (1902).
—— 'Physical Degeneration and the Poverty Line', *Contemporary Review*, 85 (1904).
—— 'The Historical Basis of English Poor Law Policy', *Economic Journal*, 20 (1910).
—— 'English Divorce Law and the Report of the Royal Commission', *International Journal of Ethics*, 23 (1913).
—— 'Reconstruction—of what?', *Hibbert Journal*, 15 (1917).

Bosanquet, H., 'Free Trade and Peace in the Nineteenth Century', *Publications de l'Institut Nobel norvégian*, 6 (Christiania, 1924).

Broad, C. D., 'The Notion of a General Will', *Mind*, NS 28 and 29 (1919 and 1920).

Brown, J., 'Charles Booth and Labour Colonies 1889–1905', *Economic History Review*, 2nd series, 21 (1968).

—— 'The Appointment of the 1905 Poor Law Commission', *Bulletin of the Institute of Historical Research*, 42 (1969).

Brown, K. D., 'The Appointment of the 1905 Poor Law Commission—a Rejoinder', *Bulletin of the Institute of Historical Research*, 44 (1971).

Burns, John, 'The Unemployed', *Nineteenth Century*, 32 (1892).

Caldwell, J. A. M., 'The Genesis of the Ministry of Labour', *Public Administration*, 37 (1959).

Collini, S., 'Hobhouse, Bosanquet and the State . . .', *Past and Present*, 72 (1976).

—— 'Political Theory and the "Science of Society" in Victorian Britain', *Historical Journal*, 23 (1980).

—— 'The Idea of "Character" in Victorian Political Thought', *Transactions of the Royal Historical Society*, 5th series, 35 (1985).

Freeden, M., 'J. A. Hobson as a New Liberal Theorist: Some Aspects of his Social Thought until 1914', *Journal of the History of Ideas*, 34 (1973).

Fry, G. K., 'The Marshallian School and the State', *Bulletin of Economic Research* (GB), 28 (1976).

Gilbert, B. B., 'Winston Churchill *versus* the Webbs: The Origins of British Unemployment Insurance', *American Historical Review*, 71 (1966).

Hobson, J. A., 'The Law of the Three Rents', *Quarterly Journal of Economics*, 5 (1891).

—— 'The Social Philosophy of Charity Organisation', *Contemporary Review*, 70 (1896).

Hoernlé, R. F. A., 'On Bosanquet's Idealism', *Philosophical Review*, 32 (1923).

Lansbury, G., 'The Position of the Poor Law in the Problem of Poverty', *Proceedings of Poor Law Conferences 1904–5*.

Loch, C. S., 'The Development of Charity Organisation', *Charity Organisation Review*, NS 15 (1904).

—— 'The Poor Law Controversy', *Local Government Review*, 1 (1910).

—— 'Mr Charles Booth on the Aged Poor', *Economic Journal*, 4 (1894).

Lummis, T., 'Charles Booth: Moralist or Social Scientist', *Economic History Review*, 2nd series 24 (1971).

Lyon, P. C., 'Provost Phelps and the Poor Law Commission 1906–9', *Oriel Record* (1959).

McBriar, A. M., 'Charles Booth and the Royal Commission on the Poor

Laws 1905–9', *Historical Studies* (Melbourne University), 15. 61 (1973).

McTaggart, J. M. E., 'The Conception of Society as an Organism', *International Journal of Ethics*, 7 (1897).

Marshall, A., 'The Poor Law in relation to State-aided Pensions', *Economic Journal*, 2 (1892).

—— 'Poor Law Reform', *Economic Journal*, 2 (1892).

—— 'The Social Possibilities of Economic Chivalry', *Economic Journal*, 17 (1907).

Phelps, L. R., 'Poor Law and Charity', *Proceedings of Poor Law Conferences 1901–2*.

Quelch, H., 'The Prevention of Destitution', *Social-Democrat*, 14 (1910).

Ricci, D. M., 'Fabian Socialism: A Theory of Rent as Exploitation', *Journal of British Studies*, 9 (1969).

Russell, B., 'Mr Charles Booth's Proposals for Fiscal Reform', *Contemporary Review*, 35 (1904).

Sabine, G. H., 'Bosanquet's Theory of the Real Will', *Philosophical Review*, 32 (1923).

Seth, J., 'The Problem of Destitution: A Plea for the Minority Report', *International Journal of Ethics*, 22 (1912).

Shove, G. F., 'The Place of Marshall's *Principles* in the Development of Economic Theory', *Economic Journal*, 52 (1942).

Simey, T. S., 'The Contribution of Sidney and Beatrice Webb to Sociology', *British Journal of Sociology*, 12 (1961).

Smart, W., 'The Dislocations of Industry', *Contemporary Review*, 53 (1888).

Stedman, R. E., 'Bosanquet's Account of Religion', *Hibbert Journal*, 29 (1930–1).

Vincent, A. W., 'The Poor Law Reports of 1909 and the Social Theory of the Charity Organisation Society', *Victorian Studies*, 27 (1984).

Webb, S., 'Rome: A Sermon in Sociology', *Our Corner*, 12 (1888).

—— 'The Rate of Interest and the Laws of Distribution', *Quarterly Journal of Economics*, 2 (1888).

—— 'Socialism in England', *Publications of the American Economic Association*, 4 (1889).

—— 'The Reform of the Poor Law', *Contemporary Review*, 58 (1890).

—— 'An English Poor Law Reform Association', *Quarterly Journal of Economics*, 5 (1891).

—— 'The Moral Aspects of Socialism: Reply to Bosanquet', *International Journal of Ethics*, 7 (1897).

—— 'The Proposed Abolition of the English Poor Law', *International*, (1909).

—— 'The End of the Poor Law', *Sociological Review*, 2 (1909).

Woodroofe, K., 'The Charity Organisation Society and the Origins of Social Casework', *Historical Studies, Australia and New Zealand*, 9 (1959).
—— 'C. S. Loch', *Social Service Review*, 32 (1958).
—— 'The Royal Commission on the Poor Laws 1905–9', *International Review of Social History*, 22 (1977).

UNPUBLISHED THESES

Abel, Emily, K., 'Canon Barnett and the First Thirty Years of Toynbee Hall', Ph.D. thesis (University of London, 1969).
Brimelow, F. A., 'The Royal Poor Law Commission 1905–1909', Ph.D. thesis (University of South Carolina, 1971).
Dober, M., 'The Unemployed in England 1880–1914', MA thesis (University of Melbourne, 1981).
Howard, S. L., 'The New Utilitarians? Studies in the Origins and Early Intellectual Associations of Fabianism', Ph.D. thesis (University of Warwick, 1976).
Maltby, A., 'The Poor Law Commission 1905–9: An Investigation of its Task and Achievements', MA thesis (University of Liverpool, 1969).
Warner, M., 'The Webbs: A Study of the Influence of Intellectuals in Politics 1889–1918', Ph.D. thesis (Cambridge, 1966).
Woodard, C., 'The Charity Organisation Society and the Rise of the Welfare State', Ph.D. thesis (Cambridge, 1961).

Index